Organized Crime
in the United States,
1865–1941

# Organized Crime in the United States, 1865–1941

KRISTOFER ALLERFELDT

McFarland & Company, Inc., Publishers
*Jefferson, North Carolina*

Library of Congress Cataloguing-in-Publication Data

Names: Allerfeldt, Kristofer, 1959– author.
Title: Organized crime in the United States, 1865–1941 / Kristofer Allerfeldt.
Description: Jefferson, North Carolina : McFarland & Company, Inc.,
Publishers, 2018. | Includes bibliographical references and index.
Identifiers: LCCN 2017053689 | ISBN 9781476670652
(softcover : acid free paper) ∞
Subjects: LCSH: Organized crime—United States—History. |
Crime—United States—History.
Classification: LCC HV6446 .A45 2018 | DDC 364.1060973/09041—dc23
LC record available at https://lccn.loc.gov/2017053689

British Library cataloguing data are available

ISBN (print) 978-1-4766-7065-2
ISBN (ebook) 978-1-4766-2996-4

Front cover: New York City skyline, 1932 (Library of Congress);
(inset) negative of Al Capone mugshot, June 17, 1931
(United States Bureau of Prisons)

Printed in the United States of America

McFarland & Company, Inc., Publishers
Box 611, Jefferson, North Carolina 28640
www.mcfarlandpub.com

# Table of Contents

# Introduction

It seems to have become a convention in nonfiction that the author writes an introduction that lays out what is to be said in the main body of the book. From there the narrative of the book progresses, gradually piling on more and more detail to reach the conclusion that had been outlined in the introduction. This is very much true of the field of the history of crime. Almost all writing on the subject, ranging from the most serious, "highbrow," academic analysis, to the more popular accounts of organized crime, seems to have adopted this convention. So, in keeping with the essentially revisionist arguments it puts forward in playing a contrarian tune, this work will reverse that process. This introduction will say what this book is not about: what it does not argue, and what it does not contain.

So, let's start with the structure. This book is not a narrative history. It is not a chronological account of how organized crime evolved. It is not even sequential. It does not explain how the "Mafia" or the "mob," the Five Families or the Snakeheads, came to dominate American criminal activity. It is not going to give a clear or particularly novel trajectory of how the Sicilians, Jews, Chinese, Russians, Colombians or other nationalities came to be seen as dominant in various criminal spheres. It is not going to show which legislation created the environment in which organized crime could thrive. It is not even going to attempt to define what organized crime is, or how that definition has changed over the years. All these things have been done elsewhere: some originally, brilliantly and eruditely, some less so.

That said, it is intended that these omissions will serve what should be seen as more instructive and original purposes. Firstly, they enable the work to focus on what the author considers the main themes in the years between the end of the Civil War and the beginning of America's involvement in the Second World War. In some ways these may be seen as rather arbitrary dates. There was no great organized criminal conspiracy detected in either 1865 or 1941—unless one counts the Japanese attack on Pearl Harbor. Neither 1865 nor 1941 saw a huge change in the law that changed the view of, or created, new criminals. They are simply years in which America as a country changed. They make good bookends for the emergence of a different nation, a more recognizably modern state.

It is hoped that this very "randomness" will avoid the temptation of putting forward an argument that highlights a rather determinist view: a history in which all things seem to be aiming at, or heading toward, a specific final outcome, or a predetermined interpretation. Put another way, this seemingly rather capricious selection of dates should escape putting historical events and their drivers into a framework that takes our present-day understanding of the nature of organized crime and then works backwards from that premise to pile up the evidence to support current views.

For instance, this work will not look at the importance of the prohibition of alcohol in the context of how the "Noble Experiment," as it was famously called, led to the consolidation of criminal activity. Instead, by looking at reports of those "dry" years, this book aims to understand what contemporary commentators, law enforcement and the general public saw as the main crimes being committed—not what we in hindsight attribute to them. It also aims to question the predetermined notions of who was actually carrying out these crimes and who constituted the true victims, as well as trying to understand why the history and impact of the organized crime of the years of national Prohibition has not necessarily been seen in these terms.

This highlights the second strand of omissions. Unlike some histories, this work will not attempt to give an encyclopedic account of organized crime in the years from 1865 to 1941. The reader will not be able to look up a particular phenomenon, gangster or event in the index and find reference to its details or his/her career in the text. Certainly, the structure will be based around individuals. It will explore the way in which their actions, experiences and images affected perceptions, molded interpretations and conditioned responses to organized crime. But the importance of these characters is contextual rather than biographical.

Of course, some of the leading figures will be there. There will be references to Al Capone, Lucky Luciano, Arnold Rothstein, J. Edgar Hoover and other well-known actors in the drama of organized crime. Yet these portraits will be concerned largely with how these figures were perceived at the time. The analysis will not be concentrated on how their legacy has been slotted into the evolution of a history of organized crime in the years since—at least not in the popularly accepted format.

Similarly, events that feed into many of our present-day notions of organized crime, events we may expect to see in a volume dedicated to the history of the phenomenon, may well seem to be missing. What is more, if they are in the text they may be handled in what seems to be a tangential or unfamiliar fashion. For example, there will be little mention of the growth and consolidation of the Mafia as the leading criminal organization. In this reading, the emergence of that shadowy organization is not seen as the inevitable result of the Castellammarese War, the Sicilian Vespers and/or the Atlantic City conference.

The book draws on the strand of current thinking about Mafia history in which these events are at best contested, and may even be irrelevant. In this interpretation the Mafia are given their minor status, not in an effort to appear revisionist, or slavish to a new reading, or even in an attempt to be controversial, but more because the organization did not figure significantly in the interpretations of organized crime at the time. The Mafia's expansion is, however, dealt with in the late nineteenth century as a part of the explosion in fraternal organizations of the time and as such is linked in with the Molly Maguires, the Tongs, the Black Hand and the KKK.

This links in with the notion of what caused organized crime, and why it seems to draw on so many of the phenomena of these years. Many accounts today lay major emphasis on the importance of such elements as urbanization, industrialization, immigration and the boom of the 1920s as spurring on already thriving areas of criminal activity. Over the years of this study, these features certainly played a major role—and some far more than others. That said, once again, their influence was not perhaps perceived in the same light at the time as it is seen today.

For example, most existing accounts place at least some emphasis on the role of the growth of the massive metropolitan areas and the emergence of political machines. They portray these as organized criminal bodies that fleeced the public purse and corrupted politics in the last quarter of the nineteenth century. They point to figures like Boss Tweed and his successors in Tammany Hall. They demonstrate how the same corrupt mix of influence peddling, graft and embezzlement characterized other bosses throughout the major cities of the nation. They argue that there was an essential relationship in which organized crime was practiced and nourished by corrupt politicians.

However, while acknowledging these connections were extraordinarily well-known to contemporaries, this study will argue that what is often overlooked is that these were politicians working within democratic systems that were dependent on partisan politics trying to win over ever-fickle electorates. Certainly some politicos were criminally corrupt and without doubt involved with illegalities other than corruption. What was more, the press loved to report these connections. But what is often overlooked is that not everything said by, or about, these figures was the unadulterated gospel truth. Like successful politicians of all parties, at all times, they exaggerated; they portrayed opponents as worse than themselves; and they used the papers and other media forms to whitewash their own images.

Obviously there were accusations—some more, some less well-founded—of organized criminal connections over these years, but this study will concentrate on analyzing the thinking of the time, in order to try to assess the veracity and motive of such claims. It will have less material devoted to Boss Tweed's antics, and more to the far later behavior of Los Angeles' Boss Parrot. It will not dwell on Thomas Nast's well-documented attacks on Tweed in *Harper's Weekly* in the 1870s, but concentrate instead on the 1920s and 1930s with Colonel Robert McCormack's vendetta against Big Bill Thompson in the *Chicago Tribune* and Harry Chandler's attacks on his political enemies in the *Los Angeles Times*.

While this conforms to the historian's task to question the past, including the opinions of other historians, again the motive behind this is this is more than simple revisionism. It is less because Nast's relentless and venomously effective cartoons are so well-known that they may be considered passé now, and more because there are other reasons for this emphasis that make the *Tribune* and the *Times* more relevant to this study. Tweed's accuser was not involved in organized criminal activity himself, but many of those whom Chandler and McCormack advocated for office in place of Mayors Thompson and Shaw certainly were. Who should we see as the true criminals when it becomes evident that both of these twentieth-century editors appeared content to skew the "facts" to suit their own political favorites and further their own fortunes by shady, if not actually illegal, means?

What is more, newspaper editors played a major role in perhaps the best-known story connected with the genesis of organized crime in the U.S. The murder of David Hennessy in New Orleans in 1890 is seen as the act that opened many people's eyes to presence of an offshoot of the activities of the Sicilian Mafia in the U.S. This is undeniable, since before that date tales of the shadowy fraternity were scarce. After that date many Americans knew exactly what the order was, how it operated, and why—or at least they knew what newspapers, politicians, novelists and other commentators had told them about such matters. In this respect, the murder of Hennessy was certainly the event that kick-started perhaps the most persistent myth in American criminal history, but it was just as certainly not the only one that created a very persistent and highly questionable narrative.

The threat posed by organized crime in the past was never as fixed or static as some commentators would have us believe—any more than it is today. In the world in which we live, there are Italian, Mexican, Russian, Chinese, Albanian and other organized, transnational criminals. They jostle for pre-eminence. They hit the headlines when the big bust or the particularly dreadful killing uncovers them—and then they fade from view. Similarly, the "main threat" posed by organized crime is just as changeable. The crimes and criminals that dominate headlines change. The same was true in the period of this study. Few at the turn of the twentieth century had not heard of the power, reach and organization of the Black Hand that brutally extorted money from the Italian communities of all U.S. cities. Most Americans knew of the so-called white slave panders who created an international network of sex slaves. Yet there is strong evidence that their influence, their reach and the nature of their threat, was certainly not as reported, and whether—indeed—many of the so-called slaves had actually been enslaved at all.

By contrast, others, for one reason or another, slipped under the radar of the press. This is particularly true of the Chinese criminal networks. The common thread is that all of these threats drew on prejudice against various ethnic or national groups in an age of massive immigration. Then, as now, stereotypes of nationalities, religions and ethnicities fed rumors of venal and amoral Eastern European Jews; drunken Poles; politically manipulative Irish; decadent French; and above all, Machiavellian, violent and clannish Sicilians and Italians. Nevertheless, this study will not concentrate on the anti–Italian sentiments that created the so-called Mafia Myth that would dominate depictions of organized crime from the Cold War onwards.

Again, there are other studies already out there that have more to say. There are investigations that can draw on deeper research and have more space to do their topics justice than this work can. Further, the "Mafia" as such was not really seen by contemporaries as a major threat during these years. There was a Mafia scare in the 1890s and the period certainly had enough anti–Italian prejudice. What was more, the Mafia was chattered about in the 1920s and 1930s, when Mussolini was allegedly wiping it out in Sicily. But there were no stories like those that would emerge later of Capone being a Mafiosi. The papers did not dwell on what would later be seen as the blood bath that accompanied the emergence of New York's notorious "Five Families." Nor did anyone detect Lucky Luciano's welding together the law-giving, law-enforcing "Commission" that would apparently rule the nation's underworld, and keep the major criminals in power—and in line.

According to the sources used in this work, it would appear that the federal, state and local police forces were more exercised over these years by other criminal activity. During Southern Reconstruction, they were distracted by the criminal networks of the native-born Ku Klux Klan. In the late nineteenth century, they put most of their effort into fighting American and foreign smugglers and counterfeiters. As the new century dawned, they saw French, "Hebrew" and Eastern European white slavers as the nadir of organized crime. During the 1920s, the bulk of commentators argued the threat came from bootleggers, gin joint owners and rum-runners of all national backgrounds, as well as largely home-bred motorized gangsters, racketeers and kidnap gangs. The Italian criminals were there, but they were just one group out of many.

It also appears that although there was a perpetual suspicion that there were organized criminals, until the very final years of this study these were seen largely as local or regional threats. This changed in 1940 when the papers published the arguably spurious confessions of a small-time crook, "Kid Twist" Reles. His sensational tales exposed hit squads capable of carrying out contracts on recalcitrant criminals anywhere in the country. This distinctly dodgy confession fed into ideas of racketeers running the Depression Era economies of most major cities.

This version of organized criminal syndication nurtured vague notions of "combinations" based on industrial management models, underworld corporations which would from then onwards replace "gangs" as the organized criminal threats in the popular imagination. With Reles's claims about what the papers christened "Murder, Inc.," there was a growing suspicion that there really might be a national criminal network, but it was still not described as what we today might call a "Mafia." However, it did play a major role in the emergence of that perception, and certainly many of the histories of organized crime looked back on Murder, Inc. as being one of the most important glimpses into the evolution of the modern threat.

Such an interpretation of organized crime disrupts many solidly held ideas about the underworld in this period. It does away with the trajectory towards a unified criminal threat, and replaces it with a fractured, disjointed, messy history. Yet, if this book does have an over-arching trajectory, a theme, it is probably simply to question why we hold the views of organized crime that we hold today and to try to understand where some of those modern conceptions originated. Perhaps it hopes to simply point out some of the inconsistencies in some of the views we generally hold, and show how shaky and flawed is the evidence that underpins them, and how odd and how illogical some of the conclusions drawn from that evidence really are.

# Prologue: The True Extent
# of Organized Crime

## Portland 1939

On a rather sticky evening in Portland, Oregon's, Multnomah Hotel, 350 delegates were listening to a keynote address given by the owner of the largest and oldest garden nursery in the United States. Major Lloyd Crow Stark took as his theme the shocking claim that the United States as a nation was forfeiting $16,000,000,000 "annually to pay for organized crime."[1] At a time when the average annual income was under $1500, his audience would no doubt have been amazed by the size of that sum. The scale of this drain on resources becomes even more surprising if this figure is placed into a context of comparison. Stark himself did not use comparatives, but others had already done this for him.

Some six years before Stark addressed the delegates, Royal S. Copeland had put the problem of organized crime into an even more startling context. Copeland, the chairman of a Senate subcommittee investigating racketeering, had told the investigation that one out of every four dollars of the entire currency in circulation in the United States was "spent because of crime." Yet it was the testimony of an expert witness to that committee—a highly controversial historian and criminologist, Harry Elmer Barnes—that gave Copeland's statement an even more surprising, alarming and certainly pertinent perspective.[2]

Barnes placed the scale of the threat of organized crime into a context to which most informed Americans could clearly relate. As the Depression bit and Europe seemed to be falling prey to the rhetoric of violent extremism, the Great War's costs and reparations were featuring in the headlines on both sides of the Atlantic. Barnes himself was no stranger to these debates. He was well known, if not notorious, for his outspoken opposition to the concept of German "War Guilt" and for his condemnation of the relentless and crippling reparations scheduled for payment to the U.S.

Nevertheless, Barnes told the inquiry that the situation was so grave that every year "organized criminal gangs and racketeers" were costing the nation three times the entire war debt owed by the Allied nations to America.[3] It was clear that for once this apparent contrarian seemed to agree with American public opinion. It looked, at least in economic terms, like the U.S. faced a far more real threat at home than the looming crisis in Europe—and that was organized crime.[4]

This can be illustrated by a quick glance at the official White House Office of Management and Budget statistics for the year in which Stark was speaking. In 1939, the total federal government expenditure—and this was during what was seen as the high-spending FDR era—was a little over half of the $16 billion cited by Stark as the annual cost of organized crime.[5] It appeared from the reporting of Stark's speech that many agreed with the nurseryman. It seemed that the prevailing opinion was that organized crime was out of control.

## Lloyd Stark of Missouri

There are several reasons why Stark's statement in particular serves as a good starting point for this study. Most obviously, it illustrates the near universal concern with the problem of organized crime. But there is more to it than that. Stark's speech also serves to highlight some of the difficulties inherent in studying organized crime as an historical concept during this or any other period. Not the least of these problems is the question of the accuracy of, and motive behind, the information used to reach the conclusions drawn about the whole idea of organized crime.

Stark was by no means unique in his interest in the subject. Scholars, law enforcers, politicians and other interested parties regularly pointed out—and tried to find ways to contain—the escalating bills caused by what they termed *organized crime*. Leading the movement, criminologists had been attempting to reach a figure for the financial, as well as social, costs of criminal activity for as long as the discipline had existed, so it was familiar, if contested, ground by the time Stark made his speech. For example, one very well-regarded analysis of the problem used the National Commission on Law Observance and Enforcement (the so-called Wickersham Commission) statistics. They had arrived at a total cost for all American "crime," which came in at a little under $13 billion for 1931.[6]

However, this was generally considered a vastly inflated figure since it included anything and everything that could be seen as vaguely "criminal," as well as the long- and short-term financial consequences of widespread lawbreaking. This broad remit meant the estimate encompassed such things as the entire annual costs of prisons ($1 billion) and the total expense of policing the nation—500,000 officers paid at an average of $1,500 a year ($750,000,000). Further, it also considered the billions that made up payments for insurance premiums to cover businesses and individuals against criminal activity, as well as the total cost to the nation of insured losses caused by all forms of "crime."[7] What is also curious to modern students is that Stark makes no mention of how he arrived at his considerably larger figure of $16 billion.[8]

This brings up another problem in the study of organized crime, or any historical study: the importance of context. Stark was making a pitch to a group of businessmen associated with horticulture, and his objective appeared to be to pique their interest and alert them to the scale of the problem of organized crime. He was not giving a lecture to criminologists, sociologists or historians. He was not addressing an audience that might be considered experts in the field, or who might go on to use the data to implement policy. With this in mind, it is clear that he neither needed, nor was he expected, to provide statistically verifiable evidence. Following on from this, it appears that the consequences of the inaccuracy or incompleteness of his information were less important than the shock they could produce.

Put simply, Stark was not in court, nor was his work being scrutinized by colleagues or examined by commissioners. He was not under oath. No one in the audience would have demanded proof that his figures were accurate, nor would they have cross-examined him to establish where he got his information, thereby establishing the weight of evidence they may have behind them. Essentially, he would have had no reason to cite or expand on his sources. Besides, even if he had revealed the source of his alarming information, the chances are that all this would have proved was that the figure was at best a "guesstimate." It would almost certainly, itself, be based on unverifiable sources. So, in essence, it is probably safe to assume that his assessment was—like most of those made before him—an overestimate.

To most of the gardeners listening to Stark, this nit-picking would most probably not have mattered. Why would it? The problem was undoubtedly there—all Americans knew that—and Stark was trying to give an idea of the extent of the threat and then outline the proposed methods being taken to tackle it. But what does matter, especially to the historian, is that like so many audiences—both before and since—the growers and gardeners, along with their spouses and guests, would probably in all sincerity have absorbed such figures. With the statistics firmly embedded, in many cases they might have gone on to repeat them as the gospel truth. Once that had happened, the guesstimates of a speaker at a meeting of gardeners might well go on to become "statistical" facts, painting a clear and threatening picture of a crime epidemic sweeping the nation.

That is not to say that his horticultural audience was composed of abnormally gullible, particularly mendacious, or even unusually idealistic people given to exceptional levels of gossip or embellishment. There is no evidence for such a view. It is probable that the conference hall in Portland was merely filled with the usual mixture of interested amateurs, who were, after all, taxpayers and citizens. Nevertheless the speech is significant, since it has become apparent over the years that the sort of overestimation, or perhaps hyperbole, that Stark employed has been a perennial problem. Even before Stark's comments, and up until the present day, this exaggeration has been seen as blighting many assessments of the nature and extent of organized crime. It has been shown that similar data of similarly questionable authenticity has all too frequently formed the basis for the analysis of organized crime from way back when.

Perhaps the problem is best highlighted in the work of the policy analyst Max Singer, who in 1971 picked up on and pointed out this phenomenon of unreliable but frequently cited data relating to crime. Singer's discovery followed his analysis of the figures bandied about by other policy advisors relating to the annual value of stolen goods. He was particularly interested in those accumulated through the examination of the costs of burglary and shoplifting by heroin addicts in New York City. The data cited seemed to him, just like Stark's figure, shockingly high. However, unlike the majority of Stark's audience, Singer was an expert; and unlike Stark's audience, he began to investigate the reliability of the data behind many assumptions in the field.

Singer set about reading through the various articles and then cross-checking the information contained within them with police records. As he verified the data within the sources, Singer discovered to his surprise that the numbers cited exceeded the total recorded value of *all* thefts that took place in the city that year. Even more surprisingly, he found that they were inaccurate not by a statistically acceptable margin of error, but by a multiple of more than ten![9] Yet what was more worrying was that no one seemed to have bothered to verify where the information had come from, let alone query its accuracy. Quite the opposite: these were figures that were regularly cited. They seemed to have entered the consciousness of those who cited them, and once firmly in their minds, they had very rarely—if ever—been questioned.

Of course, there are logical reasons for the phenomenon that Singer went on to call the "vitality of mythical numbers," and a little more investigation into what Stark was doing in Portland starts to hint at some of them. Any casual observer of the speech might well have questioned why the speaker was talking about organized crime in the first place. At first sight it does seem rather strange that at a gathering of gardeners, the keynote speaker should take it upon himself to warn the audience against the costs of organized crime. But then Stark was more than a simple—even if very successful and rich—horticulturalist. He also happened to be the governor of Missouri. What was more, he was on a national speaking tour, promoting his forthcoming campaign for election to the U.S. Senate, and he was making organized crime his campaign issue.

Once this is taken into consideration, his choice of subject matter becomes a little less baffling. Organized crime was then, as it is now, a particularly hot topic, and it was often used as a method of gaining a place in the political limelight. After all, it was a subject that had attracted press attention, which had never been more apparent than in the 1920s and 1930s, as a quick survey of articles in the *New York Times* illustrates. Perhaps unsurprisingly, "organized crime" had become an increasingly significant topic in the period of Prohibition and the Depression as the specter of the bootlegger, gangster, motorized bandit and "Public Enemy Number One" became household concerns.

The phrase "organized crime" occurs in the *New York Times* headlines some 621 times between 1865 and 1945. Five hundred and eighty-seven of those references, or 94.5 percent, fall within the period from 1920 to 1945. Similarly, the *Chicago Tribune* shows 431 total references, of which 406, or 94.2 percent, occur in the last twenty-five years of the period. The figures for the *Washington Post* and *Los Angeles Times* are also comparable at 239 and 217 (90.7 percent) and 244 and 235 (96.3 percent), respectively, although it should be noted that the *Washington Post* was not founded until 1877.[10]

Unsurprisingly—given its topicality—politicians and public servants at all levels, from City Hall to the White House, had used, and continued to use, the ill-defined menace of organized crime, particularly in the 1920s and 1930s and beyond. Stark was no exception, but his case is perhaps especially illustrative since he also had a more personal reason to attack organized crime. This motivation gave him every reason to exaggerate the costs of organized crime to the U.S. taxpayer. It gave him a motive to play up its malign influence on American life and reiterate what so many already saw as its seemingly omnipresent influence.

## Big Tom Pendergast

In his home state of Missouri, Lloyd Stark was a local celebrity, even before he ran for office. He was a leading businessman from a very prominent and wealthy local family. He was also something of a hero in his own right. He had served as a major in the American Expeditionary Force in France in the Great War, and had fought in the final stages of the war with well-recorded and medal-winning bravery in the Meuse-Argonne offensive. All this meant that he was well known in Missouri by the time he decided to enter state politics. Even so, like most Democrats of that time in that region, Stark had still needed to call on Kansas City's kingmaker and political boss to secure his support. However, unlike many other Democrats of this era, his rise to political prominence in Missouri was in large measure achieved without support from that all-powerful Kansas City-St. Louis Democrat machine. He never did secure the support of city boss Tom Pendergast.

Stark's relationship with Pendergast was never an entirely happy one. It appears Pendergast did not see the war hero as a natural ally. The political boss had refused to support Stark in a previous attempt at the governorship in 1932 and repeated this reluctance when the horticulturist ran for the U.S. Senate in 1934. So when Stark ran for the governorship in 1936, he decided he would attempt it without Pendergast's support. Instead he drew on Democrat support from outside Kansas City.

The result was that, amid what was one of the most corrupt and dirty state elections in a state with an impressive reputation for corrupt and dirty politics, Stark fell out in spectacular style with the all-powerful machine of "Big Tom." In Pendergast's mind, while he had not lent the full weight of his machine to Stark's campaigns, he had certainly never stood in his way. By contrast, Stark felt that Pendergast's support of other candidates in both the Senate and governorship campaigns illustrated hostility. Stark won both his battle with Pendergast and the Governorship.

But that wasn't the end. The undeclared dispute reached a head when the new governor refused to back an obviously corrupt and embattled Pendergast Machine lackey for the State Insurance Commission. A row ensued, and in a demonstration of a very rare brand of sang-froid in Missouri politics, Stark held his nerve against the boss. In refusing to back down, the gardener showed some of the bravery he had drawn on at the front in the Great War, and it gained him popular support, which further enraged Pendergast. By now, the battle lines were drawn, as Stark openly continued to defy Pendergast's repeated requests and refused the political appointment.

Buoyed by his success, Stark now started to question the qualifications of all Pendergast's stooges. In doing so, he broke irreparably with Pendergast. As pressure from the boss mounted, Stark fought back, all the while damning the machine and making an issue of its control of Missouri patronage.[11] The final straw came in 1937, when Stark appointed James M. Douglas to the state Supreme Court. The move was guaranteed to provoke Pendergast to fury, for as Stark himself explained: "The Pendergast Machine wanted the Supreme Court. They were not so much concerned with who was appointed just so [long as] it was an 'organization' man. Douglas was not such a man."[12]

As one local paper, sympathetic to Pendergast, put it: "After pleading for twelve years for Pendergast's endorsement, now Stark castigates that influence."[13] The result was, somewhat predictably, that Stark was ousted from the machine's all-controlling fold. Instead of bringing Stark back to heel, Pendergast's insistent sniping and constant threatening made the gardener put his considerable energy into ending the Pendergast Machine's stranglehold over political appointments in Missouri. Rather than chastening him, bullying made Stark publicly state it as his mission to do all in his power to expose the corruption of the Pendergast Machine.

True to his word, during his time in the governor's mansion (1937–1941), Stark very rarely missed an opportunity to loudly condemn the Pendergast Machine, and he did so very effectively. The result was that first local, then national, newspapers took up the crusade to clean up Missouri politics, publishing the governor's condemnation of Pendergast in a spirit driven by a cocktail of motives, which mixed factionalism and wicked glee with an eye for a good story.[14]

Stark did not find it difficult to produce evidence of the malign influence of the machine. Over the preceding decade or so, Pendergast had tolerated not only gambling and prostitution, but also in this era of national Prohibition, his machine had openly allowed the trade in booze. Bootlegging had a long tradition in Kansas City, and by the time Pendergast secured his control of the trade, networks for booze were already established. After all, Kansas went dry in 1881 and would remain dry until 1948, whereas Missouri had rejected temperance legislation in 1910, 1912 and 1918.

Perhaps one reason for this reluctance was that the illicit booze trade across the state borders in Kansas City was so lucrative. Missouri ratified the Nineteenth Amendment only after it had already got the required two-thirds of states supporting it. Nevertheless, it went dry, and Pendergast had quickly set about establishing an impressive and lucrative network of toadies, graft, corruption and kickbacks centering on what was essentially a vice empire. Under Pendergast, throughout the 1920s and into the next decade, Kansas City, Missouri, blossomed as the vital nexus for vice in the Midwest. It was the point through which illicit booze, whores and other "products" central to organized crime in the region were channeled.

However, Pendergast's real coup came in the early 1930s, when he managed to get the Kansas City Police Department under the city's, rather than the state's, governance. Arguing that as resources became more scarce in those times of austerity, it was wise for Kansas City to stop wasting them on policing policies dictated by those outside the city. Instead, as he pointed out, it made far more sense that the municipal government should control the metropolitan area's policing. Why did he support this change? The answer is simple. The policy of police "home rule" effectively meant that no matter who was in the governor's mansion, Pendergast's hold over City Hall would always give him control of law enforcement.[15]

With this built-in security, "Big Tom" now had no need to hide his illegal activities, since he was secure in his control of the region. He was also safe from outside—federal—investigation. This was staved off, Stark argued, in large part as a result of Big Tom's close connections with the powerful and influential fellow Catholic, Democratic National Committee chairman, Postmaster General and arguably one of FDR's most significant campaigners, Jim Farley. Through him he had the ear of the White House.[16] All of this meant that the stakes for Stark's attack were, therefore, extremely high. He was taking on what amounted to a criminal institution with connections at the highest levels of U.S. politics. Mounting a head-on assault on such an enemy might, under what had been the prevailing circumstances, well prove little short of political suicide. However, by 1936, Stark knew that the odds of success were shifting, and in his favor.

By the early years of the 1930s, a series of highly publicized events were fundamentally changing U.S. public opinion about organized crime. In Missouri the violence connected with gangsters had escalated dramatically. In June 1933 four policemen and their prisoner were killed in a daylight shootout at Union Station, Kansas City. On a March election day in 1934, intimidation of voters by gangsters led to another four people being killed, and eleven injured. Papers reported what they saw as running gun battles taking place between gangsters and Federal "G-men," most notably the statewide hunt for Charles "Pretty Boy" Floyd. Nor were the drivers for change exclusively local.

Across the nation, events were changing the mood from tacit support for criminals to a new intolerance. Not the least of these was the prosecution and imprisonment of Al Capone in 1931. With this momentous event it seemed that even "Crime Central," Chicago, was being liberated from the rule of gangsters. Nor was it only in the Second City that these transformations were detectable. In New York, there were high-profile, and—more surprisingly—successful prosecutions of the city's leading mobsters by the young, headline-grabbing, photogenic celebrity of a DA, Thomas Dewey.

What was more, as the decade progressed, even these considerable successes paled with the constantly advertised achievements of J. Edgar Hoover's ongoing and highly publicized "War on Crime." Public enemy after public enemy was imprisoned or killed by the methodical and modern scientific methods of Hoover's FBI, combined with the incorruptible and fearless G-men operating in the field and a perceptible and growing public support for law enforcers. The Midwest and Southwest were saved from the bank raids, gunpoint jailbreaks, and other predations of such ruthless bandits as John Dillinger, Charles "Pretty Boy" Floyd, George "Machine Gun" Kelly, George "Baby Face" Nelson, Alvin "Creepy" Karpis, Donnie "Ma" Barker, and Bonnie Parker and Clyde Barrow. The kidnappers of high-profile figures and their offspring like Charles Urschel, George Weyerhaeuser, William Hamm, Edward Bremer, and of course Charles Lindbergh Junior, were all brought to justice.[17]

All of this showed that the power of the "gangster," which had so dominated the sensationalist headlines of the 1920s and early 1930s, could be, and was being, broken. A small group of the more perceptive commentators may well have seen the motorized bandits of the Midwest, the public enemies and the tales of G-men heroics as little more than New Deal hype. The majority argued this was the result of the exposure of the political protection which had so effectively shielded celebrity gangsters and enriched their protectors within the police departments, the judiciary, and the city halls of the nation.[18] It did not require much imagination for Stark to see that this new climate represented the supreme opportunity in his feud with Pendergast.

Stark himself was aware that the tide of public impotence and indifference, if not fear, had turned. He saw that the tolerance of intimidation, and acceptance of the powerlessness and corruption of the authorities, were certainly dissipating, if not disappearing. Essentially, the laissez-faire attitude of the 1920s, which had maintained those bosses with a whiff of criminal connections—men like Pendergast—in power, had changed. It had given way to a bitter mood, driven by successful prosecutions and a new and steely puritanism tempered by economic depression.

As might be expected, Kansas City was not exempt from this change. The jobs, the booze, not to mention the jazz that the Machine sponsored, were still seen by many as beneficial to the local economy. What was less welcome was the increasing evidence that violence, corruption and graft had been essential to their production and distribution. With Stark's campaign it became evident that there might be an alternative to dominance by the Pendergast Machine. For the first time since his rise to dominance in the region in 1925, Big Tom was threatened with a genuine rival. Here was a man he could not buy off, scare off, or sack. What was even more worrying to the Boss was that he was also unable to have his friends in high places rein in or bury the evidence of his involvement in the accusations that Stark was making.

Partly as a result of Governor Stark's relentless efforts, the activities of the Kansas City Machine were now being unearthed and highlighted by grand jury and FBI investigations. As Judge Allen C. Southern put it in his report to the grand jury charged with investigating the "widespread breakdown in law enforcement" under "the big man of gambling," it was a much deeper problem than the "mere question of whether someone wants to gamble or the question of whether someone wants to buy a drink of liquor at an unlawful hour. We believe that the term 'a wide open town' implies a degree of corruption of public officials that is incompatible with their oaths of office.... [Essentially] organized crime and open violation of the law have been publically [sic] known for some time."[19]

Within a remarkably short time, Stark's relentless raising of "the corner of the curtain which enveloped the underworld ... [had] exposed a mass of corruption" and led to some 390 prosecutions.[20] Not the least of these successes was the fact that by the time of Stark's previously mentioned Portland announcement, the formerly invincible and all-powerful Pendergast was himself serving 11 months for tax evasion. Big Tom was no longer "Boss Tom"; he was now simply prisoner number 55295 in Leavenworth Federal Penitentiary.[21]

## Routes to Power

In the wake of his victory over Pendergast, Governor Stark's message was upbeat. He predicted it was "the beginning of a swing of the pendulum [away] from civic corruption, gangsterism, racketeering, graft-infested politics and contempt for law and order in state and nation." It was very much in tune with the mood of the times, and he set out to make political capital from it.[22] Not only did he announce his senatorial candidacy, but rumors emerged that the major may well be "presidential timber." The governor billed himself as the Democrats' answer—or "equalizer," as he rather dramatically put it—to the Republicans' dashing, headline-seeking and supremely ambitious candidate, the "gang-busting," "racket-bashing" New York City District Attorney, Thomas Dewey.

As a result, the Stark presidential show played to large, packed venues in St. Louis, New York City, Albany, Portland and other towns. His speeches always included details of his battles with "organized crime" in the shape of the Pendergast Machine. Yet it is telling that at no point in his diatribes did Stark clearly define what exactly he meant by organized crime. Those politicians of this era who campaigned on the organized crime issue very rarely did. This was not simply negligence. No doubt the vagueness was partly for stylistic effect. It is a well-established rhetorical trick that a nebulous, ill-defined, but all-pervasive enemy is always far more threatening—and therefore a more effective vote-winner—than a clearly drawn foe. The known and clearly defined is often by its very nature necessarily limited in its menace. However, an ill-defined threat is limited only by the imagination of the audience.

Playing up that threat was distinctly advantageous for the increasingly ambitious Stark. It almost goes without saying that the greater the threat the governor had to overcome, the greater would be his prestige for having done so. On the other hand, he may not have defined it because he simply did not feel it was necessary to do so. It would not have been a ridiculous assumption on his part that everyone in his audience would be aware of what organized crime was. They must have been, since they were so accustomed to hearing about the threat it represented to the nation.

If it had been possible to conduct a survey of what Stark's audiences on his speaking tour thought actually comprised "organized crime," the chances are that the surveyor would have encountered a variety of views. Further, many of these answers may come as a complete surprise to similarly constituted audiences today. In its classification, as well as in its prosecution, organized crime was then, and remains now, a malleable threat. It meant entirely different things to different people. This was perhaps why it was, and continues to be, a popular topic for those seeking office. Politicians, legislators, policemen, lobbyists, and academics all had differing viewpoints on what constituted organized crime. Each came at it from a different angle.

The cynic might say that all parties who spoke on the subject, all parties who used organized crime, had their own battles to fight and their own ambitions to achieve. For them, and as a result the U.S. public as a whole, the bogeymen of organized crime could, and did, range from bootleggers to Black Handers; from pirates to polygamists; from Mafiosi to machine politicians—or as in Stark's case, cronies, bootleggers, gamblers, pimps and grafters. Whichever definition or practitioner was chosen, it is clear that each speaker was engaging with his own variety of "organized crime."

It is little exaggeration to claim that defining organized crime has become something of its own subgenre in the disciplines of law, the social sciences and the humanities. It has inspired a small herd of journal articles and not a few books. For example, at the time of writing, one Internet website devoted to defining the phenomenon gives nearly 70 separate definitions. What is more, that is only for American organized crime, and the site covers some 23 other countries.[23] The British historian Mike Woodiwiss simplified this huge range of ideas in his 1999 paper to the British Criminology Conference.[24] He put forward the idea that over the years since the late 1940s, two very separate, and to a large extent incompatible, concepts of what constituted organized crime have evolved and now compete with each other in terms of the categorization of organized crime.

On the one hand, there is the idea that the definition of organized crime should be based around the notion of "systematic and illegal activity for power or profit." In this, Woodiwiss agrees with many other historians of what Mark H. Haller has called "illegal enterprise." This essentially amounts to a rather all-encompassing definition that has at its root the idea that organized crime is simply crime which is "not *dis*organized."[25] On the other hand, organized crime has also become synonymous with a far more complex world of collections of national, transnational or international gangsters, racketeers that have become known in everyday terms as "Mafias."

By contrast with the first definition, the "organization" stresses not so much the methods used in the committing of crimes, but more the structure that unites those who carry them out. This is an interpretation that implies organizations of regional, national, international or global ambitions. That in turn makes it a definition that conjures up a far more sophisticated image for organized crime. What lies at the bottom of this definition is a concentration on an image of a criminal world that's much more integrated, more sophisticated and more corporate.

The result is that this change in emphasis means the organization needs to be more structured in order to be able to support the inevitable growth that sustains and propels corporations—legal or illegal. That, in turn, means that it is often hierarchical, and that makes it far more "organized." This style of definition has the effect of turning organized crime into what Howard Abadinsky has memorably called "a bureaucracy of evil."[26] At the heart of this interpretation is the idea that these organizations are far more long-lived, since they are predicated by the needs of the network and what furthers the corporate ideals. This in turn means they are able to command far greater reach, and therefore represent far more of a threat than the simple organizations of criminals implied by Woodiwiss's first depiction.

These two styles of definition come into, and go out of, fashion and usage at various times in the broad scope of the historiography of organized crime in the U.S. Nevertheless, going back to the conference hall in Portland in 1939, it is possible to see both elements would have informed Stark's audience. At times in the period leading up to Stark's speech, there were fears that crime had been "systematized" or "syndicated" and had broken free of the usual constraints of regional or city-based allegiances, unified itself and become a national phenomenon.

To the vast majority of observers, the difference between Woodiwiss's two rather distinctive interpretations of organized crime lay in the manner in which they were reported and the time at which this reporting occurred. For example, a report dealing with the activities of a gang of horse thieves in Danville, Illinois, in the 1870s, claimed they were "one of the boldest and best organized bands ... which ever carried on business."[27] Similarly, twenty years later there was a black gang that attracted considerable attention in Knoxville, Tennessee.

Highly orderly in its methods, the gang employed 10 burglars—each of whom was allocated an area of the city in which to work. Each burglar got a prearranged share of the profits. The operation had an HQ building and a distinct hierarchy, and a strict demarcation of jobs governed the business as a whole. The scale, success and organization of the criminals excited the reporter to call them the "greatest sensation this city has known for months"—although perhaps this says as much about life in Knoxville in the 1890s as it does about organized crime.[28] That said, both were reported at the time as examples of "organized crime."

Nevertheless, while it is apparent that such reports were certainly designed to show how organized and threatening these gangs were, they also demonstrate that at the time of writing such operations still remained local in their scope, and most probably their ambitions. On the other hand, by 1911 the editor of the *Chicago Tribune* warned that if the Italian extortionists, universally called the Black Hand, were not checked, "a great criminal organization may be evolved in time ... which finally may reach a point where it can extort tribute from the greatest powers of business and wealth."[29] This editor was not alone in making such dire prophecies, and they would only get worse as time went on.

By 1926, the former governor of Illinois, Frank O. Lowden, was warning an audience in Washington, D.C., that the threat from gangsters had escalated to the point where "organized crime could overthrow the government." By way of backing up his predictions of doomsday for democracy, he pointed to what had happened in Russia in 1917.[30] His audience was no doubt thankful that the situation never quite got *that* dire, but still by 1930 a West Coast paper informed its readership that America was "helpless in the face of organized crime."[31] Even allowing for the obvious hyperbole, it appears that the threat of organized crime—or at least the perception of that threat—had evolved to break free of regional constraints.

Some feel it is possible to be more specific about where and when organized crime emerged. Historian Timothy Gilfoyle points to a time, a place and a perpetrator for the first real and repeated usage of the idea of "organized crime." Gilfoyle indicates that this is the first instance in a sense that is recognizable and compatible with most modern interpretations of the expression. What is more, he also lines up an individual he sees as coining the phrase, namely the early–1890s moral reformer, the Reverend Charles Parkhurst.[32]

In his crusade to clean up New York, Parkhurst repeatedly used phrases that resonate with ideas of modern organized crime. In a fashion similar to the perception of early twentieth century Chicago, New York and Los Angeles gangsters, Parkhurst argued that the endemic corruption of Tammany Hall and their control of the New York police force essentially created modern organized crime. He used expressions like "a superbly organized band of brigands" and pointed out the connections with politicians created a variety of "protected and entrenched crime" that could operate with effective immunity on a higher and more effective level than ever before. Essentially he argued that "the most gigantic system of organized crime known to civilized society" was being created.[33]

Others see the emergence of the phenomenon as being reactive rather than inventive. These commentators evoke what is essentially a cliché. They argue that organized crime evolved as a reaction to the fundamental changes in U.S. society over these years. It was simply the modernization of criminal activity. Most basic among such interpretations is perhaps the notion that the criminal and his methods and ambitions had become professionalized. With the growth of the wage economy, crime, like other businesses, was increasingly seen as a "career." To a proportion of the less desperate of those from the so-called "criminal classes"—and certainly in the eyes of many unsympathetic commentators—it was work.

To all intents and purposes, a life in crime was a career decision. Perhaps the most convincing and best reasoned of these accounts emerged in 1937 when the leading criminologist, Edwin H. Sutherland, edited the confessions of a career thief, Chic Conwell. This annotated autobiography described a world of professional thieves, pickpockets and con men who lived in a highly organized criminal world that had only been suspected to exist before.[34] Alongside this, it has been argued that crime expanded, becoming increasingly complex and ambitious as the nation's industrialized and commercial activity became more sophisticated.[35]

Extending this interpretation to its logical conclusion lends weight to a sort of inverted Whiggish interpretation of criminal history which has a large following. In it, commentators see an onward march to a criminal Nirvana dominated by über-criminals such as Al Capone, Arnold Rothstein and Lucky Luciano. It leads to the formation of bodies imbued with near-invincible status, organizations like the Black Hand, the Five Families, the Commission and so on, until we reach today's Mexican drug cartels, Russian Mafias, and even Islamist terrorists. While this increasing level of ambition and professionalism was certainly apparent in some—if not all—cases, it was by no means universally so, and almost certainly never as effective as the most congratulatory of accounts would have us believe.

Reports and perceptions of organized crime tended to be dependent on locality and perspective, and these, for a whole variety of reasons, were—and are—open to manipulation. A good illustration of this manipulation and its subsequent impact on the historiography of organized crime can be found in the Associated Press report of 1937 that celebrated Thomas Dewey's New York City "gang-busting." This argues that his efforts were so successful that the city's highly organized crime had been, in essence, neutered. According to this report, the threat to the city from organized crime, which had been represented by alliances of highly ambitious celebrity gangsters, was now reduced to a more or less unstructured collective of muggers and street toughs.

Over the preceding decade or so, men like Arnold Rothstein, Lepke Buchalter, Dutch Schultz and Lucky Luciano had dominated not just the New York City crimescape, but, some would argue, the nation's criminal activity. Between them they controlled imperial-scale networks directing such things as prostitution, labor racketeering, protection rackets, illegal lotteries, illegal booze, loan-sharking and narcotics. These were men who brokered national and international deals. Like the notorious managers of the huge monopolies of the late nineteenth century, the so-called robber barons, their almost limitless ambition had enabled them to set up legendary, if not mythical, crimes like Rothstein's alleged fixing of the 1919 World Series.

Similarly, like those precursors in legitimate industries, the underworld bosses were credited with having rationalized the way in which their businesses operated. Perhaps the most "rational" of these is Salvatore "Lucky" Luciano. Luciano is credited with persuading his fellow mobsters to see sense at the end of a particularly vicious series of gang wars. He gathered them together in Atlantic City and proposed the creation of a governing body—the "Commission"—to regulate and control their criminal activity. According to a whole raft of what are now seen as more or less dubious sources—including "true confessions" of mobsters and the FBI's Mafia files—this rationalization, it was claimed some years later, would launch what would become the modern Cosa Nostra.

Yet it is the very untrustworthiness of these sources that can be most instructive to the historian of organized crime. The way in which interpretations have shifted over these years is very telling, and forms the basis of this book. For example, while Luciano was apparently streamlining and rationalizing crime, most of the newspapers of the time, seemingly oblivious to these developments, boasted that New York City's organized underworld had been broken. They proclaimed that as a result of Dewey's efforts the city's organized crime was now reduced to gangs of hoodlums who simply robbed "the weak through sheer force of numbers."[36]

## The Impact of History on Crime

It is apparent that the history of organized crime, like most history, is both fluid and changeable. A considerable proportion of mainstream histories of organized crime would not agree with the dominant contemporary interpretation that saw Dewey as heroically successful in his "gangbusting." While they may agree that the level of activity of organized crime, for one reason or another, may have dropped off over the years of Dewey's crime-busting, the reasons they give for this decline are totally different. Their interpretation is often dominated by the perception that organized crime in New York in the 1930s was undergoing a period of consolidation and reorganization after the boom years of Prohibition and a bloody power struggle sparked by that bonanza.[37]

These were the years in which, after the bloody Castellammarese War, the Five Families came to dominate the Cosa Nostra. According to many of those who hold with a "Mafia-type" interpretation of organized crime, this was the decade when ruthless and well-organized, well-funded and highly ambitious gangsters changed the organization of America's underworld forever. This was the decade when truly organized criminal activity went from being seen as a local phenomenon to a national, international or transnational one—albeit quietly, insidiously, and largely undetected.[38]

Perhaps this subtlety explains why examining a range of primary sources—including newspaper articles; Crime Commission reports; congressional debates; politicians' speeches; police, court and FBI reports; and contemporary academic articles—does not make it apparent that this was the way in which organized crime was seen at the time. When "organized crime" does appear in this material, it is often associated with reports of the corruption of labor officials, lawyers and politicians. Particular attention is paid to the venality and amorality of judges, lawyers, juries and especially the police. Nevertheless, criminal actions are particularly unambitious in scope. They are normally simply related to the actions of a local gang or even a particular individual. Furthermore, these documents pay attention to the "War on Crime," "rackets" and "racketeering," and the links between crime and business, Prohibition, and urban politics, but they don't seem to be interested in, or detect, the rise of the crime families.

What is curious, given the dominance it has assumed in the interpretation of organized crime since, is that these sources do not highlight, even obliquely, the rise to prominence of Italian or Sicilian gangsters. Nor do they even mention the Cosa Nostra. Some may argue that is because, although gangsters may have used the phrase at the time, the term had yet to be introduced into the popular lexicon of the American people. They would legitimately claim that this rather peculiar and somewhat coy phrase—meaning "our thing"—would only gain prevalence some time later, during the fevered paranoia of the Cold War. The phrase really entered the public imagination in 1963 when a disgruntled Italian American gangster, Joe Valachi, used it in his evidence on organized crime given to the McClellan Committee on Government Operations.[39]

Be that as it may, the omission is still important and surprising, and the same is true of the conspicuous absence of that ubiquitous and catch-all term of organized crime today, "the Mafia." In these years, when the Mafia is mentioned, it is usually as a bloody—almost picturesque—but certainly alien phenomenon of rural Sicily. Accounts of the fraternity in the 1920s and 1930s generally accompany largely laudatory reports of Mussolini's drive to modernize Italy, make the trains run on time, and stamp out the feudal bandits of the south.

In this context, the Mafia is depicted as a medieval-style organization of blood-feuds, vendettas and honor killing. This is an organization that seems to have very little if anything to do with the cold-blooded, urban, modern U.S. gangster with his garish suits, wisecracking braggadocio, and fast cars. That said, over these years, very occasionally the Mafia is referred to in an American context. Even then it is most likely used, not in an examination of the body count or other consequences of the Castellammarese War, let alone its inexorable rise, but its association with the notorious lynching in New Orleans of eleven "Sicilians" in 1891.

Of course it is unrealistic to assume that a range of historical sources can give anything near a complete picture of a particular historical phenomenon. This must be especially true of those sources related to illegal or clandestine activity. Yet these contemporary reports do seem to highlight that the media and law enforcers of the time were more interested in changes occurring in the local nature of organized crime than they were in the emergence of any organization with global, or even national reach. In spite of previously mentioned hyperbole, the vast majority of such sources generally mention the emergence of national criminal organizations more as a threat which it was certainly still possible to avoid. They rarely describe a phenomenon which was so powerful, well-organized and established that it was only possible to talk in terms of damage limitation, as we tend to retrospectively attribute to them today.

These sources would seem to indicate other concerns. They appear to show that contemporaries were most concerned with the ways in which developments in crime changed as a response to technological development and accompanying changes in demography, lifestyle and wealth. Alongside these developments there was a growing belief that crime thrived in the new environment that was governing society. Those who held to this view saw the nation's moral compass disrupted by a new type of atheistic relativism. To them it was an amorality which brought about drastic changes in relation to both the personal and the public sphere. The media reported that it was the seeming breakdown in familial relations and an increasingly apathetic or corrupt attitude towards lawlessness that drove a nihilistic perception of the increasing power and increased prevalence of gangsters, mobsters and hoodlums in all the major cities, and even some rural areas of the nation.

It would appear that in the 1920s and 1930s the perception of organized crime veered far more towards crime which was "not disorganized" rather than the later "Mafia"-based interpretation. One typical editorial clearly illustrates this view, blaming "new conditions, the increase of motor traffic, the close of the war and the advent of prohibition" for a climate in which "organized crime is far better financed and equipped than ever before in the history of the world." Organized crime was now "calculated, violent and desperate, rather than disorganized and petty as in the past."[40]

What is evident from an overview of the 1930s is that the perception of "organized crime" over those years does not appear to be the same as that of today. Further, the differences between what constituted organized crime in documents associated with the courts, the legislatures and among law enforcers—and how these perceptions were then relayed through the media—is striking. So is the transient nature of these interpretations. Over these years, threats like the Ku Klux Klan, the Black Hand and the Industrial Workers of the World, dominate news coverage, political comment and law-enforcement effort for several years, and then seem to evaporate.

Nor is it just the groups involved in crime that emerge and submerge. Over these years the "crimescape" of America changes. This is often viewed as the result of the political, moral and economic fluctuations in the mood of the nation. It is also influenced by technological, demographic and ethnographic changes and developments. Whatever the cause, there can be no doubt that some crimes become increasingly lucrative, and therefore prevalent, like insurance and stock fraud, human trafficking, and drug-dealing. For an equally diverse series of reasons, other forms of criminal enterprise seem to emerge, to peak and to die out, like stagecoach and train-robbing, horse-poisoning and, most famously, bootlegging and rum-running.

The center of gravity of criminal enterprise that controls the headlines, preoccupies government and drives law enforcement also undergoes similar periodic shifts. There are major changes in the ethnicity, class and race of perpetrators and victims, as well as their geographic location. The crimes of the Republican carpetbaggers, White Line organizations and black freedmen in the Reconstruction South give way to the bandit gangs of the wide-open West, and all the while the threat of the urban gangsters is gestating and mutating in the metropolitan regions of the northeast, the Midwest and the West Coast. Nevertheless, some associations remain constant. There are threads of lawlessness and gangsterism associated with a variety of immigrant groups that run throughout the period.

The Irish continue to be associated with the corruption of Tammany Hall. The Chinese remain synonymous with the opium trade. Jews retain links with a variety of moral and financial crimes, blacks are tied in with cocaine, and Mexicans are perpetually connected with the "pushing" of marijuana. There are also themes that remain constant—like the association of gangsters with corrupt politicians and lawyers, and the perpetual belief that crime was getting steadily more prevalent, violent and incurable as U.S. cities rapidly grew in size and neighborhoods went in and out of fashion. Alongside this, there are some groups which always seem to be exploited, like women, unskilled laborers, and the nation's Chinese, Latino, aboriginal and black populations. Equally there were those other sections of society that always seem to be associated with the exploitation of those groups, like the city and industrial bosses, the venal politicians and the corrupt policemen.

## The Impact of Crime on History

It is apparent that organized crime represents a seemingly irresistible subject for political self-promotion and publicity—as in the cases of Governor Stark and Thomas Dewey. But that is not where the connections end. For many in positions of political power, it also represented an equally magnetic temptation to pervert the function of that public office. In newspapers of the period—as well as other sources like court transcripts and congressional reports—corruption, election fraud, graft, bribery, and jury fixing form an all-too-common strand of organized crime, and the perpetrators, organizers and beneficiaries are all too often public officials. Consequently this will form one of the major themes of this work.

Alongside this it appears that organized crime is inextricably linked to the phenomenon of the rise of the city. Cities, most notably New York, Chicago and—towards the end of the period—Los Angeles, figure centrally in the reportage of organized crime in the period. In many ways organized crime has been seen as urban in its roots and manifestation, and America's massive urbanization over this period certainly fed these fears. To most commentators of the time it was a given that organized crime was nurtured by its connections with the growth, governance and administration of cities over this period.

The city, by virtue of its fostering of anonymity, its obvious extremes of wealth and poverty (often in very close proximity), as well as its inherent overcrowding, is also seen as spawning, cultivating, encouraging and sustaining the immorality and licentiousness which create the fear of the phenomenon in the first place. The city was the home of ungodly practices and un–American vices. It was also the breeding ground of the criminal classes, gangs and syndicates. What was more, one of the most obvious features of the newly emerging and rapidly growing cities was the diversity of their populations.

Not only did the immigrants from Europe and Asia flood in and settle cheek-by-jowl with each other in these new urban melting pots, but the same elements that attracted them acted as magnets to native-born populations from all over America. Rural populations left their often uneconomic small farms to make their fortunes in the modern metropolises, reinventing themselves as entrepreneurs and workers. Black Southerners flooded north, fleeing from oppression and poverty. Men and women moved from one city to another as opportunity beckoned or the prospect of work, wealth or simply happiness withdrew from their rural surroundings.

This transient, multinational, multi-faith and multi-ethnic population was seen as another of the root causes of the moral degeneration, all too apparent poverty, and resultant desperation that condemned whole populations to a life of crime. Nor was that the only connection between the increasingly urban nation and its increasing lawlessness.

It was this ephemeral population that supplied the hoodlums with their customers and victims. Perhaps more worryingly to many commentators of the time, it was this population who, through their sheer lumpen numbers, provided camouflage for the activities of those gangsters.

Central to these migrations, which fueled so many of the problems of diversity, was the ever-increasing pace of technological change. Developments in transport and communications enabled the movement of people, as well as goods and services, at a rate unimaginable before the period of this study. These technological advances were also seen as having facilitated, inspired and enabled crimes in themselves, from train robbery to kidnapping, from auto theft to wire scams. It soon became apparent that crimes of this sort required considerable planning, as well as sophistication in their execution. In addition, the technology of industrialization applied equally to legitimate and illegitimate enterprise. This meant criminals also had considerable potential to expand to take advantage of the economies of scale. In short, these were crimes that required, benefited from and inspired organization—and this did not escape commentators of the day.

If technology brought opportunity, it also produced changes that were considered in many areas even less welcome than organized crime. Essentially it created a whole new way of life. Across the nation the skilled and dedicated artisan saw himself increasingly threatened by the unskilled industrial wage slave, and it appeared that those who stood in the way of this change were doomed. Unlike Europe, where similar change was taking place, America could rely on nearly inexhaustible sources of expendable labor: immigrants.

They were attracted by rates of pay that were generally higher than in the Old World, but often put up with working and living conditions for the lower ends of society that were frequently even worse than those endured by their European counterparts. The result was fertile ground for organized criminal activity. Not only was any radical form of unionization portrayed in many quarters as a greater or lesser form of criminal organization, but so were those who advocated political working-class solidarity—from the Knights of Labor through to the Industrial Workers of the World and the Communist Party U.S. What was more, labor's disputes attracted the seemingly legitimate, as well as downright illegitimate, suppliers of protection and muscle—both for the strikers and the bosses.

On the other hand, some commentators saw the post–Civil War explosion of industrial capitalism itself as organized crime. These critics pointed to its being based on the condoning of worker exploitation and a total neglect of the human dignity of their employees. These commentators saw a powerful criminal conspiracy in the willful disregard of the safety of both their workers and their customers in the pursuit of profit. They saw the truly threatening criminal organizations as the big business conglomerations, the so-called trusts and their plutocratic owners, that circumvented and ignored laws meant to control them. These commentators paired big businesses with the banks, which they saw as extracting usurious sums from the less well off while discounting the repayments made by the trusts and the plutocrats.

What made this situation even more unbearable was that even when union activity did emerge as a mass movement, this seemingly beneficial trend quickly became corrupted and tainted. Sometimes the bosses infiltrated the unions and made "sweetheart deals" with corrupt union officials, limiting the unions' abilities to improve conditions, raise pay or take industrial action. At other times the unions rented out muscle and blackmailed companies with threats of strikes. When unions did organize on a significant scale, the large funds accrued through members' dues sometimes attracted racketeers who subverted their aims, diverted those funds, and used unions as a way into industries capable of generating new revenue streams.

Whatever form it took, many Americans associated unionization with criminalization, and even when it grew rapidly in the 1930s, it was still seen by many as tainted by racketeering. But that is not to say that there was a total rejection of working-class movements. As in Europe, many of the American unions grew out of trade guilds, friendly societies and fraternities, and these too have an important connection with organized crime. Unlike the emerging socialism of Europe, in the U.S. fraternalism had roots that were as American as the Founding Fathers. Fraternalism, especially in the years from the Civil War to the 1920s, was seen as the more American way for workers, tradesmen and professionals to organize. Perhaps unsurprisingly, given the prevalence of these structures, they did not limit themselves to legitimate fraternities, but were also apparent in criminal organizations.

While we may use the term "criminal fraternity" today, the expression had a far more literal meaning in the times of this study. Criminal fraternities fascinated reporters on organized crime. In these years they could range from the formal, oath-bound secret societies like the Klan and the Camorra, through to the more fabled organizations like the Black Hand, the Molly Maguires, the Tongs and, of course, the Mafia. They might be simply brotherhoods of the street, gangs like the New York's Whyos or Boston's Westies.

Whatever motivated or controlled their association, there is little doubt that gangs, brotherhoods and fraternities were reported as being central to much of what was described as organized crime over these years. These were orders that, for a variety of reasons, history has either given exaggerated importance—like the Mafia—or largely sidelined them—as with the Tongs. With their codes of secrecy, their demands for absolute loyalty and total obedience, these organizations developed a peculiar ability to remain simultaneously threatening and omnipresent, whilst being largely intangible and invisible—even, as this study aims to show, mythical.

# 1

## The Birth of the Mafia

*Murder in New Orleans*

To paraphrase Mark Twain on quitting smoking: it is very easy to start a book on organized crime; I have done it several times. The narrative always begins with the murder of a policeman in New Orleans on a back street on a damp night in October 1890. His death and the subsequent trial led directly to the biggest mass lynching in American history, that of eleven supposed Sicilians. The story of what led to that murder and the mob action it precipitated, as well the subsequent interpretation of these events, seem to present a superb opportunity for shedding light on what is by necessity a shadowy and obscure history of the actions of people who wish to keep their actions shadowy and obscure. Unfortunately the elusive and speculative nature of the true background of this particular event seems to mean that the more evidence that comes to light, and the longer that information is examined, the less certain the sequence and significance of that murder seems to become.

Nevertheless the events and the way in which they have been analyzed ever since highlight some very important elements for trying to understand the nature of the history of organized crime. They show how the simple explanation of crimes committed by "bad men" and their investigation by "good men" has frequently been regarded as preferable to anything more complex. They show how—for a variety of reasons—the control of the narrative of organized crime is a political issue, and how that issue has been, and still is, manipulated. They also show the persistent dominance by one particular organization in the history of American organized crime. It is an organization that is omnipotent, omnipresent and familiar—the Mafia.

If the essence of this book is to understand what is meant by organized crime in the years from the Civil War to the Second World War, then as good a starting point as any is to examine the emergence of that perception and to look for a starting point of where this Mafia-centric view of organized crime comes from, and whether it is actually valid. This is worth doing because not only does this organization form the center of most people's perceptions of organized crime, but its early "history" in the U.S. forms a very good framework for the study of organized crime as a whole, encompassing as it does elements of murder, political and press manipulation, and xenophobia.

Perhaps more interestingly, the Mafia has become a means for a near-constant repetition of myth and an excuse for decades of genuinely inspired, as well as sloppy, historical investigation. In uncovering the debates connected with the emergence of this body—arguably, the most powerful of all symbols connected with organized crime—this study can flag up some of the other persistent problems which make historical studies of organized crime so difficult, contested and controversial.

One of the masters of American crime fiction, Raymond Chandler, famously gave some advice to would-be crime writers who found themselves in difficulty about how to progress a plot. His recommendation was characteristically terse, sinister and theatrical: "When in doubt, have a man come through the door with a gun in his hand."[1] Some historians seem to have followed a similarly simple maxim when writing about organized crime: "When in doubt about organized crime, find the Sicilians."

While this view has been largely discredited, or at least reexamined, by many academics working in the field, it retains a very considerable following with the general reading public. To them, the Mafia and organized crime are often synonymous. Even when they are not referring to the Sicilian brotherhood, the use of the word mafia, with a small "m," makes it implicit. Although this may be accidental, it nevertheless contributes to a dominant view of organized crime as a tightly structured, hierarchical and sophisticated network of criminals. The result of this narrative is the stubborn belief that all over the nation, if not all over the world, the Mafia has risen to a point where it oversees crime. It perpetuates a truly terrifying vision of an amorphous and nebulous organization that is omnipresent and omnipotent. This vision has been reinforced by government investigations, media reports and fictional portrayals ever since.[2]

In 1974, former military and police intelligence officer Dwight C. Smith published a work that put forward a series of arguments that laid bare the flaws in Mafia-based narratives of organized crime in America.[3] Since then the majority of academic historians have at least questioned the so-called "Mafia Myth." Nevertheless, even if one takes a view firmly based on Smith's position, it is undeniable that there are some benefits to the more traditional Mafia narrative for the historian of organized crime. Not the least of these is that it brings a clarity and an underlying simplicity to the distinctly garbled and opaque narrative surrounding the emergence of organized crime in the U.S.

Moreover, the Mafia-based narrative of organized crime feeds another latent but powerful appetite for many historians. It enables a precise date for the start of the emergence of the Mafia, and therefore for what many see as organized crime, in America. Those who promote it can more or less pinpoint the dawn of that body in its American context to the bloody events of one night, in one place. Certainly, in terms of that shadowy but all-pervasive entity, the "American Mafia," they are absolutely right. The Mafia came to the attention of the American public with the murder of New Orleans' popular young police chief, David Hennessy, on the rainy night of October 14, 1890. That event undisputedly took place: the unfortunate policeman *was* shot six times at close range by a group of men with shotguns. However, the rest of the conclusions drawn by adherents of the Mafia-based histories that this tragedy apparently triggered are now frequently seen as far less certain.

Although there were no eyewitnesses who came forward, the police chief's fate was very quickly linked to the Sicilians. Most accounts agree that after Hennessy was rushed to hospital, the dying man lingered on for several hours. During these hours of semi-consciousness, he gave no indication of the identity of his murderers, other than apparently rather cryptically whispering to a fellow policeman, "The dagoes did it."[4] According to most histories of these events, all those who heard the story at the time argued that by the "dagoes" he most probably meant the local Sicilians. And this was a logical conclusion, since at the time this version of events made sense from a variety of perspectives: the Sicilians might well have killed the Chief, as he was known. But that conclusion is by no means certain.

## Provenzanos and Matrangas

So who was David Hennessy, and why was he so important? According to the vast majority of newspaper accounts that emerged after his demise, Hennessy was not the typical policeman of his day. In fact, he was something of an oddity. He was popular, young and effective. Those traits were rare enough among his fellow U.S. police chiefs, but what really stood out was that, according to the biographies most papers produced after his death, he seemed to be clean-living and a teetotaler. They also maintained he was a scrupulously honest and very earnest, committed career cop. What also emerged was that he was the son of a Northerner and a Republican who had been elected on a reform ticket in the notoriously corrupt, hard-living, hedonistic and solidly Democrat capital of the postwar South, New Orleans.

As if those peculiarities didn't mark him out clearly enough, what made him truly unusual in an age when graft and racketeering were considered pretty well central features of policing, was that Hennessy had been at pains to show that he was—by the standards of the day—incorruptible. Unlike most urban policemen of these times, especially in pragmatic New Orleans, Hennessy made a point of refusing bribes. What was more, he made a show of it—and made sure it was known. A good example of this display of honesty could be seen when he played cards, as he had been doing on the night of his murder.

Although he might have a night at the card table now and then, Hennessy wanted to show that he was not a genuine gambler. He made sure that it was well recognized that he used only borrowed chips, and made certain that it was noted that at the end of the evening he had returned any winnings. According to the papers after his death, Hennessy was a true model of honest policing. Perhaps more importantly, these high personal standards seemed to be reflected in his work. Unlike many of his predecessors, he kept his election promises.

Many papers admiringly reported after his demise that he had been effective in his campaign pledge to clean up the city. They went on to hint, menacingly, that it was this dedication that was the root of his tragic fate. They linked this push to improve the city to reports that he was well on his way to solving the root cause of the murder of numerous people on the longshore. What made this even more interesting to the newspapers was that these murders had been associated with the two fractious leading families of the city's Sicilian community: the Matrangas and the Provenzanos.

Hennessy's interest in the two Sicilian families had played a part throughout his career of policing in New Orleans. However, their significance in his life—and death—came to a head when the conflict between the clans had reached the stage of a pitched battle, with one set of men being accused of having ambushed a wagon full of their rivals on their way home from work. The attack had all the hallmarks of the Sicilian civil war that was taking place at the time in New Orleans, but this time the bloodshed had spread beyond the boundaries of the Sicilian "colony."

Heedless of anyone else they may involve, the assailants had laid in wait and blasted away with shotguns, wholesale. They were surprisingly ineffectual, given the firepower employed. Remarkably, although the wagon was pretty well destroyed, only three of the eight Matrangas inside had been seriously wounded. Given the blatant and bloody nature of the attack, and the seeming spread of violence to new districts, there was a fear that it would indubitably escalate into yet another predictable series of tit-for-tat killings. With this in mind, Hennessy had mobilized his police force with uncharacteristic haste. It did not take long for the authorities to round up a suitable group of Provenzano thugs and charge them. However, rather than trying the events of that day as one incident, it was decided that there were to be three separate trials, since there had been three casualties.

The first of these three trials took place in July 1890, and it went badly for the accused members of the Provenzano clan. The prosecution had convincingly portrayed the defendants as being committed to a bloody vendetta against their rivals, but things looked set to change as the second trial loomed. Newspapers were alive with rumors that Hennessy would now tell what he knew. The July trial had been notable for his absence. In spite of his involvement in the arrest of the accused and the preparation of the case for the state, until this point Hennessy had stolidly refused to give evidence—in person. It was widely felt that in the second trial he would now give evidence that would exonerate, or at least justify the actions of, the Provenzanos, with whom rumors circulated that he was involved.

As a result, it was felt that the Matrangas would be out to silence the police chief, and given their lawless reputation, few were in any doubt that they would use violence. To add fuel to this argument, there were reports that a certain Joseph Macheca, a close ally and allegedly the chief "fixer" of the Matrangas, had been overheard threatening to personally kill chief Hennessy in order to silence him. So when news emerged that Hennessy had been shot dead that fateful night, few were surprised when the dying chief implicated the "dagoes." Even without that implied accusation, it would not have taken long for the press and the public to jump to that conclusion anyway.

As if the press could not already find enough reason to hold Macheca and his band responsible for ordering the murder, there were also other rumors swirling around the city that directly implicated them. The newspapers were alive with tales that Hennessy had tangled with the Sicilians before. They also told their readers that it was well known that once crossed, these people neither forgot nor forgave. Passionate, violent and impulsive, according to popular myth, Sicilians—more than any other group—were held to have a lust for blood feuds, a fondness for vendettas, and a predisposition to violent intrigue. What was more, it was widely known that they took their feuds and vendettas with them wherever they went.

Unluckily for Hennessy and other residents of the city, this portable hatred had particular relevance to New Orleans, which in the second half of the nineteenth century had emerged as the epicenter of Sicilian immigration in the United States. In order to better understand the incidents leading up to the murder of Hennessy and the repercussions and implications of those events, it is helpful to have at least some knowledge of why the connection between New Orleans and Sicily emerged, and how Sicilians were perceived and treated in late nineteenth-century Louisiana.

## Sicilians

The link between the Mediterranean island and the *de facto* capital of the post–Civil War South was based on a variety of elements. At the most basic level these were geographic, topographic and climatic. Put simply, many emigrating Sicilians were drawn to New Orleans because the city and its environs had a similar climate to their homeland, the landscape looked vaguely familiar, and they could enjoy a similar lifestyle to that afforded by their native island. They could also earn their livings in similar trades. As the *Daily Picayune* pointed reported in 1890: "Here [in New Orleans] they [the Sicilians] have an interior sea … furnishing every possible facility for their maritime operations in fish and fruits."[5]

Other reasons for choosing the city were cultural. Because its roots were French, the Crescent City was, unusually for the times, strongly if not predominantly Roman Catholic. While New Orleans was hardly renowned as a pious city, this feature reflected what would have been to most Sicilians a more or less recognizable culture and social structure—or at least one which would not have been quite as alien as many other American cities of the time. Sicilian immigrants would have been able to recognize and appreciate much of the cultural landscape of the city.

Not the least of this would have been the hugely popular feast days that made up the city's cultural calendar. Sicilians would have recognized celebrations like the colorful and exuberant saints' days in New Orleans. Alongside this, they would have been accustomed to the Mediterranean-style emphasis many residents placed on familial and regional ties. While this was, and is, a trait always central to dislocated first-generation immigrant groups, perhaps it is particularly associated, if not exaggerated and extended, in migrants arriving from the peasant societies of Southern Europe—not least in the minds of the host population in New Orleans.

But most importantly, as one of the main commercial ports in America, the city had developed strong trading links with Sicily. This was largely as a result of what had become the root of the island's most successful business—the lemon trade. In the nineteenth century, Sicily had developed into the world center of citrus fruit cultivation. Over these years, much of the coastal plain neighboring Palermo had been cleared and prepared for cultivation of the lucrative crop.

However, this profit did not come without investment in both labor and capital. It entailed considerable work and expertise. Groves had to be walled off and the trees planted. Tender and vulnerable saplings needed to be nurtured until they started to produce fruit. Protection from drought in the arid plains of Sicily required the preparation and installation of complex irrigation systems. The expenditure paid off for those who could afford it. Lemons had made parts of the island some of the most productive agricultural regions of Europe. By the 1880s, Sicilian citrus fruit, and lemons in particular, were exported all over the world—most notably to the capital of the reviving post–Civil War South, New Orleans.

In many ways the city was a logical choice from which to develop this trans–Atlantic citrus trade. Over the best part of the nineteenth century, New Orleans had developed large-scale docks, warehousing, skilled agents and considerable fleets of oceangoing and coastal merchant vessels for the exporting of cotton and tobacco. This made the Crescent City perhaps the logical point of entry for the citrus trade. From this well-positioned, well-equipped and well-established port city, traders not only had a suitable point of entry, but also a superbly connected hub from which to re-export to the U.S. coasts and hinterlands.

Moreover, as the trade developed, New Orleans also became an ideal base as it developed a pool of experienced manpower skilled in handling, sorting and repackaging the tender product for marketing and re-exporting. In addition, the region developed a level of middle management with skills in negotiating contracts and facilitating onward shipping to expanding markets in Central and South America. Unsurprisingly, given the nature of the trade and the special skills it necessitated, the links between Sicily and Louisiana grew.

As with so many other trade links established between so many other places, Sicily's success in the exporting of goods encouraged emigrants to follow in the wake of the product. This was nothing particularly new, since Sicily already had traditionally had a highly mobile population. Throughout its long history, many of the poorer residents of the island had spent much of their lives simply waiting to leave the island, and the situation in the last decades of the nineteenth century no different. For while the lemon groves may have made some on the island very wealthy, most Sicilians were still condemned to live in conditions that in essence had altered little since medieval times.

Leading lives characterized by the grinding poverty and the precariousness of peasant existence in much of Europe, most Sicilians were effectively tied to the same land as their ancestors had been. They were frequently controlled by the vicissitudes of similar crop cycles and the moods and demeanors of their landlords as their parents, grandparents and great-grandparents had been. In that virtually inescapable position, they were paid little—if anything—and ruled over by the whims of uncaring, often foreign or at least absentee landlords.

Sicilians were also subjected to the usual round of crop failures, droughts and outbreaks of disease that all agricultural regions suffered. The island also seemed to experience more than its share of seriously destructive epic-scale natural events. Sicily suffered some of the most frequent and devastating earthquakes, floods and volcanic eruptions in Europe—and the awful destruction they left in their wake was made all the worse by what seemed to be a blatant lack of interest in anything but profit that marked the attitude of the absent government, and absent landlords.

Nor were all these hazards products of the natural world or negligent or malevolent absent rulers. Domestic politics, war and diplomacy played a major role in creating new ones. The island had, since earliest times, been plagued by banditry on a truly legendary scale. Since medieval times, if not before, the island had been fabled and for its brigands, bandits and cutthroats. It seemed that criminals prospered on Sicily, driven by an unholy alliance of isolation, religious orthodoxy, poverty, unstable government and foreign occupation.

The resulting disruption of this reputation meant that Sicily had essentially become synonymous with backwardness, superstition, unruliness and, most famously, crime. This encompassed almost any way money could be made by breaking the law. In Sicily, cattle rustling, extortion, protection rackets, counterfeiting, blackmailing, kidnapping, rape and robbery were considered endemic. In short, there were few obvious attractions that would keep any honest, socially unconnected, but ambitious Sicilian at home. Given these conditions, it was hardly surprising that steamship company agents working out of Naples found it easy to persuade large numbers of hopeful emigrants that they could improve their lives, and even perhaps make their fortune, in the New World.

Alongside this, Sicily developed a particularly widespread version of the infamous *padrone* system for labor procurement. Although outlawed in the U.S. by the 1885 Immigration Act, this labor brokering system essentially enabled American sugar, cotton or tobacco plantation owners to use local Sicilian gang-masters to recruit cheap, robust, plentiful labor. They were essentially expendable, non-unionized workers. The uses of such gang labor were particularly obvious to the agriculturally based economy of the South, and New Orleans quickly became the center for the movement of these workers.

In the wake of reincorporation into the Union, New Orleans had emerged as the capital of a region which was still struggling to find a cost-effective and sustainable way to provide an agricultural labor force. The region's economy was based around production of labor-intensive agricultural crops like cotton, tobacco and rice in what was a post-slavery, but essentially pre-mechanized, economy.[6] That is not to say that all immigrants from Sicily ended up in this form of peonage. Many were actually enticed over by those who had gone before. A significant number of Sicilians arrived as a result of chain migration, whereby immigrants already settled in the region encouraged, vouched for and funded friends, spouses and family to emigrate as they made their own fortunes in New Orleans.

With all these causes for migration to the city, it is probable that New Orleans had the largest Sicilian community of any American city around the turn of the twentieth century—but it is difficult to prove exactly how many were there at any given time. Unofficial sources estimate that New Orleans' French Quarter—where most of the Sicilians settled—contained as many as 30,000 Southern Italians in the 1890s, with some 2,000 arriving and departing each year. Immigration records show that of the 3,878 arrivals to Louisiana recorded in 1890, no fewer than 2,611 were Italians. Of these Italian immigrants, it has been calculated that between eighty and ninety percent were Sicilian.

However, it is not always easy to decide whether all these immigrants were actually Sicilian. Sicilians were not distinguished from other Southern Italians on embarkation and disembarkation. What was more, Sicilians most did not board ships in Palermo, but rather most embarked in Naples. Therefore, on arrival in America they would be entered as originating from the mainland, not their island home. All this makes it difficult to come up with exact figures for arrivals from Sicily.

Nevertheless, the general picture of large-scale Sicilian immigration is verified by the official statistics for the 1890 census. Of the figure of 2,903 Italian immigrants arriving in Louisiana, only 35 were originally from the Italian mainland. Another set of figures claim that over 100,000 Sicilians arrived in New Orleans between 1890 and 1929. However, it should be borne in mind that some forty percent of European migrants in general returned to their country of origin within one year of arrival in the U.S., and there is no reason to suspect that Sicilians were any different. Whatever the true extent of Sicilian immigration, it is clear that by the time of Hennessy's murder, given that New Orleans was a city of around 300,000 residents at this time, it played host—by these estimates—to a pretty considerable and rapidly growing, if fluid, population from Sicily.[7]

What is even more certain is that as the numbers increased, so did the hostility these immigrants met. As with most immigrant groups, especially those from what were considered relatively unfamiliar donor countries, this immigrant population excited more or less open hostility. Predictably, the nativists—those who opposed immigration—claimed that immigrant Sicilians were a particular menace to New Orleans. To them, these incoming unintelligible, savage-looking peasants stole "white" residents' jobs. It was argued that desperate as they were, they were willing to work for less, and accept worse conditions. In addition, they brought unwelcome fellow travelers and traits with them.

Sicilians were accused of being vectors for disease; they were seen as superstitious, and with their history of being downtrodden, they brought with them the deadly seeds of revolution. What was more, as their failings became apparent, and the hostility towards them grew, they retreated into "colonies"—areas where they could be among their own kind. Nevertheless, this seemingly passive response was also seen as threatening. These colonies were increasingly seen as areas the native-born could not enter, control or comprehend—and that, in the caste-ridden South, was a particular problem.

## Mafia

Like the Japanese, Eastern European Jews, Greeks, Syrians and others arriving in increasing numbers on the eastern and western coasts, and like the Mexicans arriving from the south, the Southern Italians, and most notably the Sicilians, were neither black nor white in the traditional sense. This indeterminate status threatened the always rather precarious basis for the supremacy of the elite whites in the former slave regions: it introduced a new skin tint. Terrifyingly for a fundamentally insecure region, this new immigration injected what amounted to a new shade and a new complexity into the color basis underlying the caste system of the region.[8]

What was more, to those who had reformed their ideas of slavery, the padrone system made the already unwelcome Sicilians into peons—little more than indentured laborers or wage slaves. According to a growing mythology among American residents, the New Immigrants, as the increasing flow from the south and east of Europe became known, were unsuitable to become Americans. In this version of the American story, unlike the heroic immigrant founders of the nation and those who until the 1880s followed in their wake, this Sicilian immigration was an amorphous and undifferentiated mass. What was more, they had most probably not left home of their own volition.

To those who opposed their arrival, agents working for gang-masters paid the migrants' impoverished parents to send their children. They bribed men to leave. It was suspected that these workers may equally well have arrived simply because they had their fare paid to cross the Atlantic and were, if not slaves, then certainly modern-day "indentured servants." It is an indication of how abhorrent and threatening most Americans found this trade in contracted labor that Congress passed unequivocal legislation against it in an era of open immigration. In 1885 Washington made it "unlawful for any person, company, partnership, or corporation, in any manner whatsoever, to prepay the transportation, or in any way assist or encourage the importation or migration of any alien or aliens, any foreigner or foreigners, into the United States." The punishment was suitably strict. Any violation of this—the so-called Foran Act—would result in a fine on the gangmaster or agent of up to $1,000.[9]

Perhaps more importantly, while these gang-laborers were not exactly slaves in the true sense, they had a status that clearly threatened to challenge, or at least confuse, the nature of individuality. Further, within this menace to the white population was an intrinsic threat to the shaky and hard-won freedoms so recently gained by the local black population. This indeterminate and challenging status would prove perplexing to the Sicilians and their relations with the resident population. In the prevalent caste system of the South, blacks were considered childlike in their stupidity and subservience. But they were also very valuable. It was maintained that if "niggers" were managed correctly, they were all the more useful for the traits that singled them out as inferior. The compliant, obedient and biddable "sambo" was a well-known figure in the South.

On the other hand, Europeans, and most importantly those from the Latin regions, were seen as inherently troublesome. The relationship is perhaps most clearly demonstrated in Annie Proulx's fictionalized account of a Sicilian immigrant's fate in New Orleans. Struggling to find a workforce suitable for the grueling and relentless fieldwork in the heat and humidity of Louisiana, Proulx has an exasperated white employer claim that he'd "rather have niggers than the dago socialist rabble screaming for weekly paydays and threatening strikes and blowing up levees when they did not get what they wanted."[10]

Added to this, like many of the other immigrants arriving in the 1880s and 1890s, these Mediterranean peasants were not English-speaking. They were not familiar with American habits. Nor were they seen as understanding American ethics. Most of them were not schooled in the subtleties of representative democracy—especially those "refinements" that adapted it for the peculiar world of the post–Reconstruction South. It was apparent to most elite local observers that many of these laborers were not schooled at all: most were illiterate. When all these elements were combined with the Sicilians' legendary and prodigious reputation for violence, dishonesty and crime, it was clear to most nativists that this particular immigrant group represented an altogether new level of threat to the stability of the region.

Like most of the new immigration arriving in all areas of the U.S., these people were largely from a rural background: they were peasants. Like all those schooled in making a living from more or less fertile soil, in more or less temperate climates, under more or less hostile regimes, they were also tough, cunning, persistent, resilient and obstinate. The conditions they came from meant that they had needed to be, especially in the hardscrabble small farms dotted around the mountainous interior regions of Sicily. In the eyes of their nativist enemies, they had a form of dishonesty that was lodged intensely in their very psyche.

This ingrained dishonesty could even survive the threats of physical punishment or imprisonment. It was claimed that such measures did not seem to deter them from their genetic predisposition to thievery, bloodshed and treachery. Far from it. One article published in the wake of Hennessy's murder claimed that "dagoes" actually sought imprisonment because the clothing that they had brought with them from the Mediterranean was not suited to the rain or the cold of the southern American winter, and they frequently had no housing.

Given this shortcoming, even prison represented an unaccustomed shelter to the "dago." According to an author who opposed them, the Sicilian peasant came from a culture in which he was only used to the protection from the elements afforded at best by a tumbledown shack or the shade of a tree. In addition, in prison, of course, he would be better fed. The author claimed he had evidence to prove his claims. He explained how he had "once happened to witness the following incident: A small circus, with a few lions and tigers, exhibiting in a small town, near by where a railroad was being constructed, fed, as a part of its program, these wild beasts. The bones which the beasts gnawed were left on the ground when the circus departed between [*sic*] two days. And the 'dagoes' collected these bones and boiled them for their soup! What terrors have jails and prisons for such human beings?"[11]

But there was another, perhaps even more disquieting trait that the Sicilians portrayed. To those who opposed their arrival, there was something peculiar and very disconcerting about the way in which some leading members of this migration, this particular alien population, seemed to thrive. By the time of Hennessy's murder, the residents of New Orleans' "Little Palermo" had established themselves not only as a hardy form of imported gang labor for soft fruit, cotton, sugar and rice production, but many had also set up as fishermen, market gardeners, fruit stall vendors, and even shipping brokers.

It was in this final capacity that they were most worrying. As became increasingly apparent during the 1880s, these same Sicilians dominated the lucrative waterfront area—at least in the citrus fruit trade with Europe, Central and South America. As the staunchly Democrat *Daily Picayune* pointed out in November 1890, the local populace visiting the area were often "amazed" at the scale of the Sicilians' control of the waterfront. They had created a business which even the staid *Picayune* grudgingly admitted had "the dignity and proportions of a great commercial interest." The paper pointed out how the Sicilian companies were "employing a score and more of steamships and hundreds of thousands of capital."[12]

In the early 1890s, a visitor to the citrus fruit section of the New Orleans waterfront would almost certainly see Sicilian stevedores. They would be unloading Sicilian-owned, Sicilian-manned boats. Their work would more than likely be overseen by Sicilian foremen and all of them would probably be working for Sicilian-named companies. The names that visitor would most likely see or hear in this connection were either that of the well-established Provenzanos, or those of their competitors, the increasingly powerful Matranga family.

However, in spite of their growing wealth, the often-jealous local-born white population knew that the two clans would not contain their inherent vicious instincts for criminal intrigue. It was well known that these two families had been involved in what essentially amounted to a war for the control of this trade on the waterfront. There were rumors that the conflict was made all the more violent since it was a struggle not only for control of the considerable legitimate businesses, but also one that would enable the victor to develop the massive opportunities on the longshore for graft, smuggling, theft and other criminal undertakings that were considered so much a part of Sicilian life.

## The War of the Oranges

By the time of Hennessy's murder, the so-called War of the Oranges—as the killings among the Sicilian community had rather picturesquely become known—had been waged on the French Quarter's waterfront for at least a decade. The violence had not taken long to spill over into the produce stalls of the French Market, and it was here that it claimed its first known fatality in 1886. From then until the assassination of the police chief, it had been characterized by an escalating cycle of tit-for-tat beatings, which graduated to stabbings, then eventually escalated into shootings.

Nevertheless the authorities largely ignored the majority of this growing toll of victims. Even though it appeared that very little effort was made to hide the violence and as the struggle for control of the waterfront heated up, this neglect continued. Indeed, it appeared that the police not only ignored the mounting body count, but underplayed the extent and ferocity of the battle for the region. It would emerge in time—after Hennessy's death—that there were numerous other murders identified as being associated *with* Sicilians, and *of* Sicilians, and therefore assumed to be committed *by* Sicilians. Contemporary newspapers and other early accounts would argue that the New Orleans Police

Department's seeming negligence was largely because the crimes had been carried out by, and targeted, only those within the Sicilian community.

The usual inference was that the New Orleans police took a rather pragmatic view of the violence in Sicilian quarters of the city. Most commentators argued that since Sicilians were naturally vengeful, violent and indifferent to incarceration, it made sense to allow them to police themselves. According to many, it was preferable to let them work out their differences—no matter how bloody the consequences—than risk Anglo residents' lives and safety by intervening. This approach is perhaps most clearly demonstrated by the time it took for the murderer of the first known fatality of the War of the Oranges to be brought to justice.

Unsurprisingly, the victim was a Sicilian: a shoemaker associated with the Provenzanos. Several years passed between Vincent Raffo's shooting and the trial of the man accused of being his murderer, another Sicilian—Rocco Geraci. This delay was surprising since the police had been in possession of a sworn affidavit, given only days after the event. This document specifically identified Geraci as the killer, yet the police waited for nearly four years before they chose to act on it.[13] This delay is most important when applied to the new police administration that took over in 1888.

Most newspapers that commented on it after the death of Hennessy picked up on the fact that this evident lack of police vigilance and lack of interest in the waterfront war evaporated with the election of the "reform" administration. The charismatic new chief of police came into office as a part of Governor Francis Nicholls and New Orleans Mayor Joseph Shakespeare's successful Republican-backed reform–Democrat ticket. Those commentators who supported Mayor Shakespeare argued that this rather sudden interest in the bloodshed of Little Palermo was a clear indication of the administration's commitment to reforming the city's corrupt and violent image. That is one view. However, based on the same information, it is possible to make another, very different assumption.

Hennessy had come into power as a part of a ticket that was overthrowing a very well-established and entrenched political machine. Given its former dominance, it is clear that not everyone welcomed the overthrow of the old regime. Established interests had been upset, old elites had been overthrown. Given this upheaval, there was a considerable degree of hostility to the incoming mayor and his appointees—not least to those who took over policing the city. Those opposed to the new boss and his cronies claimed that the NOPD's newfound attentiveness to the Sicilians stemmed less from a wish to clean up the city, and more from the obligation to repay the debts.

These opponents argued that there were those who had to be paid—by whatever means—for their services to the election of the new administration. They maintained that the investigations took place as a result of Hennessy's connections to the Provenzanos, most notably the head of the clan, Vincent. The investigations reflected the new police chief's partisan wish to end the Matrangas' threat to the Provenzano dominance of the waterfront. Showing that the murders originated with the Matrangas, Hennessy—it was claimed—could imply that the newcomers' methods were typically Sicilian, with all that meant. In polite, racially aware New Orleans, this would mean that anyone with any association to the Matrangas would find his chances of progressing up the social ladder stymied, once and for all.

Given this underlying unpopularity of the Sicilian population of New Orleans, combined with their reputation for factionalism, violence and criminality, when Hennessy was shot, the obvious place to look for the assassins was in Little Palermo. Few had any doubt that the murderers were Sicilian, and it didn't take long for the anti–Sicilian sentiments that had bubbled beneath the surface of New Orleans to explode dramatically into the open. On the day of Hennessy's death, forty Sicilians were arrested. The outrage felt against their community by "decent" white residents was palpable and is apparent in an article describing those rounded up in the witch-hunt that followed the police chief's murder.

According to the account in one New Orleans paper, the local jail was now "crowded with Sicilians, whose low, repulsive countenances, and slavery attire, proclaimed their brutal nature."[14] Nor was the outrage limited to accounts in print. Within days of the murder, one Sicilian suspected of involvement in the chief's death had been shot dead by a friend of Hennessy. Others had been beaten, spat at, stoned and abused in the street. What was more, the NOPD was making itself unusually busy in the French Quarter, where the Sicilian population was centered. The area was combed for suspects, and within a week, although no one had any solid information on the identity of the killers, some four out of the five "suspected" Sicilian gunmen were under arrest for the Hennessy murder. Their arrest, like everything associated with the murder of the heroic, dedicated and incorruptible police chief, was now headline news.

## Dagoes!

At this point it is perhaps worth stepping back and re-examining some of the evidence for the involvement of Sicilians in the murder of the police chief. Closer examination of some of the facts reveals that Hennessy was, in reality—put politely—a more "pragmatic" cop than some accounts may have suggested. What was more, far from the benign and beneficent image presented in the press, Hennessy was actually—like most cops of his day—macho, reactive and quick-tempered. He could be brutal in his methods when the situation demanded it. The saintly Hennessy had actually killed a fellow New Orleans policeman in a gun battle. What was more, he was associated with well-known criminals—including the leading figure in the Provenzanos, with whom he owned a notorious gambling joint.

All the same, the press could not resist beatifying him. The murder of a pure, clean, devoted cop sold more papers than the truth would ever have done, but it would also have huge implications for the history of organized crime in America. Hennessy's picture—stern-faced and handsome—appeared on front pages alongside clearly worded accounts of his near superhuman efforts to clean up New Orleans in general, and the incorrigible Sicilians in particular. In most accounts he emerged as an incorruptible crusader dedicated to the downfall of the Sicilian "Mafia," and it was through his fate that this rather unfamiliar word gained increasing currency in the press.

There is a law of inverse proportion that would seem to indicate that the more saintly the victim, the more dastardly those responsible for his fate. In keeping with this, the media played Hennessy's squeaky-clean image for all it was worth, with the result that the murder became a sensation. Further, all the explanations of the outrage came back to the Sicilian community. The process began when the local papers ran stories of Sicilian blood feuds and vendettas crossing the Atlantic with the immigrants. The national newspapers then picked up the theme. Together they told of "conspiracies," "blood feuds" and "wars" involving old clan rivalries and shadowy fraternities dedicated to brigand-age.

Piecing together police evidence and testimony given in the first trial of the Proven-zanos, the press began to speak knowingly of an organization that they referred to as "the Mafia," which they proceeded to outline. They detailed accounts of the murderous activities and sinister membership of the traditional *Giardinieri* Mafiosi and an upstart rival, the *Stuppagghieri*. They told the public of the antics of these two Sicilian factions of the Mafia, which they explained had been transplanted to the New World and were now battling each other for control of Little Palermo.

Papers began to report how these secret and bloodthirsty brotherhoods had carried on their age-old feuds and other nefarious activities in New Orleans. They explained how centuries-old divisions in Sicily had crossed the Atlantic with the Sicilians. They gave accounts of how these rivalries worked to divide the two sides in the War of the Oranges and in turn led directly to the Hennessy murder. They explained why this feud was so relevant, pointing out how the *Giardinieri* were allied with the Provenzanos, while the *Stuppagghieri* drew their support from within the Matrangas.[15]

Like so many other aspects of this case, the handy and simple division of Mafioso feuds stemming from an allegiance to one of the two clans was at best questionable. But those who see the barrage of anti–Sicilian reportage as simply the result of sympathy for the demise of Hennessy, or even horror over his murder, are missing vital contextual points. As with so many elements in the history of American organized crime, all is not as certain as it might at first seem—or indeed, as it has subsequently been portrayed by the vast majority of commentators since. There is evidence that there might have been another, more politically partisan, and far more instructive motive at work.

Turning Hennessy into a saint and vilifying the Sicilian community was a good political move on the part of the "reforming" Shakespeare administration. Since the defeat of the Confederacy—even when judged by the tensions and corruption of other areas of the post–Reconstruction South—Louisiana politics had been extraordinarily polarized. The divisions behind this polarization are complex, deep, diverse and seem-ingly inconsistent in their roots. Nevertheless, these divisions are highly relevant to the popularity of the guilt of the Mafia in the murder of Hennessy, if not the whole concept of an all-powerful Mafia in America.

The importance of this fluidity to the murder of Hennessy centers on one of the periodic swings towards "reformists" that took place with a remarkable regularity in most major cities across the United States over these years. The electorate would get a pas-sion—for one reason or another—to have an alternative to the machine-style government that had become the norm. In New Orleans this happened in the 1888 election. The reformers in this case were centered on Joseph Ansoetegui Shakespeare's Young Man's Democratic Association. This alliance of a variety of interest groups represented the latest manifestation of the business interests in their ongoing struggle with New Orleans' powerful Tammany-style political machine, known rather ominously as the "Ring."

Yet while most cities over these years had similar machines, and most of these cities had reformers who opposed them, in many ways Shakespeare's opposition to the Ring was unique. Its enemies claimed that this mysterious cabal had been established essen-tially to maintain the control of the vast moneymaking potential of the Louisiana State Lottery—by far the largest legitimate gambling operation in the Union.

There was more than a little truth underlying this interpretation. On annual payment of $40,000 to the state coffers, the Ring, or at least the shadowy clique of powerful gamblers who controlled it, had continued to benefit from a state-sanctioned monopoly over the lottery, which it had retained since 1868.[16] By 1888, although not *always* forming the administrations, the Ring had been the driving force of Louisiana politics for twenty years. They achieved this supremacy by buying all those who could best serve their purposes. In the process they formed a powerful alliance by clearly associating themselves with the traditional virtues of the Old South.

Since this was the Jim Crow South, the Ring used a healthy dose of fear driven by the threat of "negro rule." They also cultivated the working-class vote, adroitly—and unusually—combining it with the immigrant vote. The Ring then assured that these two elements could be counted on to win the relevant elections by using good old-fashioned election rigging and bribery. As an unashamed political machine dedicated to turning votes into power, the Ring was able protect itself against periodic attempts by the traditional elites (Bourbons) and local businessmen to remove what they condemned as the dead hand of the Ring on the levers of the New Orleans economy.[17]

This polarization between the Ring and its opponents essentially underlay most struggles in the political life of the Crescent City over these years. So when Hennessy was murdered, in some ways it was bound to be used as an opportunity for his bereaved political stable-mates to make some form of political capital. The Shakespeare administration was keen to exploit whatever advantage, in whatever way, that may rescue itself from the tragedy, and using the Sicilians as a scapegoat appeared more than simply convenient—it was providential.

Like most other immigrant groups in the city, the Sicilians had traditionally been supporters and beneficiaries of the Ring's particular brand of machine politics. In that now legendary event that sealed the fate of the northern-backed Republicans in New Orleans, the so-called Battle of Liberty Place in 1874, it had been none other than a leading Sicilian who had played a—if not *the*—vital role. Leading his gang of Sicilian toughs, the rather ironically named *Innocenti*, Joseph P. Macheca captured the wounded police superintendent General Algernon Badger—an event that played a major role in changing the course of the battle. He then went on to take the weapon-laden steamship *Mississippi* docked on the waterfront—which sealed the success of the uprising.

Some of those among the elites who backed this successful rebellion went on to play leading roles in the Ring. According to their version of events, the rebels were participants in a legendary uprising. Macheca was among those who played a major part that enabled the Democrats to defeat—albeit briefly—the hated Republican-backed carpetbagger, Governor Henry Warmouth. In so doing he halted what the Ring and its supporters would argue was a regime imposed by a vengeful North which, they claimed, had threatened to empower the "black rabble" over their former masters.[18]

Since that glorious moment for Southern pride, the Ring had been closely associated with Sicilians, allowing them what more or less amounted to self-government of Little Palermo. In return, the powerful clique had demanded the support of the Sicilians at elections—which it got. However, it soon became apparent that with the death of Hennessy, the politically savvy and ruthlessly opportunist Shakespeare saw a win-win situation. By going on the offensive against the Sicilians, he and his allies would not only protect their own business interests from the increasingly powerful Sicilians on the waterfront, but also disgrace the Ring in the bargain. They set about doing this with a ruthless single-mindedness.

Perhaps the most obvious example of this exploitation was the founding of a vigilance committee, the so-called Committee of Fifty. Only three days after Hennessy's death, Mayor Shakespeare was justifying the formation of the avowedly anti–Sicilian committee, arguing that "evidence collected by the Police Department show[s] beyond doubt that he [Hennessy] was the victim of Sicilian vengeance." The mayor implied that either Mafia bosses, or maybe even the Ring, were behind the murder when he claimed, rather enigmatically, that the assassins "were mere hirelings and instruments of others higher and more powerful than they." He told the City Council at the formation of the Committee: "We must teach these people a lesson they will not forget for all time.... The instigators! Those are the men we must find at any cost."[19]

Few in the city had any doubt who those "instigators" were. Pretty soon the reformers began to whip up public opinion against all Sicilians in the city. It didn't seem to matter whether they were considered to be "Mafia" or not. It was immaterial if they were Matranga or Provenzano. Hennessy himself had shared ownership of a rather dubious club in the seedier part of New Orleans with Joseph Provenzano and arguably had been shot as a result of his preference for that family over their rivals. Yet, in the wake of his death, his fellow reformers, out to avenge him, were not so discriminating. Forgetting their fallen hero's allegiances, they apparently saw *all* Sicilians as legitimate targets.

His avengers were not simply chauvinistic in their targeting of both factions. They claimed that Chief Hennessy was killed for reasons in addition to his incriminating information against the Matrangas. They showed he had tangled with the Sicilians earlier, with his role in the abduction and extradition in chains to New York of another Sicilian brigand, Giuseppe Esposito, in 1881. As an influential and wealthy Sicilian, with or without Mafia connections, Esposito had established the Provanzanos in their prominent position on the waterfront. This, the Shakespeare faction claimed, had made Hennessy the target of not only Matranga enmity, but also a longstanding Provenzano family vendetta that he may not have known about.

Further, the reformers argued that in supporting—or at least not halting—the rise of the Provenzanos, the Ring was implicated in the aura of corruption and bloodshed surrounding the Sicilians. Although this flew in the face of much of the verifiable evidence, the undaunted supporters of the Shakespeare regime continued to press just such a case in newspapers sympathetic to their cause. Pretty soon they had managed to make it an accepted part of the myths surrounding the murder of Hennessy.

By way of response, the Ring's *Times Democrat* made an effort to counter these accusations, while at the same time trying to limit the damage to their machine that any connection with Sicilians—implied or actual—could do. Unsurprisingly, given the near-universal unpopularity of the Sicilians by this point, and the prevailing mood of a city baying for vengeance against those who murdered their saintly chief, the Ring's supporters had little success. Left with little other choice, they soon started to toe the reformers' vehemently anti–Sicilian line. Within weeks of the chief's murder, the *Times Democrat* joined the newspapers of all stripes and entered what had become a competition among them to uncover further "evidence" of other Sicilian crimes.

The result was that within weeks of Hennessy's killing the reports of murders in the city were scrutinized, picked over for evidence of "Mafia" involvement, and then effectively tied in with the blood feuds of the War of the Oranges. Murders which until this point had been seen as having nothing to do with Sicilians, Mafia or otherwise, were attributed to the "dagoes." This way the papers had soon upped the body count until, with a curious irony, the tit-for-tat cycle of violence that had supposedly marked the War of the Oranges was replicated in a retaliatory war around newspaper circulation.

The *New York Herald*, a paper not renowned for its rigorous fact-checking, had the highest tally of casualties. It detailed some "ninety-four victims of Mafia wrath" in the beleaguered Sicilian areas of the city.[20] Most papers were less ambitious. Before long the majority of accounts had settled on a figure that hovered around a total of forty fatalities. However, what is perhaps more important, accounts claimed that most—if not all—of the corpses bore the obvious marks of Mafia blood feuds, whatever they might be. However, this significant discrepancy in the body count is indicative of far more than simply historical inaccuracy or journalistic ambition.

## St. Hennessy

Re-evaluating the generally accepted evidence behind the Hennessy murder does more than just revise the historical record. It does not, of itself, justify the historian's task by showing how he or she can review and challenge our knowledge of the subject. Nor should it serve to merely implicate, or exonerate the reputations of, key historical figures. Far from simply reconsidering the reasons behind what remains a shocking murder, re-examining the details of this case has the potential to fundamentally alter the foundation for one of the most persistent myths in U.S. history. Weighing the available information behind Hennessy's murder brings up clear evidence that the underpinnings of many of the narratives of the traditional trajectory of organized crime in the U.S. are essentially unsound.

A reasonable starting place for this re-evaluation is the simple veracity of the numbers of casualties involved and why they are so widely disputed. Establishing how many Sicilians died in the War of the Oranges gives an idea of how violent that dispute really was. In turn, that data enables historians to take a view on whether the dispute may have spilled over into the killing of Hennessy, or whether that was, maybe, a fabrication—a fig leaf—perhaps hiding something even more sinister. It also gives an idea about the accuracy of the sources involved. If these figures are justifiable, verifiable, then maybe the rest of the narrative is also relatively reliable. If they are exaggerated, or underestimated, then does that mean the claims that follow from them are similarly unreliable?

In spite of the fact that the majority of commentators in the 1890s cited a minimum figure of around forty Mafia killings, there is clear evidence of misrepresentation, if not tampering, even in this comparatively conservative estimate.[21] Some of the most compelling evidence for this inaccuracy comes from the analysis of the New Orleans coroners' records for the period carried out by the noted Mafia historian, Humbert S. Nelli.

Nelli has demonstrated that the names of perpetrators and victims that appeared on a list of "assassinations, murders and affrays committed by Sicilians and Italians" carried out since 1866 were almost universally incorrect.[22] This obviously casts into doubt all those claims based on them—claims about the violence of the Sicilian community, as well as claims about the investigations Hennessy was carrying out. But it also raises the questions: who made them, why would those claims have been made, and why have they been accepted for so long?

The list of the forty murders was compiled by Hennessy's successor as chief of police, Dexter Gastor, and there is strong evidence that he or his subordinates tampered with that list. Nelli shows that there are indications that names were deliberately changed to make them sound more Sicilian. According to his research comparing the dates and places of deaths kept in the coroners' records with those reported in Gastor's list, it emerges that Frenchmen, Germans and Spaniards were portrayed as being among the victims of the Mafia. While it is perfectly feasible that foreigners were caught up in the feuds—or used by either side—it does somewhat detract from the nature of the killings as being simply the results of blood feuds. Further, according to the coroner, those who had in reality been shot were described as having been stabbed with a stiletto. This is important to the development of the birth of the Mafia tale.

The stiletto was a notorious and gruesome dagger. It was really little more than a slender spike with a handle, and it was generally seen as the favorite weapon of the Mafia and Italian gangs. They were said to favor the weapon, since in skilled hands it was more than likely to prove lethal than the shotgun or handgun, not least because the murderer could viscerally sense how effective his attempts at assassination had been. Yet, in spite of the proximity it demanded, many American commentators saw it as a particularly vicious, underhanded, and cowardly weapon. In order to be most effective, the stiletto required stealth.

It was the very essence of the notorious "stab in the back," since the slim blade was jabbed into the lower back of the victim, and its tip was moved around within the unfortunate's body, scrambling, damaging and disrupting organs. In the right hands it was almost always fatal, but it left only a trace of blood and a small puncture wound. The result was that newspapers condemned this weapon as symbolic of those who used it: assassins who lurked in the shadows, silently attacking from behind and leaving little trace of their sinister handiwork.

This malevolent reputation had served the Mafia well. In the eyes of the superstitious peasants of Sicily, the evil weapon was even more effective. It was, in many cases, as if the victim had died of natural causes: perhaps as a result of a curse for transgressing the secret society. What was more, since it was well-known that the stiletto was associated with Mafiosi, it would serve as gruesome warning to those who might seek to betray or stand in the way of the order.

With those features in mind, the stiletto would have indelibly and indisputably marked those forty killings as the work of Sicilians. While the shotgun, pistol and other weapons were frequently used by Sicilians in their banditry at home, it was the stiletto that was seen as their trademark—and most contemporary histories of the Mafia mention the weapon. What was more, the motive behind these killings was frequently slanted—sometimes with little obvious evidence—to make it appear that the murder resulted from a vendetta or turf war killing, rather than what it most probably was—perhaps a robbery or even a crime of passion.[23]

Obviously if Macheca and his fellow Mafiosi were responsible for these murders, they also had reason to kill Hennessy. If the police chief knew the details of their crimes, as most contemporary newspapers suggested, then it was in their interests to silence the policeman most likely to know—Hennessy. There is evidence—although largely circumstantial—that supports this interpretation. It is known that Hennessy was investigating the activities of the Sicilians. It is also established that he was in contact with the Italian authorities—most notably the Italian Consul in New Orleans, Pasquale Corte.[24]

What was more, he had an ongoing correspondence with one of the most famous detectives in the U.S. at the time, William Pinkerton. Pinkerton was the son of the founder of the eponymous national detective agency, Allan Pinkerton, and there is evidence that Hennessy met with the famous detective in October 1890. There is also evidence that he received information from him on Mafioso activity in other regions of the U.S. As William Pinkerton put it, Hennessy "had dug deeper into the order than any outsider ever had dared…. [H]e said he had the evidence to root up the Mafia in this country."[25] But since the content of those conversations and letters has been lost, the impact of this line of inquiry has to remain largely speculative.

All that is left are snippets revealed in more or less unverifiable newspaper accounts. These are for the most part based on information released by Hennessy's loyal secretary, George Washington Vandervoort. Hardly surprisingly, Vandervoort was both a staunch supporter of Shakespeare and tremendously devoted to the legacy of his dead boss. He also shared the almost universal animosity towards Sicilians in the wake of Hennessy's murder. Mix in the fact that most of these versions center on the nebulous role of Joseph Macheca and the Matrangas and their involvement with the highly secretive *Stuppagghieri* Mafia clan, and it is impossible to avoid the conclusion that most of these accounts should be treated as speculative at best.

For example, much is made of Hennessy's correspondence with the head of police in Rome, Louis Bertin. The information he gathered there almost certainly drew on the same information as that cited by Consul Corte, who had referred to over one "hundred criminal fugitives" on the run from the Italian authorities, and known to be resident in New Orleans.[26] Yet it would have been obvious to Hennessy that any investigation of the criminal records or Mafia activity for Macheca in Rome, or any other area of Italy, would necessarily draw a blank. This was a certainty since, if Hennessy had done even the most rudimentary investigation into the roots of the Matrangas and their history, he would have known that Macheca was in fact a U.S. citizen who had actually been born in the U.S.

Hennessy may have also been aware that when Macheca's mother remarried, her young son had developed what Mediterranean connections he had via his stepfather, yet these were not even with Sicily. Macheca's European links were with the British colony in Malta, not the Italian island of Sicily. What was more, he would also have discovered that the Matranga brothers were only infants when their parents left Sicily to settle in New Orleans and their connections with the "motherland" can be seen as tenuous, at best. So very little genuine evidence to directly incriminate any of them could have been gained from those Italian connections.

It is, however, possible that Hennessy's investigations really did uncover something about Macheca's shady past: something which only became apparent through his Pinkerton and Italian connections. In her own investigations into her ancestors' role in the murder of Hennessy and the subsequent Mafia panic, Martha Macheca Sheldon—Joseph Macheca's granddaughter—argues that Hennessy may well have uncovered the role that Macheca played in the disappearance of his own father. Macheca's father, who had Anglicized his name to Peter Carvanna, among other aliases, was a small-time Sicilian crook. Shortly after his arrival in New Orleans, on the eve of the Civil War, he was arrested for an unspecified crime, and sentenced to a lengthy prison sentence, the details of which remain sketchy.

Believing that Peter would not return from prison, and probably somewhat relieved to be able to start a new life for herself and her son, Macheca's mother, Marietta, remarried an upright and industrious Maltese fruit trader, Guzeppi Mercieca. Guzeppi later Anglicized his name to Joseph Macheca and passed on that name, his standing in the New Orleans community, and his pride in his Maltese background to his stepson, the younger Joseph. However, Peter—or perhaps someone posing as him—was released at the end of Civil War, and that man uncovered the whereabouts of the unfortunate Marietta. He then went to visit her and, by Sheldon's account, the shock of the subsequent meeting visibly altered Marietta's behavior for the rest of her life.

Although little in this sad saga can be verified beyond doubt, it is possible—and given his history and nature, probable—that the ex-prisoner, seeing his estranged wife's good fortune and wealth, attempted to blackmail Marietta. It could be that he beat her up, or perhaps he even raped her. Maybe he did all three. Whatever happened, it is not inconceivable that in order to end what he saw as the source of his mother's suffering, Macheca killed Carvanna. If Hennessy pieced these bits of information together, then there is no doubt that Macheca would have had reason to kill him, or order his execution.[27]

Macheca would certainly have had the ability and means to carry out such a murder. According to local understanding, he was allegedly central to the cycle of vendetta killings in the Sicilian community. Even if he was not a Mafioso, Macheca could have carried out the murder. After all, Joseph Macheca was a powerful man of action and used to violence. It was also well known that since his early days as leader of a gang of political strong-arm thugs—the Innocenti—he had been only too happy to use violence. He was involved in smuggling operations during and after the Civil War, and had often shown a willingness to operate outside the law. What was more, New Orleans was a violent city where disputes were all too frequently resolved with guns. There is no need to assume that he was a Mafioso or that he killed Hennessy in order to preserve the secrecy and safety of his fraternity.[27]

## Shakespeare

Historians have also pieced together the evidence to come up with other motives for Hennessy's murder. One of the most intriguing of these alternatives puts the whole issue of Sicilian, and consequently Mafia, involvement into question—at least in the usually accepted format. In this version the New Orleans "Mafiosi" are dupes of higher powers who were carrying on their own feud. The evidence for these accounts all stem from the same place. They see the shooting of the New Orleans Chief of Detectives (Chief of Aides, as it was known at the time) Captain Thomas Devereux by Hennessy in October 1881 as playing a central role in the subsequent murder of the police chief nearly a decade later.

Eyewitnesses of that event were left in no doubt that Hennessy shot Devereux. They also claim, pretty unanimously, that he was "aided and abetted" by his cousin, Mike. The Hennessy cousins did not attempt to deny that they carried out the killing either.[28] However, the subsequent investigation and trial found them both not guilty of murder. It was agreed Devereux had provoked them. The victim was generally held to be an objectionable man in the best of times. On his last afternoon in October 1881, Devereux's natural cussedness was exaggerated by the unanimous opinion of all witnesses that he was also very drunk and was picking a fight with the Hennessys.

The result was that at the subsequent trial, Justice Baker ruled the cousins had acted in self-defense. They were found not guilty and allowed to leave the court and resume their posts in the police.[29] Yet in spite of this verdict, the factionalism of the New Orleans Police Department that had culminated in this killing continued to haunt Hennessy until his own murder. Rather wisely, given their well-known political allegiances and the fact that the Ring's political star was in the ascendancy, both David and Mike Hennessy had opted to leave the police force and quit New Orleans until the storm died down. In this they were only partially successful, since many in the NOPD refused to hold with the verdict and these men were determined not to forgive the cousins, or forget the killing. One detective in particular, Dominick O'Malley, kept up the feud.

O'Malley hated Hennessy and never made any bones about it. A Ring tool, an ally of the Matrangas and a close friend of Captain Devereux, O'Malley was furious when he was passed over as police chief in favor of Hennessy in 1888. Further, according to Hennessy's secretary, the ever-faithful George Washington Vandervort: "Hennessy always thought that O'Malley directed most of his enmity against him [with the result that Hennessy] refused to work the Matranga [ambush] case [of July 1890] alongside of O'Malley, and believed that if he was killed O'Malley would have a hand in the job."[30]

When the surprise judgment at the murder trial for Hennessy's death was delivered on March 13, 1891, it found Macheca and eight co-defendants not guilty. In the shocked mood that followed the decision, the local anti–Ring press accused O'Malley of having bribed the jury. Nor was that the end of the accusations. By May of that year a grand jury was charged with reopening the investigation of the murder. The object was to try to get a better understanding of the trial, and attempt to explain why it provoked a mob to kill eleven alleged "Mafia" who they saw as responsible for the chief's death.

The grand jury heard evidence that backed up allegations of irregularities in the trial. The blame for these was placed squarely on O'Malley. They uncovered O'Malley's previous convictions for jury tampering and argued: "With his skill, as acquired by years of experience, the most cunningly devised schemes were planned and executed for defeating the legitimate course of justice, the chief aim and object being to place unworthy men upon the jury in the trial of the nine accused."[31]

The grand jury then went on to detail his associates in the police force and the Mafia, but stopped short of any indictments of either O'Malley or others connected with him. The embattled detective had fled New Orleans a few days after the verdict was announced in order to avoid punishment for his alleged crime. He would have known that whether guilty or not—given the mood of the mob—he would have stood a very high chance of being hanged, either way. Nevertheless, as a parting shot before he left town, O'Malley did bring a case against the anti–Ring *New Orleans States*—the main source of the accusations—for some $10,000 in damages.[32]

Some accused O'Malley of being guilty of even worse crimes. The Italian Consul to the U.S., Pasquale Corte, claimed that O'Malley himself killed Hennessy. He said he had a letter from a prisoner being held in Baton Rouge that proved O'Malley's guilt. John Duffy's letter was dated November 4, 1890—about 2 weeks after Hennessy's murder. In it the prisoner said a "reliable friend who writes me" had information which could "help your dago friends." Duffy had told the Consul that O'Malley, along with four "American" accomplices, dressed themselves as Mafiosi and used Mafia techniques—in this case massed shotguns at very close range—to kill the police chief.[33]

Judging by the events that followed, those who had known of the contents of Duffy's letter before it was published had dismissed it as fantasy. Maybe Duffy's status as prisoner cast doubt on the reliability of his claims. No doubt there were also those who saw the revelation as little more than a blatant attempt by Consul Corte to rehabilitate the rapidly declining reputation of Italians in New Orleans. Perhaps most importantly there were many who would rather believe the findings of Shakespeare's Committee of Fifty, with their stream of anti–Sicilian, anti–Ring and anti–Mafia rhetoric.

The Committee flooded the papers with lurid tales of death threats issued against those who sought to shine light on the secret order's diabolical doings. They stridently called for action to clean up the city, limit the activities of the corrupt and violent Sicilians prospering in their midst, and drive the Mafia out for good. Unsurprisingly, given the city's mood, the campaign was effective. It appeared that the vast majority of the city's population was behind the vigilante actions of the anti–Mafia mob that formed following the acquittals of the Sicilians accused of Hennessy's murder. They supported the shooting and the hanging of eleven "Sicilians" (technically, three Italian citizens and eight American citizens) in and outside the parish prison where they were being held for their own safety.

Essentially those leading the mob argued that O'Malley and his Mafia paymasters had bribed, intimidated and corrupted the jury, making the verdict a mockery of justice and necessitating the extreme extra-legal measures they had undertaken. They produced evidence that O'Malley paid $150 to three jurymen. Perhaps more tellingly, in keeping with emerging reports of Mafia techniques, they also argued that O'Malley had imported unrecognizable Mafia thugs from New York in order to intimidate witnesses.[34]

For his part, O'Malley denied these charges, arguing—with irrefutable logic—that if the prosecution had had evidence of jury tampering, why had they waited until *after* the trial to produce it? He was convinced, as of course he would be, of the innocence of the Sicilians on trial, claiming: "Those men were innocent, and the people made a great mistake, for which I hope they will properly apologize to the widows and orphans hereafter. Each one of the nineteen men made a statement to me, which I investigated and reported upon…. I had such confidence in their innocence that I offered small bets that all of the accused would be acquitted."[35] The mood was, however, against him. O'Malley was seen as a stooge of the all-powerful Mafia, and his statements were held to be blatant attempts to save his own skin by protecting his brutal paymasters. This is perhaps best summed up in the words of one local paper that saw America's largest mass lynching as a spontaneous outburst of Jacksonian democracy, when it echoed the Founding Fathers, claiming that "the voice of the people *is* the law of the land."[36]

Even the usually neutral *New York Times* went with the majority opinion when it claimed, "Lynch law was the only course open to the people of New Orleans."[37] The grand jury set to investigate Hennessy's murder and the "Parish Prison Killings" agreed. It found the incident to be a "popular movement," and the report concluded, "The verdict has been rendered. The power of the Mafia is broken. It must be destroyed as an element of danger, a creation of leprous growth in this community."[38]

Nationally, there was a mood of grudging support for the lynchings that was perhaps best shown in the editorial of the *New York Times*, which argued: "Orderly and law-abiding persons will not pretend that the butchery of Italians was either 'justifiable or proper.' Yet while every good citizen will readily assent that the affair is to be deplored, it would be difficult to find any one individual who confess that privately he deplores it very much."[39] Perhaps one of the clearest demonstrations of popular support is shown by the humorous weekly, *Texas Siftings*, in April 1891. The paper ran a cartoon that showed the Mafia as a dragon with knives for claws. The vigilantes are represented in the form of a modern St. George mounted on a steed emblazoned with the title "New Orleans." Rather anachronistically, although clad in a suit of armor, George is firing his shotgun into the writhing beast.[40] It seemed that this was just the way the incident was seen by most observers. It was put forward as a clear stand by native-born Americans against the expansion of a foreign threat—the Mafia. Certainly, it was bloody and it was brutal, but it was also a necessary and effective reaction to a deep-rooted threat that was aimed at the very essence of American law and order and justice.

A constant stream of information poured out of City Hall in New Orleans. Sensing that they were on the verge of conclusively breaking their enemies, the Shakespeare administration was determined to keep up the pressure. In part this was no doubt to press home their political advantage, but it was also in part perhaps to justify the actions of the vigilantes with whom they were now indelibly associated. Whatever slant historians choose to place on these events, there is little doubt that in a majority of the American press for the next decade or so, the events surrounding the revenge of the Hennessy murder were portrayed as the first victory in an ongoing battle with an insidious, foreign, invisible and violent secret society.

For example, some eight years after the Parish Prison murders—as the Mafia lynchings may more accurately be called—in 1899, five more Sicilians were lynched in Tallulah, Louisiana, accused of the attempted murder of a local doctor. The *Picayune* justified the action as a reaction to another incursion into the state by the Mafia. The evidence behind the vigilantes' actions was purely circumstantial, and not very convincing at that. In fact, there is little to show that Sicilians were involved at all.

On the basis of nothing other than hearsay, their accusers created a plot featuring a malevolent conspiracy of Italians who, in reality, were unrelated and unknown to each other. Drawing on this, the paper still accused the Sicilians of acting together in a previous murder. The *Picayune* argued that the vigilantes were particularly incensed because they claimed the so-called Mafiosi had bragged of their murderous deeds and said that they were secure from retribution since they had sufficient money and protection at a high enough level to clear their names. In light of this, the paper drew the conclusion that the victims were obviously Mafiosi, and defended the lynchings by saying: "The people of Louisiana have a very lively sense of resentment and outrage at the fact that the Mafia or any other foreign murder society should be in operation in their State, and they are determined, whenever it shows its dreadful head, that they will crush it."[41]

Typical of the way in which the administration behaved with regard to the 1891 lynchings was the action of William Parkerson. Parkerson was one of the city's leading lawyers, a staunch supporter of Shakespeare, and a leading figure in the Committee of Fifty. He was also the leader of the lynch mob that cornered the "Mafiosi" in the Parish Prison. It was Parkerson who organized the shooting and hanging of the cowering "Italians." For this deed he was carried home in triumph on the shoulders of the mob.

Nevertheless, the day after "the work at the prison was over," Parkerson claimed that he received a mysterious and oddly phrased letter. The letter was a warning that had all the hallmarks of a Mafia threat: "You are a doomed man. God almighty can't save you. We have it sworn, our comrades you killed and we will kill you and your family will be poisoned. The stillette [sic] will do the rest."[42] Nor was the heroic Parkerson alone in claiming to have received such threats. Shakespeare, Vandervoort and several other "reformist" politicians of various ranks told of similarly intimidating letters speaking of Mafia retribution.

## The Birth of the American Mafia

It is telling that this threat to Parkerson was not run as a story in any of the main Louisiana newspapers. Instead it was published in some of the leading papers of the northeast. This can be seen as more than an oversight. A closer examination in a certain light could actually reveal it as one of the most striking elements of the whole tragic affair. It is probable that many of the residents of New Orleans were eager for these killings in particular to be justified in minds of the rest of the nation. To them it was vital that their actions in the Parish Prison should continue to be seen as part of the solution to what they insisted was a national problem.

Many of the leading local actors in the drama had made links between the dead Mafiosi and Sicilian secret societies in other regions of the U.S. The New Orleans press seemed to relish detailing Mafia activity in places as far apart as Atlanta and Chicago; Brooklyn and San Francisco. These reports can be seen as an attempt to shift the emphasis away from those all too familiar racial issues that plagued the post-bellum South. It was undeniably true that reports of vigilante violence in the South had been widely reported nationwide ever since the last Federal troops had been withdrawn from the region in 1877.

An idea of the scale of this violence can be gathered by averaging out the number of lynchings recorded state by state across the area south of the Mason-Dixon line by the Tuskegee Institute. It emerges that in the years between 1882 (when records began) and the end of 1891, there was at least one lynching every other week in the South.[43] Since the vast majority of these killings involved white-on-black violence—more often than not in response to reports of black-on-white violence—Southern lynchings were seen fundamentally in racial terms.

Yet far from condemning the Mafia Lynchings, as the Parish Prison murders become universally known, the Shakespeare administration had capitalized on them. In order to further justify their support for those who perpetrated the killings, the reformist regime was at pains to maintain that the vigilantes were not racially motivated, but were *American* people who were enforcing *American* laws. The unusual and violent action was only necessary because the usual *American* processes of law had been subverted by criminals.

For instance, Louisiana's Governor Francis Nicholls reassured the *London Times* that "the race or nationality of the parties did not enter as a factor into the disturbances."[44] The city clerk of New Orleans told the press in Boston, "This was not a wild uprising of a crazy mob. It was a calm, deliberate action of the best element of the city. Lawyers, doctors, merchants and the higher grades of society were there and felt that something must be done."[45] This campaign seemed to work. The *New York Herald* argued that the swift and deliberate action of Parkerson and his fellow vigilantes had prevented "a war upon the [Italian] race" from breaking out in the city. The paper went on to argue that New Orleans was not unique: the national sentiment was vehemently anti–Mafia and anti–Italian. Further, it was not generally condemnatory or even particularly opposed to either Shakespeare or the vigilantes.[46]

On the other hand, the Italian government demanded that the New Orleans vigilantes be tried for their crimes and argued for some form of compensation for the families of the victims. Particularly outraged Italians even saw the events as a cause for war with the United States. The result was that in March and April 1891 there was an escalation of the issue of war with Italy in the American press and the emergence of a jingoism that in many ways can be seen as similar to that which would take America to war with Spain a few years later. However, in this case the fever broke and the jingoism dissipated.[47]

It is plain the motives behind and even the identity of the perpetrators of the Hennessy murder meant some held that the case may well be open to reinterpretation. This is perhaps most clear in the efforts made to calm the situation in 1891. Determined war with Italy be avoided, U.S. Attorney General William H.H. Miller questioned any connection between organized crime and the death of Hennessy. He also argued that most of the victims had been naturalized Americans, so he found Italy's outrage rather odd.[48]

Nevertheless, Miller was in a minority, for while the vigilantes could never produce any concrete evidence of Mafia involvement, there is little doubt that, thanks to the press coverage of the murder, trial and lynchings, the average American now had the word "Mafia" firmly placed in his lexicon. He knew this shady organization was ruthless and clannish. He also knew it was Sicilian—or at least Italian—and he was beginning to be convinced that it was also highly organized and omnipresent. The fear of the organization seems to have run deep all over the nation.

In 1896, while awaiting trial for the killing of a public official, a Sicilian in Hahnville, Louisiana, was taken from his cell by a lynch mob. So were two other unrelated and unconnected Sicilians awaiting trial in the same prison. All of them were hanged. All were accused of having Mafia connections and using Mafia methods.[49] When, over the next decade or so, Italians were involved in any crime, there would frequently be a Mafia connection made in the public mind. The synapses that created one of the most persistent mental images of organized crime had already been formed in the minds of many Americans, all over the nation.

For example, less than a week after the lynchings, police broke up a peaceful demonstration in Troy, New York, by firing into the crowd. One man was killed and police responded with the accusation that the largely Italian protesters had been "armed with knives and guns." The implication was that they were Mafia.[50] A month later in West Virginia, a group of Italian laborers were accused of slitting the throats of an entire local family. The accusations led directly to a gunfight between a posse and these "Mafiosi."[51] Nearly three months after the lynchings in the Parish Prison, in Pennsylvania some forty deputies were needed to protect Italian coal miners. The locals objected to them as "scabs," but referred to them as "Mafia."[52] Nor did these accusations die out as the events in New Orleans receded further into history.

A quick glance at the national press over a single month nearly a year after the lynchings gives some idea of the scale of the perception of the Mafia. Mafia membership was seen as a trait of any violent Sicilian, or even anyone of Sicilian descent. Perhaps one of the best examples of how far this went was the report that a ship had docked in Tacoma, Washington, after a lengthy trip from the Far East. It emerged from stories told by the crew that was it was skippered by a particularly brutal Sicilian captain. Sure enough, the *Tacoma Times* could not resist the completely unfounded allegation that the brute "may be a Mafia man."[53]

A policeman in San Francisco reported that a Sicilian who'd shot at him was obviously a "member of a Mafia gang." He told the *San Francisco Chronicle* that he knew this because the man had warned him: "You have hurt me, and my people will have your life within three days."[54] A couple of days later in Newark, New Jersey, an overextended Italian bank was struggling to pay its largely immigrant investors. Although there was no evidence produced to back this allegation up, one local commentator claimed that the bank had always been little more than the front for Mafia activity.[55]

Essentially, the press had made sure that the stage was now set for the Mafia: Sicilians and organized crime were on their way to becoming synonymous. Nor would this would be the only time this would happen. The idea of the link became stubbornly ingrained in the American mind, nailed home by a variety of individual crimes; vivid depictions in novels and films; congressional investigations; pronouncements by law enforcers; and all sorts of other reminders. Occasionally leaders of the Italian community and academics would argue that the Mafia did not exist. Perhaps most famously, even J. Edgar Hoover argued that the popular belief in the Mafia was erroneous. But the public seemed to want this particular bogeyman, and the result was that the connection between Italians and organized crime would stubbornly re-emerge throughout the twentieth century.

In pretty well every decade of this study and in the years beyond, certainly from the turn of the twentieth century to the 1940s, the connection would be remade. From the "Barrel Murders" of the 1900s, to the murder of Joe Petrosino, to Murder, Inc.; from the Black Hand scare, to the Prohibition gangsters of Chicago, there would be incidents which reinforced this connection. The Mafia legend is without doubt the most enduring of all organized criminal myths of the twentieth century, and it owed its origins to the unexplained incidents of that rainy night in New Orleans. Whatever the truth of the events of that October night in 1890, it was without doubt the date the American Mafia was born, or at least it was the birthday of its mythological status.

# 2

## Crime Rings

### Rings and Bosses

The reanalysis of Hennessy's murder clearly serves to question, if not alter, the validity of the initial evidence for a Mafia-type model of organized crime. However, equally importantly, it also highlights one of the most important preconditions necessary for its very emergence and survival: the link between the criminal and the politician. The Ring had used—or had been accused of using—criminal connections, not the least of which were the Mafiosi, to further its own political aims. Shakespeare and Hennessy's opposition to the Ring and the criminal methods it used to achieve dominance of Louisiana politics enabled them to have a solid political platform. What is also interesting about the Ring is that it—perhaps deliberately, maybe accidentally—lent its name to an entire genre of organized crime that emerged some years before the Mafia scare of 1891.

This was clearly illustrated on Good Friday 1876, when in Boston, the Rev. Dr. James Freeman Clarke delivered a fire-and-brimstone sermon attacking political corruption. Titled "The Ring, the Lobby and the Caucus: The Three Enemies of the Nation," it made newspaper headlines all over New England. In it the Harvard professor of natural religion told his fashionable Unitarian congregation: "The phrase 'Ring' is a new one: but the thing itself is as old as covetousness and knavery … [because] a ring is only a corrupt combination of several persons in power [who] unite their strength for purposes of plunder."[1]

Perhaps the most famous ring was Boss Tweed's Tammany Ring, which dominated the headlines of 1871–1872. The success of the prosecution and the scandalous revelations concerned with it kept the public's interest and fueled a search for similar scandalous rings in almost every major city of the Union. By 1876, there is little doubt that the minister had chosen a hot topic for his Good Friday sermon. Wherever he had been in the U.S. at the time of his sermon, the congregation he addressed would have been familiar with the term, for throughout the 1870s "rings" would most likely have been the main form of organized crime on people's minds. They were certainly the form that excited the most press attention.

The term ring came from the practice of "ring bidding" at auctions, where a group of bidders would collude in order to exclude other bidders, and in so doing gain unfair advantage. In many ways it was a very apt word since it indicates how insiders could manipulate information, position or contacts to gain financial or political advantage. As such, rings are perhaps one of the most glaring and sophisticated examples of true organized crime in the second half of the nineteenth century. They certainly fit with many of the models which are used to define organized crime—both historically and in the present day.

Present-day Russian gangsters refer to the shielding of criminals by politicians as the provision of *krysha*—literally "roof," but perhaps more accurately in this context translated as "shelter." This in turn enables the criminals to function, thrive and hopefully repay their political patrons for that protection. They gauge their own status and power by the level of *krysha* which they have achieved and measure allies or competitors in the same way.[2] This has clear historical roots. It has been argued that it was influential political protection and political influence that propelled and sustained the rise of the Sicilian Mafia in the nineteenth century.[3]

Perhaps the most blatant ring activity can be found in the activities of organized crime in modern Nigeria. Here highly sophisticated illegal trading or "bunkering" operations can steal, store and ship the vast quantities of oil that make them such effective multi-billion-dollar operations. This is only achievable with the knowledge, collusion and protection of high-ranking Nigerian politicians.[4] However, like some other types of organized criminal activity of the late nineteenth century in America, the ring scams seem to have slipped under the radar of the historians of organized crime.

Most likely this is because they don't fit the prevailing, if constrained, public perception of organized crime as centered around mobs, gangsters and Mafias. Nevertheless, casting aside these restraints, there can be little doubt that in terms of the diversity of criminal activity, the extent of newsprint they excited, and in contemporary public perception, the ring scandals of the Grant administrations (1868–1876) must certainly rank as some of the most important demonstrations of the intersections of organized criminal activity and political power in U.S. history.

What is more, if the decision to include the rings in the pantheon of organized crime was to be made solely on grounds of prevalence and diversity, then the range of products covered and the geographic spread of the ring scandals of this period make a pretty convincing argument for their inclusion. Rings covered a range of commodities from beef to gold, quarried marble to silver coinage, as well as railroads, canals, grain, customs revenues, warships and civil service salaries. They are found in the most rural communities and in the huge metropolitan areas—in the West, the South and the North.

Equally impressive are the variety of government agencies implicated in scandals surrounding rings. They included the Treasury Department, the Indian Agency, the Postal Service, the Secret Service, the Department of the Navy and the War Department. Further, although Grant himself was never connected—at least directly—a large proportion of his administration most certainly were. The result of all these scandals was that by the end of his second term, the president had been obliged to either discipline or defend members of his cabinet extending from his attorney general to his war secretary, interior secretary, naval secretary and treasury secretary. Alongside them, association with rings also tainted Grant's personal secretaries, his vice-president, and his own son-in-law. "Grantism"—as the administration's corruption, nepotism, greed, price skimming, tax evasion, perjury and patronage became known—appeared to be ubiquitous.

## The Whiskey Ring

Arguably the most widely known, certainly the most publicized, and perhaps the ring which best illustrates the links of organized crime and politics, must be the Whiskey

Ring. It is well known because in many ways this scandal became the final straw for the reputation of the Grant regime. It certainly spelt the very public disgrace, and contributed to the downfall, of one of the prime movers in many of the regime's other scandals. A military engineer and expert in siege warfare, Orville E. Babcock had a distinguished Civil War career, serving in several theaters of operations before coming to the attention of U.S. Grant and serving on his personal staff. The two developed a close relationship, so much so that the supreme commander even entrusted Babcock to deliver the coup de grace for the Confederate regime. It was Babcock who conveyed the demand for the surrender of Robert E. Lee at Appomattox.

After the war's end, Babcock remained a close advisor and confidant, rising to become Grant's aide-de-camp in 1866. After entering the White House, from 1869 Grant promoted his friend to make him his private secretary. In this position he was entrusted with controlling personal access to the president in this era of increasing pressure from job-seekers and lobbyists. It was this powerful, influential close friend and intimate of the president who linked many of the rings together, operating a favor bank system that took graft as a form of tribute for his own benefit. As one contemporary, a member of Grant's cabinet, memorably put it, it was Babcock who had always been at the center of an "eternal cabal" linked with the worst of the administration's outrages.[5]

Nevertheless, the role of the Whiskey Ring, or rather Whiskey *Rings*, scandal is instructive in ways other than its terminal impact on high-ranking and corrupt members of the administration. In order to assess its other lessons, it is necessary to also understand at least some of the details of the fiddle. In essence, the whiskey scams associated with the ring revolved around deliberate underreporting of whiskey production to the Treasury Department officials. Depending on the proportions of this deceit, the whiskey distillers could reduce their costs by between 50 and 75 cents per gallon through the saving of the federally imposed duty. Those storekeepers and bar owners who colluded—and a great many, if not most, did—were in turn often rewarded with a price discounted by an agreed and universal 17 cents a gallon. This was a saving that they could choose to pass on to their customers, or not.

But this service came at a cost. In order for the fraud to work, the officials at every level of regulation had to agree to take part in the scam, and there were a wide range who needed to be brought in. It included all those who carried out the recording and measuring of production, as well as those charged with assessing and collecting the tax and—of course—those who were meant to fine those who didn't pay. In order for the scheme to work, they would all be paid a fee for turning a blind eye to that untaxed overproduction. It was also necessary for those officials who were not involved in the scam to be persuaded, by financial or physical pressure, to remain silent.

Unsurprisingly, this pressure was usually financial, since it was often more effective and inclusive, and it frequently left less difficult questions behind it than violence that stopped short of murder. Yet that price could be significant. According to the testimony of the former supervisor of Internal Revenue, in 1874 alone, Babcock was paid some $26,000 as well as "many valuable presents," including a $1,000 cigar case. It was estimated that in the single year from November 1871 the five top officials involved, including Babcock, pocketed some $45,000 to $60,000 apiece in bribes, kickbacks and gifts. The same amount was paid to the heads of four of the major distilleries involved. When it is considered that a dollar in 1875 was worth twenty dollars in 2000, that equates to about a million dollars apiece in today's money.[6]

Yet the scheme was nothing new. Moonshining, bootlegging, rum-running and other forms of crime associated with liquor had been pretty commonplace in a society in which whiskey represented a very portable, almost universally valued commodity, and one that had always been subject to regulation and some form of levy. What was new was the level of the charge, and therefore the profits available in the 1860s, because in that decade the nature of that duty had changed.

Waging a modern, industrial, total war, as the Union had done with the Civil War, the federal government had been required to find entirely new levels of income. The result was that unprecedented new taxes were placed on a variety of everyday items. Under the Internal Revenue Act of 1862, duties of between 0.3 and 1.5 percent were charged on income, manufactured goods, official documents, transport and financial transactions, as well as alcohol. Whiskey duties had peaked at $2 a gallon in 1865, and although slowly reduced, unlike many of the other revenue streams imposed during the war, they remained as a hated but permanent source of federal income from then onwards.[7]

One result of this taxation was that "whiskey rings," whereby politicians and other federal "officers connive at robbery of the revenue and divide the plunder with the robbers," had been reported as early as 1867. The phenomenon was widespread, too. Examples of them were uncovered in, among other places, New York, Chicago (and the rest of Illinois), Louisiana, Wisconsin and Iowa, and it is highly probable that many other undetected scams also existed.

Nor was the scale of the fraud involved in the exposures of 1875 anything that could be called unique. According to one estimate, somewhere around 152 million gallons of whiskey were produced in 1867—for a variety of reasons, not least the excise issue itself, exact figures are difficult to come by. Federal accounts show that a mere 14 million gallons, less than ten percent of that production, was declared for duty that fiscal year.[8] So, even allowing for inaccuracies, that figure shows that there had been a considerable scale of evasion nearly ten years before Babcock met his demise.

However, the 1875 Whiskey Ring scandal clearly demonstrates a selection of the facets that underlie the symbiotic nature of organized crime and the gaining and maintaining of political power that are so vital, and such a defining feature of *successful* organized crime. The connections between organized crime and politics are well established and the whiskey frauds are no different. Politicians and politically appointed officials were implicated, prosecuted and shamed when the scandal broke, but its origins were not simply political; they were also very much partisan. The gradual uncovering of the details of the Whiskey Ring reveal it as a good example of the way in which organized crime both requires and feeds off political protection.

Nothing shows this more clearly than the confession of General John McDonald. Confronted by irrefutable evidence showing him to be a key player in the scam, McDonald, the supervisor of Internal Revenue in St. Louis, claimed it was actually a way for politicians to raise money for political campaigning. According to him, it was Republican party workers in Missouri who in 1870 organized the entire scam. McDonald argued that these organizers set up their revenue evasion scheme with the clear purpose of raising a war chest in order to fight off an insurgent Republican rebellion by members of a liberal wing of the party. Disillusioned with the policies of the Grant administration, these liberals under a previously loyal and influential supporter of the administration, Carl Schurz, had formed a splinter group. Perhaps more worryingly, they had been gaining considerable support, and had succeeded in dividing the majority Republican vote in the key state of Missouri just in time to have a major influence on the 1872 election.[9]

These claims may have been a way of persuading reluctant officials into the scheme by showing them that breaking the law served a higher purpose than mere financial gain. Or they may have simply been a way for McDonald to justify his own actions. Whatever the truth of the matter, the White House was worryingly close to the whole affair. Officials high up in the Grant administration had essentially shielded the fraudsters, since the fraud served the interests of those in power. The result was that for some time nothing was done to investigate it, let alone stop it.[10]

However, McDonald argued that this was only true as long as the activities of those involved in the ring could be condoned and concealed, if not controlled, by their allies in the White House. This situation of shielding by the upper echelons of the administration lasted until the beginning of 1874, when it became increasingly apparent to the beneficiaries in the White House that the motive behind the fraud was changing. It was becoming ever more obvious that the scheme was now financial and criminal rather than political. With this change in perception, calls around Washington grew for an investigation and the prosecution of those found to be involved.

The organized criminality of the scandal began to become apparent to the political village in Washington, as all the while in the background, newspapers ran recurring and worryingly resilient accusations of wrongdoing. Typically this exposure drove politicians of all hues scrambling to be the first to make further exposés of the perpetrators in their midst. In this they were driven by the usual motive—personal ambition: either by a thirst for political advantage, or in order to shelter themselves from the inevitable fallout. These wishes went right to the top, with the by now beleaguered president fighting hard to protect his friend Babcock.

Nevertheless, it became increasingly evident that Grant was going to have to allow further inquiries and exploration of what was really going on. Announcing that he would "let no guilty man escape," on June 3, 1874, the president appointed Benjamin Helm Bristow to head up the Treasury and lead the investigation into the Whiskey Rings.[11] As the nation's first solicitor general, the ambitious Bristow had already shown himself to be meticulous, ruthless and inventive in, among other things, his successful prosecution of the South Carolina Ku Klux Klan. Now, with one eye on running for the White House himself, Bristow made it his mission to unravel and expose all those who'd been involved in the scams.

Using a combination of informants and undercover agents, as well as employing journalists eager for a chance to expose yet more scandal, Bristow managed to collect enough information to mount a series of highly effective raids on the Missouri Ring in May 1875. Some three hundred ring members at all levels were netted. Among them were the local Revenue Supervisor General John McDonald, the Revenue Agent John A. Joyce, and the Revenue Collector Constantine Maguire.

As the evidence from these trials crept ever closer to implicating Babcock and other White House staff, it left the public convinced that central government and organized crime were more or less synonymous. One commentator at the time summed it up, saying: "Senators, representatives, local politicians in swarms, the whole Washington lobby with its ramifications reaching every part of the land, thieves, detectives, officials at the White House," were all implicated in the scam.[12]

Regardless of this growing evidence and the hostility of much of the press—even the Republican press—Grant still intervened to protect Babcock. He effectively sabotaged the prosecution's case by withdrawing immunity from those who turned state's evidence—including McDonald. Ever faithful to his friend, confidante and secretary, Grant was persuaded only with difficulty not to appear in the St. Louis criminal court. He was finally persuaded that the president must remain above such scandals. The advice was good: Babcock was eventually tried in one of the most sensational and high-profile trials of the age, and Grant's appearance would not have enhanced the office of the president.

In what was in many ways a commendable demonstration of loyalty, Grant remained determined to the last to defend his friend. The president broke with protocol and made a sworn deposition in Babcock's defense. Some felt that even in doing this Grant did himself no favors. When confronted by pretty well irrefutable evidence of Babcock's misdemeanors, the president's famous "photographic memory," which had served him so well in the Civil War, spectacularly failed him. He claimed to have forgotten almost every detail that might have been used to convict his friend. As the *New York Times* put it, if "Babcock had been engaged in any wrong transactions the president had no knowledge of it, and he did not believe it."[13]

In the end the president's amnesia and staunch belief in his friend gave a stay of execution for the irrepressible Babcock. His secretary was found not guilty. Some measure of how influential Grant's protection proved can be gathered from the fact that Babcock was the only one of Bristow's haul of prosecutions—that numbered nearly two hundred Whiskey Ring defendants—who was entirely exonerated of the charges. Furthermore, within three days of his acquittal, he was back in the White House, once again guarding access to his loyal friend, the president. But even such a narrow escape couldn't dull Babcock's extraordinarily gluttonous instinct for intrigue. In fact, far from it; it seems to have given him a new sense of invulnerability.

Babcock was now the victim of what can only be seen as either his own pathological inability to hide his machinations, or a continuation of Bristow's witch hunt against him. Within two weeks of his acquittal the secretary was once again in court, and once again facing a criminal jury. This time it was for a bungled attempt to smear one of the prosecuting attorneys involved in the ring trial which had so nearly cost him his career.

He was accused of having planted incriminating evidence in a safe, ordering it blown open, and then distributing the contents to the press. Again he was acquitted. But this time he didn't return to his job guarding access to the president. It appears he was just too controversial and just too tainted. Instead Grant made him Inspector of Lighthouses, a job that eventually killed him. He drowned off the coast of Central America in 1885.

## The Tweed Ring

The corruption of the federal government in Washington, D.C., and its ties with the rural regions of the nation as demonstrated by the Whiskey Ring had a municipal government and urban counterpart. It did not draw on the increased potential of expanded central, federal government, but instead centered on local and regional politics. The metropolitan political "machines" that converted interest groups into votes represented one of the purest forms of organized crime in the period. This was true inasmuch as they were, by any of the huge variety of definitions, organized, and many of their actions were also indisputably criminal.

What is more, they were frequently described as "organized crime" in contemporary accounts. There is no doubt that the possibilities for such mischief grew over the early years of this study. Immigration, internal migration, industrialization and the transport revolution of the railroads drew unprecedented numbers into the metropolitan areas of the northeast and Midwest, quickly transforming the leading American cities from "walking cities" into the massive metropolises of the late nineteenth and early twentieth centuries.

With that growth and outward prosperity came opportunity and power for those charged with regulating and administering. With those changes came a new level of temptation, since it was not simply the population that had grown. City halls across the nation now controlled increasingly large budgets. Municipal administrations oversaw huge-scale infrastructural works and other public projects. In addition to that, they represented another element that is seen to feed organized crime—change. These were times of flux for city administration. They took on increasingly wide-ranging responsibilities. In order to do this they had growing workforces who were in turn administered by expanding bureaucracies with vastly expanded budgets. At the same time, the old power networks based on reputation and inherited status, models of administration that had worked for smaller cities, no longer applied.

The result was that municipal politicians at a variety of levels now had unheard-of patronage within their influence. To many traditional observers it appeared that Thomas Jefferson's dire warnings to James Madison against urbanization had come true. It appeared that just as he predicted, Americans had become "piled upon one another in large cities," and as a result it seemed that the New World Eden had "become corrupt as in Europe."[14] The form this corruption took was arguably one of the most apparent, obvious and concerning sorts of organized crime of the last quarter of the nineteenth century—at least according to the press, who labeled the phenomenon "bossism."

Commentators began to see bossism as one of the defining features of the age. In the mid–1880s one Southern minister complained it was getting so that "no man can talk politics for five minutes without using it [the word 'bossism'] and in an ordinary or extraordinary political editorial or speech it occurs more conspicuously than any other word." He went on to say he counted the word used twenty-nine times on the front page of his local paper, in one single week.[15] The New York Times uses the phrase in headlines over six hundred and fifty times in the period from the end of the Civil War to the turn of the twentieth century, and in a selection of newspapers across the nation for the same period, the expression occurs in headlines over 7,000 times.[16]

Some argued that bossism was simply an inevitable result of urban expansion in a democratic state. As the crusading English journalist William Stead put it, the political boss was "a natural product of the elemental forces of his time."[17] Others saw the boss as a perversion that fed corruption and political gangsterism—"a sinister and withering influence that has been felt in every department of political affairs."[18] In part the phenomenon gained such prominence in the United States as a result of the growth of democracy. The traits inherent in bossism were magnified by the newfound power of those at the top of this pile. It was perpetuated by their having to seek re-election within relatively short periods of time. What was more, the electorate had changed. Over these years those seeking elected office had to appeal to an increasingly diverse and self-interested collection of voters.

This meant that in order to satisfy their various electorates, the bosses needed to achieve visible, tangible, quantifiable results within their term of office. They needed to get results that yielded beneficial outcomes, results that could be traced back *directly* to them. It didn't matter how short-term these benefits really were; they simply needed to be seen to satisfy the demands of the electorate at the time of the election. In order to achieve these goals, political expediencies, sectional influences, and the overwhelming effects of the "favor bank" frequently supplanted the legal niceties and ethical considerations that had previously been held to govern society. Manufacturing alliances and building a power base became the central concerns of these bosses. As a result of this, a new form of urban feudalism emerged, ruled over by the oligarchy of the political machine commanded by the city "boss."

Considered by many as too direct and too populist, and therefore "man-made" rather than constitutional, this innovative form of democracy was pretty soon condemned by its enemies as criminal. In the eyes of its wide range of opponents, under bossism, City Hall was ruled by the oligarchy of the political machine: "Nothing can be clearer than that boss government, as it is administered in several of our States today, is destructive of popular government.... [It] obtains power by means which are not only not authorized by the people, but have been declared by them, in their laws, to be criminal."[19] They argued that the constant need to get re-elected created a system of politics which "profits by, and encourages, any manner of fraud, any sort of vile corruption, any outrage against decency, any crime against the ballot, violence, repeating [votes], bribery, theft, and whatever in the category of crime is necessary to give one political faction victory over another."[20]

James, later Lord, Bryce—arguably one of the most astute contemporary observers and analysts of U.S. politics—perhaps most clearly summed up what was wrong with bossism. He essentially saw it as the personalization of public duty. To him it was a self-serving parody of democracy imposed by the oversimplification and mechanization of politics to meet short-term goals. He called the phenomenon the "most conspicuous failing of American democracy," arguing that while it promised democracy, it "delivered autocracy and corruption." He saw it as a criminal perversion of democracy, and for many of those reading his works at the time, its criminality took on a personal form.[21]

Bryce was writing in the wake of the exposure of the corruption and graft of the archetypal "boss," William Magear Tweed. A career politician from his election in 1852 as an alderman for New York City's Seventh Ward, Tweed flourished and came to exemplify a post–Civil War world of spoils systems, graft and cronies. He, and the "Forty Thieves" with whom he was associated, personally bought land and voted to resell it to the municipality—at a huge profit.

The so-called Tweed Ring inflated the cost of public works and pocketed the difference. They took kickbacks for municipal jobs and contracts. They skimmed off money from City Hall contracts. They took and paid bribes and made illegal payments safe in the knowledge they controlled the police and criminal courts in their wards. They leased buildings they personally owned to the municipality at extortionate rates. They both took and gave money to quash legislation which threatened their own interests or those of their allies. In short, they never missed an opportunity to utilize their powers of office for personal gain. It was simply what one turn-of-the-century commentator would call "the systematic robbery of the public purse."[22]

Under Tweed's regime it was estimated that the New York taxpayers stumped up an unprecedented $160 million that was spent on municipal projects. Nevertheless, at the same time, New York City's debt increased by over $100 million. When he was charged with some 200-odd counts of corruption, the prosecution demanded that Tweed *personally* pay back over $6.5 million—nearly $110 million at today's values—which they estimated he personally had accumulated through corruption over his twenty-year political career.[23] Yet Tweed was unapologetic. In his reputed last words, he rather enigmatically said, "I've tried to do some good, if I have not had good luck."[24] In this lack of contrition he was not alone: the bosses' attitudes to the law were at best ambivalent, which has perhaps been a contributory factor to their equally ambivalent reception they have been given by historians since.[25]

While Tweed and his Tammany Hall cronies were largely discredited or punished, their successors, using similar if less blatant machines, would continue to be re-elected for decades after their demise. What was more, variations of their system of urban organization would be imitated throughout America pretty well until the last quarter of the twentieth century—and arguably beyond.[26] Yet while there were contributory factors that were ubiquitous to American urban democratic politics in any era, there were also elements behind their rise that were unique to these times.

Essentially their success was due to their provision of a valuable service. They exuded "men of the people" approachability. This was combined with bonhomie and a backslapping style that played well with their extensive network of responsive and sensitive "ward heelers" and grassroots workers. Nor was this familiarity entirely manufactured. Many of the bosses had been raised in the poorer regions of their cities. They knew the hardships, aspirations and objectives of their constituents. They understood the insecurity that poverty, dislocation and alienation represented in the growing "mega-tropolises." In many ways they were the epitome of truly representative democracy for an increasing number of residents of most major cities, but in particular, New York.

In part this was due to a shift in the nature and power balance of the electorate. Over these years the so-called urban underclass had emerged as a considerable force in urban politics. Their rise to representation drew on the removal of property qualifications for municipal elections in New York in 1821. They then grew with the extension of the franchise to all naturalized residents with the 14th Amendment (1868). Pretty soon it became apparent that New York's largely patrician leadership was not only becoming increasingly irrelevant, but also seemed terrified by these new voters. Even when driven by necessity to realize the unavoidability of having to harness the power of this alien population, the erstwhile overlords were exposed as being increasingly unable to gauge their needs. Effectively lacking a mouthpiece, this electorate was ripe for the picking by a new breed of politician—and the boss was just that creature.

These men generally grew up in poverty. They often came from working-class backgrounds. Most were brought up surrounded by those who would become their constituents. With this constituency firmly in their sights, the Machine calculatingly built up political organizations run and led by men like themselves. The machine's precinct captains and ward heelers became a point of contact for supporters—and would-be supporters—who previously would have had no representative, even if they had had the franchise. Understanding the immediacy and hand-to-mouth existence of many of their constituents, they could be the savior of the underclass in times of unemployment, poverty, homelessness and other distress. At just such times these representatives of the local ward boss could offer solace and advice; they could supply shelter, fuel, and work; and, above all, they could give them protection. All the boss required in return was their vote.

To most of these new voters this was a pretty good deal, especially when down on their luck. Most were unfamiliar with, or uninterested in, the democratic system of America. They felt that as long as the boss and his machine continued to protect them and their family, whatever else the politician did with the power he attained with their vote was his concern. On the other hand, to those whose power, influence or livelihood was curtailed by this new creature, the boss and the political machine were not only immoral and opportunistic, they were also criminal. Furthermore, the whole machine, the apparatus with which the boss gained and retained power, was itself a criminal organization. It was organized crime and it drew in dwellers from the underworld, the criminal classes, who brought with them criminal tendencies, and their own criminal organizations.

## The Machine

Intrinsically linked with the expansion of the cities and empowering the image of municipal government as organized criminals were another unpopular group: the metropolises' vastly expanding immigrant populations. In the mid–nineteenth century, famine and poverty drove large numbers of Irish to seek a better life in the New World. Throughout the century, opportunity and intermittent religious and political persecution at home caused German liberals, Jews from the Pale of Settlement, and then Catholics from Poland and Italy to arrive in unprecedented numbers in New York. As the century drew to a close, improved transport technology on land and sea, the American industrial emergence, the relaxation of emigration restrictions in Europe, and the creation of trans–Atlantic networks allowed the nation's great cities to expand in hitherto unimaginable ways.

Boston, New York, Chicago, San Francisco, New Orleans, Pittsburgh, Baltimore, Cleveland, St. Louis and other burgeoning cities sucked in vast numbers of Italians, Poles, Greeks, Russians and other southern and eastern Europeans. By 1900, on average a quarter of the entire population of America's 50 largest cities had been born abroad. In some cities, the proportion was closer to half.[27] Often newly arrived, frequently ostracized by the existing residents, and more often than not impoverished, they were also numerous, unenfranchised, unrepresented and unpopular.

Nevertheless, such a numerous group of outsiders was perfect fuel for the expanding machine. The immigrant "colonies" became the ideal recruiting ground for the machines. Confused and friendless, these immigrants could easily be brought into their political fold. As became evident, all that was necessary was to help them naturalize and enfranchise them and then reap the rewards as they turned into loyal supporters. The opportunity presented by the near-constant flow of immigrants is spectacularly demonstrated by Tammany's campaign to elect their favored candidate for governor of New York in 1868.

In preparation for that particular election, the Tammany Machine cranked into action, firing up its printing presses. Within days they had printed off an estimated 70,000 sets of naturalization papers. This foresight enabled them to naturalize over 40,000 potential new voters in the runup to the election. In turn it was estimated that some thirty-two thousand of these grateful new citizens then went on to vote for the Democrat candidate and add to Tammany's haul.[28] Although nothing really came close to this scale, the practice of naturalizing supporters continued to operate until the 1920s, when Congress closed the Golden Door of virtually unrestricted European immigration. But that is not to say that the foreign-born were simply dupes of the machine; they were frequently the most ardent of its supporters.

In the so-called "immigrant colonies," it was familiarity and understanding that counted, and ward heelers and precinct captains would frequently be drawn from those immigrant communities. In this situation, as organized crime historian Mark Haller argues, "[A] person's ethnic background was often an advantage rather than a liability. Neighborhood roots could be the basis for a career that might lead from poverty to great local power, considerable wealth, or both."[29] The result was that by the 1860s, Tweed's prototypical Tammany Machine was often directly associated with the Irish at all levels—although he himself was neither Irish, nor an immigrant. Irish organizers and workers were utilized at the precinct, ward and municipal levels.

Having acclimatized to the New World by the last half of the nineteenth century, Irish immigrants and their descendants were perfectly placed for this role in Tammany's expansion of democracy. They were already near universal in the city's other points of contact with the urban poor—the police and fire services, as well as many of the saloons. This meant that during the period of this study, Tammany became increasingly associated with Irish bosses, many of them men who had been inducted during the Tweed days and earlier, and then worked their ways up. This pattern was replicated in the machines that came to govern other urban areas, most notably Boston, San Francisco, Jersey City, Albany, Pittsburgh and, perhaps most notoriously, Chicago.

By the turn of the twentieth century the "New Immigration" from southern and eastern Europe was replacing the Irish in many of the areas they had previously dominated. In New York and San Francisco, two Irish machine strongholds, the New Immigrants represented some 60 percent of the manual workforce and proved an obvious, if not always successful, target for the machines with their working-class image. In the early twentieth century, Boston's Irish machine politician, James Michael Curley, solidly represented the New Immigrant as both a congressman and mayor, even going so far as to fly the flags of immigrant donor nations outside city hall.

From 1900 to 1920, Irish Chicago bosses like George Brennan and Roger Sullivan worked hard at naturalizing Poles and other white immigrants. They and their successors made a show of putting New Immigrants in prominent clerical and administrative positions in order demonstrate their pro-immigrant stance and hopefully reap the benefits.[30] Nevertheless, there can be no doubt that simply being associated with the unpopular, impoverished and largely excluded underclasses of the urban environment added to the association of political machines with criminal activity. As one newspaper commented as the "Tweed Ring" was being investigated in 1871: "The dangerous classes, shoulder-bitters, thieves, gamblers, whisky-sellers and rowdies generally, have for years been assiduously cultivated by the ring and secured against the law ... fully under the control of Tweed and at his bidding willing to do anything from repeating [votes] to mob-violence.... It is a sorry fact that the chief city on the continent should be virtually subject to such control. But the worst elements of the entire population naturally flock to such a city, and there have as much weight, and, through frauds, even greater than the decent population."[31] Twenty years later the situation had changed very little. Opponents of machine politics still claimed that New York was governed by "the blind allegiance ... the passionate devotion ... of the saloons, the houses of vice, the racecourses and the gambling-houses ... [and that a] great army of men, [were] employed directly or indirectly, by the machine."[32]

Ironic as it may seem, given their working-class power base, in addition to this extension of "basic democracy" their more worldly backers argued that the machine also provided stability and continuity for the business community. They maintained that this was an essential advantage of this form of municipal government in a challenging era of dog-eat-dog competition. They claimed that through their roles as "fixers," the machines facilitated, enabled and encouraged entrepreneurs, investors and financiers to provide jobs, infrastructure and stability for the city.[33]

That said, while few would have argued that they were entirely altruistic, or even entirely legitimate, it was easy to see their appeal: they were often mutually beneficial to the boss and the voter. One Tammany boss, Richard Croker, was asked whether he was "working for his own pocket." The question came from a wealthy Republican inquisitor in 1899, during the course of investigations into political corruption carried out by New York State's Mazet Committee. With disarming honesty, Croker replied, "All the time." That straightforward admission was tempered with the notion that he was also working for the benefit of all politicians. Staring pointedly at his interrogator, he added he was collecting for "you too."[34]

Some felt that corruption was part and parcel of the flawed American system of local government, and as long as that system remained flawed it would be a necessary incentive to attract the most able leaders. They contended that the ever-expanding size and complexity of cities required professional bureaucrats, not pretty well unpaid aldermen. The contemporary political scientist, David M. Means, writing somewhat satirically—although taking the precaution of using a pseudonym—argued that the boss of the 1890s was very similar to the ubiquitous Prince of Machiavelli's era.

In true Machiavellian fashion, Means advised the aspiring boss that in order to maximize his power, the politician should not be afraid to break those laws that stood in his way. He even includes a chapter dedicated to "The revenue from the citizens and how far it may be appropriated by a boss." In this he explains how courting and smoothing the path of the wealthy aids philanthropy, with the result that it should be obvious to both the beneficiaries and the benefactors that a proportion of that largesse rightfully belongs to the boss for his endeavors.[35]

One of the more articulate and persuasive Tammany successors to Tweed, George Washington Plunkett, famously expanded this justification when he spoke to the reporter William Riordan. The politician told the reporter that he saw politics as simply another business. Plunkett told him that he had invested a great deal of his time and effort—as well as his money—in his political career, and like any investor he expected those investments to yield a return. Plunkett saw nothing wrong with that objective, arguing that this was the way of the modern world.

Plunkett still put forward a clear argument that he was a politician—strenuously arguing he was not, as many portrayed him, an amoral gangster. In his mind—and no doubt in the minds of his supporters—he had strong principles and integrity. Essentially he regarded it as legitimate to make money from some sources and not from others. For example, he condoned the utilization of privileged information or taking payments to "speed up" the political decision-making processes for those he "represented." On the other hand, he condemned extracting protection money, or other payments from illicit enterprises like gambling or prostitution. With refinements like this he drew his now famous distinction between "honest graft" and "dishonest graft."[36]

Not that all those connected with the new urban politics even pretended to have had such scruples. Other machine politicians were well and truly, not to say blatantly, integrated into the criminal world of their cities. Bosses whose wards lay in vice districts were rarely troubled by such nice distinctions as those Plunkett claimed he lived by. In Chicago's Levee District, the semi-legitimate red-light area of the city's First Ward, the pimps, gamblers, dive owners and prostitutes were very effectively represented by the machine of Aldermen "Bathhouse" John Coughlin and Michael "Hinky Dink" Kenna. In return for their protection and representation, the business owners of the district enabled the so-called "Lords of the Levee" to remain in power from the 1890s until the 1920s, again amassing considerable personal fortunes in the bargain.

There was nothing new about this in Chicago. The city had a history of close ties between vice and politics. In 1873, Michael Cassius McDonald had organized the city's gambling, saloon and vice interests into a powerful coalition. "Mike McDonald's Democrats" pretty well ruled Chicago, and continued to do so until "King Mike's" death in 1907, when his baton was passed on to "Big Jim" O'Leary. Under McDonald's "Tammany By the Lake," as his machine was sometimes aptly called, the link between vice and party politics was central. The money from the one financed the other.

It was a highly organized operation. McDonald's machine took a set monthly fee from the city's bookies, brothels, saloons, gambling houses and opium dens. In return they could rest assured that they would suffer no interference from the law, and that their "turf" would be protected. It is even rumored that his power over the underworld extended to allocating "patches" to the pickpockets, muggers and other criminals at the Chicago Columbia Exposition of 1893.[37] What is more certain is that his machine's criminal activities financed the party, paid off the police, and maintained a generally compliant legislature and judiciary.

This in turn kept out the reformers—most of the time. The system worked so well that the investigative journalist and moral crusader William T. Stead could not help being impressed by the sheer *chutzpah* of the operation. He told his readers that the McDonald syndicate operated a near perfect kleptocracy in which "gaming is utilized as an engine of party finance. Chicago taught the world how to make the dice box, wheel of fortune, and pack of cards a resource of partisan finance. It is ingenious and immoral. It is simply the adoption by the Mayor of the city [McDonald tool Carter Harrison] of the methods and morals of the policeman who levies blackmail on the streetwalkers on his beat.... The principle in both cases is exactly the same. The gaming house has no more right to exist in Chicago than the woman has to solicit vice in the public streets. The law against gaming houses is much more precise than that which forbids solicitation."[38]

Such an association was by no means unique to Chicago. In the rapidly growing city of Omaha, Nebraska, another gambler turned politician was essentially running the government. Tom Dennison ran the city for the first three decades of the twentieth century, although he never ran for elected office himself. He acted as an interface, middleman and power broker between politicians, newspapermen, the financial elites and the underworld of gamblers, gangsters and other criminals.

In the 1910s it had an estimated 6,000 prostitutes concentrated largely in Omaha's "crib" district, and even during Prohibition there were 1,600 saloons operating with impunity. Nevertheless, Dennison successfully enabled Omaha to shake off an image of a blue-collar city, regularly traumatized by riots, with outbreaks of lynch law, and ruled by the Union Pacific Railroad. What he created was the image of the town as a middle-class and wholesome regional capital, with safe streets and good business prospects. At the same time, the city also provided all the pleasures that would later gain it the reputation as "Las Vegas-East" for the "sporting man," a town that maintained a thriving underworld.[39]

An even closer relationship with gambling was essential to the Democrat machine in New Orleans. Known simply as the "Ring," the machine had bought Louisiana's politics since 1868. Through the profit on an investment of $40,000 a year, they generated sufficient funds from the Louisiana State Lottery to control the thrust of Louisiana politics until the 1890s. This was in spite of intermittent "reform" administrations, who found it easy to make frequent and persistent exposes of the Ring's blatant criminal activities, which included nepotism on a grand scale, election rigging, and needless to say, embezzlement and corruption of all sorts.[40]

Nor was the connection between machine politics and vice necessarily essentially limited to the larger cities. In the newly emerging townships of the western frontier, the "law," such as it was, was notoriously pragmatic. It was frequently based—at least in the initial stages—on protecting social and economic order, rather than projecting or enforcing any moral or political message. More blatant and often more violent—but nonetheless identifiable—machines and bosses evolved very quickly after the founding of the towns. In some respects these machines were similar to the Chicago or New Orleans models. In other ways they were very different. A good example of these can be found in the evolution of the boomtown from the mining camp of Deadwood.

In the years before the settlement became a part of South Dakota, Deadwood's famous political boss, Ellis Albert "Al" Swearengen, drew his financial backing from—and sought to protect his interests in—gambling and prostitution. Neither activity was illegal in the town. Rather, the girls and the card tables were the main distractions of most of the residents and were the main income streams for a considerable portion of the population. However, empowered by the nature of the frontier, Swearengen broke the laws of the land in a variety of ways. Controlling the settlement—according to legend—he bribed federal and state officials to do his bidding; he took kickbacks; he defrauded businesses; he beat his whores; and he ordered, if not personally committed, several murders.[41]

# 3

## Chicago: Crime Central

### *Prohibition Chicago*

If the idea of the boss and his connections with crime became cemented in the minds of Americans in the late nineteenth century, that tie was never clearer in the public mind in the twentieth century than during the years of Prohibition. Most commentators felt that without at least some level of political protection, violators of the Volstead Act could not have functioned, let alone thrived. The police, the judiciary, City Hall and Washington were all seen to be involved in either actively or passively subverting Prohibition. It seemed that newspapers constantly reported more or less apocryphal stories in which community leaders and law enforcers were caught red-handed taking or giving bribes, buying booze or protecting bootleggers.

Typical of these stories was the discovery in September 1920, near Austin, Texas, of a "monster" whiskey still capable of producing 130 gallons of moonshine a day. Alongside this was some 400 gallons of whiskey left behind by the fleeing bootleggers. In an era when hooch production was at a peak, in an area where illicit whiskey had a long history, this was nothing unusual. However, it made headlines because the still had been found on a ranch belonging to the local U.S. Senator, J. Morris Sheppard. Sheppard was a big catch because he was one of the most famous, outspoken and committed "drys" in the nation.[1]

Touted as the "father of national Prohibition," Sheppard had sponsored anti-booze legislation since 1912. His commitment to the cause had culminated in his Senate sponsorship of the Volstead Act itself. Critics ignored the fact that the still was later traced to a cousin of Sheppard. Instead, political opponents and other detractors claimed the discovery was clear evidence that the Yale-educated, erudite and earnest Texan must be on the take. They argued that he was being paid off by organized crime. Others claimed he was in the bootleg business himself, running the still safe in the cover his position in the Senate gave him.[2]

The reality is that it was unlikely that this most staunch of prohibitionists was aware of the still. He would remain one of the most outspoken supporters of the policy. Nothing demonstrates this better than the way in which he remained in favor of the "Noble Experiment" even in the 1930s, when support for the issue was essentially seen as political poison. In the teeth of the Depression, Sheppard was in favor of "jailing highbrow drinkers" and proposed a $1.5 million fund for lobbying Congress to keep the nation dry.[3]

But that is not the real question here. Whether guilty or not, Sheppard was lampooned, condemned and mistrusted by many, often simply as a result of his choice of career. Over these years, the reputation of politicians had rarely been lower. In the middle of the decade, the Secretary of the Interior was convicted of selling off government oil reserves in the Teapot Dome scandal. Linked to this infamous scandal were President Harding's Ohio Gang, who, led by Attorney General Harry M. Dougherty, seemed to be involved in a whole range of dodgy deals and political malfeasance at the very highest levels of government.

What was more, the leading organization that crusaded for clean, open politics was itself mired in financial and moral scandals that caused its huge membership to leave the order in droves. Throughout the 1920s the reimagined Ku Klux Klan sponsored "clean," "American" politicians and attracted upwards of four million members. It made repeated accusations of political corruption and sought to uphold what it saw as the essential principles of the Republic—including Prohibition. Arguably, the exposure of the reality of venality, nepotism, corruption and immorality at all levels of the Klan was shocking. It was little short of a body blow to the faith of many "ordinary" Americans in the ability and motives of all those involved in politics. Seldom in the history of the Republic had the media been more rife with rumors, accusations and counterclaims of the connections between organized crime and politicians of all ranks.

Perhaps these connections thrived most vigorously in Chicago. The American public, and those abroad who'd heard of Chicago, probably knew it equally well by its other names. In popular imagination the metropolis was not just the "Windy City" or the "Jewel of the Prairies," but also "Sin City," the "Wicked City," or "Crime Central." With an already formidable reputation for crime, Prohibition-era Chicago became—and has largely remained—the byword for organized crime, home to the most violent turf wars of the period and some of the most notorious criminals. What was more, the city's gangsters reveled in their status as brutal killers.

Hoodlums rejoiced in names like "Ammunition Eddie" Wheed; Claude "Screwy" Maddox; Johnny "The Terror" Torrio; "Machine Gun Jack" McGurn; "Bloody Angelo" Genna; and Louis "Two Guns" Alterie. The antics of the 42-Gang, the North Side Gang, the Druggan Lake Gang, the Maddox Circus Gang, and the Saltis Gang all flared up in the headlines—often very briefly. Frequently they made the news only as they were "rubbed out" by rivals in what seemed like the city's perpetual turf wars.[4] But as the press latched onto tales of the city's "Beer Wars" and the "St. Valentines Day Massacre," it was one name that emerged to become near ubiquitous whenever organized crime in Prohibition-era Chicago was mentioned: "Scarface" Al Capone.

What seemed evident to commentators, then and since, was that Capone could not have functioned as openly as he did without political protection of the highest order in the city. Many thought that his protection emanated from Chicago's pragmatic, charismatic and larger-than-life mayor. Controversial and flamboyant, William Hale "Big Bill" Thompson was in office for much of the Prohibition era and in many ways has become synonymous with those years of lawbreaking, violence and bloodshed—especially by Capone and his "Outfit." However, how deep that association went, how close their relationship was, is open to interpretation—and that interpretation has been manipulated, interpreted and revised by a variety of journalists, politicians, historians and biographers, creating another of the most persistent of organized crime's many controversies.

Some commentators at the time show this association to be a close, deep friendship, verging on hero worship. It has also been seen as, at the very least, the symbiosis of two kindred spirits operating for their own benefit on either side of the law—nothing more than a convenient business relationship.[5] They argue it was born simply of political and financial expediency—the one taking full advantage of all the other could give him.[6] Others see it as a vague connection essentially founded on accusations made by commentators with their roots in the increasingly dirty partisan politics of the brashest of modern cities.[7] Whichever interpretation is given preference, there's no doubt that the connection between the mayor and the gangster was, and still is, an important theme in most accounts of urban organized crime during Prohibition.

It was not simply journalists and writers who made this connection. Powerful and influential figures utilized this association at the time. At the height of Capone's authority in Chicago, Big Bill's most constant critics were to be found in the *Chicago Tribune*. The *Tribune* repeatedly sketched a direct line between the flamboyant Thompson's populist policies and the undesirable and unshakeable reputation of the city as the crime capital of the USA.

"Colonel" Robert R. McCormick frequently used uncompromising language to condemn Big Bill's regime. Although both were ostensibly Republicans, they were pretty near polar opposites in character. McCormick came from an established Chicago family. He was a Chicago blueblood. Thompson—although from wealthy stock—had arrived in the city as a drifter, and their characters and manner clearly demonstrated these different backgrounds. The imposing, misanthropic, haughty, opinionated and irascible McCormick was deeply, viscerally—almost irrationally—opposed to the charismatic, dramatic and garrulous Thompson.

Some idea of how deep this dislike went can be seen in his statements about the influence of the mayor on Chicago. He claimed: "For Chicago, Thompson has meant filth, corruption, obscenity, idiocy … barbaric crime, triumphant hooliganism, unchecked graft and dejected citizenship." Not content with leaving that legacy in the minds of his readers, he argued that with his criminal connections Thompson had achieved nothing short of making "Chicago a byword for the collapse of American civilization."[8]

This take is reinforced by Thompson's opponent in the runoffs for the 1919 Republican mayoral candidacy. Charles Merriam was equally scathing of Thompson. He had accused Big Bill, even before the advent of national Prohibition, of being intimately and profitably connected with "grafters and gunmen, gangsters and thugs."[9] Nor has this condemnation disappeared over the years. Far from it. Thompson's association with the underworld is truly hammered home in a large number of biographies of the mayor's most famous erstwhile "ally" and "protégé"—Al Capone.

These profiles often repeat an observation made at a meeting in 1931 between Capone and Frank J. Loesch, a prominent Chicago attorney and founder of the Chicago Crime Commission. Loesch was struck by the fact that Capone had a portrait in oils of Mayor Thompson on the wall of his office in the Lexington Hotels—alongside those of his other heroes, George Washington and Abraham Lincoln.[10] They also frequently echo the rumor put forward in 1929 by John Landesco: "In circles close to Capone it was well known that he [Capone] had contributed to the [1927] Thompson [mayoral] campaign."[11]

By the 1940s the popular gang historian, Herbert Asbury, was claiming that Capone's Outfit "dominated the political machines of Chicago … during most of Thompson's third term."[12] The association is even more closely drawn in the 1960s by historian Kenneth Allsop. Allsop told his readers, "Without stretching the logical sequence too far, to Thompson may be attributed Capone's eventual terrorization of Chicago."[13] Similarly one of the most recent large-scale treatments of Chicago's organized crime reiterates the connection between Thompson's 1927 election victory and finances from Capone. It even goes as far as saying that "a number of Capone gangsters actually worked in Thompson's campaign headquarters."[14]

Understandably, and possibly forgivably, biographers of Thompson tend to be more sympathetic to their subject. They are certainly more circumspect in assessing his connections with organized crime in general, and Capone in particular. The most hostile treat Thompson as something of an "idiot savant": a sort of holy fool of urban politics. They portray him as being simple in many of his statements, but astute in his understanding of the nature of the voters of Chicago. As the Kansas "sage" William Allen White put it, Thompson possessed a "bland, blithe, deceptive puerility."[15] These sentiments are echoed in the first book-length biography of the mayor, *Hizzoner Big Bill Thompson* (1930). In this, John Bright argued that Chicago—brash, rough, pushy and gauche—got what it deserved with reckless, loud-mouthed and self-serving Thompson.

Thompson's relationship with Capone, according to Bright, was perfectly in keeping with this view. He argued Capone and other gangsters duped the mayor, and his political enemies played up that hoodwinking for all the political capital it was worth.[16] This depiction is equally true of *Big Bill of Chicago* (1953), which repeats and attacks as myths the expansion of Chicago ganglands under the Thompson regimes. It also questions the veracity of the umbilical link between the politician and the gangster.

The two journalists who wrote this generally Thompson-friendly portrait, Herman Kogan and Lloyd Wendt, attribute the ineradicable connection with gangland largely to the mayor's dreadful relationship with the highly influential *Chicago Tribune* and the *Chicago Daily News*.[17] This view is backed up by the most recent biography of Thompson–Douglas Bukowski's 1998 reappraisal. Bukowski asserts that—in spite of extensive searching—neither he, nor the FBI at the time, could find any real evidence of criminal behavior by the mayor, let alone close links to the city's underworld.[18]

Other sources point out that on his death in 1944 his estate was worth some two million dollars. Gold certificates, currency, stocks and bonds—the readily transferable, portable and anonymous forms of cash favored by racketeers and corrupt politicians and mobsters—made up nearly three-quarters of the value. Real estate made up the rest. Commentators are divided on where these funds came from. Some see them as the result of shrewd investments and point out that Thompson had inherited considerable wealth from his father, a real estate developer. Others see his considerable wealth in terms of the mayoral salaries of the day. They claim that no one could legally amass that amount of money whilst serving the public rather than themselves. They see the root of this corruption as lying with Chicago's gangland, and that most notorious of Chicago mobsters—Al Capone.[19]

In 2009, supposedly irrefutable evidence of the connection between Thompson and Capone emerged in the form of a photograph discovered in the garbage of a vacant Chicago lot. The picture was supposedly taken in December 1930 at St. Joseph's Health Resort in Wedron, Illinois, when Thompson was there recovering from appendix surgery. It shows several hundred people standing in front and on top of the resort. In the center is Thompson. Among the others are figures who resemble John Torrio and Claude "Screwy" Maddox—close associates of Capone.

Close to Thompson is a tall, heavy figure, dressed in trademark overcoat and fedora, who some observers are convinced is Al Capone himself. It is, according to John Binder of the University of Illinois, "conclusive proof of how strong the links were" between Capone and Thompson. Other commentators—interestingly, including relatives of Capone—dispute this view.[20]

What is clear is that the relationship needs investigation, since it acts as one of the pivots of organized crime in America. Any mention of organized crime inevitably seems to draw on the legacy of Prohibition. Any depiction of Prohibition sooner or later mentions Capone. Central to Capone's image is the city he made his home, his base of operations, and the scene of most of his crimes. Chicago and Capone have become synonymous with openly criminal gangsterism in the 1920s, and that could not have taken place without the collusion of the authorities. So, QED, Capone and Thompson must have been in cahoots. Yet if Capone's reputation is founded on less than secure evidence, then where does that leave our understanding of the central role of politics in the development of organized crime as a whole?

## Big Bill the Builder

> In a criminal sense, Chicago is a big spider with a huge web radiating its contamination out as far as the Atlantic seacoast. Every city of size and importance within an extensive area is a worse city because of this spider at the southern tip of Lake Michigan.—Carl Schurz Lowden, "Chicago, The Nation's Crime Center," *Current History* 28:6 (September 1, 1928): 892.

Given his mercurial nature and the ever-shifting trends of his biographers, it would be difficult to establish the extent to which controversy dogged or made the career of William Hale Thompson. What is certain is that it played a major role, both at the time of his office in City Hall, and since. A Republican machine boss, Thompson was the archetypical extravagant, larger-than-life politician of the era. Born into a wealthy family, Thompson was not a career politician. In his youth he wandered from job to job, punching cattle, working on steamships, and doing other manual labor all around the western states before settling in the Second City of the U.S.—Chicago. His experiences in the blue-collar West made him robust in his build—as well as his language, and his take on life.

Once he settled down in Chicago, it became obvious what course his life would take. With an easy charm and an open bonhomie, Big Bill, as he became known, was the very model of an early twentieth-century American demagogue. From his trademark ten-gallon hat to his ostentatious boots, he oozed showmanship. By the second decade of the twentieth century he had become known for his booming, plain-speaking, "whiskey-soaked" voice, his wisecracking, clownish publicity stunts, and an outspoken, proletarian, folksy, down-home wisdom. A man of the people, he squeezed the flesh and appeared to have ready solutions for all the different problems for all the different elements of Chicago society.

In fact, this was the secret of his success. "Big Bill, The Builder," as he liked to be known, was a political alchemist, an artist in a peculiar form of diplomacy. Thompson was peerless at forming alliances with a variety of the disparate elements of the diverse population of Chicago. He appeared to have a knack for finding a common thread between groups whose interests seemed totally incompatible. At various times in his career, according to the mood of the times, he was able to weld together a series of short-lived coalitions.

Among these coalitions he included considerable numbers of the city's Irish, Italian, Swedish, German, Russian and Czech voters, not to mention the city's black population.

In creating these alliances it seemed he appealed to an electoral base that was united by nothing more than the promises and threats made by Big Bill himself. Seeing common interests where others could only see conflict, he merged interests as disparate as the city's workingmen and the Republican Party faithful; the pacifists and the patriots; and other seeming enemies. His talents drew on his ability to appear to be all things to all men. However, he also knew his limits. He knew there were those whom he could never win over. A true politician, those Thompson could not ally himself with, he never lost an opportunity to attack, insult and—above all—ridicule.

Sometimes this played to a specific audience, often one which had been considered hostile. A good example of this was when he showed his patriotism by going against Republican calls for military action and vociferously opposing American entry into the Great War in the wake of the Lusitania's sinking in 1915. It was a tactic that did his reputation absolutely no harm with the disaffected German-American electorate—a staunchly Democrat group that up until that point he suspected were already lost to him. After the war ended, capitalizing on his popularity, he opportunistically stated his opposition to the "punitive" Treaty of Versailles and the dangerously interventionist League of Nations. Similarly, he reassured the Irish community that just like them he felt the British to be "seedy and untrustworthy," even going as far as to famously threaten to "bust King George on the snoot."[21]

Yet, while often fierce and always colorfully vocal in his opinions, he was also fickle in his beliefs and frequently short-term and opportunistic in his objectives. As one biographer of Al Capone put it, when Thompson was electioneering: "Practically every plank in Big Bill's platform invalidated some other plank."[22] This is illustrated by his final political campaign. Some years after his declaring his support for the plight of hyphenated Americans, he found himself confronted with a Bohemian-born rival for office, Anton Cermak. Typically during the election, he condemned Cermak in explicit and highly insulting terms that concentrated on his Eastern European roots. Referring to him as "pushcart Tony," he proceeded to tell voters he would "not take a back seat to that *Bohunk*, Chairmock, Chermack or whatever his name is."[23] Unsurprisingly, this upset and alienated many of the very minorities he had earlier professed to support. Equally unsurprisingly, and not that unusually, he lost that particular election.

Although Thompson may have made a point of courting controversy, it was never for its own sake. There was always a deliberate and strategic aim to what appeared to be his seemingly random pronouncements. He always had a clear target in mind, no matter how reckless his attack, or how odd his statements sounded to those uncertain of their context. In fact it was that very fearlessness that generated his distinctly unorthodox but memorable approach to publicity. For instance, while he was out of office in the mid–1920s, Thompson's name slipped from the headlines. In order to correct this, he renamed his personal yacht *Big Bill*, put a carving of his own face as a figurehead on the bow, and said he was taking it off on a scientific expedition to Borneo.

As if that was not strange enough, he went on to challenge all comers to match his $25,000 wager that the boat could return with a specimen of the island's legendary tree-climbing fish. Even in a city legendary for its gamblers and risk takers, it seemed no one was up for this particular challenge. Perhaps this was just as well for Thompson. The expedition was doomed to failure from the outset. Leaving the Windy City with all the hoopla

Thompson could manage, Big Bill and the *Big Bill* quickly lost impetus. They got no further than the Mississippi Delta, and then turned around and slunk back to Chicago with very little comment. However, the unique nature of the venture and the name of the boat ensured Thompson's name, picture and comments were once again back in the papers.

There can be no doubt that this media manipulation, this coalition forming, and his fluidity of policy served its purpose, but at a price. His unorthodox and highly confrontational style made him enemies. Thompson was in office for two terms from 1915, but it is his campaign for City Hall in 1927, and his hubristic shot at the Republican presidential nomination the following year, that did most to seal his distinctly shady reputation. Big Bill quickly discovered that this reputation was linked with the leading distasteful elements of the underworld. Unsurprisingly, in the nation's most crime-wracked city in the 1920s, much of that reputation had to do with the enforcement of alcohol prohibition.

Yet, in some ways this is surprising, since this was one issue on which Thompson, at least initially, voiced no opinion. When the Volstead Act came into force in January 1920, Thompson, forsaking his typically opportunistic and populist style, remained uncharacteristically silent. Although a "man of the people" in a working-class city that knew how to enjoy itself, he made no public statements opposing the Volstead Act. In all likelihood he was waiting to see which way the political wind blew before committing himself. After nearly a year of the Noble Experiment, at the height of a brief post–Volstead dry-euphoria, he had made up his mind and made a pronouncement. He assured Chicago's citizens he would "close all the hellholes where liquor and moonshine are alleged and proven to be sold."[24]

Ten days later it seemed he had honored this promise. He extravagantly praised the arrest of over 550 offenders, and perhaps more significantly, he won the support of the Chicago Crime Commission.[25] This puritanical zeal was rather surprising since he was on record as reassuring the wet voters in the runup to Prohibition that he saw "no harm in a friendly little drink in a friendly little saloon."[26] It seemed that in common with so many of his fellow politicians of the era, Thompson's actual view of Prohibition was to be found more in his rhetoric than in his actions.

There can be no doubt that Big Bill treated the enforcement of Prohibition as a tactical weapon in his quest for City Hall. When he lost his position in 1923 to the reform candidate, Superior Court Judge William Emmet Dever, he and many others saw it as a result of the rather dour "Decent" Dever's having concentrated his electioneering on Thompson's cavalier attitude to the law and the scandals which that such "pragmatism" had precipitated. These accusations were sustained by events in the very last stages of the race. As the election day loomed, a special grand jury indicted Thompson's "silent boss," the so-called "Poor Swede," Fred Lundin, as well as twenty-one of his associates. The charges centered around claims they had defrauded the Chicago Education Board.[27] The result of this debacle was that at the last minute Big Bill withdrew from the election, and the rather unlikely, and distinctly uncharismatic, Dever was elected into City Hall.

## Reformers and Grafters

The essence of Dever's campaign against Thompson was law and order, and clean politics. The judge had sold himself as the squeaky-clean option. As a central part of this image he had made the issue of Prohibition enforcement the main plank of his campaign. However, even the rather bloodless and strait-laced judge could see the difficulty of his position. The result was that he could never really commit to this platform in the hard-working, hard-drinking, blue-collar "city of broad shoulders." As the cowboy philosopher Will Rogers argued when Dever ran for his second term in 1927, "They [Dever's Democrats] was trying to beat Bill [Thompson] with the Better Element vote. Trouble is, in Chicago there ain't much Better Element."[28]

Instead of coming out with outright support for Prohibition, Dever argued that although to his mind the Volstead Act was illogical, he still felt the law of the land had to be obeyed, and instead he steered his administration to reversing Chicago's reputation as *the* city of vice. He now had the problem of making good on those promises, and his tactic was to hit the gangsters hard right from the start. In the first two months of the new administration, Dever's newly appointed police chief, Morgan Collins, started by transferring seventeen Chicago Police Department precinct captains to new districts, along with over one hundred beat cops. He went on to close down five breweries, arrest 450 dive owners, and put 4,000 speakeasies out of business.

Flushed with these successes, in 1925 Dever then appointed a new Prohibition director who added to these achievements. By the end of the year he had tightened up the notoriously corrupt procedures for issuing medicinal alcohol permits; he had padlocked those premises suspected of selling illegal booze; and he had closed many of the most notorious gambling dens.[29] Yet even these highly publicized successes had not seemed to halt the problem of gangsters and gangland violence; if anything, it seemed to make it worse.

In spite of this increasingly active stance emanating from City Hall, the *New York Times* reckoned that the returns from bootlegging were continuing to grow, and not just marginally, but very significantly. While the *Times* was looking at the national picture, the situation in Chicago was even more dramatic than elsewhere—or so the papers claimed. One Chicago paper was quoted as claiming that at the height of Prohibition there were at least 6,000 speakeasies and another 15,000 other "blind pigs" and "gin joints." Together it was estimated that these outlets generating nearly $6 million *a week* for the Chicago gangs.[30]

As with so many organized crime statistics, such figures were at best guesstimates—there is no way of verifying them. That said, local figures could be more reliable and by way of illustration, it was estimated that one not particularly large or well-known gang—the Guilfoyle-Winge-Kolb gang, in the northwest of the city—was reported to be *clearing* over $2 million a year from its booze sales.[31] What is certain is that the result of this huge bonanza was that turf wars and tit-for-tat killings became everyday news in Chicago. The city was plunged ever deeper into the so-called Beer Wars.

The carnage was shocking. In June 1926, it was reported that "unsupported and generally violated prohibition laws were [the cause of] ... upward of 100 gang murders in Chicago."[32] What was particularly worrying was that the suspiciously round figure was for the years from 1923 through to 1925—the years of Dever's crackdown. By October the following year another estimate claimed that gangsters over the previous three years had murdered 215 other gangsters.[33] Even more alarming was the claim in the same article that Chicago's police had killed a further 160.[34] With these figures before the public, there was almost unanimous agreement that the situation regarding the city's organized crime had got considerably worse when enforcement of the law was at its most rigid.

There was a growing suspicion that, at the very least, in part this escalation was the fault of over-zealous enforcement of an already unenforceable policy. Yet determined to show that he had not lost control of the situation, Police Chief Collins—veteran of over 35 years police experience—had adopted the standard policing technique. He moved to using ever more violent law enforcement methods that would culminate in the formation of ten "machine gun squads."[35] The result was that it appeared Chicago was at war, and the national and international press was only too keen to report such great copy. According to some there was "gang warfare" on the streets of Chicago.[36] A Canadian paper reported criminality had become so inbuilt in the Chicago psyche that even minor traffic offenses were liable to lead to the situation where "organized crime is set in motion to defeat the ends of justice and secure immunity for the criminal."[37]

Not one to miss such a blatant opportunity for political capital, running against Dever again in 1927, Big Bill, the astute politician, realized that he had the perfect political issue in Prohibition. Telling his audiences that "the prohibition law … has been directly or indirectly at the bottom of all the bombing assassinations here in recent months," he stood on an openly "wet" platform.[38] Over the coming weeks, as he warmed to his theme, Thompson's language became characteristically extravagant and his promises ever more outlandish. He famously told his prospective voters that he was as "wet as the middle of the Atlantic Ocean" and went on to promise them that he would open 10,000 speakeasies to replace that number of saloons which he claimed had operated in the city before Volstead.[39] Thompson was using his very fancy political footwork to wrong-foot his rather ponderous opponents, and the battleground was organized crime.

True to his previous form, with his penchant for showy, high-profile, populist rhetoric and his love of grandiose policies, Thompson declared he had a solution to the escalating violence. He would make Chicago a "wide open city" and clean it up by reassigning the forces of law and order to catching those who carried out the major crimes rather than using valuable manpower chasing those who simply supplied booze. A West Coast paper summed up the difference between the two candidates: "The idea of the Thompson party was if the police forgot about minor prohibition law slips, the backroom games and other infractions of laws affecting 'personal liberty,' they could concentrate on major crimes and clean up the city. [On the other hand] … the idea of the Dever administration had been that major crime grew out of gambling, liquor and vice rings in large measure."[40]

It was also, Big Bill argued, a case of local autonomy and safety. It was Prohibition's enforcement that lay at the root of lawlessness in Chicago. As he would later explain, Chicago did not need "Dry agents from Washington, who run around like a lot of cowboys with revolvers and shotguns. Our opponents would have us believe we don't know how to run our town."[41] Many agreed with him, including the pragmatic western philosopher, William Allen White. In an article in *Collier's* he stated: "We have come to a stage in the enforcement of prohibition in our great cities when it is necessary for a community to choose between wholesale homicide following uncontrolled bootlegging and wholesale bootlegging under blackmail without the homicide."[42]

By contrast, Dever countered this inclusive, populist and logical platform with the same arguments—now even more bloodless and unappealing—with which he had won his 1923 campaign. He claimed that while he realized the situation was worsening, his sense of "civic responsibility" to continue to apply the law outweighed his own "personal inclinations" to ignore its deleterious effects. This moral duty made him support the continuation and enforcement of Prohibition, even though he confessed to feeling that "a world of harm has come to American cities because of the eighteenth amendment."[43] Rather predictably, Thompson was voted back into office with a majority of over 80,000.

## Capone and Thompson

*A new chapter of the report on "Organized Crime" released yesterday by the Illinois Association of Criminal Justice, contains the charge that Scarface Al Capone contributed to the campaign fund of Mayor Thompson in his last race for office.—Chicago Tribune, June 8, 1928.*

With that background, and what seemed like his irrepressible penchant for hyperbole and exaggerated promises, the legend of Thompson being in league with the mobsters was bound to grow legs and a tail. But there was of course some foundation. Given that the spotlight was to be turned away from their main business, the city's gangsters were bound to support Thompson. In essence he was allowing them to continue to trade, unmolested. What was more, since Thompson didn't promise to fight to repeal Prohibition, he was not threatening to kill the goose that laid the golden eggs—the Eighteenth Amendment. It was a win-win situation for them.

This confluence of interests between the bootlegger and the politician is not—of itself—an indication that Thompson was being paid off by Capone. However, rather predictably, the elements of the press hostile to Thompson reported that Capone and the mayor's mutual benefits matched so thoroughly that it could not be simple coincidence. There were accusations that Thompson's sponsor for the mayoralty, Robert Crowe, was also in league with Capone, and that he, Thompson and Police Chief Charles Fitzmorris were all in the pay of Capone.[44]

The press, and most notably the influential *Tribune*, cited examples of Capone's actions that seemed to back up the theory of a Capone-Thompson axis. In April 1927, the Associated Press reported that no sooner had Thompson returned to City Hall than "Scarface"—the sinister name they insisted on calling Capone—moved his operation's headquarters from their Dever-era quarters in the Hawthorne Hotel in the suburb of Cicero. They came back to the Metropole Hotel in Chicago's Levee district. The hostile press reported that this was because, as one mobster put it: "Who's going to go out there [Cicero] when I can find anything I want right here in the city?"[45] Rumors surfaced of Capone's having bankrolled Thompson's campaign, and accusations of the connection emerged again when Big Bill began to wind up the region for his 1928 Republican presidential bid.[46]

Nevertheless, it was not until Thompson ran for a fourth term as mayor in 1931 that his reputation for fostering crime and being allied to the mob was truly cemented. Under a banner "Gangdom is Campaign Issue," the *Chicago Tribune* showed two pictures, one of Big Bill and the other of Capone, side by side. Underneath the photos were comments made by the self-proclaimed "nemesis of the gangster"—and Republican mayoral candidate—Judge John H. Lyle. The *New York Times* had published a piece in which Lyle claimed "gangsters are gnashing their teeth and frothing at the mouth" at the thought of his election. He also went on to claim that he laid "at the door of the present [Thompson] administration … every murder by gangsters in the last twelve years."[47]

To back up this connection to gangland, Lyle claimed that Capone had contributed

$150,000 to the Thompson campaign fund.[48] Such partisan rumors need to be seen in the light of a hard-fought election. But they have nonetheless persisted, even though there is no conclusive evidence of Thompson's alliance with Capone, or—for that matter—any other bootlegger. This persistence has gained them the status of fact. There is a school of historical interpretation that sees Capone's return to the Levee on Big Bill's return to City Hall as near incontrovertible proof of the gangster's payments to Thompson's campaign funds.[49] But as Big Bill himself put it, "It's all newspaper talk," and other influential contemporaries took a similar view.[50] One of the most vocal and convincing of these was William Allen White.

The Progressivist "Sage of Emporia," White argued that all city governments sooner or later acquired a "Big Bill." To him Thompson was, like Tammany's Plunkett had claimed to be, honest in spirit if not in deed, and more importantly he delivered what the electorate wanted. White also argued that the implication that Thompson had been on the take in the School Board scandal in 1923 was simply a smear provoked by Big Bill's populism frightening the city's elites.

White frankly admitted that the Big Bill type of mayor "steals a little, wastes more, shames us all; brawls, wrangles and blunders and bulls his way through the years of public service." Nevertheless, White had an enduring belief in the power of American institutions. In the end he believed that while "public opinion does constrain his folly," Thompson was also a public servant, and that same opinion "does more or less direct his energy." He reasoned that Thompson was the very essence of the classlessness of America. While Thompson was a demagogue, White was also convinced that such characters as Thompson were seen in essence as "big-hearted, free-handed, fair-minded defender[s] of the common people against the pharisaical, tight-fisted, long-nosed interference of a lot of snobs and snoopers."[51]

Leaving aside White's somewhat gushy view of Big Bill, it is also possible to challenge the veracity of the claims that link him with organized crime by examining their origins. The claim that Thompson was linked with Capone via Fitzmorris and Crowe stemmed from his severely disgruntled opponent in the 1927 Republican mayoral runoffs, Dr. John Dill Robertson. Thompson had upset his former health commissioner in the election campaign. The ever-outrageous Thompson represented Robertson and the other leading Republican candidate, Fred Lundin, his former campaign manager, as two caged rats.

Having allegedly found the pair of rodents in a local city dump, Big Bill made them one of the central features of his campaign. He would throw his voice through the two rats, named Fred and Doc, and make them squabble and bicker in a strange variation on the Punch and Judy show, entertaining his audiences and mocking his opponents and their policies. Infuriated, Robertson hit back by accusing Thompson of close association with the underworld. He simply repeated the phrase "Who killed Bill McSwiggen?" whenever he could. The campaign was also taken up by Thompson's nemesis, the *Chicago Tribune*. The paper echoed the same phrase as a banner in bold type on its editorial page. They ran it every day over the final two weeks of the election campaign.

The question would have had resonance in the city, relating as it did to murder of a popular young law enforcer—a situation in many ways reminiscent of the David Hennessy case in New Orleans a quarter of a century earlier. In 1926 William McSwiggen, the highly effective twenty-six-year-old assistant state's attorney, was shot dead close to what was then Capone's HQ in Cicero. While the link between the murder and the mayor was tenuous, what it demonstrated was indicative of suspicions already in the mind of many of the Chicago electorate: the ineffectual and seemingly corrupt attitude of the Thompson administration towards the mob. It focused attention on Thompson and his "cronies" and their alleged connections with the city's law enforcers, as demonstrated by their failure to solve even the most open and shut gangland murder case.

McSwiggen was known as the "Hanging Prosecutor" for the efficiency with which he achieved the death penalty for seven of city's gangsters in the ten months before his death. The blatant way in which McSwiggen met his "martyrdom" shocked even the most hard-boiled residents of Chicago. The result was that the Chicago public rapidly beatified the self-made boy wonder and clamored for his killers to be brought to justice. However, Crowe, as state attorney, and Fitzmorris, as police chief, had been singularly ineffective in bringing the perpetrators to justice. The whole department dragged its heels over the case and, if nothing else, they made themselves look extraordinarily suspicious.

The chief suspect, Capone, was only interviewed after having been given time to flee the city to California. What was more, when the case came to court, no convictions were achieved. To his enemies Thompson was deeply connected. As the candidate most closely associated with Crowe and Fitzmorris, like them, he was equally guilty either of spectacular dereliction of duty, or of being in the pay of the mob. Given these allegations, the rumors and the suspicions, it is not altogether surprising that without any real evidence, Robertson was able to create a connection between Capone and Thompson which has become one of the most enduring assumptions in the history of American organized crime.

It was easy for Thompson's enemies to put across the idea that the mayor was dodgy, if not actually criminal. Thompson's flip-flopping policies and brash style made him an easy target, yet by contrast, the reputation of his most influential critics was often above reproach. John Landesco, who first reported Capone's role in bankrolling Thompson, was one such enemy. Landesco was the author of the highly influential "Organized Crime" section of the *Illinois Crime Survey*, and had been embedded so fundamentally in the world of Chicago's gangs that his information is generally taken as accurate and his conclusions are seen as sound. However, the accusation that Thompson was bankrolled by Capone in the 1927 election was little more than rumor, and Landesco more or less admits as much with his "sources close to Capone" approach.[52]

As the organized crime historian Mark Haller has shown, the *Crime Survey*, while a revolutionary and invaluable analysis of the criminality of Chicago in the 1920s, takes as a given its premise of organized crime's crucial linkage with politicians at all levels.[53] While this was pretty good starting point, using it as a yardstick with which to analyze all gang activity is not necessarily productive, or conducive to an accurate picture. The danger is that the accusation of the involvement of a politician with, or in, organized crime can very easily move from being a supposition to a statement of fact.

This is borne out by the fact that some mention of the bribery of Thompson via campaign funding has been given in most accounts of Prohibition Era organized crime in Chicago ever since. Sure enough, given the general acceptance of the claims, it was not long before the undisclosed figure had been quantified. According to Herbert Asbury, a not always reliable journalist and virtuoso recorder of gangster myth, Frank J. Loesch, the president of the Chicago Crime Commission, said the figure was $250,000. Asbury also claims that Judge John Lyle put it at $150,000.[54]

However, Asbury—or his informants—may well be confusing the bribe with the *Tribune*'s accusation of a similar backhander given by Capone to Thompson in 1931.

Inevitably there has been inflation over the years. One recent account puts the figure at $260,000, and that figure seems set to go into the popular version of the "wicked city in Prohibition"–type accounts that populate the Internet and popular history, and was cited as fact in a recent bestseller.[55] No one, however, states where these figures come from.

That is not to say that there was no evidence that Thompson was "on the take." Far from it. Although he and Fred Lundin were eventually cleared of the 1923 School Board fraud, in 1933 he and another set of associates were ordered to repay the city nearly two and a half million dollars. However, it is interesting that these funds were not traced back to Capone or any other "bootlegger." According to the memoirs of perhaps one of his most committed, articulate and relentless enemies, Judge John Lyle, these millions originated from rake-offs. They were, it appears, garnered from a scam that involved corrupt consultants and the valuations of condemned buildings that belonged to the city.[56]

Unethical, dishonest and venal as Thompson undoubtedly was—and even one of his most staunch supporters, William Allen White, admits he was seriously corrupt—the connection of Big Bill to Capone is based more on speculation, rumor and political invective than genuine evidence. As David Ruth has shown with so many aspects of organized crime, the analysis of the context, contemporary mores, fads and fashions is paramount when attempting to understand the reasons behind the portrayal of mobs and mobsters at the time and since.[57]

## Tough Tony's Assassination

> A casual glance at the gang map of Chicago of three years ago, and of the gang map today, is overwhelming evidence. The gang population of Chicago has been cut 40 percent.—William F. Russell (Chicago Police Commissioner), "Gangs and Crime," *True Detective* (January 1930): 95.

> The idea of 6,000 policemen, ninety-eight judges and nearly 2,000 bailiffs, clerks and attaches of the court and law enforcement machinery not being able to suppress even the leading twenty-eight public enemies of this city [Chicago] is outrageous. It can only be charged to influence with this present City Administration.—Judge John Lyle cited in the *New York Times*, February 4, 1931.

Perhaps the association of Thompson and Capone is simply the result of a tendency that commentators and their followers demonstrate: a trend to prefer their political leaders to be more powerful and intelligent than their criminals. Many would like to presume that those in power are authoritative enough to prevent the rise of a "public enemy" like Capone. If those officials choose not to cope with the criminals, in this reading that must mean they are colluding with them. On the other hand, maybe it is simply that politicians of the 1920s, as now, were considered intrinsically untrustworthy, especially when the Dollar Decade over which they had presided imploded so spectacularly in 1929.

It could also be that it was simply that Thompson was seen as a new breed of machine politician, just as Capone was a new breed of criminal. Both could be products of the vast temptations of the city and the huge profits available through the bonanza that was Prohibition. More prosaically, maybe it is simply the result of political mudslinging, where historically the mud has stuck. In what can be seen as a curiously ironic addendum to the reputation of Thompson, the career of his successor has been linked even more directly with organized crime, with the result that his reputation in this area is just as contested. Yet history generally sees Anton Cermak as fighting the criminals, rather than colluding with them.

Anton "Tough Tony" Cermak was a Bohemian immigrant who arrived in the U.S. with his coal-miner father in Chicago at the age of eleven. A rough and ready political brawler, he had grown up in Chicago's Valley district. In this notorious immigrant ghetto, the young Cermak mingled with many of the young toughs who would grow up to become major players in Chicago's all-powerful gangland. This experience, according to one interpretation, left Cermak with a burning desire to break the power of the gangs in the city, and especially the successors to Capone's organization.

He told reporters on winning City Hall that he would "shake up the police department and end [the] prosperity enjoyed by organized crime" in the city. One reporter went on to tell his readers that "the gunman is in for a rough time of it when Chicago sets seriously about the task of ridding itself of the underworld leeches … [and] the chaotic conditions of taxation and extortion is destined to fade from the picture, judging by the spirit shown in the city since Big Bill pulled out."[58] To this end the new mayor, according to the sympathetic *Chicago Tribune*, gave orders to the city's police to "break up all meetings of gangsters."[59] According to this pro–Cermak version of the controversial and violent events that followed, there was no direct connection between the recently elected mayor and those whose influence he sought to curb. According to this account, the mayor was simply cleaning up the aftermath of years of corrupt and collusive municipal government under Big Bill.

The events that would form the center of the *Tribune*'s analysis focus on December 19, 1932. On that afternoon a police detective, Harry Lang, along with three fellow detectives from the Special Gang Detail, raided the La Salle Wacker Building on La Salle Street. The target was room 554, which was generally known to be the "headquarters of the Nitti organization"—the successor "outfit" to the jailed Capone's operation. In the room the police found seven "hoodlums" including Frank "The Enforcer" Nitti, the then leader of the Outfit.

According to the testimony of the policemen, as reported in the *Tribune*, when the police burst in, they ordered the gangsters to put up their hands. While his six lieutenants did as requested, Nitti instead started to cram paper into his mouth. Amid the confusion, the police alleged Nitti drew his gun, shooting Lang and wounding him in the arm. In response, Lang fired off five rounds at Nitti, three of which found their mark. Although wounded seriously enough to be given the last rites that night in hospital, Nitti survived.[60]

In April 1933 a sufficiently recovered Nitti was brought to trial for his part in the incident. The mobster was charged with assault with a deadly weapon. However, in the ensuing trial, the police could not get their story straight and the gangster was acquitted. But that was by no means the end of the story. On the strength of the evidence that emerged from testimony given at Nitti's trial, after 14 successful pleas for delay, Lang was eventually prosecuted for his part in the events. Yet again the evidence was contradictory and this time it was the detective who walked away from the court. Instead of serving time for attempted murder, Lang was convicted of simple assault and ordered to pay a $100 fine.[61]

The story now gets convoluted. Mayor Cermak proved less lucky than Nitti. In February 1933 he was standing on a podium next to the newly elected President Franklin

Delano Roosevelt in Miami, Florida. While the president was delivering his speech, the bullet of a deranged, unemployed Italian anarchist assassin, Giuseppe Zangara, struck the mayor of Chicago. According to most commentators who picked over the dramatic events in the weeks which followed, the target was meant to be the president. Some accounts had the assassin standing on a wobbly chair which, when it moved, upset his aim. Others argued that he was simply inexperienced, overexcited and incapable. At least that was how events were reported in the *Chicago Tribune* in 1933.[62]

Whomever the assassin was aiming for, the bullet found a target. Two weeks after the shooting, Cermak died of his wounds. Eighty years later, those same events were given a very different slant, even in the same newspaper. It came to light when the *Chicago Tribune*'s columnist John Kass questioned the Chicago alderman and political historian Edward Burke about the assassination of Cermak and how it related to the mayor's connections with Nitti. Burke reiterated a very different story, first alleged in 1957 by no less a figure than former Cook County Circuit Court Judge and sworn enemy of Thompson, John H. Lyle.

In this version of the assassination, the bullet shot in Miami had actually found its intended mark. Cermak was targeted in a contract killing arranged by Nitti. He ordered the contract as revenge for Mayor Cermak's ordering of the raid which had so nearly led to the gang boss's death. According to Lyle, the assassination took place while the president was speaking because those behind it knew that would increase the publicity. Seemingly getting into the part, and using a curious patois, Lyle argued the killing was designed to warn any prospective reformer: "The mafia [*sic*] doesn't have to kill you inside the Chicago City limits. It can kill you in New York or Miami or at the big fights or the World Series, cause you always go places like that."[63]

Chicago gang historian Gus Russo came up with another interpretation in 2001. While he agrees that Cermak *was* the target in Miami, he does not see his death as being linked to any attempt on the mayor's part to get rid of the gangs. In his account, "Ten Percent Tony"—as Cermak was also known—was less interested in cleaning up Chicago than in cleaning up for himself. Cermak, Russo claims, made significant money bootlegging during Prohibition, chairing an organization dedicated to representation of saloon keepers as a vaguely disguised front for his activities.

Russo also links Cermak with many of the leading underworld figures, especially of the notorious Irish mobsters, the Touhy brothers. According to Russo, like Pendergast in Kansas City, Cermak sold the idea of an open city in order to gain personal control of Chicago's vice industry. Once he had achieved this, he could—like Pendergast—take his cut from all the city's gambling and prostitution enterprises. To this end, Russo claims that Cermak's much-vaunted personal oversight and direction of the clampdown on vice and racketeering operations was simply the most logical way of protecting his own investments and allies. It was not aimed at preventing lawbreaking as such, only lawbreaking by those not controlled by, or affiliated with, him and his operation.

In this version, Cermak was interested in wresting control of the city's vice from the Italians, and placing it in the hands of more controllable and accountable elements of the criminal world. The Cermak that Russo details is only interested in his own fortune and simply seeks to further that aim. With this goal in sight, he is willing to make deals with the devil. Cermak gains power using the support of the Capone gang, but once in City Hall he turns on them. In office he instigates policies which will only benefit himself and his cronies. The result is that Russo's Cermak has Nitti shot by Lang simply to remove the competition. In turn, according to this version, Nitti has Cermak killed in order to protect his own business interests from predatory threats emanating from, and protected by, City Hall.[64]

It is interesting that at the time of writing Cermak's reputation as a gang-busting mayor seems to be undergoing something of a revival. Robert M. Lombardo's study of Chicago organized crime claims that while Cermak "was anti-mob, he was not anti-vice." Writing in 2013, Lombardo argues that Cermak was genuinely committed to the idea of the open city, and saw the rationalization and control of vice as the only way of defeating organized crime and breaking a cycle of corruption in a city which had become synonymous with vice and violent crime.[65]

While partisan politics and the preservation of reputation both play a major role in the way in which these two mayors are portrayed, that is not the entirety of their importance to this study. In part it is possible to see these fluctuations of legacy and accusations of criminality as reflecting the course of historical investigation. New documentation can alter the evidence, and that in turn can provide fresh insight. In Russo's case it is claimed that the journals of Capone associate Murray Humphreys offered a radically different perspective on the events surrounding Cermak's activities and demise than had previously been the case.

At other times the same evidence may well just be interpreted in a different way, perhaps to illustrate a different thesis. Lombardo's study of Chicago organized crime sets out to challenge the prevailing belief in the Cold War era that organized crime and the Mafia were synonymous. It aims to question the wisdom behind narratives of the time that the Sicilians and their allies were in control of criminal activity, coast to coast—including Chicago. Lombardo rejects the stubbornly immovable "Mafia controlling all crime" type of interpretation prevalent from the 1950s onwards.

Lombardo shows how the assassination highlights changes what for so long had been the prevailing narrative: a picture of all-powerful mobs overseen by commissions of Mafia Dons whose whims and wishes are performed and enforced by a host of foot soldiers. He sees organized crime as a series of autonomous gangs of which Nitti's "Outfit" was but one. Like most contemporary historians, he maintains that they are interconnected only inasmuch as it suits their immediate aims and ambitions. To Lombardo, Cermak's death in Miami was not an instance of the national reach of the mob, as Lyle and then Russo argued. Instead he sees it as the playing out of a local turf war—just in another area.

# 4

## New York: The Night Mayor and the Big Policeman

### The Parable of the Night Mayor

> *Whenever a major crime is committed in any part of the country, nine times out of ten, it is traced to some member of a Chicago gang. The Windy City seems to be the crime center of the nation.... There is something wrong with Chicago. Either the political organization is rotten or criminals have become so strongly organized that officials are unable to hold them in check.—Aberdeen Daily News, January 17, 1931*

The contemporary perception in the Prohibition Era was that Chicago was "crime central," with its ingrained and seemingly endemic links between hoodlums, gangsters and corrupt politicians. This view has survived to the present day. It has given the city an image connecting its politicians with organized crime that is verging on the unique. In reality even the most cursory scrutinizing of the governance of other major cities shows that this was certainly not the case. The accusations leveled against Big Bill Thompson and Anton Cermak regarding their supposed ties with organized crime are actually more the norm than the exception in most of the larger cities of the times.

Corruption and more direct links between City Hall and organized crime are readily apparent in Boston, Philadelphia, Kansas City, Omaha, Detroit, Milwaukee, New Orleans, Cleveland and many other cities. However, it is probably the two most rapidly expanding seaboard metropolises—New York and Los Angeles—that yield the most convincing evidence that Chicago was neither the most "infected" city, nor was it entirely unique in terms of its connections with organized criminal activity. Both cities show clear evidence, not only of the connections between City Hall and the underworld, but also that crucial association hinted at in the career of Big Bill, and crucial to the ambitions of Anton Cermak: the control of the city police force.

In New York the dandified, flamboyant mayor with film-star good looks, James J. "Jimmy" Walker, earned a reputation for mixing with the city's party elements. Rarely if ever seen before four in the afternoon, he usually appeared at City Hall after spending the night with Ziegfeld Follies chorus girl Betty Compton. The night before, the pair would have frequently kept themselves entertained in the company of movie stars, boxers and gangsters in a Broadway theater or perhaps one of Harlem's mushrooming speakeasies and nightclubs. Walker was in many ways the high-profile, Jazz Age personification of the city that never sleeps. As the muckraker Henry Pringle put it, Walker was "the personification of all that the timid bookkeeper who lives in the suburbs and goes nowhere would like to be in the eyes of his Kansas cousins."[1]

As a result of this modern image, his constituency—like that of Big Bill in Chicago—voted for his man-of-the-people policies that were liberal, populist and libertarian in an age of puritanical hypocrisy. For while Walker was handsome, glamorous and hedonistic, he still had something of the old-style city boss about him. "Beau James" would still involve himself in the most basic problems of running a rapidly expanding metropolis in a time of change.

It was Walker who set up the city's municipal sanitation department. Further, he was the mayor who rearranged and brought order to New York's rather chaotic hospital system, turning it into a coherent and effective network. It was Walker who expanded the subway system, while simultaneously keeping the fares at an affordable level. Walker improved the range and quality of the city's open spaces. He put considerable time and funding into the city's increasingly impressive parks and playgrounds. More contentiously, as a keen sports fan and a friend of the black heavyweight contender "Battling" Jimmy Johnson, Walker legalized boxing in the city. In this he bumped up against considerable opposition.

Forever at war with the city's moral reformers, the "Night Mayor"—as he became known—achieved some major victories. Perhaps his most significant triumph was repealing the Puritanical "Blue Laws." These bylaws had outlawed most sporting and recreational activities on Sundays. This was no mean feat since, while these Sabbath restrictions were sacrosanct to many of the city's elite austere "bluenoses," in practice, they had been largely ignored by the working men of the city. Alongside this largely popular measure, he also ran up against the moral lobbies in his defeat of a measure that proposed a separate New York film censorship to run in conjunction with the Hayes Code that was emerging in Hollywood. In a similar vein, he opposed and defeated a proposed measure in the State Legislature to censor books sold in the city, claiming—rather peculiarly—that he knew of no girl who had been corrupted by what she read in a book.

Predictably, given his opposition to morally based legislation, he controversially, but openly, attacked Prohibition. He went on record attacking the Volstead Act as a "measure born in hypocrisy." What was more, like Big Bill, in his election speeches he promised to make the city "wide open." To Walker, law enforcers and policy makers should concentrate on public safety, security and prosperity, rather than dictating morals and investigating the private lives of citizens. However, unlike Thompson, he used subtle and politically adroit measures to make sure his policies worked. And again unlike his Chicago counterparts, Walker was sincere and consistent in his take on these issues, most particularly on booze. Since he personally did not see drinking as a crime, he didn't see the necessity of enforcing the Volstead Act.

Committed as Walker was to "wet" policies, he was nevertheless pragmatic in how he went about supporting the removal of Volstead—or at least making it unworkable. As president of the state Senate, he had supported Governor Al Smith's repeal of the "Little Volstead" Mullan-Gage Law. Passed in the euphoria that followed the introduction of the booze ban in January 1920, this 1921 legislation had made Volstead violations in the city a state as well as federal crime. Highly unpopular with most New Yorkers, it had clogged up the city's judicial system and arguably done much to make the city's reputation as one of the most booze-soaked towns in the Union.

True to his principles, Walker kept up his opposition to Prohibition once he entered

City Hall in 1926. He reversed the aggressive enforcement policies of his puritanical predecessor, but he did so by sleight of political hand. In part he achieved his aim with a policy based around lethargy. He essentially made sure there was a new approach by replacing his predecessor's highly effective proactive and go-getting police chief. Commissioner Richard Enright was a staunch defender of the Volstead Act who frequently ran up against the inertia and corruption of his own force. Frustrated at being blocked in his attempt to bring prosecutions against thirteen inspectors, a handful of deputy inspectors and some precinct captains for failing to enforce vice and Volstead laws, he resigned his post the day before his term ended.[2]

By contrast, the man Walker chose to succeed Enright was a rather disinterested, stolid bureaucrat. George Vincent McLaughlin's previous experience had been in jobs involving finance, and then as the state superintendent of banking. His rather laissez-faire attitude towards policing in general was summed up by his comments on a spate of police killed on duty. After the twelfth murder in eight months, McLaughlin rather diffidently told reporters: "We are getting all the bad breaks so far. The police are making splendid arrests, but the luck is against them."[3] His performance in chasing up Volstead violations followed that pattern.

Walker also rather ironically introduced a so-called "Cabaret Law." This required the annual licensing of night clubs and introduced a mandatory closing time of 3:00 a.m. across the board. Given his lifestyle, at first glance this move seemed at the very least hypocritical, if not actually politically damaging. In fact it was, on closer examination, a highly adroit maneuver that actually protected many of those whom it seemed to most restrict. Through this legislation Walker managed to reclaim the implementation of the dry laws for the City of New York, wresting it back from the Federal Prohibition Agency. Using the Cabaret Law, Walker effectively put the enforcement of Volstead back into the province of his newly disinterested, but essentially sympathetic, NYPD. The result of this shift in enforcement was that the city's nightlife continued without a great deal of interference or influence by the law.[4]

Unsurprisingly, such behavior laid the Tammany-backed "Night Mayor" open to accusations of mob connections. However, it was his relations with law-keeping rather than his supposed connections with lawbreaking that fueled his downfall. Walker would be connected with police corruption, vice and organized crime. While Walker may well have had such connections, a close examination of the evidence shows once again how organized criminal activity was often the most effective way to smear a political opponent. In all too many cases it appears that the smearing has lost its crucial connection with partisan politics and has gone into the historical record as simply the reporting of fact. The reputation of Jimmy Walker is one such incident.

## The Murder of Vivian Gordon

It all began with what seems like a typical "Gotham noir" moment on the morning of February 26, 1931. While out for an early morning stroll, a man stumbled on the bludgeoned and strangled, semi-naked body of a woman in Van Cortlandt Park in the Bronx. Very quickly the corpse was identified as the forty-two-year-old local resident Vivian Gordon. A probable explanation and backstory for her demise followed equally fast. Central to the speculation were Gordon's connections with the city's vice industry. The woman had served prison time as a prostitute and was known by the police to be running a series of blackmail operations. Predictably, as with all good detective stories in this genre, it also turned into far more than a simple murder case.

The gruesome discovery set in motion a series of events that culminated in a major investigation into the NYPD's involvement in "Dry Manhattan's" booming night life–fueled vice industry. Diaries and other documents found in the downtown apartment of the murdered woman told of her intention to expose a "frame-up by police officers and others."[5] This suggestion was corroborated in a letter dated some three weeks before her murder. In this she warned her ex-husband that she would be "going before the investigation committee this week and intend[ed] to tell the whole story of this dirty frame-up.... I intend to go to the limit."[6]

Gordon's accusations came at a time when the links between the city's judiciary, City Hall and the vice industry were already being investigated by the Hofstadter Commission. This inquiry was given the task of looking into the functioning of the city's magistrate's court system. The inquiry was presided over by Samuel Seabury, a dogged, crusading, left-wing, but patrician and rather pompous retired judge with presidential ambitions. It had simple but unambiguous objectives, which Seabury himself had summed up in two overriding questions: "What are the conditions in the Magistrate's [courts]?" And: "Is justice being done?"[7] To answer these simple questions, the Commission would interview over 1,000 witnesses.

It would uncover, among other crimes, a huge conspiracy in which innocent women were arrested for prostitution and forced to pay large sums of money in order to clear their names. The scam the Commission had uncovered had been running for quite some time when Gordon was murdered, and through a variety of what could be coincidences, she was linked to the emerging scandal in a variety of ways—both in life and death. The first coincidence was her own death as a victim of the racket. Eight years before her murder in 1923, Gordon was in the middle of a very nasty divorce from her estranged husband, deputy U.S. Marshal John Bischoff. Furious that Gordon was resisting his attempts and struggling to get a favorable settlement, Bischoff used his expertise to try to disgrace his soon to be ex-wife. He arranged to have her caught and photographed *in flagrante* in a hotel room with her lover. What was more, he took this fairly commonplace strategy—the Badger Game, as it was known—one step further.

The vindictive Bischoff, in cahoots with a corrupt NYPD vice lieutenant, Andrew McLaughlin, then used this evidence to set in train a successful prosecution of Gordon for prostitution. An equally corrupt magistrate's court had then tried her. In spite of three separate appeals, the doomed woman had served two years of a three-year sentence in Bedford Reformatory in upstate New York. The court had also ruled that she should also lose the custody of her only daughter. Given this treatment, it was perfectly understandable that Vivian would have taken the first opportunity to expose the scam to the Seabury Commission—which she did. Not only that, but she was due to appear again and give potentially even more explosive evidence.

Crucially, this meant that authorities undertaking investigations into the NYPD already knew most of the accusations contained within her diaries. This had the effect of making it impossible for those involved in the scam to follow their usual practice, and bury Vivian's potentially disastrous accusations.[8] Instead, the police adopted another strategy. Attempting to exonerate itself, the NYPD put the maximum number of men and resources onto the case. All this sudden flurry of interest in a single murder initially succeeded in doing was making the department look even more suspicious and appear even more guilty.

This is where it came back to City Hall. By the end of February the moral guardians in the city pointed to the laxity of the Walker regime's approach to law and order. On behalf of the City Affairs Committee, Rabbi Stephen S. Wise and the Rev. John Haynes Holmes argued:

> The murder of Vivian Gordon lights up … the alliance between "the forces of law" and the forces of lawlessness…. This is not so much the murder of a woman as notice served by criminals and gangsters inside and outside of the Police Department, on and off the magistrate's bench, that inquiry into and exposure of all organized criminality will meet with swift and awful punishment.
>
> This is a challenge to the city of New York. How shall we meet the challenge? As the Chief Magistrate of New York is wont to meet every exposure of lawlessness—with a merry quip to a press super-tolerant of Mayoral wise-cracking, or with a mock-serious homily to his faithful underlings?[9]

By the middle of March, the two clergymen were sure enough of this connection to present their findings to Governor Roosevelt and formally demand the resignation of James J. Walker as mayor of New York.[10]

There was suspicion that Roosevelt would happily comply with this demand. Governor Franklin Delano Roosevelt had instigated the judicial commission and he repeatedly defended its actions. What was more, he widened the remit of the committees which stemmed from the original Hofstadter Commission to investigate collusions between corrupt law-enforcers and City Hall. He did this even though both he and Mayor Walker were nominally part of the same administration.

While they were both Democrats, Roosevelt and Walker came from opposite ends of the party. FDR liked to be seen as an anti–Tammany reformer. He played to the perception that claimed, as many Americans of his generation believed, Tammany was a corrupt, nepotistic and self-serving organization that, in the traditions of bossism, had had a distinctly malign influence on U.S. politics in general, and New York City in particular. Walker had risen through the ranks of Tammany and was committed to the controversial organization. It would pay FDR to take Walker down.

However, by April it appeared that FDR had missed his chance to pin anything on Tammany or Walker. The NYPD's huge investigative efforts seemed to have paid off. Detectives had arrested and indicted a suspect, Harry Stein. They made a press statement telling the city Stein was "a racketeer" with "a record as long as your arm." These included—most tellingly—a conviction for the chloroforming and robbery of a woman some years before Vivian's murder. The circumstances appeared very similar.

To corroborate this, the police claimed that when questioned, Stein had made a detailed confession in which he admitted to committing the murder with an accomplice, cab driver Harry Schlitten. He was adamant that their motive was simply the robbery of a well-dressed, bejeweled woman out at night on her own. They also produced detailed evidence directly linking Stein to the murder. They uncovered receipts that showed he had sold Vivian's watch for $50, her diamond ring for $500, and her fur coat for an undisclosed figure. It seemed the mystery was solved.

Backing this interpretation, a coalition of Tammany-appointed bosses took the stand at a press conference in May. Bronx District Attorney McLaughlin, Police Commissioner Mulrooney, and Mayor Jimmy Walker—who had to cut short a break in Los Angeles—jointly declared that the standard of "detective work reflects the highest credit on the [New York Police] department." They also played up Vivian's record "as an expert racketeer" and her operation of "a blackmail machine along the lines the old badger game," for which she had previously been convicted.

In addition they detailed their discovery of her diaries containing the names of "several hundred men" alongside "about forty women, whom she was accustomed to supply for gay [in the 1930s sense] parties." They declared that all this, when added to Stein's confession, showed that there was absolutely no truth in the intimation "that the police had caused this woman to be done away with, because she might be a witness against them."[11] By July the case had gone through the courts, but as they read alternative accounts, New Yorkers became increasingly uncertain about the mayor's view of the fatal night's events. They also increasingly doubted the NYPD's enhanced reputation.

There was a growing sentiment in the press that the detectives' construction of the events was, according to Stein's counsel Samuel Liebowitz, "a concocted story, manufactured out of cloth by the cops ... a contemptible frame-up ... a liaison between the cops and the underworld."[12] The jury on the Stein trial agreed, unanimously acquitting the suspect and his accomplice after only three and a half hours' deliberation.[13] This verdict effectively swung the attention of the public back onto the NYPD and its ultimate boss, Jimmy Walker. What was more, the embattled mayor now faced a triumvirate of ambitious anti–Tammany politicians only too willing to show how corrupt both the police and the mayor were.

Once again, as so often in the history of organized crime, personal ambition drove the version of events the public were sold. Judge Seabury felt that a real purge of corruption in the NYPD would enable him to run for the Democrat nomination in 1932. Tammany was in many ways ideal as a scapegoat for—or at least a distraction from—the dire state of the nation. When it was personified in a figure whose extravagant and hedonistic lifestyle seemed out of step with the national mood, so much the better. Nor was Seabury the only one with such ambitions.

A more sure-fire Democratic presidential nominee, and perhaps the most pragmatically skillful politician of the day, Franklin Roosevelt saw the downfall of Walker as essential to his radical bid to renew national confidence. The overthrow of Walker would cement FDR's distancing of his own image from that of his previous running mate—the Wet Tammany Catholic and ally of Walker, Alfred E. "Al" Smith. It was felt by many of his advisors that connection with Smith still tainted Roosevelt's name through memories of his train wreck of a presidential campaign in 1928. Nevertheless, the timing of the impending political execution needed to reflect an image of Democrat solidarity, or it could allow a Republican rally in New York.

The final member of the anti–Walker triumvirate was a highly ambitious Republican. Mayoral aspirant Fiorello LaGuardia had already lost one bid for City Hall to Gentleman Jimmy in 1929. Half-Jewish, half–Italian, LaGuardia drew on a similar demographic to Tammany's, and he was only too willing to see Walker fall from office. The downfall and disgrace of the Night Mayor would create a mayoral vacancy in which a Republican candidate in Democrat New York might stand a real chance. If that fall from grace was linked to corruption, it would certainly help gain support for LaGuardia's ongoing populist, reformist agenda. It was clear that the mix of corruption and policing was tied to political ambition and organized crime.

Predictably, given the way in which the forces arraigned against him were all in the ascendant, it was hardly surprising that on September 1, 1932, the Night Mayor resigned. Matters had come to a head in mid-presidential campaign, when FDR was forced at last to choose whether to go to war with Walker and Tammany. If he did, he showed himself disloyal to his old friend and running mate, Al Smith. If he did not, he risked having an increasingly unpopular Walker ruining his campaign anyway. Events overtook his having to make such a decision. Walker had appeared in front of the Seabury inquisition and had been found wanting. He was accused of accepting bribes totaling around one million dollars, and when questioned about the funds, he'd given at best only partial and very slippery explanations.

Like so many Tammany politicians before him, the Night Mayor had probably been on the take. Walker could not explain how he'd made a small fortune out of oil shares when it emerged that he had put up none of his own money. He was unable to explain why a bus company director gave him a $10,000 European vacation, or why a Brooklyn financier had given him nearly a quarter of a million dollars.[14] Disgraced, he left City Hall for Europe, vowing he would return and exonerate himself. He came back, but never regained his status, yet another municipal government figure destroyed by his connection with organized crime.

## Big Bill Devery

It was probably the connections with the inherently corrupt NYPD and their ruthless organized criminal activity, as exposed by the Gordon murder, that really did it for Walker. In this there was very little unique, or even particularly new. The NYPD had a notoriously bad reputation for its involvement with graft, corruption and kickbacks that had frequently broken into public view and led to spectacular scandals. To illustrate this, it is probably worth examining one that took place some fifty years before the demise of Walker.

One of the most notorious of these exposures took place in 1894 and 1895, when the extent of police department corruption had been highlighted by the investigations of the New York State Senate probe under Republican lawyer Clarence Lexow. It should come as little surprise that the investigation was undertaken in large part at the insistence of the Rev. Charles H. Parkhurst—a reformer sometimes seen the originator of the term "organized crime" in its modern sense.

In essence, Parkhurst coined the term with reference to the interaction of the police with Tammany Hall. To his and many other minds, the police *were* organized crime. Parkhurst was charged with bringing to justice a police department that was very often more likely to be the conduit by which criminals escaped reckoning. As Parkhurst pointed out:

> Experience had shown the directors [of Parkhurst's Society for the Prevention of Crime] that very little could be accomplished by the occasional closing of a saloon illegally run, or by the prosecution of any single gambler or disreputable housekeeper so long as the conditions exist which render it possible for illegal practices of the sort to maintain themselves so unconcernedly, so confidently, and so diffidently. If an attempt is made to suppress a gambling-house, the prime difficulty we encounter is not in dealing with the proprietor himself, but the support, which he receives, from the authorities whose sworn duty it is detect and arrest him and to breakup his illegal business.
>
> Until this alliance is broken which exists between criminals and their proper prosecutors it is like bailing out water with a sieve to attempt the extinguishment of individual gambling houses…. It is only because that department [the NYPD] is either negligent or criminal that there is present urgent occasion for such a society as ours.[15]

As Parkhurst claimed, and Lexow laid bare, the NYPD was tolerating and in many cases even effectively licensing prostitution, gambling and other vices. New York's Finest blackmailed and extorted the general public. They utilized the underworld at all levels with a truly egalitarian enthusiasm and a democratic rapacity. They operated protection rackets and ran fencing operations for stolen and contraband and confiscated goods. The sale of offices in the department was so commonplace as to be the norm, as was the sharing of the spoils of corruption on a hierarchical basis within the force. It was accepted that policemen could be hired for strong-arm voter intimidation and other forms of election fraud.

What was more, paying off policemen for perjury and other collusion with defendants, attorneys and judges was more or less expected, with the consequence that it was often built in by lawyers, detailed on invoices, and it was often charged and claimed back as a legal expense. The NYPD were seen as grasping, brutal, often drunken and always corruptible criminals. Essentially they were simply yet another—and particularly unpleasant—variety of the criminal classes which made up, and many cases directed and commanded, the city's expanding underworld.

While police brutality, dishonesty, corruption and venality were generally a given and more often than not often expected at every level, there were some whose exploits took them above the common herd. One of most outstanding of these, and one of the most prominent of Parkhurst's targets, was the ebullient, truly larger-than-life, two hundred and fifty–pound captain of Eldridge Street Station. Based as he was in the heart of the red-light district, William Stephen (yet another "Big Bill") Devery was a well-known and powerful presence in the city's police. He was also one of the most openly corrupt of the NYPD, and, largely as a result of that, one of the best protected. These were both elements that made him a prime target of the Lexow committee, and a prime illustration of the level of corruption in the force.

Devery realized that with 6,400 police officers and a budget of $11.5 million, the opportunities for skimming off money in the NYPD were impressive. Lexow exposed the captain as presiding over, and profiting from, a system of payment for progression in the NYPD. The committee exposed a system of promotion in which the prospects for an individual's rising through the ranks rested on a tariff of fees ranging from $300 to become a beat cop, up to $14,000 to make captain. While the initial outlay was extortionate—in all senses—the expectation was that the pickings when in post were so great that these figures were by no means unrealistic. At least they certainly hadn't been in Devery's case.

A pragmatic policeman, Devery was also an opportunistic believer in the Open City approach to vice. He saw his job as the protection of property, not the guidance of the city's morals. To him, whorehouses, gambling dens and round-the-clock bars only needed policing in order that they could remain in business—and in order for Devery to be able to retain them as a source of personal revenue. This attitude came across clearly when he was summoned to the Lexow Committee. Devery seemed confused by the whole process. Why was he being investigated for what was to him standard policing technique? He waved aside a truly impressive stream of accusations detailing graft, kickbacks and dodgy deals with a cavalier air, claiming when caught out that he—using a starkly contemporary phrase—simply "disremembered."[16]

His lack of recall failed to convince those overseeing him. Shocked by the extent of his corruption, the Board of Police Commissioners fired him. Then they indicted him for extortion. But the Commissioners had severely underestimated the depth of Superintendent Devery's network of graft, the power of his cronies, and his huge reserves in the Tammany Hall favor bank. They also ignored his incredible instinct for reinvention and survival. It must have come as a surprise to few observers who knew of his record up until this point that Devery was acquitted on all the charges brought by the Commissioners.

In spite of such setbacks, his persecutors did not give up. They made another attempt to prosecute him the following year. This time they were met by an even more impressive and emphatic obstruction. The accusations triggered a New York State Supreme Court order expressly prohibiting any further prosecution of the embattled police captain. It was plain that continued harassment meant nothing to the indomitable Devery. Far from it: his career blossomed. As the century closed, Richard Crocker's Tammany machine realized the potential of the big policeman. Under that regime, Devery rose to become chief of police.

In an attempt to check his rise, the post of chief of police itself was abolished by the anti–Tammany reform-minded Republican administration in 1901. Yet even this seemed to aid Devery. The seemingly invincible policeman simply bounced back, appointed by his network of allies to what he then turned into an even more powerful position—that of Deputy Police Chief. In that post, together with professional gambler Frank Farrell and the Tammany boss Timothy (this time a "Big Tim" rather than "Big Bill") Sullivan, he reached his zenith of corruption. He established one of the most sophisticated—if short-lived—graft machines the nation had ever known.

Between the three members of the syndicate that Sullivan welded together, they took over the administration of the New York State Gambling Commission, the essential control of New York State Legislature, and the day-to-day running of the New York City Police Department. With this power, for as long as the triumvirate remained in their posts, they were to all intents and purposes safe from investigation and prosecution from any angle and at any level. The result was that the operation netted the three over $3 million in the year 1901 alone. Essentially an operation of this nature was foolproof.

And so it proved until Tammany lost the 1902 election. To make his mark in terms of his reformist credentials, the incoming reformist mayor, Seth Low, looked around for a high-level scalp. He went further than any of his predecessors: he fired Devery. Loss of the job in real terms didn't actually make that much difference to Devery. By this point the constant skimming, extorting and grafting had made him a very rich man. Nor did it seem to dent his confidence. He behaved like a victorious general after a popular war: used to wielding power, he simply shifted his attention to politics. He turned his authority and his talents to getting himself elected into a suitable position.

After using considerable money to get himself elected as Democrat district leader in the Ninth Assembly District in Chelsea, he then ran for mayor of New York. But by this point, Devery's star was waning. In spite of liberal use of money and some spectacularly flamboyant and outlandish parties for his supporters, he failed to gain the mayor's office. This failure hit him, not just once, but twice—first as a Democrat and then as an independent candidate. It appeared Devery's former allies had either lost their power, or pulled away from the steadily decreasing attraction of his orbit. Realizing the futility of his ambitions, Devery retired, living a comfortable existence until his death from a heart attack in 1919.

In the years since he had left the force, things had changed. Most notably the NYPD had suffered what was arguably its most inglorious moment in 1915, when one of its men had been sent to the electric chair. Charlie Becker had been convicted of ordering the murder of a well-known gambler, Herman Rosenthal. Rosenthal had publicly complained that Becker had been skimming off an unacceptable take to protect his operation. Becker had hired a Jewish gang to have him killed. The ensuing case showed the depth, organization and extent of the corruption of the NYPD, and had led to a serious and largely effective reform that did away with the Devery world—at least in the public's mind.

Devery's obituary in the *New York Times* was in keeping with this view of steady implosion of the old system of graft. In essence it portrayed Devery as a quaint anachronism: a relic of a previous age of brutality and corruption. He was paraded to be a dinosaur who had learned his craft when policing was a matter of containing and controlling the "criminal classes," occasionally using his nightstick to protect the life and property of the privileged upperworld from the predations and incursions of the criminal underworld. Policing to Devery, according to this almost eulogeic tribute, was not a question of monitoring morality or protecting the sensibilities of a more "civilized" population. He was in essence a man whose time and thinking had passed: policing had moved on.[17]

Big Bill Devery took a practical approach to policing. Like many other law enforcers of his generation, he saw policing as operating so close to the criminal world that it necessitated the recruitment of a peculiar brand of officer, with a particular set of "virtues." By the time of his obituary, these "virtues" were seen as vices, if not as organized criminal behavior. In Devery's mind, to control the underclasses required a policeman who would not be overly concerned with red tape and regulation. The ideal officer could not afford be too fastidious or fainthearted in his dealings with the "criminal classes." It was more important that the man could maintain order and exert authority, and in order to do that he needed to understand the motives and behavior and be able to move among those people.

Devery summed up this attitude when he discussed the lack of these qualities in the Commissioner of New York Police from 1914 to 1918, Colonel Arthur Hale Woods. Woods was the opposite to the lowly-born Devery. He was from a distinguished Boston family. He was a Harvard graduate and had mixed with the great and the good as a teacher at the prestigious Groton private school. Given this pedigree, it should have come as no surprise that the down-to-earth Devery described him as "a classy gentleman in every shape and form." He went on to explain that this apparent virtue was not necessarily an advantage when overseeing the NYPD. As he detailed: "To take a banker, a broker, Admiral, General, Colonel, Captain or any other classy gentleman [as many of his successors were], and put him in charge of that quasi-body of wild Indians which is the New York police force, and them quasi-Indians will pull wool over his eyes."[18]

There can be little doubt that "them quasi–Indians" pulled no wool over Devery's eyes. Devery had worked his way up through the ranks and had learned how to scam the system. He had run a tight operation, knowing the most effective methods of hoovering up money from *all* police of all the ranks under his command. It was also apparent that he had learned how to make sure that reformers did not put any serious obstacles in place that might block the flow of his healthy, if illegal, income stream. Devery had managed very briefly to show the potential in New York for a true marriage of corrupt politicians and corrupt police in a more or less perfect version of organized crime. But at the time of his death, on the opposite side of the country, a similar marriage seemed to flourish more spectacularly, more violently and for far longer.

# 5

## Los Angeles Noir

### L.A. Noir

By the 1940s the focus of popular interest in organized crime had shifted from New York to Los Angeles via Chicago. In many ways this focused on the interface of police and city hall. In his novel *Perfidia* (2014), set in L.A. in December 1941, James Ellroy describes what a *New York Times* reviewer memorably calls "a Los Angeles Police Department of order, if little law."[1] Elroy's LAPD is a place where the cops are on a testosterone, drug and booze–fueled course of corruption, ambition, violence and self-interest. They are linked to, controlled by and in the pay of corrupt politicos. Despite the embellishment, it is still a pretty good historical analysis of one aspect of the city's organized criminal history—albeit from one very popular perspective.[2]

Yet the accusations of organized criminal activity within and involving the LAPD, as well as the headlines to prove it, can be found well before the Japanese attack on Pearl Harbor that forms the background to Ellroy's book. In the two decades leading up to the events of December 1941—if not before—the city's police at all levels had developed an unenviable reputation for corruption. The now ubiquitous L.A. Noir genre is in large measure fueled by, and set against, the epic venality, wholesale corruption, and appalling dereliction of duty that characterizes the city's police department in almost all the genre. It is clear that many of these assumptions stem from what was generally presumed to be the well-established associations of the LAPD with the city's organized criminal underworld. In order to fully understand this, it is probably best to have a bit of background.

It is possible to find some accounts that trace this symbiosis to the nature of the city itself. It was a magnet for those down on their luck and also those on the make, and was—in similar fashion to turn-of-the-century New York—undergoing a boom of truly epic proportions in the 1920s and 1930s.[3] Some explanations of L.A.'s apparently unique criminal history concentrate on a section of this struggling mass—those at the top. They detail the relentless and destructive struggles for power, money and influence within a powerful oligopoly of politicians, businessmen and other influential citizens and the dire impact such a struggle has on the city.[4] Another group of commentators lay the emphasis on the way in which the events of these years were reported at the time, especially by the leading paper of the region, the *Los Angeles Times*.[5]

Maybe predictably, this history will take the view that all three of these elements need to be considered, and that none was really more important than the other. Without the boom and growth of the city, the means and motive to fuel the huge wealth and influence of the local oligarchs and enable them to reach new levels of corruption would have been absent. Without the reportage, these events would not have reached public knowledge; they would not have been imitated in fiction and film.

Nevertheless the investigation must logically start with the city itself. With its alluring beach-life, near permanent sunshine, and the fabulously glamorous Hollywood stars, by the 1920s L.A. had become the iconic embodiment of the much-vaunted California Dream. Its magnetism was apparent both in the U.S. and abroad, and during the inter-war period it lured hundreds of thousands west in search of what would prove an all-too-often illusory quest for the perfect life. As the *Saturday Evening Post* commented, the city grew because of an "extraordinary and almost unprecedented pouring of population, money and prosperity into one section of the country and more particularly into one city."[6]

From the perspective of boosters and those they sought to attract, Southern California had the climate; it had the scenery; it had the jobs; and it had the character. Throughout the early decades of the twentieth century, it had the power to suck in massive numbers of expectant individuals from the polluted, crowded, cold and essentially miserable older cities of the U.S. It also drew in escapees from the increasingly intolerant governments and stagnating economies of Europe. Each one of these immigrants was driven by an urge to find fame and fortune in the glamorous, racy and thoroughly modern playground. The regional capital, Los Angeles, grew from a minor California coastal *pueblo* to become the very model of the sprawling twentieth-century megatropolis. In the 1920s L.A. was the fastest-growing city in the world, comparable perhaps only to its northern California rival, San Francisco, in the middle of the previous century.

The speed of this growth was truly phenomenal. In the last decade of the nineteenth century, the city had contained a little over 50,000 inhabitants. Ten years later, in 1900, the number of residents had doubled, and that population in turn doubled again over the next decade. By 1920 it had passed the half-million mark. But it really took off during that decade as the glamour and modernity of the city chimed with the mythical hedonism of the 1920s. By 1930 Los Angeles had added another 80 square miles to its total area in a largely low-rise suburban sprawl, which extended by a network of roads to reach nearly 450 square miles.

By the time of the Great Depression, this massive expansion had made the city stretch out in all directions to become even bigger in area than all five New York boroughs, *and* the entire footprint of Boston *and* San Francisco's Bay Area—*combined*. With a shade under a million and a quarter inhabitants, it was also already the fifth largest city in the U.S. Yet the true picture was even more dramatic. If the whole of Los Angeles County was included in these figures—an area which took in Santa Monica, Beverly Hills, Venice and Culver City—the city's population grew to over two and a half million citizens.

This made it rank as third largest in the U.S., with only Chicago and New York exceeding it in population. Nor was this the end. While its growth slowed down during the 1930s, it certainly did not stop. The city would still expand by another quarter of million by 1940, as people continued to chase the "good life" and the "California Dream" and yearned to escape the gloom of the Depression decade in other areas of the nation.[7] Entering the top three metropolitan centers in terms of population, it also joined them in terms of its reputation for organized crime. In part, like its two bigger competitors, the engine for this criminal activity was a combination of a booming economy, massive opportunity, amorality, venal and corrupt partisan politics, and simple avarice clashing with thwarted ambition and lack of opportunity.

Spectacular oil discoveries, the emergence of the aviation industry, the manufacture of "modern" goods like car parts and tires, and of course the making of movies—as well as a range of other businesses—combined to make L.A. the ninth-largest industrial center of the U.S. In keeping with the scale of the industrial enterprises, the city played host to large corporations that undertook most of the employment. The result was that, like most city dwellers, a large, if not dominant proportion of Angelinos were corporate employees. The "good life" was paid for by a shift-work paycheck or a corporate salary. Nevertheless, in true California style, it was still a speculator's paradise, and it was certainly not shift or secretarial work or even middle management that drew expectant migrants west to the L.A. El Dorado.

The scandalous and glamorous—and to many observers essentially vacuous—movie industry could, and did, make fortunes for a tiny section of the population, who produced, financed, starred in and distributed films to what appeared an endlessly fantasy-hungry population. To those involved in it at the higher end, it was essentially a modern-day alchemy: a dark art that transformed limited talent, glamour and celluloid into money—for limited effort. But perhaps more importantly it was an illusion that enabled others—less fortunate, astute, beautiful or gifted—to dream of fame and fortune. Nor was this the only local industry capable of quickly transforming rags to riches. South of the city another happy few struck oil, and consequently netted equally massive wealth and lived only marginally less conspicuously glamorous lives.

Both industries more or less directly fed organized criminal activity. The film industry produced seemingly unlimited numbers of hopeful and gullible, attractive and beautiful failed or has-been actors and actresses with little other than their physical magnetism to sell. One contemporary source spoke of "50,000 wonder-struck girls" being sucked in by Hollywood in the 1920s.[8] Three quarters of those girls were under 25 years old, and they soon found that the glamorous work they had searched for was elusive to the point of nonexistent. For example, it was estimated that during the 1920s an average of 30,000 extras sought 1,000 jobs within the studios. Those who failed to get them would end up waiting tables, working as salesgirls, or, all too frequently, selling their most valuable commodity—themselves. While some argued that they were corrupted, others claimed that they manipulated others with their "charms" as a way of getting ahead. These were the girls—but in reality it was both sexes—Theodore Dreiser called "hard-boiled savage climbers."[9]

Ironically, the very problem of desperate girls being lured into prostitution created its own genre of films. The prostitute became a stock character in Hollywood with many of the most glamorous stars playing the role—and some, including Garbo, Dietrich and Swanson, gaining Oscars. In turn, many of those prostitutes on the street also modeled their image on those screen goddesses. It also created a new and predatory class of wealthy and entitled, hedonistic and sybaritic, egotistical and demanding, and frequently amoral pleasure seekers. The predictable result was that Hollywood fueled a massive surge in sex for sale—both in the reality of the flesh and on the more ethereal but no less demeaning celluloid of pornography. It was a trade that a salacious press claimed—and still claims—catered to all tastes and most pockets, with all perversions.

There was a large body of American and foreign commentators who claimed that L.A. had a shiny exterior that was largely façade. They argued that it was a deception that relied on a certain perception. In this land of make-believe that "Tinsel Town" seemed to be rapidly becoming, drugs and (for much of this time, illegal) booze could have the capacity to alter perceptions, provide Dutch courage, and inspire the stamina to continue. They also made the dream seem real—or at least make the misery of the existence in the netherworld of purchasable intimacy a little more bearable.

Carey McWilliams called L.A. "Harlot City," and depicted its well-developed vice industry as fertile ground for the city to become entirely "mob minded."[10] More prurient and judgmental sources than McWilliams argued the movie studios themselves were actually organized criminals. They apparently used the infamous "casting couch," dangling the lure of a glamorous career in film to sexually exploit attractive people of both genders. They perverted the morals of the nation and cynically permitted, profited from and financed—if not encouraged—criminal perversions and immorality in their work and play. They provided work for panders, pimps, drug pushers and abortionists.[11]

When this facet was added to the corruption and protection of vice by local politicians and police, L.A. was quickly ranked as one of the most depraved cities in the U.S., with one of the most highly developed criminal vice "syndicates" in the country. But vice was not the only area that could be exploited by organized crime. The opportunities in organized crime to be had by orbiting the hopeful young girls in vice were equally apparent to those who preyed off equally gullible and perhaps innocent speculators in the concurrent oil and property booms, and pretty soon the three became linked.

By the dawn of the 1920s, an entire industry had grown up in the area in more-or-less honest, more-or-less legal, boosting and selling of more-or-less desirable property lots and more-or-less viable oil wells. One of the best examples of these opportunities fell into the lap of Chauncey C. Julian. Julian was probably the most blatant of the boosters. He summed up the situation in one of his daily adverts for stock in oil wells that told his readership: "We're all out here in California where the gushers are and we ought to clean up…. Come on folks get aboard for the big ride."[12] Predictably, the bumptious salesman CC—as he became known—took those "folks" for a *very* "big ride," and in the process demonstrated the depth of dishonesty at all levels in the "City of Angels."

Initially successful and providing impressive returns for his clients, Julian sold millions of shares in oil wells. However, from the mid–1920s onwards his lucky streak faded, and the stock sold was simply part of what amounted to a huge Ponzi scheme—but it took on a particularly L.A. style. Typically, given the nature of the city, the true reality of the "Julian Pete"—as the scheme became known—was uncovered by an equally unscrupulous Texan lawyer and his partner. Instead of going public with that knowledge and instigating legal proceedings against CC, they went public with the information in a very different way, and cashed in on it. They took over running the scam from Julian, bigged up the profits themselves, and inflated the bubble to an entirely new level.

It was estimated that the scheme at its peak had sucked in 40,000 investors and was worth over $200 million—over three times the most exuberantly generous valuation of the wells themselves. Still, according to one version, even when the true scale of the fraud was brought to light in 1927, District Attorney Asa Keyes managed to persuade the jury to drop the charges against the two leading conspirators in the Julian Pete scam. Commentators saw little new in this, for as one lawyer associated with the oil industry who became a hostile journalist put it: "So pock-marked was this slimy business with fraud and faithlessness, so infiltrated with shuffling and trimming, with bad faith and treachery, money-juggling and moral back-sliding, that few citizens were greatly surprised at this dramatic turn."[13]

At heart, underneath the glitz and glamour, inter-war Los Angeles was essentially a low-brow, populist town lifted up by wonderful climate, some big spenders, and a taste for the exotic. Still expanding and finding its true essence, it had all the features of a western boom town. L.A.'s very engine was reminiscent of Deadwood or Tombstone. It was a city driven along by a series of explosions caused by the bursting of speculation bubbles. As one contemporary described it, the city was a sexed-up, pumped-up, permanently blue sky, sunshiny version of the speculation fever that grabbed the whole nation in standard histories of the 1920s: "The easy money carnival spirit gripped them … sent them hell-bent along their deluded way. The jargon of the easy money votaries became their daily rehearsed song. They sang it from every real estate and stock-peddling platform, in every glittering café and club, in banks and at news-stands, in the homes of the opulent and the places where the wage-earners do their turn at the treadmill. Sobriety … the quiet voice of reason … had fled."[14] All these ways to get rich quick gave the city an air of what Carey McWilliams evocatively called a "truly bonanza affair … one long drunken orgy, one protracted debauch."[15]

As McWilliams's language implies, Los Angeles in the 1920s and 1930s had the "devil take the hindmost" air of the Gold Rush of a little under a century before. The difference was that these were times when the expectations of the public, as expressed through the rhetoric of the politicians, the self-righteous tone of their newspapers, and the actions of vigilantes, were thoroughly twentieth century. This was democratic populism. Actions that would have attracted no mention in the mining camps and shantytowns of Northern California of 1849 were seen as deeply troubling in the election-conscious City Hall and the customer-centered boardrooms, as well as the churches and news offices of Southern California in 1929.

As if re-election or profit were not enough, there were other very important drivers, all very typical of the late 1920s and early 1930s. There were worries that were driven by a genuine wish to see the city modernize and prosper. There were progressive politicians and social-gospel churchmen who wanted to clean up the vice areas. There was an equally powerful urge that pressed to keep the city "white," to control and contain the Mexican, African American and Asian populations of the city, as well as the internal migrants, refugees of rural poverty and the dust storms of Midwest. But perhaps most importantly there was the simple and all-prevailing wish to put one over on business rivals and political opponents.

Together these elements sounded warnings that this modern-day Gomorrah was being run by a powerful cartel of politicians, businessmen and lawyers. Essentially in the more "civilized" climate of America in the 1910s and 1920s, these were no longer the "bosses" like those who had ruled New York from the 1870s through to the 1900s. At least they were no longer perceived in the same way. Nevertheless, to those outside the governing circles of this cartel, this was "organized crime," and those charged with controlling it were periodically exposed as being deeply involved in organizing it.

## Chandler and Cryer

Arguably the most powerful and influential of the city's ruling oligopoly was the property magnate, press baron, and self-serving, politically connected oligarch, Harry

Chandler. Chandler was undoubtedly the largest landowner in the rapidly urbanizing Golden State. Aside from owning the controlling interest in the world's largest cotton plantation, an 862,000 acre estate in "Lower" California, he also owned the 281,000-acre Tejon Ranch that sprawled over the boundaries between Los Angeles and Kern Counties. Further, he controlled, then sold, 49,000 acres of land adjacent to the expanding metropolis, and then built many of the houses in the suburbs that were developed on that land.

Chandler also sat on the board of an assortment of more than three dozen banks, construction, transport and irrigation companies, as well as having widespread influence in oil production and manufacturing enterprises. He also controlled—one way or another—a large number of other businesses, either directly or remotely. All these combined to make his estimated wealth anywhere between $200 and 500 million—a figure that meant, it was also claimed by his own newspaper, he was ranked as the eleventh richest man in the world.

In keeping with such wealth, Chandler was also one of California's social elite. With his father-in-law and other business partners, he could claim a heritage that, while short even by American standards, was impressive and absolutely central in terms of Anglocentric Los Angeles. Together he and his associates had not only developed, sold and managed vast chunks of desert, coastal and inland farmland that became prime L.A. real estate, but they crucially controlled the element that had the power to make these areas habitable. The secret purchase of over 100,000 acres of the San Fernando Valley and the building of the Mulholland Aqueduct from the Owens Valley put Chandler in charge of the most valuable resource in this parched land—water. This in turn cemented his position at the top of the regional elite, a position that he jealously guarded.[16]

As the *Saturday Evening Post* put it, "When the large and passionate California moon rises majestically into the heavens and smiles a golden smile … one wonders whether Harry Chandler owns 51% of said moon."[17] The quote perfectly sums up the speculation and hyperbole connected with the tycoon, there was, nevertheless, little doubt that he was a very powerful, very wealthy and very well-connected man. But most importantly, in terms of this study, since 1917 and the death of his father-in-law, Harrison Gray Otis, he had also been the owner of the region's most influential newspaper, the *Los Angeles Times*. Chandler used his mouthpiece, *Times* editor Kyle Palmer, to, quite naturally, further his own interests, and they were essentially simple: to protect and expand his empire, and to realize his vision of what L.A. should be and become. As one commentator would later put it: "Working in tandem, Harry Chandler and his father-in-law, Harrison Gray Otis, nurtured a union-busting, water-rustling, fortune-making enterprise, never shying from wielding their mighty creation, the *Los Angeles Times*, as a tool to shape L.A."[18]

In the early 1920s Harry Chandler's business empire seemed to grow in lockstep with the apparently unstoppable expansion of the metropolis. In an effort to protect his fortune, the tycoon also developed political ambitions. Using the considerable advantage of owning the region's leading newspaper, the *Los Angeles Times*, Chandler became Southern California's political kingmaker. He also became a central player in the evolution of the city's organized criminal network—if not in his own right, then certainly through the accusations and publicity his newspaper gave to it.

This connection had begun in earnest when, in 1921, Chandler had thrown his considerable influence and funds behind the election to the mayorship of a former Los Angeles County district attorney. George Edward Cryer was a reformer of proven credentials. This was an image that was reinforced by his scholarly, ascetic and earnest looks, which were reminiscent to many of a youthful Woodrow Wilson. Suitably, given the appearance and platform of the challenging candidate, the tone of the election was set, with the *Times* promising Cryer would close "the dens of vice." What was more, it was the *Times* that assured the public that Cryer would not play politics, but govern "quietly, effectively, efficiently."

Alongside this, the paper set about attacking the incumbent mayor, a previous darling of organized labor, Meredith "Pinky" Snyder, for corruption and his abject failure to tackle the city's endemic vice.[19] Arguably that was not the real reason behind the *Times'*—and Chandler's—objections to the mayor. In reality, the animosity focused on the mayor's increasingly vocal support for the public ownership of utilities. This was very much against Chandler's interests. The owner of the *Times* drew much of his fortune from a deal that had arguably swindled landowners in the Owens Valley out their water rights. Chandler then effectively turned their fertile region into a desert by shipping that water to regions he and his cronies developed; they could then charge residents for the vital water for these former deserts.

The campaign against Snyder was successful. While Cryer only managed to narrowly squeak into City Hall, he consolidated his position to the extent that he was able to remain there until 1929. Like the then mayor of Chicago, Big Bill Thompson, he in great measure achieved this by gaining the backing of a rather peculiar and outwardly contradictory coalition of interests and seemingly mutually exclusive backers. Spearheaded by the *Times*, Cryer also claimed the support of both the super-patriotic, bitterly anti-union Better America Federation, and at the same time drew in the unions through the local Central Labor Council. Similarly, Cryer had the votes of the local Anti-Saloon League as well as the most influential and powerful local bootleggers. He also included powerful local ministers and leaders of the black community as well as a variety of others in this rather unwieldy alliance of interests.

However, there was one fundamental difference between Thompson and Cryer. It was not Cryer's charisma, eloquence or charm that had welded together these disparate electorates. For while Chandler gave Cryer the voice, his strategy was put together by his other important asset, Kent Kane Parrot, and it was he who would emerge as the leader of the bloc that later formed in opposition to Chandler. In spite of having such an unfortunate name—which, in order to defuse its comic potential, he and his friends insisted should be pronounced "Perrot"—Parrot was a shrewd and Machiavellian maneuverer. Throughout Cryer's time in office he was essentially the power behind the mayor's throne.

Initially the ambitious lawyer was simply another Chandler placeman—but as his CV seemed to indicate, this was not a man who would stay a lackey. Parrot was also a former SoCal football star, husband of the future author of children's classic *My Friend Flicka*, and the rising star on the progressive wing of Republican L.A. politics. Parrot would first act as Cryer's campaign organizer, then once he was in office he became his political advisor, and finally he essentially developed into his "Svengali."

However, no sooner had Cryer tasted triumph in the 1921 election and gained City Hall than his campaign manager began to show a real mind of his own. Almost immediately he demonstrated that he was guided by his own needs not those of their rather invisible ally at the *Times*—Chandler. Pretty quickly, Parrot started to flex that considerable political muscle that had enabled the unlikely coalition. He started dictating appointments that were not necessarily in the interests of, or sanctioned by, his political paymasters. To Chandler and Cryer, these were way outside his purview. Perhaps more importantly, they realized that their opposition may very quickly pick up on the fact that they were also outside the law.

These activities first began to be hinted at when Parrot tried to have himself appointed Harbor Board attorney, a move that he made, according to his enemies, in order to steer auditors away from his own corruption. He then went on to make sure that his own LAPD bagman, Captain Lee Heath, was protected, and was enabled to collect the dues Parrot raked in with the minimum of interruption. The sums that Heath collected were soon large enough to attract the attention of his superiors, who either felt cut out of the take, or simply annoyed by Parrot's patent disregard for procedure—even if that was being applied to what were by then well-established pathways of corruption.

Either way, when the incumbent chief of police, Louis D. Oaks, started showing signs of interest in Heath's activities, neither Heath nor Parrot even bothered to deny the accusations. They simply pulled rank. Parrot just made sure that Cryer fired Oaks. He then promoted his protégé Heath to the vacancy, showing to both his bosses a worrying and ruthlessness streak that complemented that well-developed contempt for procedure. Perhaps more worrying to outside observers was that both of these actions were so obviously and blatantly way beyond his official concern. Further, each had a whiff of empire building about them, but the *Times*, embroiled as it now was with the Cryer regime, chose to ignore them until after the 1923 municipal elections.

Both Chandler and Parrot shared a more important agenda, and that was—as so often with Chandler—centered on anti-radicalism. The increasingly fractious pair were united in opposing a potentially mutually devastating strike. On the city's waterfront the anarcho-syndicalist Industrial Workers of the World had organized a particularly effective strike. This temporarily reunited the triumvirate. The strike threatened the very essence of the Chandler empire while also playing into the hands of those Cryer had condemned in order to gain office in the first place, as well as threatening Parrot's lucrative waterfront racket. Further, since Parrot and Cryer were still fundamentally sharing Chandler's anti-union stance, it made sense to simply sideline the potential problem areas of Parrot's self-interest and concentrate on excluding what would undoubtedly be a more pro-labor mayor from City Hall. United, they broke the strike.

But predictably, after Cryer's second victory in 1923, Parrot's allegiances changed and the fracture in the relationship with Chandler became increasingly more likely. A month after Cryer's re-election, at the end of July 1923, the *Times* shifted to become actively hostile to City Hall. It ran a series of articles that not only accused Parrot of being a corrupt megalomaniac, but also cited clear examples of his involvement with leading underworld figures. From this point onwards the *Times* never missed an opportunity to refer to "City Hall Gang" and the "Parrot Machine" as well as always calling Parrot "Boss Parrot" and referring to Mayor Cryer as "Parrot's Puppet." Through this language Chandler sought to bring up ideas redolent of Tammany Hall–style corruption and the toadies of city bosses.[20] The association with the underworld of organized crime was as obvious as it was ubiquitous.

When Parrot retaliated and made his views on municipal ownership of utilities more prevalent in the runup to the 1925 election, the rhetoric in the *Times* became even more hostile. A considerable part of Chandler's fortune came from his stake in the Owens Valley aqueduct, which supplied the lion's share of Los Angeles's water. When Parrot came out in support of the proposed publicly owned Boulder Dam scheme, Chandler knew this control would be severely challenged. Unsurprisingly, he stepped up the campaign against Parrot, and once again the accusations, or perhaps revelations, of connections with organized crime played a central role.

## Tinsel Town's Underworld

The power of the press to make accusations about politicians' connections with the underworld was never far from the surface in any major American city in the 1920s and 1930s. As this study has demonstrated, New York and Chicago were perhaps epicenters of such accusations, but St. Louis, Philadelphia, Cleveland, Atlantic City, Boston, Baltimore, Detroit, Galveston, and most other sizeable cities had their politico-mobster connections. Boo-Boo Hoff, Abe Berstein, John Lazia, Nucky Johnson, Jonny Jack Nounes and others all needed "protection" in the police department, the press and City Hall. Arguably, however, in Tinsel Town, it was most celebrated and most blatant. Only in L.A. did the depiction of scandal, crime and even murder become an industry. Only in "La-La Land" could organized crime make the careers of those who committed crime in make believe.

This environment seemed to have an effect on the nature of organized crime in the city—or at least the way in which it was portrayed. In the municipal primary election campaign of 1925, the *Times* came out swinging with accusations about the "Parrot-Kinney [the mayoral secretary and Parrot crony]-Cryer Machine." The paper led a campaign focused on the "danger of the Farmer Pages [Milton "Farmer" Page was a notorious local "gambling hell" owner], the bootleggers, the confidence men and others of this vicious ilk dominating the administration of Los Angeles."[21] Sometime later the *Times* would flesh out these accusations, but at this point it was largely insinuation.

The paper argued that Parrot used his control of the LAPD to benefit a coalition of bootleggers, gamblers and pimps. The *Times* argued the LAPD's direct connection with the bootleggers enabled them to regulate the trade in the favor of their bootlegger-paymasters. They could also use their position to contain and harass competitors of those whom they represented. The LAPD would prosecute the leading bootlegger, the flamboyant and outspoken young dandy Tony "The Hat" Cornero, at every given opportunity.

In the days of the Chandler-Cryer alliance, Cornero had become "the wealthiest bootlegger on the Pacific Coast," having moved down from his native San Francisco to the more promising territory of L.A. before the Volstead Act. But, by early 1926, he was complaining that police harassment was costing him $500,000 a year in lost business. This may well be true. For an example of the techniques the LAPD used, Chandler's now overtly anti–Cryer-Parrot *Los Angeles Times* pointed to the actions of what he argued were the Parrot-controlled LAPD on a single night in April 1926.

While stopped in their "large touring car" at a traffic light, Cornero's brother Frank and his passengers were all arrested and charged with having committed a suspected robbery. As Frank was being booked, his sister Catherine was brought in and charged with running an unlicensed nightclub. Both were subsequently released and all charges dropped, but not until they were thoroughly humiliated by the LAPD. Tony Cornero would later express outrage over the incident. The arrests of his family were bad enough, but the events were made particularly egregious since, as he explained, he'd paid $100,000 towards Cryer's 1923 campaign and a further $100,000 since in bribes directly to the LAPD.[22]

By contrast, it was possible to find examples of where the Parrot allies had been favored. Those opposed to City Hall were quick to show that Milton "Farmer" Page—one of the leading lights in the "L.A. System" of local gang lords—was acquitted of malicious involvement in a shoot-out with other gangsters. To Parrot's opponents, the whole thing smelled very suspicious. There was little doubt in the minds of his political—and underworld—opponents that Parrot's former mentor, Judge Gavin Craig, who was presiding over the case, had been acting in the interests of the alliance between the leading underworld vice bosses and the political boss.

Page's acquittal was seen as proof of the operation of a more-or-less formal organization, known as "The Combination," which supposedly linked the "City Hall Gang" with allies in the underworld who funded much of City Hall's campaigning in return for protection and freedom to operate. Further evidence of the "Combination" was implied by reports that LAPD squad cars were usually seen quietly leaving Page-owned casinos just prior to law-enforcement raids. No doubt they were removing incriminating evidence before the same boys in blue rushed back, sirens blaring, to make a show of looking for the items that they had just taken away.

There was also the time that the pimp Albert Marco, another alleged and senior member of the shadowy coalition, was arrested for pistol-whipping a police officer. The inexperienced young policeman had pressed for the "Tsar of Vice" to be put on a charge of assault with a deadly weapon. However, after the intervention of two more "experienced" detectives, the charges were subsequently reduced to "disturbing the peace." This was particularly suspicious because, since Marco was a non-citizen, his possession of a pistol on its own was a felony offense. What was more, the revised charge completely ignored the extraordinarily violent and lawless nature of the assault he carried out on a uniformed officer of the law.

These were but nothing compared with the most lucrative and potentially damning of the connections drawn between Parrot and the underworld. These largely focused on the upbeat, charming, rather incongruously effeminate lord of L.A. vice, "Sunshine" Charlie Crawford.[23] A veteran of the Klondike gold rush, Charlie had made his first foray into vice in the jumpoff point for Alaska: the rough and ready emerging capital of the Northwest, Seattle. Yet, even with the massive numbers of gullible fortune seekers ready to part with their money, Charlie's ventures there had not been a great success. Crawford had been too blatant in his bribes—even for a frontier town like Seattle. But the experience had set him up with a useful connection. While in the Northwest, Crawford had met and formed a working relationship with the pimp, Albert Marco.

The pair came into their own during Prohibition when Charlie—who had previously moved to L.A.—used Marco as a conduit for shipping British Columbian booze south. With the support of Parrot and his cronies in the LAPD, Crawford quickly gained the pole position in the city's bootlegging. What was more, with the money that the sophisticated operation provided, he then set about forming a crime cartel that ruled vice in L.A. throughout the 1920s by forming close links with City Hall and the LAPD and using them to provide an *almost* impenetrable—if expensive—carapace that bootleggers and mobsters in other regions of the country could only dream of.

Marco joined Charlie in L.A., and between them the pair ran, or had oversight of, the lion's share of the city's booming prostitution business. With this angle of vice covered, Crawford now brought in the "slot machine kings," the brothers Robert and Joseph Gans. He added the teetotal family man Ezekiel "Zeke" Caress to run bookmaking as well as the cartel's bookkeeping. As blatant as he had been in Seattle, Crawford was hardly less circumspect in L.A. He used uniformed LAPD officers, driven in LAPD squad cars, under the gaze of their fellow policemen, to provide protection and supervise the collection of income by other uniformed officers. Most notable of these were the gangly and supremely corrupt Guy "Stringbean" McAfee and Thompson machine gun–wielding Richard "Dirty Dick" Lucas.[24]

Reaching the height of his influence in early 1928, Crawford was outed by the *Examiner* as "the city's outstanding underworld boss."[25] Yet even with his connections in City Hall, Crawford's supremacy was essentially unsustainable. The virtual monopoly and the exclusive protection by the LAPD on which that authority was founded could only last as long as the police were in the pocket of his partner, Parrot. That, in turn, was conditional on the boss's remaining capable of controlling elected officials and staving off what had become a constant sniping from Harry Chandler in the *Los Angeles Times*.

Sure enough, by 1929 the situation in L.A. was changing, and Parrot's carefully crafted alliances were coming apart. The first sign of the decline of the "Combination" was apparent when Parrot lost his tame district attorney, Asa Keyes—the man who had failed to convict the two Texan lawyers at the Julian Pete trial. Keyes fell prey to a reformist urge, sponsored in large measure by Harry Chandler's anti–Parrot *Times*. Chandler had hated Keyes ever since the DA had threatened to expose the reality of those in on the scam, and Keyes was convinced that Chandler was one of the leading figures.

What really aggravated Chandler was that whatever information Keyes chose to expose would have a damaging impact. Even if Keyes couldn't prove that the tycoon himself had been in on the scheme, many of Chandler's cronies had made vast profits from the "Julian Pete" scam, and it would not do to have them ruffled. The diffident and ineffectual Keyes had challenged the wrong man. Chandler was as vindictive and willing to play dirty as he was greedy. The *Times* delighted in passing on the details of a secret grand jury's discovery that Keyes had apparently taken not just $100,000 in cash, but two cars, as well as a set of monogrammed golf clubs, a chaise longue, and a watch as payment in order to get him to throw the case.

Pleading his innocence, Keyes argued not only had he not had that money, but that the problem with the trial lay with the court system itself. He reasoned that the case was far too technical in its financial twists and turns to have been tried in a normal court. He maintained that the evidence presented to the jury in the 1927 case had just been too complex to be offered in a form that could be explained to, and understood by, a non-specialist jury. This had rendered him incapable of securing a conviction. The judge at the Grand Jury hearing two years later was unconvinced by this explanation, and Keyes became prisoner 48218 in San Quentin.

All the time Keyes was in prison, the Chandler machine argued that Keyes had always been "a crook of the first water." It put out stories that the DA had been involved in perverting the course of justice throughout his career. When he tried to appeal his conviction, the *Los Angeles Times* linked him with one of the most infamous murders of the 1920s, the unsolved killing of the gay film director Desmond Taylor. Taylor had been shot dead in his Hollywood bungalow in 1922, and no one had been convicted of the crime. The *Times*, with the national press following suit, kept up a stream of exposés, based on undisclosed evidence. They claimed that Keyes had been bought off to protect the identity of the "mystery woman" or the "narcotic ring" who'd allegedly killed Taylor.[26] The result was that Keyes served two years, and on his release died a broken man in 1934, still professing his innocence and arguing he was yet another victim of the sinister and secret machinations of Chandler.

## Two Gun Davis

Whichever way one views it, the comeuppance or human tragedy of Asa Keyes had major political fallout for Parrot and huge implications for organized crime in L.A. His network of mob connections started to unravel. The "boss" next lost his man in City Hall. In a backlash, fueled in large measure by the *Times'* accusations of criminal connections in the mayor's office, L.A. underwent something of a religiously-based witch hunt. Mayor Cryer was replaced by the jury foreman in the Keyes conviction, John Clinton Porter. A rabidly anti–Catholic, anti–Semitic Klansman, Porter was part of a reform movement spearheaded by a former member of Parrot's coalition, the Southern Methodist preacher, "Fighting" Bob Shuler.

Shuler was a fire-and-brimstone preacher who, in keeping with his stance as an outspoken supporter of the revivified Ku Klux Klan, attacked Jews, blacks and libertines with equal venom. Dubbed "Savonarola" by H.L. Mencken's *American Mercury*, after the apocalyptic 15th-century Florentine friar, Shuler ranted from the pulpit to his 9,000-strong congregation. In the process he shouted his lavish support for Porter. Shuler was essentially an intolerant demagogue, but in these troubled times he had a huge following. What was more, those who couldn't attend his church could join the hundreds of thousands tuning in to his radio show, which also declared for Porter. The preacher's message rang out loudly in synch with the increasingly anti-corruption and moralistic mood, as he never overlooked a chance to draw the connections between Cryer, Parrot and the underworld.[27]

By the time the election actually came around, the change in atmosphere was so all-pervasive that Cryer decided not to run. Porter was not Chandler's choice for mayor, but he may as well have been, since with Cryer gone, Parrot's power evaporated and what remained of the Combination unraveled. However, as with so much connected with organized crime in L.A., the regime in power in the police department was crucial. Once he was able to wield any power, Porter took an even more hands-on approach to the running of the LAPD than the Cryer-Parrot regime.

On coming to office, Porter moved the police chief's office into City Hall. He then installed a buzzer to summon the head of the LAPD to his own office—which he did all too frequently. He would berate LAPD chief James E. "Two Gun" Davis over the city's "upward crime curve," and told him the solution lay in "cleaning up" the LAPD. He instigated his cleanup and hired a former LAPD detective to head up a team of "super-snoopers." The ominously titled Efficiency and Personnel Committee was an internal investigation charged to carry out permanent surveillance within and on the department itself. Such a tight reign proved too much for the incumbent police chief. After sixteen months under this new regime, Davis resigned, as Porter knew he would. Davis then accepted the post as head of the Traffic Division and was replaced by his deputy assistant, Roy Edmund "Strongarm Dick" Steckel. Chandler's initial approval was registered in the *Times*.[28]

Davis's tolerance of Crawford and his hatred of Reds had made him a compromise candidate at the time of his appointment. His removal, and the control of the LAPD by a reforming City Hall dictated to by a populist, moralist and dictatorial preacher, were potentially even more damaging to Chandler than the *status quo ante*. Chandler knew this, and it did not take long before he started to become hostile to the new police chief. By November 1930, the *Times* was calling Steckel a "yes-man" who "made no protest, presumably realizing he would lose his job if he did."[29] He now started to defend Davis, preaching that his removal would give "notice to the racketeers, crooks, grafters and underworld generally that the police department of this city is leaderless and likely to remain so for an indefinite period."[30] The reality was a slight variation on that picture, but it required a change of leadership in the underworld, not the police force.

The final nail in the coffin of the Combination came when Charlie Crawford and the editor of a friendly journal were shot dead on May 20, 1931. A "mob-hunting," suave and successful former deputy district attorney, "Debonair Dave" Clark, confessed to the murder. The celebrated case played out in a courtroom drama worthy of any Hollywood film—and indeed, the events sparked *noir* writers to use it as a starting point for a variety of novels. While he never denied shooting the gangster, Clark argued it was carried out in self-defense. He also exposed the fact that he had been blackmailed by Crawford for some years. After a heated discussion over the lawyer's threat to expose the gang lord's involvement in corrupt deals with the LAPD and other lawyers, Crawford had threatened him with a gun, but Clark had shot first.

Rather unsurprisingly, it all went back to accusations of Crawford's involvement in the ubiquitous Julian Pete scam, but things got nasty when the mobster tried to persuade Clark to double-cross LAPD chief Steckel, a close friend of the lawyer's. When Crawford drew the gun, and his companion blocked Clark's way out, Clark had shot the two in self-defense, and his legal team played up his courageous loyalty to the "reformer" of the LAPD, Chief Steckel. The jury could not reach a verdict. After 15 counts, they were still eleven to one. After a second trial, Clark was acquitted of all charges, and Shuler and the *Times* rejoiced at the death of the gang lord.

While Crawford's murder seemed to benefit Chandler and the reformers in City Hall in that it would perhaps clean up the city, in fact the collapse of the Combination was not good news for the policing of L.A. Criminal enterprises that had been concentrated in one set of hands were now up for grabs. The price of bootleg booze dropped like a stone, reducing by as much as two-thirds in a matter of weeks, as new sources and new bootleggers entered a wide-open market. Lacking protection from City Hall in the courts, and the LAPD on the streets, the dominance of the Combination was very soon challenged. Turf wars broke out and even the leading members of the "System" suffered personal attacks.

In December 1930, Zeke Caress, his wife Helen and their chauffer were kidnapped. They were freed on a ransom of $50,000—after Zeke, ever the accountant, had beaten the kidnappers down from $100,000.[31] Next it was the turn of Combination "slot-machine king" Robert Gans. Gans was held up with fifteen of his employees at gunpoint after he walked into his own shop. One of his employees was shot as the robbers had spooked and shot, wildly. The raid netted a mere $1200, a figure hardly worth talking about when it is considered what Gans was making.[32]

## The Combination

Even though he seemed to have broken organized crime in L.A., Porter lost the 1932 election. Some argue this was the result of his Republican roots, at a time when the Grand

Old Party was out of favor. Others blame his Hoover-type utterances that the downturn in the economy was only temporary when over time it continued to get increasingly worse.[33] Others see it as the simple result of a desire for a change from the reformist rhetoric.[34] Those interested in organized crime would claim it was connected with the steep rise in criminal activity, and the abject failure of the reformist regime to do anything but make it worse.[35] It appeared that the Combination's demise had led to chaos in the underworld and there was talk of L.A.'s descending to the levels of violence created by organized crime in Chicago or Philadelphia—especially in the Porter-hostile *Times*.[36]

Whatever the real cause, Davis was reinstated, ostensibly as a peace offering to the all-powerful Chandler, by the incoming mayor Frank Shaw. A New Dealer who talked about putting utilities under public ownership, Shaw also drew support from organized labor: he was not a natural ally of Chandler's. Davis's anti-labor credentials could go some way to smooth over these traits in the oligarch's eyes. Nevertheless, the situation was volatile, and there is little doubt that Shaw's dreadful reputation for being tangled up with the mob owes something the inevitable breakdown in relations between the tycoon and the mayor.

Shaw would be the first mayor in the U.S. to be voted from office by popular dismissal. Davis and twenty-two other senior police would follow him into the wilderness. With the reform bit firmly clamped in their mouths, the regime of Fletcher Bowron that replaced Shaw did not hold back on portraying both Shaw's City Hall and Davis's LAPD as corrupt, venal and ineffective, and picturing themselves as the only truly effective reformers capable of changing the situation. That portrayal has largely become accepted as fact. It has given a dynamism to L.A. organized crime by providing a watershed moment in City Hall corruption that in turn feeds a unique romanticism.

This sleazy, macho, self-serving, cynical inefficiency has colored the L.A. crimescape, the LAPD and L.A. organized crime in the way it has been portrayed in classic noir literature from Dashiell Hammett to James Ellroy, and films from *The Maltese Falcon* (1931) to *Gangster Squad* (2013). From these vivid and hard-boiled yet distinctly romantic roots, this picture of the "mean streets" has entered the traditional view of LA's underworld in the 1920s, 1930s and into the 1940s. That depiction of the events characterized and cemented by Shaw's demise rather inflexibly persists in a similar style to tales of the ubiquitous Mafia and Capone's unchallenged dominance of gangland Chicago.[37]

As with much in history—and especially in the history of a subject as shadowy, mired in controversy and misconception, and generally popular as organized crime—this version of events is open to reinterpretation. Shaw's successor was determined he would be seen in history as a reformer, especially with regard to the disgraced LAPD and, through them, the thorny issue of organized crime. In this he has been remarkably successful. His ousting of Davis, and most other leading figures in the department, was and largely *is* still, seen as a cleansing. The Bowron administration has been portrayed as having removed the last remnants of the Combination and in the process cleaned up the city's underworld.

In the wake of the demise of Parrot and Crawford, the old underworld monopoly had stumbled on briefly under the ex-cop Guy McAfee, and then had fragmented. However, the story went that once Frank Shaw got into office, these disparate elements had been increasingly managed and milked by City Hall. It was apparently the mayor's supremely corrupt brother, Joseph "Sailor Joe" Shaw, who controlled this process. According to the most prevalent interpretation, he set himself up as the administrator of the

City Hall favor bank. As Frank Shaw's secretary and the gateway to the mayor, Joe would reward those who toed the party line in ways that, it was alleged, went beyond methods used in City Hall even in the Parrot days.

The accusations were varied. He sold exam questions to policemen and firemen, which not only netted income, but also served to keep them in his pocket, for fear that he might disclose how they gained their posts. For those too dumb to benefit from this, he would even alter exam scores to ensure a preponderance of lackeys. Those who helped him in other ways would often be rewarded with jobs—frequently in what became the bloated Department of Water and Power. Nor did the accusations end there; it was claimed that he would help party donors in their business lives—notoriously being accused of condemning the products of the competitor of one poultry-producing supporter. He was also accused, personally, of giving bribes to members of the school board and was said to have personal contacts with the underworld. All of the accusations are largely based on hearsay, rumor or the allegations of political foes or those already implicated in graft, like former Mayor Porter, and of course the *Times*.[38]

His enemies found even more fertile ground in the relations of City Hall and the underworld. The Shaw regime continued the operation of what were essentially Open City policies that had dominated the city's netherworld since the turn of the century. Having taken the support of those bookmakers, madams and other moral criminals infuriated by the day-to-day harassment of the Porter regime, City Hall essentially tolerated vice almost by default. Under Davis—overseen by Sailor Joe—the LAPD was allowed to continue its usual lax policies of enforcement and its own versions of racketeering, while the city administration stalled the anti-vice legislation proposed by moralists from pretty nearly entering City Hall until December 1937.

As one very well-informed commentator has put it, throughout the 1930s, seemingly with the support of the majority of the city's voters, City Hall chose to treat vice "as a business enterprise and [consequently] extracted funds for election campaigns from underworld figures in return for allowing vice interests to provide these services to their customers.... Any attempt to eradicate these operations would call for more policemen, more courts, and more jails at a time when revenues were declining and other priorities, such as jobs and relief payments, were considered to be more important to Shaw. As an overall policy, Shaw decided to keep city government out of its citizens' bedrooms and amusement centers, and to let them choose their own pastimes."[39] Given this commitment to what appears to modern readers a genuine open-city policy, using the cloak of reform it was possible to attack the Shaw regime as linked with organized crime. It was a tried and tested policy that had been used with great effect against Thompson in Chicago and Walker in New York, and these instances proved it was a supremely effective tool if used correctly.

Yet just as it is possible to challenge orthodox opinion with the regard to Chicago and New York, it is equally possible in to put forward another view in the case of L.A. At the most basic level, some of those who see organized crime as ubiquitous and monolithic have put forward an argument that at least Los Angeles organized crime managed to avoid becoming syndicated. They argue that the Los Angeles underworld maintained its independence from, and avoided being sucked into, what was at the time the vastly expanding and significantly more brutal nationalized "mob." This rather optimistic view is upheld by the comments of what is perhaps the Holy Grail of such opinion, the 1951 Kefauver Committee. That august body approvingly commented on how L.A. remained relatively "Mafia"-free, with consequently less organized criminal violence and mayhem than Chicago or New York for the majority of the 1920s and 1930s.[40]

This is backed up in the canon of mythology that centers around the "Mafia" interpretation of organized crime. In 1927 Capone arrived on a "fact-finding mission" in L.A. After a week of scouting around to see the possibilities the city offered for his Outfit, he was essentially scared off by a posse of LAPD. The *Los Angeles Daily News* scooped the story and, bragging that the city's police had proved too much for the Eastern gangster, ran the headline in block capitals: CAPONE TOLD TO BLOW; GANG CHIEF ROUSTED. Those who hold with the nationwide organization of crime theory see this as delaying the syndication of organized crime in L.A. They would point to the "fact" that two years later at Atlantic City, where Mafia orthodoxy puts the initial meeting of the big Mob players, Los Angeles has no presence. This is considered strange, since far less populous and wealthy cities like Cleveland, Kansas City and Philadelphia sent their own delegates.

However, assuming that the tale is even true and Capone really did scope out the opportunities in L.A., the cause of his retreat is still open to a considerable variety of different interpretations. The *Daily News*'s leading columnist, Matt Weinstock, later argued that even this achievement—such as it was, at a time when the concept of the "Mafia" did not make headlines—was the result of corruption. To him it was simply the Combination protecting its own investments via the LAPD.[41] The city editor of the *Examiner* agreed. As he saw it: "The syndicate owned the police department. I knew all the boys in the syndicate. They had been around a long time, and they really had the town organized. They had it so well organized that when Scarface Al Capone came out from Chicago to look the field over with the thought of taking charge himself, he was rousted out of his hotel room and put on a train back to Chicago. And the boys who did the rousting and who told him to get out and stay out were the cops owned body and soul by the syndicate."[42]

As Weinstock eloquently put it, it was just the best way of ensuring that those "with the biggest manure pile in the village" remained in charge. He saw nothing to differentiate the Shaw regime from the Bowron regime that replaced it. To him Bowron simply utilized the stink emanating from the "manure pile" more effectively than Shaw, and therefore replaced him.[43]

## L.A.'s Most Corrupt Mayor?

According to the leading Hearst columnist in Los Angeles, neither Shaw nor Bowron were truly reformers: both were actually demagogues and products of a brand of highly pragmatic *realpolitik* that American metropolitan management required. Extending and sanitizing this view, it has been argued that Shaw was simply operating a more modern form of consensus politics. Lacking a natural power base, he is said to share the same *modus operandi* as FDR meticulously crafted when he forged his New Deal coalition. Elected to office in the same year, they both operated a form of what Theodore Lowi calls "Interest Group Liberalism." This is a natural, tolerant and matter-of-fact offshoot of Progressivism by which "any group representing anything at all, is dealt with and judged according the political resources it brings to the table and not for the moral or rationalist strength of its interest."[44]

This pragmatic approach essentially meant that, as with the Parrot coalition, such alliances could only be temporary. There are other similarities. Very like the situation with Parrot, as the coalition deteriorated, those opposed to the regime sought to further encourage the decay of the alliance and speed it along. One of the best ways of doing this was the already proven technique of playing the "organized crime card." It worked against Thompson in Chicago, and Walker in New York—why shouldn't it work in L.A.?

In the case of Shaw, this approach has had a far longer historical half-life, since Shaw had the dubious honor of being the first mayor to lose his post through recall. This, combined with the reputation Los Angeles had as what U.S. Attorney General Frank Murphy claimed was "one of the most corrupt and graft-ridden cities in the U.S.," has more or less sealed the reputation of Shaw. The mayor has found himself as being inextricably linked to organized crime, and made those who ousted him, by default, are reformers.[45] There is an alternative view, and analysis of it is constructive in terms of attitudes to organized crime.

The start point for such an argument should be what Shaw claimed he wanted to achieve. An ardent supporter of FDR and committed New Dealer, Shaw pushed through legislative programs that included the completion of municipal utilities by 1937, state-funded construction projects and outright support for organized labor in their fight with the open shop. Such policies inevitably brought him up against L.A.'s conservatives who, by the end his term, were given voice by both the *Examiner* and the *Times*. However, this was only one of his problems. He also succeeded in alienating many on the left upon whose support he had risen to power.

Allowing LAPD Chief Davis to exclude job-seeking migrants with his notorious "Bum Blockade" brought Shaw up against the American Civil Liberties Union (ACLU), labor leaders and other liberals. This hostility was also fed by his continuing to use the LAPD's brutal and intrusive Red Squad that had been so active under Porter. The Davis version of this anti-labor unit was even more intrusive and even more brutal. Its very existence under a mayor who touted his New Deal credentials, let alone its expansion, made him particularly hated by the left. The final straw came in 1937, when Shaw refused to pay union-level wages on Works Progress Administration projects and the Central Labor Council withdrew its support.[46]

In true L.A. style, Shaw was of course open to attack by the moral reformers. As usual, vice was one of the most important battlegrounds; after all, it was an easy target. Davis took a robustly Open City approach, and refused to police what he called the "poor man's sports" of prostitution and bookmaking. Instead he preferred to show his tough policies in targeting Reds and "Eastern gunmen." The tone was set in his first term when he had promised to "hold court on gunmen in the Los Angeles streets" and told his officers, "I want them brought in dead, not alive."[47]

All the while, when City Hall dictated the city was "closed," the LAPD continued to collect revenue from those prostitutes and gamblers who paid protection. They also managed to make themselves look busy by harassing those who did not pay them.[48] The sums were considerable. *The Hollywood Citizen-News* estimated that in 1933, when the Porter clampdown was still operative, L.A. vice generated some $2 million a month, and out of that the LAPD and a handful of journalists, as well as politicians, took 20 percent.[49]

However, in 1937, when the Citizens Independent Vice Investigating Committee (CIVIC) announced they had discovered that the city had 1800 bookmakers and 200 gambling houses, as well as 600 brothels, they gained massive popular support for their cleanup campaign. The LAPD was charged with negligence and CIVIC demanded powers to set up vigilance groups to outlaw such activity. What was overlooked was that since 1935 gambling was legal within Los Angeles. Further, prostitution by this point was a misdemeanor, not a felony, and hardly worthy of the attempts to whip up public outrage and create fears of working girls representing a "crime wave."[50]

In a city like 1930s Los Angeles it was always going to be difficult for reformers to maintain an entirely pure image. It can be argued that in claiming the moral high ground, yet trying to show the sleaziness and immorality of its opponents, the Minutemen and CIVIC were forced to use methods and associates which laid them open to accusations of being as entangled with organized crime as the Shaw regime itself. The offer of $1,000 for information leading to the arrest of a public official was an open invitation for those disaffected with not only Shaw, but also Police Chief Davis—which, it was argued, may well include ex-convicts and other criminal elements.

What is more, some of the CIVIC activists seemed to be directly connected with vice themselves. For example, CIVIC threatened to "unleash" its co-founder, the puritanical physician Dr. A.M. Wilkinson, on Santa Monica and Venice if the authorities in the suburb refused to withdraw an ordinance outlawing "Tango"—a variation introduced to subvert and avoid the ban on bingo introduced earlier in the year. Some made a connection between this out-of-character move and a "very large donation" or "loan" of $4,400 made to Wilkinson by none other than Guy McAfee to "help defray the costs of a fireworks pageant."[51]

There can be little doubt that at the very least this was a good example of poor judgment, if not actual corruption, on the part of CIVIC. But as if that was not demonstration enough, further evidence of this ineptitude emerged the following year. In 1937 the good doctor's personal assistant, William R. Coyne, started a prison sentence for six counts of theft, extortion and attempted bribery. Coyne was convicted of using Wilkinson's Federated Church Brotherhood as a front for racketeering.[52]

Perhaps political naivety and susceptibility to corruption can be expected when inexperienced zealots try to gain political office by using a single issue. But there is no doubt that the most notorious agent that CIVIC and the Minutemen used was certainly connected with the underworld. Harry Raymond, whose death would spark the real downfall of both Shaw and Davis, was a dirty ex-cop who definitely had gangster connections. He had been fired from both the Venice and San Diego Police Departments for extortion, and he was almost certainly trying to blackmail members of the LAPD at the time of his death. There is also reason to suspect that Raymond had close connections with Eastern gangsters like Bugsy Siegel and played a role in their infiltration of Los Angeles.

On the other hand, there was certainly an element of exaggeration about the nature of the underworld deals made by the Shaw regime. The fact that former vice squad officer turned "vice Tsar" Guy McAfee and "slot machine king" Bob Gans gave $15,000 to the Shaw campaign was not illegal. As Assistant U.S. Attorney Hugh Dickenson ruled: "Any citizen, including a gambler, may contribute to [political] campaign funds."[53] It has been argued that those accused of being "underworld bosses" were not always as murky as the reformers painted them. The anti–Shaw Municipal League was forced to admit that McAfee made most of his money as a legitimate bail bondsman, as did Gans. Both were also seen as philanthropists and had considerable standing in their communities. What was more, and probably most infuriating to the reformers, with City Hall protection they conducted most of their activities in the open.[54]

It was Raymond Chandler, the ultimate chronicler of L.A.'s seamier side, who had one of his characters sum up the situation. To him even the most honest and genuine reformers had targeted the wrong elements in L.A. society. As he saw it, simple, knee-jerk solutions rarely worked because: "We [in L.A.] don't have mobs and crime syndicates and goon squads because we have crooked politicians and their stooges in City Hall and the legislatures. Crime isn't a disease, it's a symptom.... We're a big, rough, rich wild people and crime is the price we pay for it, and organized crime is the price we pay for organization. We'll have it with us a long time. Organized crime is just the dirty side of the sharp dollar."[55] He could have added that in LA the more dollars someone owned, the more that dirty side came out. He also could have said that the more they had, the more they seemed willing to use those dollars to put down those who stood in the way of their making even more dollars. It seemed that in turn, linking those enemies to organized crime was one of the most effective ways of putting down those opponents.

# 6

## Prohibition

### The Cradle of Organized Crime?

Many commentators do not find it difficult to understand the origins of organized crime in America. To them, they are not really that complex. A vast array of books, magazine articles, Internet sites, films, television shows and other sources have explained the history and origins of the phenomenon. They explain why gangsterism thrived and expanded as America modernized in the three quarters of a century following the Civil War. These sources have repeatedly told of the evolution of the Mafia families from their simple roots among Sicilian immigrants in New York and New Orleans. They describe how these men became warring bosses, but saved themselves from mutual destruction by evolving systems of cooperation and shared organizational structures that enabled them to coexist, regulate trade and expand triumphantly across the nation.

Other interpreters explain how it was that Irish and Jewish backstreet hoodlums made massive fortunes and carved out empires that permitted them to take control, among other things, of the fleshpots of Havana, Hollywood and Las Vegas. Some detail how organized American crime prospered as a result of agreements made between corrupt police, lawyers, and municipal as well as national governments on the one hand, and ruthless crime lords on the other. Organized crime was, in these accounts, one of the many less desirable results of the age. It was a side effect of mass immigration, industrialization and the rise of urban America in the last decades of the nineteenth century and the first half of the twentieth. It was the downside of America's laissez-faire capitalism and an unpredicted result of participatory democracy.

As usual with simple explanations in history, these accounts are, at best, selective. While much of the material they contain is irrefutable, and many of the conclusions they reach are eminently sensible, they do not give the full picture—if that is ever possible in history. They are open to reinterpretation, and several scholars have undertaken to re-evaluate them, offering more sophisticated, sensitive, complex, and ultimately satisfying analysis.

For example, Timothy Gilfoyle has shown how the ties between vice, political corruption and immigration—while undeniably pervasive and intrinsic to the successful operation of criminal networks—are also far more subtle in their contribution to the growth of organized crime in New York over these years.[1] Jeffrey Adler finds that the Italian district in Chicago did have a higher than average homicide rate. But he argues that it was due more to individual circumstances within the Italian communities, rather than any inherent or inherited propensity to form themselves into secret and violent societies.[2] In a variety of contexts, including the Italians in early 20th-century New York, Federico Varese has shown that organized crime is usually reluctant to expand beyond its homeland, and often fails when it attempts to do so.[3]

Perhaps most significantly, Michael Woodiwiss has disputed the simplistic approaches by broadening the parameters of what constitutes organized crime. He sees the debates over the origins of organized crime as inherently flawed by a pervasive belief that it is in the interests of various elite groups—both legitimate and criminal—to keep any definition narrowly focused within the considerations of the dominant Mafia-style organizations of the popular imagination.[4]

To illustrate more clearly the manner in which the attitudes toward the history of organized crime have altered over these years, perhaps it is constructive to take one of what has been seen as the "givens" of the subject—the impact of the prohibition of alcohol and its centrality to the emergence of the modern "mob." In examining this, there are some elements that are undeniable, verifiable, historical facts. On the other hand, there are some which open to re-evaluation, either because of new information, or simply radical reappraisal of existing research. But there are other features of the accepted history that it is difficult to see as anything less than the result of deliberate misinformation and/or the product of simple prejudice.

It is an incontestable fact that the nationwide prohibition on the manufacture, sale or transport of intoxicating liquor came into law in full on January 16, 1920, under the provisions of the Eighteenth Amendment, enabled by the Volstead Act. Further, it is a fact that in many ways this enforced puritanism and its subversion can be seen as the backdrop for the decade. It is certainly true that it had a huge impact on the population as a whole, and equally certain that for many, then and now, this influence was associated with crime.

What is more, there is no doubt that during the years until the repeal of Prohibition in 1933, huge numbers of Americans and others knowingly broke the "Dry" laws. It is equally true that many made illegal fortunes. The records show that thousands of American residents were prosecuted and imprisoned. Some of those criminals, along with bystanders, were injured and were killed—or injured and killed others—as a direct result of contravening the legislation. But what is less certain is the impact of this legislation on the phenomenon of organized crime. With this uncertainty comes opportunity: an opportunity to use Prohibition as a tool to examine not only the roots and motors of organized crime in America, but what actually constitutes "organized crime," who perpetrated it, and why it has been depicted the way it has been depicted—then and since.

## A Nation on the Take

While it is undeniable that Prohibition had a major influence on organized crime, it is less easy to define with absolute certainty *what* that influence was, or *who* composed the organizations upon which the legislation most clearly singled out as criminals. The usual picture of organized crime inspired by this period is one of rum-runners, bootleggers and other gangsters bribing, fighting with and eluding corrupt police, Prohibition agents and politicians. These gangsters are equipped with fast cars with running boards, tommy guns, Brooklyn, Chicago or New Jersey accents, sassy and brassy molls, and call each other by outlandish nicknames.

The Prohibition gangsters are universally brutal and violent. They are usually from one or another of the main immigrant groups of the time—more often than not Italian or Jewish. Similarly, the corrupt officials and police are collectively smarmy, fast-talking, just as brutal—and almost all either first- or second-generation Irish. Although founded in truth, such generalizations have essentially been turned over the years into a series of caricatures that in their dominance of the historical literature and imagery skew and stunt the causality and historical debate surrounding the nature of organized crime in these years and those that followed.[5]

Even when the dry laws were in force, Americans at all levels of society questioned their real efficacy and their impact on reforming lawlessness in U.S. society. According to many expert commentators, it appeared that the country was being overrun by a "crime wave." For example, in 1926, Judge Alfred J. Talley appeared at the Senate's National Prohibition Law Hearings to give his impression of the success of the policy. A famous conservative and advocate of Prohibition, Talley told a Senate subcommittee that like most of the country's largest cities, it appeared that New York City was in the grip of a huge surge in criminal activity. He went on to detail statistics that illustrated a massive increase in drunkenness, violence, and most worryingly, homicide. What was more, this was a phenomenon that the forces of law and order appeared powerless to control. He argued, "[T]he conclusion is irresistible, examining these figures, that the increase of crimes of violence or passion, the increase of intoxication, the breakdown of the administration of the law, can be traced primarily to the disrespect for law which has been engendered in the minds of young and old, of high and low, especially by the operation of this prohibition law.... I mean the Eighteenth Amendment and the enabling act that has followed it, which is called the Volstead Act."[6] Judge Talley was not unusual in his conclusions. Many of the witnesses called to the subcommittee seemed to concur—often reluctantly— with his conclusions that crime had increased as a result of Volstead, and they were as diverse a group as states' attorneys, U.S. congressmen, and representatives of the American Federation of Labor and the American Medical Association.

Perhaps the most interesting evidence, however, came from General Lincoln C. Andrews, Assistant Secretary of Customs, Coast Guard and Prohibition, and an obvious and committed supporter of Prohibition. Andrews told the committee that nearly 900 out of "about 3,600 to 3,800" men serving as federal Prohibition agents had been sacked for "crookedness or incompetency" at a time when there had barely been six "dry" years. Aware that this confession did not make him look very impressive, Andrews argued that with staff turnover, there had been a total of some 10,000 men working as agents. He claimed that this meant that the figure for dismissal was less than 10 percent of the entire number. Justifying his administration of the situation, he piously argued that such a level of corruption was acceptable since, with the betrayal of Jesus by Judas Iscariot, even the Twelve Apostles had evinced a similar rate of corruption. But as Senator James A. Reed, a leading wet Democrat from Missouri, pointed out, what made his admission all the more worrying was that this figure represented not all the agents who had been detected and prosecuted, but simply those who had been found guilty.[7]

Like many other Americans, Reed may well have suspected that the figure was low, and that the reality may have been that thousands of officials in a variety of administrations, at all levels, throughout the nation, were actually "on the take." However, while the numbers involved in this systematic and systemic corruption may have been open to question, few doubted that with the opportunities presented by Prohibition, crime had become more organized. What was clear was that the huge profits available through breaking the dry laws meant that there were a growing number of large-scale bootleggers, rumrunners and moonshiners who could afford to pay off officials. And the scale was impressive.

## Big Bill Dwyer and George Remus

In the year before the Senate's investigations into the efficacy and effects of Prohibition, two trials had reached the national headlines highlighting the way in which crime had organized and developed as a result of the Volstead Act. Both involved huge-scale bootlegging operations. Both indicated the extent, size and sophistication of the large-scale criminal operations dedicated to importing, shipping and selling Americans their booze. Both also conclusively show that Prohibition's influence on organized crime was certainly not confined to the cartoon rumrunner, with his fast cars, funny accent and Tommy gun. But perhaps most importantly, both indicate that the real growth in "organized crime" lay in the facilitation of bootlegging by public officials, and both show that the real expansion of criminal activity lay with activity of government officials.

The first case centered around William Vincent "Big Bill" Dwyer. Raised in Hell's Kitchen in New York and having worked as a stevedore, Dwyer was exposed in 1925 as running a "liquor ring" that had successfully supplied imported European and Canadian booze more or less since the Volstead Act came into force. His model was simple. Through contacts he'd made while growing up in one of New York's roughest districts and then at work on the waterfront, he established a system that bought off the relevant members of the U.S. Coast Guard, the New York Police Department, and the all-pervasive and ever-powerful Democrat political machine at Tammany Hall. Considering himself safe from prosecution, he then imported good quality booze wholesale, distributed it around the country, and retailed it for a considerable fortune.[8]

By contrast, Cincinnati-based George Remus had trained as a lawyer. Born into a family of German immigrants, George made it clear from an early age that he was possessed of a peculiar, but brilliant, mind. Almost certainly on the autistic spectrum, George habitually referred to himself in the third person, using his surname. Leaving a room he might tell those around him: "Remus is going now." If he wanted something he might say: "Remus would like..." In keeping with that eccentricity, he showed little or no respect for the moral duties of his chosen profession, openly viewing the law as a problem to be circumvented, rather than a solution to maintain society's equanimity.

So, when the nation went dry, Remus went to work. Applying his imagination and legal training, he studied the legislation. To Remus this meant learning the Volstead Act by rote, and citing it to those who would listen. Within the terse wording of the Act, he found loopholes. Remus discovered areas he could profitably exploit and yet technically remain within the law. Satisfied with his research, he then went out and bought distilleries and their warehouses filled with bonded alcohol, which, while the country was dry, were suitably cheap.

This meant he had a totally legal supply of booze, but in order to remain within the law, he needed to find some way of selling this booze to a thirsty public. The answer lay in pharmacies, and Remus quickly established his own chain. Using these he could sell the bonded stocks by branding them "medicinal" alcohol. Under this method it was perfectly legal for him to sell to all those who had the paperwork to buy it. And there were plenty who did.

In a pre-antibiotic age, efficacious drugs centered on a few specific "cures" like quinine, a variety of stimulants like cocaine and amphetamines, and a handful of more-or-less effective and more-or-less quack medicines. One of the main weapons in the physicians' armory remained the cure-all of a good stiff drink. With this in mind, it is hardly surprising that within the first six months of Prohibition, over 15,000 doctors and nearly 60,000 druggists and drug manufacturers applied for licenses to sell "medicinal" alcohol.

In this period, in Chicago alone, some half a million prescriptions were written solely for medicinal whiskey.[9] Not content with servicing this need, and in order to maximize profits, Remus also ran a lucrative scam, whereby his own workers would "hijack" his own booze consignments and spirit them away to his own secret distribution centers. From there, unfettered by the expensive legal niceties of prescriptions, he could then sell it—albeit illegally—to anyone he chose, and for far better money.

What united the unlikely pair—the legal professional and the dockyard laborer— apart from the booze business itself, was the money involved and those whom they paid in order to safely make it. The careers of both of these criminal entrepreneurs demonstrate clearly that the bootlegger could not have survived without the connivance, complicity and venality of the authorities. It was elected officials and their minions at a variety of levels who really enabled bootlegging—bringing into question *who* were the organized criminals, and *what* was the true nature of the organized crime. To maintain his freedom and grease the palms of all those involved, Dwyer's operation must have paid out millions. While it is difficult to put a figure on what he distributed to ensure a comfortable level of security, perhaps the results speak for themselves.

He was so generous that the authorities invariably looked the other way. Sometimes they went even further. On one legendary occasion, the rumrunner bribed the entire crew of a U.S. Coast Guard cutter to fetch 700 cases of liquor from a vessel out on "Rum Row." The conditions were rough and Dwyer had no suitable boat with which to bring in his booze. He had nothing capable of getting out through the swell and reaching the U.S. twelve-mile limit where the Canadian and transoceanic ships hovered, waiting for smaller vessels to bring their illegal cargoes of booze into American waters.

What Dwyer did have was friends who could and would do this for him. On this evening, it was officers and ratings of the compliant Coast Guard who brought Big Bill's cargo into harbor. Using a U.S. Coast Guard vessel, they went out to Rum Row. When they reached the twelve-mile limit, the somewhat baffled crew of the ship that was smuggling the precious cargo loaded it onto the deck of the cutter. Once on the quay, the Coast Guard handed over their cutter to Bill's men, who unloaded it. Nor did the authorities' help end here. While working on the dockside, the bootleggers were guarded by a squad of officers from the NYPD, who made sure that they were safe from prying eyes and thieving hands.

It did not take long for Dwyer's bravado and investments to pay off. He had quickly earned sufficient money to expand beyond his bootlegging enterprise. By the time of his going to trial in December 1925, Dwyer was earning enough to buy a race track, several casinos, and other legitimate sporting interests. Even after having paid for these investments, he still had sufficient money for their expansion and development. He became so prosperous that one account claimed that he owed the Internal Revenue Service over $2 million by the end of only his second year in the rumrunning business.

While that figure was obviously an estimate, what *is* known is that by 1934—in the wake of Al Capone's incarceration for tax evasion—Dwyer reached a deal on unpaid taxes with the IRS. Legend has it that Big Bill didn't haggle; he seemed only too eager to pay. His behavior made many speculate that he felt he was getting off lightly. Nevertheless, the sum was considerable. Dwyer agreed to a figure within ten minutes of their making the offer, even though he was paying the IRS a little under $4 million for his income tax debts since 1922—a figure which is made even more impressive when it is understood that it was calculated at the lower rate of 25 percent and can be equated to twenty times that amount in today's values.[10]

More is known about the financial intricacies of Remus's dealings. This is partly because the ex-lawyer was implicated with so many high-up officials who were also subsequently investigated, which enabled the cross-checking of the figures involved. Remus famously told the court in his 1925 trial that he paid the attorney general's aide, Jess Smith, between $1.50 and $2.50 per case for all his liquor permits. Some idea of the scale of this exchange can be gathered from his admission about his production figures for booze. Just one of the seven distilleries he owned at this time turned out 18,000 cases and 3,200 barrels of liquor in less than three months in the summer of 1921. This meant that by the end of that year, according to Remus's own testimony, he had paid Smith "between $200,000 and $300,000" and a further $50,000 in the mistaken belief that it would immunize him from prosecution.[11]

Remus's largesse did not end there. It seemed that he was paying out huge bribes to everyone. At the height of his activity, a wiretap on his hotel room revealed his paying off forty-four separate individuals. These included policemen, prohibition agents, officers of the Internal Revenue Bureau, warehouse guards, local and national politicians, as well as other government agents and officials.[12] This bribery was central to his business. As one commentator later explained, "During a two-year period in which Remus acquired three million gallons of bonded whisky for 20 million dollars and sold it for 75 million dollars, not less than 20 million dollars was paid to various Federal, State, and local enforcement officers for their silence. 'The fix' was the key to the entire operation."[13] Remus himself realized this, lamenting after his empire imploded that he'd "tried to corner the graft market, only to find that there is not enough money in the world to buy up all the public officials who demand a share in the graft."[14] In fact—as New York's egalitarian Republican U.S. congressman, the outspoken Fiorella LaGuardia, pointed out— it was simply one public official whose greed got the better of him that did him in. But that one man telling the story was enough to see Remus off to the Atlanta Penitentiary.

It was also enough to lead many to question about who it was that were the *real* criminals. A convinced "wet" and the son of poor Italian immigrant parents, La Guardia saw Prohibition as representing the worst aspects of what he saw as the self-righteous, patronizing puritanism so rife in the U.S. of the 1920s. He was an outsider who repeatedly condemned the closing of the ranks by the ruling elites. He attacked the way they had of protecting themselves and their buddies from prosecution even thought they broke the Volstead law with enthusiasm. He also saw Prohibition on a practical level as an idiotic policy, "impossible of enforcement." This, he argued, would do nothing except create "contempt and disregard for law all over the country."[15] He pointed out some of the intersections in this network of corruption and showed how it had become ingrained at all levels of law enforcement.

LaGuardia described in Congress how the "ace" Justice Department Prohibition enforcement agent, Franklin L. Dodge—the fêted hero of the biggest booze bust to date, that of the "Savannah Four"—had confiscated a large shipment of Remus's booze. He also detailed how it had emerged at Remus's subsequent trial for the murder of his own wife, that Dodge had purloined 350 cases of the whiskey of that shipment, worth an estimated $200,000. He then went on to sell that whiskey and use the proceeds to make further deals. In the meantime, the heroic lawman had given evidence to convict Remus of bootlegging, and then he'd run off with Remus's wife. Subsequently, to counter the increasing likelihood that Remus would tell his side of the story, Dodge tried to hire members of Detroit's Purple Gang to get a "hit" placed on the bootlegger.[16]

LaGuardia had no doubt where the real criminal organizations were. He placed the blame squarely on the "authorities entrusted with the enforcement of the law."[17] He pointed out that while criminals like Remus and Dwyer knowingly and inexcusably broke the law, they could not have done so without the collusion of almost every branch of government, from the lowliest sailor in the U.S. Coast Guard (as with Dwyer), to the Attorney General of the Department of Justice (as with Remus). As the only "wet" on the House Committee on the Alcohol Liquor Traffic, he repeatedly detailed how this worked and who was to blame. Speaking to the Senate in 1926, he argued:

> It is common talk in my part of the country that from $7.50 to $12 a case is paid in graft from the time the liquor leaves the 12-mile limit until it reaches the ultimate consumer. There seems to be a varying market price for this service created by the degree of vigilance or the degree of greed of the public officials in charge.
>
> It is my calculation that at least a million dollars a day is paid in graft and corruption to Federal, State, and local officers. Such a condition is not only intolerable, but it is demoralizing and dangerous to organized government.[18]

LaGuardia went on to claim that collusion in this graft went to the highest levels of the federal government. He argued that Congress not only turned a blind eye to infractions of the dry laws, but deliberately eased the graft that lubricated them.

> The Government even goes to the trouble to facilitate the financing end of the bootlegging industry. In 1925, $286,950,000 more of $10,000 bills were issued than in 1920 and $25,000,000 more of $5,000 bills were issued. What honest businessman deals in $10,000 bills? Surely these bills were not used to pay the salaries of ministers. The bootlegging industry has created a demand for bills of large denominations, and the Treasury Department accommodates them....
>
> I have been in public office for a great many years. I have had the opportunity to observe first the making of the present prohibition laws as a member of Congress, and later, as president of the Board of Aldermen of the largest city in this country, its attempted enforcement. In order to enforce prohibition in New York City I estimated at the time would require a police force of 250,000 men and a force of 200,000 men to police the police.[19]

LaGuardia perpetually and eloquently showed how venal, corrupt and hypocritical the establishment was with regard to Prohibition. Few would have been surprised by his findings. At the time of LaGuardia's accusations, faith in the probity of government was at one of its lowest ebbs in U.S. history, with stories constantly emerging about corruption, graft and kickbacks throughout the highest levels of the administration. Jess Smith—the personal assistant to the attorney general whom Remus had paid off—had committed suicide. His boss, Attorney General Harry Daugherty, had been forced to resign, as had the Secretary of the Interior, the Alien Property Custodian, and the head of the Veterans' Bureau.

Much of the scandal related to booze, and it ran through to the highest levels of the administration. The Prohibition Bureau was so corrupt that within a year of Prohibition, permits for the sale of "medicinal" alcohol, like those used by Remus, had essentially become the equivalent of transferable bonds. Even the recently deceased President Warren G. Harding was rumored to have been involved in breaking the dry laws. There was strong evidence that he participated in drink-fueled poker nights at the government-run speakeasy, the infamous "Little Green House" at 1625 K Street. Here confiscated booze was served to him and his "Ohio Gang," allegedly supplied by Prohibition Commissioner Roy Haynes.[20]

## Italians and Other Bootleggers

Nevertheless, LaGuardia's accusations not only subjected him to the hatred of the "drys" in Congress but also those at large in the nation. Their attacks on him pointed up one of the great truisms of Prohibition that has glimmered on in a surprisingly long, if surreptitious, half-life in the popular image of the era ever since. In the minds of LaGuardia's contemporaries, the vast majority of Volstead lawbreaking was carried out by "aliens," or at least "hyphenates," whose culture, education and morality naturally made them less honest and more greedy. It also gave them the wherewithal to defy this beneficial and charitable legislation.

In many ways this is to be expected. Arguably there are few times in U.S. history when xenophobia and isolationism have had stronger currency in the popular imagination. Developments in communications and transport had combined with relaxations of immigration laws and an era of globalized trade to create an unprecedented wave of immigration into the United States in the first decades of the twentieth century. In the period before this new surge, tens or occasionally hundreds of thousands had annually arrived at U.S. ports. In the years leading up to the Great War, the arrivals regularly totaled over a million a year. To those already settled in the nation, these immigrants appeared like a never-ending stream. Moreover, they were different.

These impoverished and illiterate hordes came from unfamiliar parts of Europe and Asia. Where British, Scots and Swedes had arrived, now there were Poles, Greeks, Russians and Japanese. Southern Italians replaced the Germans as the most numerous nationality of immigrants, and in the minds of a growing number of Americans, the consequences of that shift did not bode well for the nation. Cowed by authoritarian regimes in their native lands, the new immigrants were seen as ill-educated, mistrusting and superstitious. In addition, they brought cholera, diphtheria, typhus, tuberculosis and the other ghastly and virulent diseases indicative of poverty and poor hygiene. In short, they looked, sounded and acted like dangerous aliens. They were incapable of being assimilated into American society, and as a result, they congregated in the cities, creating colonies where "true" Americans hardly dared go—even if they had wanted to.

Nor was it simply their numbers, habits or appearance that generated hostility. The mistrust of foreigners had been spurred by revulsion at the slaughter of the Great War and feelings of the betrayal of American altruism at the Paris Peace Conference. In the wake of the Russian Revolution and its repercussions, there was increasing evidence that foreign agents were fomenting revolution among the nation's lower orders. On top of this, massive tests of the IQs of the foreign-born and huge surveys of the nation's comprehensive immigration statistical evidence demonstrated—"scientifically"—that the immigrant was inferior to the native-born in almost every way. The result was that in 1921 and 1924, both of the main parties had backed comprehensive immigration restriction, and organizations as diverse as the American Federation of Labor, the Daughters of the American Revolution, and the revived Knights of the Ku Klux Klan were calling for further expansions of these laws.

Given this general consensus, it would be a brave man who would dispute that aliens, foreigners and the un–Americanized hyphenates were not at the root of the crime wave. For example, in 1927, an article in H.L. Mencken's scurrilous *American Mercury* cited comments made by a "Babbit" in the House of Representatives claiming that, as a New Yorker and an Italian, LaGuardia was "wet" simply in order to defend his fellow immigrants. The author quoted the Maine representative as saying, "After all … he's from New York, where there are few real Americans. He has the commonest of all foreigners for his constituents—Italian wine-bibbers who have sent him to Congress to recover for them their lost beverage."[21] This association of Italians and other immigrants as one of the leading sources of Volstead violations has tinted many peoples' visions of Prohibition, and especially organized crime in the Prohibition era.

There is a great deal of evidence to indicate how widespread this view was at the time. As William J. McSorley of the American Federation of Labor told the Senate Judiciary Subcommittee in 1926: "You will find that the workingmen of this country [Italy], 90 per cent of them, are either making wines, beer or whisky out of every known vegetable and fruit that exists. Everyone has his own special concoction. They even make wine out of parsnips and such stuff."[22] Much of this, he confessed, was pretty undrinkable, and many would-be drinkers with the money turned to those who they felt knew about such things.

The Italian-owned wineries of California in particular cashed in on the craze for domestically produced booze. They could produce wine semi-legally under the "fruit juice clause" of the Volstead Act. Under this section of the Act, farmers were allowed to "conserve their fruit," a practice which had often meant either brewing—as with hard cider—or pickling it in alcohol. Either way, if it was sold it became legal booze, and yet producers were allowed to make up to two hundred gallons of the stuff every year. This had the effect of fueling a hugely lucrative trade in unprocessed grapes and grape juice that could be exported largely from the Italian-dominated wine region of California, to end up on the handcarts and market stalls of the Italian fruit-sellers in all major American cities. Adding sugar and allowing fermentation meant the purchaser could produce a drinkable red wine, which became known as the ubiquitous "Dago Red."

The result was that in the Italian districts of cities there was a veritable cottage industry producing wines and other spirits for neighbors as well as, in many cases, the large bootlegging concerns. One report by New York social workers in the early years of Prohibition estimated that all Italian households spent between $50 to $300 on wine-making supplies per year. It seemed that everyone knew about it, and many gained from it.

Court records showed that in terms of wine production during Prohibition, the Italians led the way, and although much of it was for home consumption, there were also those who produced hundreds of gallons, giving them a surplus. Many were selling this for between $3 and $5 a gallon, giving them a nice source of income on the side.

There were also urban myths about Italians and their homemade wine. It was said that every fall, the gutters in Italian districts ran red with the dregs of wine production, and that Italian shop assistants would frequently apologize to customers for their giveaway wine-stained hands.[23] Needless to say, the law took its cut. As one policeman said of working in the Italian quarter of Chicago in 1922: "No one wanted to take Saturdays off because on Saturday you just drove up in front of a place [where someone was making illegal booze], and someone came out with an envelope. They threw it in the car, and you drove away."[24]

While this domestic booze production was associated with small-scale production, it also linked in with more sinister suspicions about the foreign-born, particularly the Italians. Many were convinced—with reason—that the cottage industry viticulture fed the more organized crime of bootlegging. As early as January 1920, New York's Prohibition commissioner told the *New York Times* that eighty percent of illegal alcohol sales were being committed by "aliens."[25] Little seemed to have changed by 1926, when a survey—based on the "names and speech" of defendants—claimed that between sixty-five and seventy-five percent of all those tried for bootlegging crimes in the Philadelphia district were "aliens."

Similar figures emerged for other regions—with Connecticut and New Jersey registering upwards of eighty percent. The survey settled on a "conservative figure" of sixty-five percent nationwide. Before arriving at a total for native-born Americans, this figure also needed to take into consideration that "at least fifteen per cent [of the bootleggers and vendors of "hooch"] however, must be accredited to the Afro-Americans." This meant that according to this survey, in spite of their overwhelming numbers in the general population, a mere twenty percent of the nation's bootleggers were probably native, white Americans.[26]

As can be gathered from the logic of this "survey," at least part of its findings can be seen as little other than simple anti-immigrant prejudice, but these were widely held prejudices and they had very deep roots. The fundamentally Protestant, middle-class, native-born temperance movement had had close links with the powerful immigration restriction movement since the turn of the twentieth century. By the 1920s, these restrictionists had built an exceedingly powerful alliance that managed to push through legislation—in both fields—that had been vetoed since the turn of the twentieth century. Using a mixture of pseudo-sciences that purportedly pointed up both the cultural and racial inferiority of the largely southern and eastern European immigrants, the restrictionists had managed to reduce their numbers from their peak at over a million a year to 150,000. Central to this restrictionist victory was the relationship of the so-called New Immigrant to alcohol.

To some commentators it was the circumstances they encountered in America that drove the recent arrivals to drink. It was the poverty, the ignorance, the constant rejection and the resultant despair that confronted them as they sought a better life. This was what made the immigrant the ideal "victim" of the saloon. In the novel *The Jungle* (New York, 1906), Upton Sinclair graphically illustrated this sad phenomenon with the tragic decline of his hardworking Lithuanian hero, Jurgis Rudkus. Rudkus attempts to provide for his young family by grafting in the stockyards of Chicago, only to find himself thwarted by unscrupulous bosses, dishonest realtors and, ultimately, predatory saloon owners.

Less charitable critics claimed the immigrant tie to alcohol was the result of their inherent nature and the environments in which these people had grown up. Many within the immigration restrictionist movement believed the foreigner had always been ignorant of the virtues of moderation—let alone abstinence—and claimed that the relative declines in Italian and French power and culture were associated with wine production and consumption. Bohemians and Germans were synonymous with beer drinking and brewing, which was demonstrated by their rowdiness and aggression. Nevertheless, as a less alcoholic option, it suited their generally sensible and industrious natures. On the other hand, Poles, Irish and other Catholics were simply seen as drunkards—lacking any of the Protestants' natural propensity toward moderation and self-control.

To many true Americans, the immigrant would be indelibly linked with booze—for he or she was essentially an addict. The urge to drink was so strong among the immigrant population that the *New York Times* reported rumors of a large number of aliens who had left the U.S. in the first year of Prohibition because they could not bear to live in a dry country. According to their sources, these emigrants felt that the Volstead Act was the action of "a tyranny."[27] Yet to many drys, this was a mirror image of their own beliefs. To them, these immigrants had no experience of what it was like to live in a democratic civilization.

These were people who had been brought up in impoverished regions like the Pale of Settlement or the slums of southern Italy where they were assured by "experts" that if there was any law at all, it was enforced solely through repression, brutality and fear. To these benighted people laws were designed simply to retain the power of the autocrats and their cronies who ran the states they had inhabited. The result was that not only did this "new" immigrant population have an inherent ignorance of the benefits of Prohibition, but they had a mistrust of the law itself and would surely feel no compunction about breaking it.

## Prohibition and Mafia

According to its advocates, the Volstead Act promised a more sober population. These idealists had been convinced that closing the saloons would lead to a utopia in which there would be increased prosperity, improved health, better family life, less crime and greater happiness for all Americans. These hopes were clearly expressed by the baseball star turned evangelist preacher, Billy Sunday. On hearing of the passage of the Volstead Act, he gushed to his congregation that Prohibition was essentially the Second Coming, the Welfare State and women's rights rolled into one. In the Promised Land that was dry America it meant: "The reign of tears is over. The slums will soon be a memory. We will turn our prisons into factories and our jails into storehouses and corncribs. Men will walk upright now, women will smile and children will laugh. Hell will be forever for rent."[28]

Given this vision it was reasonable for some to fall back on the inherited prejudices of alien inferiority and foreign immorality to explain why it was that as the 1920s wore on, in spite of the inherent logic of Prohibition, the Noble Experiment seemed to be failing. Reports of the antics of bootleggers, gangsters and hooligans multiplied every week. Drys argued that it was only necessary to look at the names of the gangsters to see how vital the immigrant gangs were to the demise of Volstead. Jews like "King" Solomon, Samuel Cohen, "Boo-Boo" Hoff, Abe Bernstein and other "foreign-sounding" names dominated bootlegging in cities as diverse as Cleveland, Detroit, Minneapolis, Newark and Philadelphia.

But it was in the "melting pot" of New York that this foreign domination was clearest.

The Irish bootleggers "Big Bill" Dwyer, Charles Higgins, John Nolan (aka "Legs" Diamond) and "Owney" Madden shared the trade with Abner Zwillman, Joseph Reinfeld, Meyer Lansky, Irving Wexler (aka "Waxey" Gordon), Max Greenberg, Arthur Flegenheimer (aka "Dutch" Schultz), Al Lilien and Charles J. Steinberg. The entire city's booze business was overseen by the son of one of the city's best-known rabbis, the criminal "fixer" known as the "Big Bankroll," Arnold Rothstein—at least until his murder in 1928.

Yet in spite of Rothstein's undeniable influence, it was the Italians who headed up this list in terms of notoriety, if not numbers. "Lucky" Luciano (born Salvatore Luciana), Francesco Uale (aka Frankie Yale) and Frank Costello (born Francesco Castiglia) became increasingly well-known and powerful. But it was Johnny Torrio, and his more famous one-time lieutenant Al Capone, who, with their Chicago operation, really placed the Italian mobster center-stage in the public imagination.[29]

The threat of Italian gangs was nothing new. The "mafia" murder of New Orleans police chief David Hennessy in 1890, the Black Hand scares of the early twentieth century, and the growing fear of Italian anarchists, all fed an American prejudice that organized crime was an essentially Italian phenomenon. Prohibition apparently cemented that idea. Many accounts of American organized crime date the real rise of the "Mafia" in the U.S. from this point.[30] According to these interpretations, the opportunities presented in Prohibition promoted ambition and spawned undreamed-of wealth, and—by reducing respect for the law—to a certain extent gave legitimacy to the gangsters.

What was more, some accounts claim that Prohibition came at the right time to have a truly dynamic effect. Gangs had lost much of their clout in the nineteen-teens. By 1914, Progressive political reform had reduced the efficacy and demand for that staple of organized criminal income—the political gangster, the strong arm of the election. In addition, the profits of prostitution and gambling had been hammered by the vice crusades that characterized the home front in the Great War. The essential turning off of these sources of revenue, combined with a more than usually successful run of gang-busting administrations in many of the nation's metropolitan regions, had put paid to many of the old mobs.

In short, Prohibition offered the gangster the ideal escape route from this gloomy future. It made way for a new breed of younger, more ruthless, more ambitious and more organized mobster.[31] In these readings of the history of the era, gangsters of all ethnicities benefitted from a "Volstead bonanza," but it was the Italians who seemed to be best positioned to take full advantage. Italians—most notably those from the south, and particularly Sicily—were frequently portrayed as innately criminal, with their inherently violent nature, their peasant cunning and instinctive aptitude for intrigue, and their established criminal fraternities.

With a more sophisticated reading of both the importance of the Progressive clampdown and the importance of the Italian community, David Critchley and Federico Varese point to the example of New York City in the 1910s and 1920s.[32] They show how the Italians—Sicilians and others—moved in to replace the corrupt police when the NYPD was cleaned up in the early years of the century. Rather counterintuitively, the growth of the mob was in great measure the result of the successful reforms of Mayor William Gaynor.

Gaynor's administration had outlawed the on-the-spot fine, a staple of illegal funds for beat cops and their superiors. This fundamentally altered the hierarchy of the police precinct. It meant that petty graft and corruption, which had up to that point made up the vast majority of the individual policeman's income, essentially dried up, as did the dividing up of graft spoils between the beat cop and those above him in the station. It also meant that prostitutes, pimps and gamblers, as well as bars opening against the law on Sundays, found themselves without the "security" provided by their payments to the NYPD. These lawbreakers now had to ply their trades open to the vicissitudes and pressures of the law and each other, enabling Mafiosi to resort to their favorite criminal activity: providing protection.

This developed further when the Volstead Act came into force. One of the main problems facing bootleggers in their lucrative trade was hijacking. Relatively easy to organize, it could take place anywhere in the shipping process from Rum Row to the point of the final sale. Further, for the hijackers, it was a relatively low-risk activity, since the product was high value, pretty well untraceable, and in high demand. What was more, there was, of course, no recourse to the law—unless the forces of law and order had already been paid to provide protection. As the problem grew, the Jewish criminal mastermind Arnold Rothstein, always quick to see an opportunity, hired out guards to bootleggers and set up safe areas where buyers could meet sellers.

But it was Joe "The Boss" Masseria who really benefited from providing protection and mediation services to the bootleggers. He established "curb exchanges" based on a stock exchange model for potential customers. Meeting deep in the Italian quarter, protected by his own strong-arm thugs and with no visible product on display, his clients were safe and secure. The idea caught on. It was this brokerage that, according to Critchley and Varese, essentially created the modern New York Mafia. However, this is not how popular perception sees their genesis. In most popular histories, in most documentary and film accounts, and consequently in most people's minds, it was the Italian bootlegger who made the Mafia, and, of course, it was Prohibition, the Volstead Bonanza, that enabled him to move out of the shadowy underworld and into the big time.

## Capone as Mafiosa

The rise of the most famous of all of the Italian gangsters of Prohibition, Al Capone, perfectly illustrates many of these perceptions about the role of Prohibition and the rise of Italian organized crime. Having been brought up in the Italian gangs of Brooklyn and lower Manhattan, Capone was tough and ultra-violent. He was also ruthless, cunning and—above all—connected. He learned early that street fighting was not simply a question of youthful brawling. As a contemporary of his put it, to him—as with other Italians— violence was used to deliberately "maim or kill" the enemy. Any attack needed to be brutal enough to make sure it left the opponent either thoroughly terrified or verifiably dead, ensuring he would never be troublesome again.[33]

Nevertheless, as the stereotype of the Italian gangster also implied, Capone was a shrewd political operator. For example, arriving in Chicago, the twenty-year-old Capone demonstrated a Machiavellian *sang-froid* beyond his years, a trait for which he would become legendary. Obedient to his New York mentor, the equally shrewd and similarly violent Johnny "The Fox" Torrio, he was content on his arrival to bide his time. He watched the city's small fry kill each other off before making his own bid for power, which probably involved murdering Chicago boss "Big Jim" Colosimo, and at least two others.

What reinforced this stereotype of the Italian criminal community transplanted was that Torrio was Colosimo's nephew. He was called up to the Windy City from New York to take care of a Black Hand outfit that was blackmailing Big Jim. After all, what could more clearly illustrate the structure of Italian lawlessness than a relative's being summoned to help resolve the unwelcome attentions of a rival Italian secret criminal society?[34] This stereotypical image of the most famous of Prohibition-era gangsters clearly illustrates the way in which many commentators portrayed the gangster—a foreign figure, driven by elemental, un–American urges.

Yet, as Capone often said, he thought of himself as being just as "American" as the next entrepreneur. He liked to claim he was an American businessman in an age when President Calvin Coolidge had urged the country to remember that the "chief business of the American people is business." Capone had been born in America, brought up and educated in America, and his background made him "legally" American. What was more, he was at pains to be seen to defend American values, making comments that showed how anti-radical he was and how he stood for the free market—albeit in an illegal commodity.

Nor was Capone alone in his view that he was a part of an *American* tradition. As a renowned short story and essayist of the time put it: "It is not because Capone is different that he takes the imagination: it is because he is so gorgeously and typically American.... Of course he was born in this country: could anyone but a native American have adopted so whole-heartedly American principles of action? An immigrant would have taken years to assimilate our ideals; whereas Capone was born to them.... There are analogies for Al Capone among the American immortals."[35]

Not treating Capone as a true American highlights many of the problems encountered in interpreting organized crime in the U.S. over these years. After a brief period as the media darling, Capone had become the symbol of all that was rotten with Prohibition America, and has continued to be seen as the epitome of organized crime in an era that has become synonymous with organized criminal activity and gangsters. As a 1930 biography of the controversial figure had him say, "They've hung everything on me except the [Great 1871] Chicago fire."[36]

Capone's reputation as a foreigner not only chimed with many of the prejudices of the day, as detailed above, but fed and informed more modern versions that in turn have fueled interpretations of organized crime ever since. Capone has become the poster boy for a particular interpretation. This stresses that his Italian roots made Capone a Mafiosi, even though his ancestors were Neapolitan, not Sicilian, and there is no real evidence to link his "Outfit" with the Cosa Nostra, Camorra or any other brand of Italian criminal fraternity. That said, such views are firmly entrenched, frequently reinforced, and informed largely by two of the most popular—and in many ways unreliable—depictions of organized crime in the second half of the twentieth century.

The 1959 hit television series *The Untouchables*, with its heroic Elliot Ness and his team of incorruptible G-men, tied the "Scarface Mob" squarely with the Mafia. In this portrayal, the series followed the idea put forward by such "experts" as the Pulitzer Prize–winning *Brooklyn Eagle* journalist Ed Reid, in his 1952 *Mafia*. Reid's bestseller argued that the Mafia was "a super-government of crime that is more powerful than any formally constituted government on earth."[37] In the world of TV fantasy, only such an exaggerated vision of the Mafia and its tendrils burrowing deeply into the very fabric of the city could possibly represent a genuine challenge for Capone's nemesis: Elliot Ness, superhero.

Nevertheless, in this case the fantastical took on an aura of historical fact. Throughout the decade, the American public lapped up such hyperbole. They had been sensitized to such ideas in 1951 by the shocking statement that "Organized Crime" existed as a real threat to their safety. They were told this by no less a figure than J. Edgar Hoover at the Kefauver hearings. Further credence was lent by the real Elliot Ness, who died in 1957. By this time he was a good-looking but bankrupt and booze-soaked figure—known to his less sympathetic workmates as "Elegant Mess."

That said, there were some truths that lay behind the myth. Ness *had been* a genuine G-man. He had not only battled Capone, but also, to prove it, had co-written a book about his experiences that became a best seller. But the myth went far further than acknowledging the facts about this all-too-human G-man. The TV series made of his exploits played him as a granite-jawed, morally upright, teetotal superman, played by the heroic-looking Robert Stack. Each episode culminated in his killing or capturing another member of the Scarface Gang and was lent authority by having an introduction by the FBI propagandist, McCarthyite Red-baiter, and superstar journalist Walter Winchell.[38]

Similarly, Mario Puzo's 1969 novel *The Godfather* has the fictional Don Vito Corleone broadly in alliance with Capone. Although Corleone fends off an attempt by the imprisoned Capone to intervene in the Mafia civil war that rages in the early years in which the book is set, Corleone essentially sees Capone as parochial and insignificant in the real power games of the era.[39] Puzo himself never made any great claims for the veracity of his works. He admitted that he based his accounts on hearsay, mythology and imagination. Puzo himself told reporters, "My Mafia is a romanticized myth."[40]

However, this is not the way that the public tend to view his work. Sales of some thirty million copies, followed by Francis Ford Coppola's hugely successful films, have meant that his interpretation of the Mafia has now become the gold standard. Any interpretation of the Mafia written in the years since Puzo's books must either expand this version of organized crime that they portray or produce evidence to show they are incomplete or erroneous.

Given the immense popularity of his books, "Puzo-Mafia" expressions like "he sleeps with the fishes" and "make him an offer he can't refuse" have become synonymous with the Cosa Nostra in the modern criminal jargon. Similarly, Puzo's depictions of The Family's "ethics," their loyalty, and their almost infinite and inescapable power, are those that most interpretations since—whether they admit it or not—have had to prove or refute.

That refutation may be simply an exposure of the inaccuracies and half-truths of *The Godfather* through archival research. The proof could be the perpetuation of the myth of the moral boundaries that lie at the heart of the novels or, as will be discussed later, it could be the denial of their very existence. Still, in terms of the myths surrounding the Mafia in Prohibition, it remains largely true that if Puzo said that Capone was Mafioso—or in some way linked him to the "Family"—then in the vast majority of minds, that remains fixedly the case.[41]

Even if these ideas have entered those minds by cultural osmosis, they are still firmly implanted and have been, and are being, reinforced by all forms of the popular media ever since. These ideas, and a great many other assumptions, have fed the conviction that Capone's motives, actions, successes and subsequent demise, were all somehow connected with a shadowy super-secret, super-violent and all-powerful centralized criminal network.

## Roy Olmstead

The Capone model of exaggerated threat was not unique. According to a variety of accounts, Prohibition gave a whole range of gangsters from a whole range of backgrounds "the opportunity to organize on a national scale."[42] Nevertheless the organization that was credited with the greatest expansion was the Mafia, and as a result, studies of organized crime have tended to concentrate on a "Mafia-centric" interpretation, either sidelining or subsuming other gangs. There are a variety of reasons for this, including the previously mentioned xenophobic anti–Italianism inspired by the climate of the years leading up to Prohibition and the way in which those sentiments were used by commentators, lawmakers and law-enforcers. It has also been seen as a legacy of the excitement caused by the Kefauver Committee "confessions," coinciding as it did with the paranoia and insecurities of the McCarthy Era. But, as Michael Woodiwiss and others have pointed out, it is also clearly detectable earlier.[43]

Even before the Cold War, it had been clearly obvious to a diverse and powerful group of opinion formers that a growing menace was threatening the nation in the form of a huge criminal network that operated alongside and within all elements and levels of legitimate businesses and elected government. Whether or not those who espoused this opinion genuinely believed in the existence of this threat, there is no doubt that a huge, nebulous, all-pervasive, ruthless and alien criminal organization attracted the public imagination to a far greater extent than a couple of local hoodlums, no matter how alien, no matter how brutal, no matter how successful, and no matter how blatant those criminals were.

During the years of Prohibition, such an argument served the forces of law and order at a variety of levels. They could argue that they were unable to control the "crime wave" unleashed by Prohibition. In part this impotence resulted from the notion that those participating in that lawlessness were part of a huge organization that was so wide-ranging, so highly disciplined, so alien and so ruthless that it had greater human, financial and political resources available than either the local or federal government. Given this superiority, how could they be expected to control it and remain within the niceties of the law?

This argument is well exemplified by the rather peculiar career of a high-flying young police lieutenant in the Pacific Northwest. Although Roy Olmstead was neither foreign-born, nor associated in any way with the Mafia, his career can be seen as a clear indicator of a variety of the legacies and myths of organized crime that became associated with the Prohibition years in most histories. Not the least of these, Olmstead's success and eventual very controversial demise illustrates very clearly how powerless the law-keepers felt, and were perceived as being, in their battle against the organized bootleggers.

Olmstead lived and worked in Washington State, which had gone dry in 1916, and like many of his colleagues, the young policemen had seen the potentially huge profits generated by rumrunning firsthand. Even before the Volstead Act came into force, Olmstead became involved in a minor way in the thriving trade in illicit whiskey from neighboring Canada. Retaining his post in Seattle's Finest, on his days off, he was buying small shipments, personally smuggling them down through Puget Sound, and stashing them on one of the numerous densely wooded and uninhabited islands of the area.

However, this rather ad-hoc weekend activity changed once federal agents became involved. His simple and rather casual methods became outdated, especially in the early days of Prohibition when the authorities were determined to enforce the ban. Like many others, Olmstead discovered it was no longer feasible to smuggle on this essentially opportunistic scale. This change in the nature of the trade was demonstrated in March 1920, when the young police officer was caught red-handed with a shipment of whiskey. He was convicted and fined $500, then cashiered out of the police force.

It did not take long for Olmstead to realize that this seeming misfortune could be turned to work distinctly to his advantage. Recognizing that in order to succeed he would have to be more organized, within a year he had set up a highly sophisticated bootlegging business. Getting an initial investment of $1,000 from each of his eleven backers, Olmstead soon established what the *New York Times* would later call "one of the most gigantic rum-running conspiracies in the country."[44] With its shipping, warehousing, transport, packaging and clerical operations, it rapidly became one of the largest single employers in the Seattle area. Each week's work bootlegging earned Olmstead what would have been a lifetime's salary as a police lieutenant. He proved to have all the attributes necessary for the successful bootlegger—he was ambitious, innovative and meticulous in his planning. But unlike many others in the "trade," he was also, in his own way, scrupulously honest.

With his success, Olmstead became a celebrity in his hometown. Ostentatiously wealthy, seriously well-connected, he became known as a gregarious party-giver. He was a popular, young, attractive and cheerful figure and was seen by many residents as something of a philanthropist. Those who dealt with him on a business level—including the aircraft magnate William Boeing—knew that he did not adulterate or tamper with the branded booze he shipped in from Canada. They also learned that he prided himself on his word being his bond. It was said that unlike his competitors, he was even honest enough to pass on the savings that he made through the scale and efficiency of his operation. These allegedly included those discounts on shipments that avoided the Canadian export tax on shipments to the U.S.—something he achieved by fictitiously routing his whiskey via Mexico.

Olmstead was a bootlegger who fought no turf wars. Here was a rumrunner who was not interested in expanding his operation into narcotics, gambling, prostitution or any other form of illicit behavior. What was more, unlike Capone, Luciano, Masseria or any of the other big city gangsters, Olmstead never retaliated with violence to the (very) occasional hijackings of his booze. He relied instead on controlling the local market so tightly, and providing such a good service—serving up nothing other than the genuine article—that he built up a loyal and contented customer base. He knew no one would be able to sell liquor in the region without his say-so. However, he did not enforce this monopoly with violence, and he would not allow his men to carry side arms. In fact, he allegedly scolded one of his workers he found carrying a weapon, telling him that "no amount of money was worth a human life."[45]

However, in other ways he carried out the same trade, using many of the same methods as other violators of the Volstead laws. Like most other bootleggers, in order to protect his business, he put a large number of a variety of public officials on his payroll. It later emerged that "Olmstead and his Gang" had laid out an estimated $6,000 a month in bribes.[46] In Olmstead's case this was predominantly paid over to his former police colleagues. It is instructive that even in doing this, as with all other aspects of his operation, he made sure that he was seen to be both meticulously practical and scrupulously fair.

His former colleagues and their superior officers were paid regularly and with the minimum of fuss. Those whose services were bought simply received a second salary that reflected their rank and pay as a policeman. This meant those at the level of the beat-cop got proportionately less than the sergeant, the sergeant got less than the lieutenant, and so on. Soon he had expanded this network of pliable public servants to include most local and federal officials who would have been charged with his capture and prosecution.

Yet, as with Remus and Dwyer, sheltering under this carapace of corrupt officialdom did not serve to grant him total immunity from prosecution. In Olmstead's case, it turned out that one of the popular bootlegger's closest lieutenants—his accountant, Al Hubbard—had been working for the Prohibition Agency and reporting to them about almost all the details of the Olmstead operation. On November 17, 1924, Olmstead and forty-three other members of his organization, including his wife and his lawyer, were arrested.

In what became the case of the year, they were charged with violations of the Volstead Act and criminal conspiracy. In spite of Olmstead's pleas to a huge variety of influential friends, he was convicted. In a highly controversial decision, Judge Jeremiah Neterer told Olmstead that the damage he and his "conspiracy" had done "to organized society and the government of this country was incalculable."[47] With those words, he sentenced Olmstead to four years' hard labor on McNeil Island in Puget Sound. In addition, Neterer fined him $8,000. The bootlegger took this decision stoically. With typical fatalism, he told reporters, "I'm not complaining, I broke the law."[48]

## "Prohibition Portia"

Olmstead's conviction and imprisonment can be seen as something of an epiphany in terms of public opinion with regard to Prohibition. His treatment divided a nation that was rapidly getting more and more disillusioned with what they saw as an unenforceable, undesirable law. Inevitably those opposed to Prohibition viewed him as something of a martyr, but even those who supported the ban were divided. To many of the less committed drys, the harsh sentence given to an amiable and appealing young man was regrettable and probably counterproductive, even if he was a bootlegger. Others were less than convinced about how effective such arrests and convictions might be. They pointed to the fact that the "sting" had run for over two years. During that time, it later emerged, Olmstead shipped in nearly 100,000 cases of whiskey, with a street value estimated at $6 million.[49]

Nevertheless, staunch drys justified the decision as a victory for law and order over just one of the ever more powerful and seemingly ubiquitous organized criminal networks that threatened the constitutional underpinnings of the Union. Among these vengeful hardliners was the "First Lady of the Law," Mrs. Mabel Willebrandt, the ultra-efficient and incorruptible Assistant Attorney General of the United States. Willebrandt was the person charged with making Prohibition work, and she was—unlike many of those she commanded—fully committed to its success.

This high-minded "Prohibition Portia"—as her nemesis, the "wet" Democrat presidential candidate, Al Smith, called her—crowed that jailing Olmstead "was a prohibition victory of no small proportions." Willebrandt had argued tirelessly in favor of targeting the big bootleggers, those who hit the headlines and made the money. To her, these were the epitome of organized crime. Their ruthlessness and disregard for the laws of the land, and blatant pursuit of money, made them a huge threat to the very fabric of the United States. Any victory over them, whoever they were, was a victory for the forces of law and order.

Willebrandt essentially believed that policies of enforcement that targeted these large-scale operations would ultimately be far more effective. They would have more impact, stop more booze and make bigger headlines, than trying to enforce Prohibition through piecemeal raids on speakeasies, smashing up stills, and arresting those caught bootlegging. This previous policy of targeting of the myriad points of sale she had likened to "trying to dry up the Atlantic Ocean with a blotter," and saw it as a strategy that—as she implied—was doomed to failure.

However, even Willebrandt was forced to admit that the methods by which the arrest of Olmstead had been achieved were "dangerous and unwarranted" and advised that they should not be used in future cases.[50] Nor was Willebrandt alone in these doubts. Olmstead's legal team felt sufficiently confident in the flaws of Neterer's judgment to take his decision to the Supreme Court. What was more, where Willebrandt saw the bootleggers as the organized criminals, others saw the total opposite. They saw the Olmstead conviction and other—to their minds—dodgy decisions as demonstrating that those forces ranged against the young bootlegger were actually demonstrating far more damaging traits. The most extreme opponents saw the courts, the police, the Prohibition agents, and the other forces hounding the bootleggers as organized criminals themselves.

With regard to Olmstead, the controversy surrounding the case largely centered around the legality of the wiretaps that had been used to provide the most damning evidence. While there was no doubt that the material showed Olmstead to be guilty of breaking the Volstead Act, many saw the evidence as flawed. It was questionable whether the unsanctioned, uncorroborated and questionably recorded evidence that they provided was admissible in a U.S. court. It was doubtful, to say the least, that such methods were sanctioned under the Fourth Amendment's prohibition of "unreasonable search and seizure," let alone the Fifth Amendment's safeguards against unlawful self-incrimination.

What was more, they had been made even more questionable because the notes and recordings that had been made of the conversations had been transcribed. After this process of transcription, the originals had been destroyed, rendering the transcribed contents totally unverifiable by those who would later read them. Essentially anyone could have tampered with the reports, altering them to highlight whatever they wished and/or omit whatever they wanted left unsaid, before they were presented at the Olmstead trial. As Olmstead's defense showed at his appeal, many of the other reports and documents that represented essential aspects of the evidence for the prosecution's case had been mislaid, or perhaps never even existed.[51]

Yet, in spite of these claims, eventually the Supreme Court justices decided that Olmstead's conviction was safe. The nation's leading judicial minds determined that Olmstead's conviction lay within the boundaries of the Constitution. Predictably, when given the questionable methods used to enforce such a highly contentious and increasingly unpopular policy as Prohibition, the decision created a blaze of controversy and has excited comment ever since.

Some idea of the arguments it sparked can be gathered from the *Literary Digest's* roundup of newspaper articles dealing with Olmstead in the week the Supreme Court announced its verdict on the legality of the wiretaps. Some, like the *Cleveland Plain*

*Dealer*, argued that the decision stretched the parameters of the law. On the other hand, the paper also argued that the risks to the Constitution posed by the taps were a small price to pay in order to break the stranglehold that organized crime had on the morals of the nation.

Most commentators, however, like the *New York Times*, saw Olmstead's conviction as just plain wrong. To them it was a reiteration of the legal sentiments that had protected slavery with the *Dred Scott* case. They saw it as a charter for what they condemned as the state's "universal snooping" and agreed with Justice Brandeis's worries that upholding the legality of the methods used to convict the bootlegger meant that "the government [itself] becomes a lawbreaker."[52] Those who denounced the decision frequently argued that it fed a swelling record of dissatisfaction with the government's attitude to law and order, and displayed their growing inability to tell who were the actual criminals.

## *"This Government Murder Must Stop"*

To the rising number of opponents of Prohibition, it seemed that it was becoming ever more difficult to tell the lawbreakers and law-enforcers apart. The corruption associated with such cases as Remus's conviction was compounded by the methods and the justifications used in Olmstead's prosecution. It seemed that almost every day there were reports of the dubious practices used to entrap those violating the Volstead laws. Gone were the rather comically approving reports of the antics of the two Prohibition agents, Izzy Einstein and Moe Smith. Izzy and Moe used joke-shop false beards and stage props.

In the initial flush of enthusiasm for Prohibition, most Americans read of their antics and their impromptu disguises, agreeing with each other that they would only serve to fool and ensnare a "sap" or a "lush." Nevertheless, to the reading public's delight, the pair's quick-fire one-liners succeeded in entrapping over 4,000 foolish and drunken victims. The antics of the pair made them seem something of a symbol of the innocence of the first years of Prohibition.[53] It seemed that after Olmstead, the two clownish agents were replaced by an altogether more sinister set of enforcers.

Unlike the less protected bootleggers, it appeared that the more-or-less corrupt Prohibition agents, as well as large numbers of the police and the judiciary, had the law behind them—no matter what they did. Knowing this, they indulged in crimes that were equally, if not more, egregious as those they were meant to be preventing, detecting and prosecuting, including bribery or beatings, corruption or even murder. As the *New York World* quipped in February 1931, the Volstead Act was useless: "It's left a trail of graft and slime, It don't prohibit worth a dime."[54]

Added to this, it was very, very expensive. As the National Commission on Law Observance and Enforcement (Wickersham Commission) revealed that same year, the grossly inefficient and corrupt Bureau of Prohibition took two-thirds of the entire law enforcement budget of the federal government. It was estimated it cost some $300 million to enforce Prohibition from 1920 to its repeal in 1933. To its opponents, that money achieved shockingly few convictions while enforcing a principle that many by now opposed as undesirable anyway. What was more, the outlawing of the sale of alcohol cut the federal income from excise duties by around $11 billion over its 13-year reign. At a state level the impact was just as dramatic. The state of New York lost nearly 75 percent of its pre–1920 budget. Such drops in income had to be made up, and doing so alienated many of Volstead's wealthier supporters, since they had to make up that funding through income tax and other financial burdens.[55]

Perhaps the most spectacularly damning accusations against the federal government came from expert witnesses who argued that the government's misguided policies were far worse than any form of organized criminal activity that was brought about by the bootlegging gangs. They argued that, unlike the gangsters whose motives were greed, the cruelty of the government was not limited by financial constraints, but had free reign. Instead it was being driven by a fanaticism which was leading to mass murder. The evidence for this hinged on the testimony of the nation's foremost toxicologist, Alexander Gettler, and New York's chief medical examiner, Charles Norris.

The pair argued that the government was responsible for a huge spike in deaths by alcohol poisoning. Every year the federal government sanctioned the production of sixty million gallons of industrial alcohol for use in products from hair tonic and perfume, to paint thinner and cleaning fluids. That alcohol was "denatured" by adding increasingly toxic chemicals to what could otherwise be used to manufacture highly dangerous "white lightning." This had quickly developed into a cat-and-mouse game with the government trying to stop the bootleggers from using it to manufacture booze.

Toxins related to kerosene, benzene and strychnine soon replaced compounds that simply made the product bitter and unpalatable. What was more, manufacturers increased the proportion of those toxins in the product, from two to four percent. As Wayne B. Wheeler put it, the government relied on making hard-core drinkers run the same risk as "the man who walks into a drug store, buys a bottle of carbolic acid with the label on it marked 'poisonous,' and drinks the contents."[56] The theory was that word would soon get round that boozing wasn't worth the risk to your health or even your life, even for the most die-hard alky.

On the other hand, as stocks of legal alcohol ran dry, and the money involved in the "Alky Racket" grew, bootleggers could afford to employ better scientists to filter out those poisons. What was more, they grew bolder in their claims to have done so, whether this was true or not—and most claims were not. Evidence of this was made public in 1927. That year, as Prohibition really bit, Charles Norris and his team analyzed booze from a variety of sources. They took samples from speakeasies, police hauls and, most ghoulishly, bottles found on the corpses of dead boozers. They discovered that *all* samples contained deadly methyl alcohol in variable quantities. Alongside this they found traces of gasoline, benzene, formaldehyde, acetone, mercury salts and carbolic acid, as well as many other deadly compounds.[57]

To make this situation far worse, as the toxicologists told the public, the government continued the practice of denaturing. They did this knowing that at least ten percent of that industrial alcohol would be used by bootleggers to produce alcohol for human consumption. The federal government must also have been aware that their actions fatally poisoned anywhere between 3,000 and 12,000 residents of the U.S. in the calendar year of 1926 alone. Opponents of the practice demonstrated that the year cited 750 deaths as a direct result of this policy in New York City alone. They pointed out that this was over four times the number that died that year from alcohol poisoning in the "wet" United Kingdom. A pretty horrific figure when it was considered that the city had slightly more than one-eighth of the population of Great Britain, and that the UK had been denaturing its industrial alcohol since 1855.[58]

These voices against the practice were not simply public health officials. That incorrigible "wet" Senator Reed of Missouri condemned the policy, saying, "Only one possessing the instincts of a wild beast would desire to kill or make blind the man who takes a drink of liquor, even though he purchased it from one violating the Prohibition statutes." Others said that the Eighteenth was the only amendment that carried a death penalty. Some asked why burglars were not routinely given rat poison or counterfeiters were spared being shot when violators of the Volstead laws were being so casually poisoned by their own government. The *New York Herald Tribune* summed up their arguments, demanding "This Government Murder Must Stop."[59]

While it is probably not really tenable to accuse the federal government of genuine mass murder, these claims indicate how it was no longer entirely evident to many previously law-abiding citizens that the government in Washington was really dedicated to the "pursuit of happiness" for all its citizens. Given that Prohibition seemed to have singularly failed to "alter the customs, habits, morals, and religious observances of millions of people by some miraculous psychological transformation," was disobeying those inherent inclinations by drinking a crime that should involve risks of injury or even death? Further, should that penalty be sanctioned and abetted by the federal government?[60] If it wasn't, as many believed, then who were the real criminals?

On the other hand, those who supported the policies in principle could also argue that the whole sorry demise of Prohibition was the result of organized criminals. In the light of what were clearly vocal, logical, deep-seated and widespread murmurings and doubts about the moral underpinnings of Prohibition, it was also becoming increasingly politically astute for those who had implemented the dry laws to claim that the legislation had "failed"—and not because it was, of itself, flawed. They could argue that failure was at least partly because of the rise of insurmountable, unconquerable and nearly invisible organizations dedicated to crime.

How could the forces of law and order continue the dry policies when there were criminal masterminds whose agents penetrated all aspects of society and all levels of government and were subverting them at every turn? With specific relation to the opposition to the Olmstead decisions, how could the forces of law and order be asked to fight these criminal networks while effectively having one arm tied behind their backs? How could the law enforcers possibly contain what was clearly an epidemic of lawlessness if they were repeatedly being forced to prove that all their actions fell within the strictest interpretations of the Constitution? They argued that if the public officials charged with enforcing Prohibition had to work within "nice ethical" constraints, then U.S. "society would suffer," and as a result, criminals would have "greater immunity" to prosper and expand.[61]

# 7

# Racketeering

## A Different Kind of Organized Crime

> *One should bear in mind that gangsterism was a vital factor early in the American*
> *class struggle, first on the capitalist side and then on the side of labor; and that its history*
> *is inextricably bound up with the history of organized labor.*—Louis Adamic, 1930[1]

Alongside the ubiquitous gangster of Prohibition, there was another brand of organized criminal who exercised the journalists, the public and government—the racketeer. By the 1930s the term "racket" already had a long history in the American criminal dictionary. According to many newspapers of the early thirties it seemed racketeering had largely replaced "gangsterism" and "organized crime" as the leading criminal threat to the nation. Yet the term was not considered an easy concept to define. One commentator argued: "The expression "racket" is used so loosely as to include a great variety of things one does not like—graft, violence, monopolistic practices, etc." He added that even though—or perhaps because of—its nebulous nature, the racket was still "a substantial and sinister reality" in the United States.[2]

Some claimed this confusion was somehow linked with the rather dubious explanations given for the origin of the term "racketeer" itself. Without a clear root, how can the term have a clear meaning? It is generally thought that the expression derived from the raucous fund-raising parties held for political and charitable causes in the mid–1800s. The noise created by the events led to them being called "rackets." Soon, these interpreters changed the meaning of the word. The dishonesty and threats of violence coming from over-zealous ticket touts and organizers arranging these parties led to a direct connection in street slang with the gangs with which they associated.

In time the term was associated with gangsterism and then, of course, organized crime. By the 1920s a more specific set of principles became associated with racketeering. A definition emerged that portrayed a racket as the act of offering of a dishonest service to solve a problem that wouldn't otherwise exist without the enterprise offering the service. This is best exemplified in the well-known protection racket, whereby the criminal threatens or carries out damage or loss to person or property and demands money to protect the victim or premises from just the same eventuality in the future.

Yet over the next decades a series of attempts were made to outlaw racketeering that took a far more inclusive definition. The most relevant of these was the 1934 Anti-Racketeering Act. This measure essentially took a definition of racketeering that incorporated any illicit interstate trade within its purview. This drew more on the findings of the 1933 subcommittee of the Commerce Committee into organized crime, and that body essentially conflated racketeering with organized crime. What is more, it has been argued that it only introduced the interstate element into the 1934 Act because otherwise Congress as a federal body would have had no tangible result to show for the subcommittee's months of hearings. In an era of visceral austerity, such seeming profligacy by politicians and "experts" was hardly justifiable.[3]

It is also feasible that an explanation for this fluidity of definition can be the evolution of language. By the early 1930s the term "racketeer" had largely become more or less synonymous with "gangster." Arguably, this was the result of newspapers and other media searching for new terms to differentiate between the old-fashioned street gangs and the new organized criminal. Using a different word could perhaps go some way to explaining how it was that "organized crime" had evolved from the province of local thugs into the complex operations of criminal businessmen.

Reflecting these changes, the media portrayed organized crime as growing ever more sophisticated. This change was reflected in a noticeable difference in the language used to explain this refinement. In order to deal with the growing "perception of organized crime as systematic illegal activity," it was necessary to have "crude shifts of grammar and image."[4] "Gangs" changed into "mobs." "Mobs" then morphed into "syndicates," until the actual business of "gangsterism" became "racketeering."

According to those "in the know" at the time, fueled by the vast profits made available through Prohibition—profits derived from what become known as the ubiquitous "alky racket"—over the 1920s, organized crime changed beyond recognition. It was no longer a question of loosely united, but constantly bickering, groups of street-corner hoodlums carrying out opportunistic crimes. Many of those "street gang members" had now become "gangsters." The most successful had learned that a lower profile made it easier to make bigger money. They had realized that skimming off money from banks was generally more profitable than holding them up, and paying off the law was better than fighting the law.

Gone was the mindless ultra-violent building of a reputation as a "psycho" that had enabled "Monk" Eastman to retain control of his gang. Gangsters no longer paraded the gouged eyes or severed ears of their enemies in public as the Whyos had in the 1870s. Capone, Torio and Luciano would not steal a wallet on the street, or mug a passer-by. When they used violence it was with a longer-term aim in mind: disciplining a gang member or intimidating a reluctant payer. To them, time in the "big house" was time when someone else was running their racket. In short, they'd learned it was better to rob smartly than rob violently, and that arrest, battle scars and infamy were less badges of honor than indications of carelessness and stupidity.

## The Atlantic City Legend

This is probably a good point to challenge another of the myths about organized crime. In spite of these changes in the way they saw themselves, and the way they operated, the gangsters of the 1920s and 1930s were not *that* organized—at least not in a national sense. There is a persistent rumor that in 1929 all the leading American crime bosses gathered in Atlantic City, New Jersey, in an effort to staunch the blood flow caused by what was becoming a national turf war. It was meant to be hosted by Enoch "Nucky"

Johnson—the inspiration for Nucky Thompson of HBO's *Boardwalk Empire*—in the Ritz and Ambassador Hotels on the city's famous boardwalk.

According to one source, there were representatives from all over the nation. "Greasy Thumb" Guzik came from Chicago, "Nig" Rosen and "Boo-Boo" Hoff attended from Philadelphia, and "King" Solomon traveled from Boston. There were representatives of Detroit's Purple Gang, and New York's Lucky Luciano, Joe Adonis, Louis Lepke, "Dutch" Schultz, Albert Anastasia, Meyer Lansky, Frank Scalise and others were at the meeting. Representatives also came from Kansas City; Providence, Rhode Island; Cleveland, Ohio; as well as another New Jersey gangster to keep Nucky company.

According to this source, this roll-call of the bad and the badder importantly did *not* include "Joe the Boss Masseria and Salvatore Maranzano, two old line Mafiosi ready to square off in New York in a war to claim the position boss of bosses. Their obsession with such a claim ran counter to the Atlantic City conferees who were looking for a confederation of forces that left each [crime lord] supreme in his own area."[5]

This view of a consensus amongst criminal bosses, and their formation of a "confederation," has taken root in the history of organized crime. Perhaps even more important than the treaty meeting itself were the implications the Atlantic City agreement had for American organized crime. With the old guard, represented by Masseria and Maranzano, effectively sidelined, a new breed of Mafia could emerge. This revolution also took physical form. Within two years of the meeting, Masseria and Maranzano were dead, killed in the final act of bloody Mafia civil war, melodramatically christened the Sicilian Vespers. What was more, a commission was formed to oversee the agreements made in Atlantic City—and meetings yet to held. This was indeed a brave new (under)world.

Over the years this view of the development of organized crime has had some very impressive and powerful advocates. These include several "ex–Mafia" informants and the vast majority of historians of organized crime, as well as a selection of federal government committee reports on organized crime. Nevertheless, the veracity of the event is questionable. Although it is unlikely anyone would have advertised his participation in this secret meeting at the time, there is only one report from one attendee of the conference that can be verified by a contemporary source.

Shortly after the conference was meant to have taken place, in Moyamensing Prison in Philadelphia, prisoner 90725, Alphone Capone, was serving his first prison sentence: a year for carrying a concealed weapon. After his arrest, for some reason, Capone talked openly about a meeting in Atlantic City to Director Schofield of the Philadelphia Public Safety Department. The conversation was reported on the front page of the *Chicago Tribune* under the headline "HOODLUM PEACE PACT." Capone had told him, "I've been trying to get out of the racket for two years, but I couldn't do it.... I'm tired of gang shootings. I'm willing to live and let live. I have a wife and an eleven year old kid, a boy, whom I idolize and a beautiful home on Palm Island in Florida. If I could go there and forget it all I would be the happiest man in the world. It was with the idea in mind of making peace amongst the gangsters in Chicago that I spent a week in Atlantic City and got word to each of the leaders that there shall be no more shootings." The *Tribune* identified the "Chicago crime chieftains" represented at the conference, "either in person or by proxy," as "Joseph Atello, Earl McErlane, Joe Saltis, Bugs Moran and John Torrio." The result was the formation of a "compact [that] parceled out the territory to be controlled by the various gang chieftains." All "signed on the dotted line," Capone said, to quit shooting."[6]

Capone's version of events at the conference applied only to Chicago. In 1931 a

*Chicago Tribune* journalist upped the number of Chicago gang-lords in Atlantic City to "about 30," but he still argued it was essentially held to patch local differences.[7] In the final years of this study, another wider-ranging version of the conference emerged. In 1939 the journalist Hickman Powell wrote a book detailing his role in covering the trial of mobster Charles "Lucky" Luciano for white slavery. In his version, supported since by many eminent criminologists, the Atlantic City meeting was called to patch up national problems like the killing of Frankie Yale in New York, not simply Chicago turf wars.[8]

In *Ninety Times Guilty*, Powell claims that the Atlantic City meeting was the first of a series of underworld summit meetings that resulted in the formation of a national "Commission." In putting forward this depiction, Powell not only managed to create a storyline that placed Luciano center stage, but also one that tied American crime back to the Mafia by association of the now supreme crime lord with a mysterious body called the Unione Siciliano. Powell maintains that through this process Lucky Luciano managed to establish the "Pax Siciliano" that would dominate and regulate the American crime scene from then onwards.

However, Dwight C. Smith, David Critchley and Mike Woodiwiss have uncovered evidence that demonstrates that Powell's view is not just flawed, but may well be entirely fictitious. By the time he wrote this piece, Powell was working as a speechwriter for Thomas Dewey, the gang-busting New York District Attorney with presidential ambitions. Dewey's most famous coup as DA had been the conviction and imprisonment of the man now identified as the nation's leading crime lord—Charles "Lucky" Luciano.

Having convicted Luciano of sixty-two counts of prostitution (out of the ninety that made up the title of the book), and sentenced him to thirty to fifty years, was a coup that had boosted Dewey's career. Three years later, discovering that the pimp in prison in upstate New York was actually the boss of bosses, was political dynamite. As Dewey's campaign ramped up, so did the necessity for Powell to back up his story. He turned to a notorious New York attorney for whom he already ghostwrote.

Richard "Dixie" Davis was down on his luck. He had famously been on a retainer to act as the attorney for Arthur Flegenheimer, the notorious bootlegger and later racketeer better known as Dutch Schultz. But in October 1936, having been implicated in Schultz's illegal operations, he was struck off the New York Bar and sentenced to a year in prison. On the advice of Thomas Dewey, this was reduced to six months, but he was also given an "indeterminate suspended sentence."[9] Well known to Powell from his days as court reporter for the *New York Tribune*, the rather desperate Davis, calling himself "Kid Mouthpiece," lent his name to a series of articles Powell wrote for *Collier's Magazine*.

In five articles, running in July and August 1939 under the title "Things I Couldn't Tell Till Now," Powell told the confessions of mob-lawyer turned informant Davis. In them the journalist placed "evidence" from Davis's mob connections that his claims in *Ninety Times Guilty* were actually based on hard fact. He made claims that, as Woodiwiss puts, it showed "that Luciano *did* organize the conference rather than *may* have organized the conference." The Unione Sicilione was, in the articles, "the mysterious, all-pervading reality," which organized the underworld on a national scale during and after Prohibition. Its leader was Salvatore Maranzano, who was shot dead on September 10, 1931, "at the very same hour there was about ninety guineas knocked off all over the country." After orchestrating this purge, Luciano, according to Powell and Davis, "set up a system of underworld co-operation that spread from coast to coast." Luciano was then compared to "Hitler developing the system of axis powers."[10]

Powell's book received a favorable reception in the nation's newspapers and magazines. What was more, *Collier's* had a good reputation for the accuracy of its content, and an even better circulation. Most of the reviews seem to indicate that both his comments and conjecture were generally accepted at face value at the time. So much so that there were remarkably few commentators who even questioned, let alone condemned, the reliability of the claims of a political speech-writer and a disbarred lawyer that they understood the most intricate workings of the underworld. Further, no one seemed to notice the unmistakable evidence that these were claims that just happened to benefit the politician who had employed Powell since 1937 and was paying him $10,000 "to be number one typewriter in his campaign" for the highest office in the nation.[11]

There was, however, as Woodiwiss indicates, at least one hostile paper that held a different view of what it all meant. The *Evening Standard* of Uniontown, Pennsylvania, pointed out at the time that Powell's "so-called 'inside story' of the gangster lawyer was in reality a piece of lurid, sensational 'expose' used as a vehicle for publicizing and boosting the energetic, ambitious and spotlight-seeking District Attorney Tom Dewey…. 'What a grand guy this Dewey is' was the sum and substance of the alleged Dixie Davis memoirs."[12]

These controversies have carried on ever since, essentially dividing historians, criminologists and other interested interpreters. At their most extreme, the interpretations that grow from these events divide commentators into two camps. There are those who see organized crime as a monolithic, highly organized, centralized and controlled operation, or a series of operations under the auspices of criminal bosses so powerful they have become almost untouchable. On the other hand, there are those who see organized crime as a fundamentally fluid and unstable series of alliances that have no permanent, over-arching governance or leadership, other than at a local level.

## John Landesco

In spite of the arguments that developed around the importance of the Atlantic City conference, there was no doubt in the minds of most Americans that by the 1930s organized crime was big business. In some ways it was like the hated trusts of the turn of the twentieth century. Like the trusts, the bloated and highly protected large-scale criminal syndicates spent their time gobbling up the smaller competitor criminals. Like the trusts, they created cartels with those they could not devour, and it became common knowledge that they got ever more ruthless and amoral as they grew larger. In other ways they were like the newspapers: they were "syndicated" across regions of the nation, if not the whole nation. Each "syndicate"—or "the syndicate," depending on the account being used—controlled territories, enforced rules of behavior, and dictated the "racket," or area of business.[13]

In a highly influential book of 1929, one "informed" observer claimed that the money at stake in bootlegging and the consequent creation of criminal empires in the 1920s had meant that "[b]eer and alcohol running, bombing, bank robbing, murder for pay, window smashing, and a score of other crimes that can be carried on successfully only by organized gangs or 'syndicates,' are all rackets."[14] Unsurprisingly, over the years of Prohibition, this fear of rackets seemed to be concentrated around what most Americans were told was the epicenter of the nation's gangsterism—Chicago. The local papers backed up this view. As early as 1927, the *Chicago Tribune* claimed the city was paying out between eight and ten million dollars a year to the racketeers.[15]

As usual with reports of organized crime, as the editors got into their stride on a long-running story, they allowed the figures to escalate. Three years later, by 1930, under the headline "Huge Sum Is Received Every Seven Days For Gang Operations," the *Chicago Daily News* claimed that "beer, booze and alcohol" generated $3,510,000 per week for Chicago's "racketeers." They made this extortion appear all the more terrifying by telling their readers that the funds raised formed the "war chest whence comes the money that corrupts police, politicians and prohibition agents," as well the funding for other rackets.[16]

The University of Chicago sociologist and pioneer investigator of organized crime, John Landesco, went further. He insinuated that in Chicago and its environs, and he suspected probably other regions, "the gunman and the ex-convict have seized control of business associations … and have exploited these organizations for personal profit." He explained this line of reasoning, arguing that these criminal elements were awash with cash and looking for ventures through which racketeers could launder bootlegging money. They were after businesses that could provide room for expansion and diversification—especially if the source of their original wealth, the 18th Amendment, was repealed. Landesco claimed that "the gunman and gangster are, at the present time [1929], in control of the destinies of over ninety necessary economic activities" in the city and its hinterlands. He went on to list twenty-three gangster-controlled industries in Chicago that ranged from the city's butchers and bakers to window-shade makers, and a whole range of trades in between.[17]

Landesco goes into some detail about the techniques used by gangsters. He explains how they worked their way into the confidence of the struggling business owner. Even while the economy boomed through the years of the 1920s, there were still those who fought to keep their heads above the financial tide. When the downturn hit, these pressures became so much worse. To the small businessman struggling with debts, slow payers or troublesome workers, the racketeer often appeared something of a godsend. With cash, contacts and a reputation for seemingly simple solutions—the mechanics of which were best kept vague—this new "associate" seemed like the knight in shining armor. Landesco shows how the racketeer could help businesses. He pointed out that while "the transformation of gunmen, bombers and gangsters into 'racketeers' was sometimes at their own initiative, [more] often [it was] upon invitation to solve a problem in competitive co-operation with which many groups of small businessmen were unsuccessfully struggling."[18]

Through a series of examples, he demonstrates that gangsters enabled business owners to create and defend cartels, or what they euphemistically called "protective associations." However, that defensive-sounding name barely disguised methods that were, more often than not, predictably violent but highly effective.

In Landesco's explanation, initial contact was frequently made through a third party who would arrange a loan. The interest on that money would inevitably escalate and become increasingly impossible to repay. This had the effect of drawing the legitimate businessman ever closer to the mobster. The mob would then set about expanding its share of the business, a process that centered on intimidating any competition.

To achieve this, they would fix prices, and use their muscle and reputation for violence to guarantee these charges, assuring that there was no undercutting of the rates that they set. They would also choose who it was that the business would buy from and who it was that they could sell to. For a number of reasons, racketeers were selective about those with whom they traded. Sometimes they would allocate contracts to those who paid them the most for the privilege; at other times they'd award them to those who ran other businesses they already controlled, or those who funneled funds back into their own businesses.

## Chicago's Dry Cleaning Racket

For the mobsters, racketeering had another great advantage—the system was self-perpetuating. As the cartel grew, so it became more difficult to resist its expansion still further. Smaller operations were forced to either join the association or pay a percentage of their takings over as protection. If they did not, they would find their staff would suffer a rash of "sluggings"; their premises would be smashed; they would be subject to bombings and other intimidations. To illustrate his theory of the emergence of racketeering, Landesco used the example of Chicago's dyeing and dry cleaning business in the 1920s and showed how the gangsters muscled their way into this industry.

Citing the *Chicago Daily Journal*, Landesco claims that none other than Al Capone was called in to aid the businessman Morris Becker in his dispute with the manager of the Master Cleaners and Dyers Association, Walter Crowley. Built up over a fifteen-year period, Becker's company—Sanitary Cleaning Shops, Inc.—was by the middle of the twenties the largest independent cleaners in Chicago. Sanitary ran all of the city's ten biggest dry cleaning premises. Perhaps more importantly, Becker's businesses remained an independent enterprise.

In 1925, Crowley decided that Sanitary ought to be in his Association. Since Becker was already trading very profitably, the advantages of this membership eluded him. He saw no sense in Crowley's prompting that he raise his prices by an additional 50 percent, and saw no benefit to be gained by paying the $5,000 (cash) "initiation fee." Becker refused Crowley's overtures, and that was when that the Association started showing its less appealing side. Crowley ordered a concerted campaign of intimidation against Becker, who recorded him as threatening that "he could make all our property valueless, by simply giving the word."[19] It appeared that Crowley was not bluffing. Association thugs bombed Becker's buildings. They beat and robbed his workers. Finally they demanded that those intimidated workers came out on strike, which—to a man—they did.

Trusting, as he put it, that "this was America" and these things would not go unpunished, Becker reported his treatment to the authorities. Going to court, Becker and his son produced a large amount of evidence clearly demonstrating the tactics and behavior of Crowley's thugs. But it soon became apparent to all involved, including Becker, that the Association was capable of producing far more powerful weapons. Not only did all the witnesses for the prosecution mysteriously and unanimously refuse to testify, but when confronted by this mass refusal, the state's prosecutor had become markedly uninterested, if not hostile. He allegedly snapped at Becker to search for his own witnesses, telling him: "I am a prosecutor, not a process server."[20]

To make matters even worse, this surly and singularly unhelpful public official was ranged against the skill and reputation of America's most famous lawyer. Convincing Clarence Darrow, that celebrity defendant of the rights of the put-upon American "working stiff," to represent Crowley was a coup. No doubt he was told that Becker was a typical oppressor of Chicago's working-man, and that Crowley was merely trying to unionize the industry. Whatever the reasoning, when combined with the money that had been paid to silence the prosecution, it made the defense team seem pretty well unassailable. Sure enough, given these investments made by the defense, the jury acquitted Crowley in less than a quarter of an hour.

Becker was understandably furious. He was also out of pocket and forced into a disgruntled and disillusioned retirement. However, it was not long before he had found a solution, and one so effective that it enabled him not only to remain independent, but to build new premises, including what would become the city's largest dry cleaning depot. The solution is perhaps best explained by Becker himself, who later famously told reporters, "I now have no need of the state's attorney or police department, or the employers' association. I have the best protection in the world."[21] As a *Washington Evening Star* editorial explained, "He hit on the brilliant idea of taking Mr. Capone into business with him: in other words, fighting fire with fire."[22] The *Tribune* put it more succinctly: "He tried law and order and it didn't go, so he tried the other."[23]

That said, by all accounts, Capone's protection *was* as effective as Becker claimed. As one commentator later claimed, arrangements like these were normally pretty satisfactory for both parties, since the "alliance of organized gangdom and organized industry was probably, however, not of the parasitic type of racketeering. It was of the collusive type, with the organized gang acting as a fairly effective hired 'policeman.' This policeman would of course receive excellent remuneration but would enforce the objective of the employer-employee combination."[24] Landesco shows how this "combination" outraged many of the most powerful residents of Chicago, with its invasion of legitimate business and its reversion to the law of the jungle.

## Simon Gorman

In many ways it is really rather odd that Landesco and his readers were so surprised, or that they saw the alliance as anything unusual or novel. Such arrangements had a long history in the city. There had pretty well always been a connection between Chicago crime lords and labor organizations. In fact, Capone's own criminal antecedents were even more directly linked to racketeering of this "collusive" brand than most. The grassroots power of the founder of the empire that would evolve into Capone's "Outfit" had been founded on just such a "combination."

"Diamond Jim" Colosimo had drawn his most reliable support, much of his muscle and many of his votes from his control of a street sweepers' organization. His nominated successor, "Dago Mike" Corrozzo, had control of twenty-five locals of the International Hod-carriers, Builders and Common Laborers Union, which brought him the allegiance of an estimated 20,000 workers, along with their funds. Yet the real innovator in this sphere was Colosimo's actual successor, "Terrible" Johnny Torrio, the same Torrio who had brought the brutal young thug, Capone, from Brooklyn to Chicago.[25]

It was also Torrio who had eventually handed over power to "Scarface." Torrio was a meticulous organizer and efficient manager. He had quickly seen the criminal potential of labor organizing. As a consequence, he had put more faith than any of his predecessors in the power of a wide-ranging alliance between labor and the syndicate. It was estimated that at his peak he controlled almost two hundred different labor associations. These included the rather unlikely cartoonish-sounding Soda Dispensers and Table Girls Brotherhood and the Bread, Yeast, Cracker and Pie Wagon Drivers' Union.[26]

Capone himself wasn't unfamiliar with or averse to union rackets before Becker had called him in. One of his most important advisors had operated as a very successful labor racketeer for years before he hooked up with Capone, and in fact it was probably this expertise that attracted the boss to him. The mysterious, highly intelligent, well-connected and dapper Murray "Curly the Camel" Humphreys was a trusted lieutenant of Capone's and had almost certainly advised Capone on the Becker takeover. Humphreys had quickly become a vital associate of Capone's as the key to the logistics of Scarface's growing empire. When labor trouble threatened, Humphreys was the fixer, charged with smoothing the path of Capone's relations with unions in distribution and warehousing operations when the outfit was still establishing its alky racket.[27]

Nor was it simply Capone and his associates who were involved in Chicago's labor racketeering. Crowley had only decided to target Becker because he had come off worse in a tussle with Capone's enemy, George "Bugs" Moran, again in a battle associated with the city's cleaning industry. The confrontation had centered on a group of independent cleaners who had decided to form their own association. This "Central Cleaning Company" had been targeted by Crowley, who used his usual tactics of intimidation, only this time the victims had called in help at an early stage. Negotiating with Moran's Northsiders, they hired armed guards who very publicly and effectively rode shotgun for their vans and guarded their premises. Unwilling to tangle with such public displays of power, Crowley admitted when he was beaten, gave up on Central Cleaning, and to save face moved in on Becker's businesses.

While it is possible to see the actions of Capone and other mobsters simply as an extension of their traditional protection rackets, Landesco and other commentators found another type of racketeer emerging in the early twentieth-century Chicago laundry business. Landesco details the rise of the "Czar of the laundry business," Simon J. Gorman, as an illustration of those who, like Walter Crowley, ran the union as his fiefdom by "election" from within, rather than taking them over from the outside—but with considerable input from the mob. Gorman bragged about his association with the notoriously violent Chicago-Irish gang, Ragen's Colts, a boast he used to great effect to cow his enemies into submission.

Nevertheless, Gorman's background was not that of a gangster, nor business owner. He was a union organizer. Born into a poor Jewish family, he had worked as a blacksmith, becoming president of Local Number 4 of the International Horse Shoers of the United States and Canada. Ambitious and brutal in equal measure, he linked himself to the "Hinky Dink" Kenna—"Bathhouse John" Coughlin machine that controlled the Levee district of Chicago. The two bosses provided him with a successful saloon in Chicago's "Loop" district, which gave him a center for his services for the machine. However, unwilling to remain a subordinate—a ward heeler—the ambitious young man used his newly learned political skills to move on and set himself up in what was by then the rapidly expanding "laundry racket."

As the labor secretary of the Chicago Laundry Owners Association, Gorman had a reputation for "direct action" and shrewd maneuvering. Pretty soon, through a combination of guile and more-or-less overt brutality, he had made himself essential to the functioning of Chicago's laundry, dry cleaning and linen supply businesses. As he convinced others to recognize the advantages of membership, by the end of the 1920s some 240 laundry-related businesses had joined his Association. Those who decided to join paid ten percent of all their takings and agreed to only trade with other association members. It was estimated that they each paid dues to Gorman, at a rate of $350 to $700 a week. Those businesses that tried to evade Gorman's association found it cost them even more.

However, to Chicago's business leaders this was simply another route to take to becoming a racketeer. As the *Chicago Journal of Commerce* put it: "A 'racketeer' may be the boss of a supposedly legitimate business association; he may be a labor union organizer; he may pretend to be either, or both."[28] Most of the techniques for recruitment were the same. Those who refused to join found their drivers were "slugged," their "bundles" were hijacked, their windows were smashed, acid was thrown into their laundry baskets, and they may even have received an "exploding suit" or two. This last, rather comical-sounding affair was actually an incendiary bomb concealed within the laundry they took in, and could be highly destructive, if not lethal.

If these inducements proved insufficient, Gorman used his significant connections within City Hall to persuade reluctant businesses. Zoning arrangements were made which conspicuously helped expansion of those businesses connected with Gorman, and just as obviously penalized those outside his association. Further, official certification for such indispensible items as boilers would be withheld from nonmembers. Fire and safety inspections would find infractions of city codes in those laundries that did not join the Association. The result was that non–Gorman premises would be closed down because of such "oversights." For those associated with Gorman, such matters were mere formalities. Unsurprisingly, given these pressures, most laundries joined the Chicago Laundry Association.[29]

## Gordon Hostetter and Labor Racketeering

As with many aspects of the history of organized criminal activity, in order to be able to better assess the reality of the situation and to remain more objective, it can often be instructive to look into the motives of those doing the accusing. While the accusations may seem well-founded and the context in which they are made may well be relatively clear, the motive for making the accusations and the way in which they emerge may be more opaque. It is instructive, therefore, to ask some basic questions like: what is their relationship with the criminal under investigation? Or perhaps, even more blatantly, how might they benefit from making the accusation?

As historian Andrew W. Cohen has argued, it may not have been simple disapproval of Gorman's brutal and underhanded methods that lay at the root of the link many people made between Gorman and organized crime. Cohen shows that in this age of unrestrained and unfettered capitalism, it could well have merely been the success of the Association that prompted the condemnation.[30] Cohen points out how Landesco and other influential commentators relied—at least in part—for their information about Gorman and other racketeers in Chicago on the expert industrial relations specialist and executive director of the Employers' Association of Chicago, Gordon Leslie Hostetter.

Rather grandly styling himself as an "industrial relations engineer," Hostetter had a long experience of dealing with industrial disputes, having worked in a variety of posts where he represented management's interests. He served an instructive stint in Major

General George Washington Goethals' War Industries Board. In the 1920s, Hostetter moved to Chicago, where by 1927 he claimed he had coined the expression "racketeer"— although this has subsequently been disputed. He also presciently bragged that he "foresaw the rise of racketeering" in the running of labor unions.[31]

This was hardly surprising, since Hostetter essentially viewed a politicized, organized labor force as a crime in itself. To him the union itself was a threat to American society rather than a benefit to the working man.[32] With this premise in mind, he advised members of the Employers' Association, or EA, as his association was known, on how to keep the unions out of their businesses. In this capacity Hostetter acted as the protector of the nonunionized business, variously known as the "open shop," or "American" system. In order to protect this hallowed institution, he even offered low-cost counterunionizing services—including strikebreakers—to members. He also bragged of organizing "businessmen to protect themselves against the hoodlums."[33]

Unsurprisingly, not everyone saw Hostetter's union-bashing achievements in this light. The Illinois State Federation of Labor argued that he had turned the Employers' Association of Chicago into an "organization [that] specializes in attacks upon labor unions." They argued that the EA was an organization that "stands for the ruthless annihilation of organization among working people."[34] The Chicago Federation of Labor went even further, arguing that Hostetter aimed to "vilify labor representatives as 'racketeers'" and to conflate in the public's minds "the racketeers whom labor condemns and the legitimate labor unions."[35] They saw his actions as part of a larger scheme to dismantle American unionism altogether. Not that this rather apocalyptic stance was anything unusual; the national mood was generally downbeat, if not hostile, when it came to trade unionism.

It was a sign of the times. The First World War had been kind to the American economy. As the "Protector of Democracy," American industry, finance and agriculture had thrived. Perhaps inevitably, the 1920s had started with a postwar slump as wartime orders dried up, and the costs of war had to be met. Alongside this slump came fears of revolution, manifesting itself in the Great Red Scare. Once the world's leading economy had powered itself past these problems, the decade had transformed into one of the nation's most spectacular economic booms—at least for most industries. In some measure this "dollar decade" had been fueled by the mechanization and organization triumphs that lay behind the production lines and other labor-saving practices. But it had also seen "scientific management" lead to record levels of employment and prosperity for American workers, without their direct input.

The result was that for American organized labor, the 1920s were wilderness years. Over the decade the courts generally ruled against unions in industrial disputes, and most legislation coming from Congress seemed hostile to their cause. Union membership figures tell the story. By 1923 the nation's unions had hemorrhaged over one and a half million members, or nearly thirty percent of the total workforce they had represented in 1920. By 1930 nonagricultural union membership had nearly halved.[36] No doubt gloating, Hostetter argued that this was a clear indication that most unions no longer represented the needs of the American people. Further, he claimed that unions were being driven to ever more desperate schemes in order win disputes and demonstrate the necessity of union membership to the "working stiff." Given this situation, he argued that these weakened unions represented easy pickings for his new breed of racketeers.

Chicago's laundry business was by no means unique in the attention it attracted from organized crime, but it is a good starting point. Most major cities, most major industries and most major unions played host to their own variety of labor racketeering. Yet Chicago's laundry racket is arguably most valuable as an example because it clearly shows the fears that this form of crime produced through the detailed, contemporary, pioneering analysis of commentators like Landesco and Hostetter, but it is by no means alone in that status. As the *Boston Globe*'s columnist Uncle Dudley put it: "Because Chicago is the first victim and has suffered most, the remedy should be found there first."[37] Nevertheless, as was so often the case over the period of this study, in all forms of crime, especially organized crime, New York vied with Chicago. It did so in terms of its reputation for violence, corruption, venality and criminality—and labor racketeering was no exception.

However, while New York's variety of labor racketeering in many ways mirrors Chicago, it also serves to illustrate a different set of characteristics. It is perhaps an irony that where the Chicago rackets originated in the cleaning of clothes, New York's centered on the manufacture of clothing. What is more important is that in the public's mind there was a crucial difference. Where Chicago's union rackets were seen as using industrial disputes to create monopolies for self-serving individuals, New York's versions were associated with union muscle and the power of the unions themselves. The distinction is probably best illustrated by the career of Benjamin "Dopey Benny" Fein.

For the five years leading up to 1915, Fein was employed by the United Hebrew Trades (UHT). This organization was a radically socialist umbrella group with a membership fluctuating anywhere between 60,000 to 150,000 workers. Its members were drawn almost entirely from those employed within the burgeoning sweatshops of the lower East Side garment industry. The workers, of both sexes and all ages, were largely poor first-generation immigrants. The work was seasonal, piece-rate and poorly paid. Conditions were atrocious, sweltering in summer and freezing cold in winter.

Until a tragic fire in 1912, there was scant safety regulation, and even less attention paid to what little there was that existed. Production was subject to volatile swings in demand—meaning a worker could be laid off with no notice at all. In the event of industrial action—which was all too frequent in this unpredictable industry—Dopey Benny could allegedly call upon a force of up to 1200 street toughs. This formidable collection of thugs was drawn from among the city's flourishing street gangs, predominantly from the dominant Jewish gang of the time, the Eastmans. Their function was primarily to provide muscle for the UHT.

As the UHT's strike force, these toughs served a variety of purposes. Benny's mob would defend the striking employees of their union paymasters from rival toughs hired by the owners. They would intimidate and beat up "scab labor" hired by the bosses to break the strike. They would terrorize the foremen and managers loyal to the bosses and, frequently the owners themselves. They would also operate as the UHT's own police force, making sure that union dues were paid, ensuring that strikes remained solid and that their own strong-arm techniques were not reported to the authorities or questioned by wavering members. What is notable about Fein is that unlike Gorman or Humphreys, he was seen, even by his ideological enemies, as committed to the cause of radical unionism.

While Fein had a strict tariff for the level of mayhem he visited on those he was charged to intimidate—including a set fee of $200 for throwing an unsympathetic foreman or manager down an elevator shaft—it was argued that he was not for hire by those outside the UHT. Legend had it that he had refused a $15,000 fee from an employer to remain neutral in a particular strike. Further, at his trial for extortion in 1915, the assistant district attorney was reported as claiming, "The man really had a conviction that he was helping in his own way in a cause in which he believed ... [and] he tried to convince me that he would have made the raids for the union leaders for nothing, except he found it easier to get pay for them." However, this was qualified by the comments of a retired police captain who had frequently dealt with Fein. Cornelius Willemse recognized in 1931 that Fein "was New York's first real racketeer." But even he could not help adding, admiringly, "and he made it pay."[38]

## *"It's a Racket"*

> [Arnold Rothstein was] the Monarch of Easy Money–America's super-gambler, racketeer and underworld King ... "The Brain" who had his finger in every criminal pie.... Known to honest policemen as a "cop shooter"; known to big thieves as a "fence"; known to Wall Street as the planner and backer of the only $5,000,000 bond theft in financial annals; known to gamblers as the greatest crap shooter of all time; known to organized baseball as the instigator of the worst scandal ever recorded in sport; known to prohibition authorities as the largest single banker of bootleggers in the country; known to the County and Federal District Attorneys as the brain behind the pitiful swindling of poor people in one of the most flagrant of bucket-shop collapses; known as the largest and trickiest bettor in all turf legend.—Edward Dean Sullivan, "The Real Truth about Rothstein" *True Detective Mysteries* (October 1930), 20

If the style of Chicago's rackets differed from New York's, so did the nature of those involved in them. Both cities provide models for the type of criminal who was to evolve into the modern organized criminal, at least in the mind of the press and the public. For if Capone represents the zenith, or nadir, of the Chicago mobster in the 1920s, Arnold Rothstein represents New York's most successful version, and the two could not have been more different.

A second-generation Jewish immigrant, Rothstein was chiefly a professional gambler, but that was certainly not the extent of his activities or ambitions. Essentially Rothstein was the embodiment, the very archetype, of the new crime boss, but he differed from Capone. Although motivated purely by money, he didn't indulge in gangster bling. He dressed in a quiet, expensively tailored business suit. He wore none of the flashy diamond cufflinks and tie-pins or garishly colored silk shirts that would soon become a part of the legend and go on to play a crucial role in the downfall of Capone. In his dealings with associates, Rothstein acted calmly and demonstrated the ruthless efficiency of a bookkeeper, but one who would allow no questioning or argument. If he didn't look like the Capone-era gangster, nor did he act like one. There are no tales of Rothstein bludgeoning a suspected stool pigeon to death, or wielding a Tommy gun in a red rage. He didn't even drink, preferring milk to alcohol.

Nor is that where the differences ended. Unlike Capone, Rothstein shunned publicity. Capone could never resist giving his opinion to a reporter, or being photographed with a blonde or a boxer, but the newspaper-buying public would almost certainly not have recognized a picture of Rothstein. The "Brain" or the "Big Bankroll," as his associates knew him, did not seek that form of recognition. Most New Yorkers would not know that this pale, pudgy-faced, nondescript man was—according to legend—controlling much of the criminal activity in the nation's first city. And that was the way he wanted it. Rothstein would certainly have done all he could to have avoided any photograph of him appearing in the papers. He was a man who operated in the background, organizing deals, forming business alliances, and sniffing out new angles for illicit profit.

It is both supremely ironic and yet typical that this mysterious figure should be most notorious for something he may well never have done. If the public had heard of him, it would most probably be for the rigging of the 1919 World Series, and that they likely knew because they'd been told he was *allegedly* the model for F. Scott Fitzgerald's Meyer Wolfshiem in his 1924 classic, *The Great Gatsby*. What is less well known about him is what he really did, how he really operated. In part this was a result of his trademark secrecy, which also has similarities with Capone. In the legend he distributed about himself, Capone drew his entire fortune from bootlegging—an activity many saw as meeting a "legitimate" demand for something which had mistakenly been made illegal. The celebrity gangster was careful to protect his public image, not mentioning his less savory involvement in white slavery, protection and gambling rackets.

Perhaps the "Brain" had similar misgivings about being associated with anything other than gambling. This was not because he saw it as immoral, but because he wasn't familiar with the risks and therefore could not alter the odds to suit him. At least he could not be sure that he had rigged the odds in other fields in the way in which he skillfully and surreptitiously did in most games in which he participated—a habit that would eventually cost him his life. Nevertheless, one central but shadowy aspect of his criminal portfolio was made up, like Capone, by labor racketeering. In many ways this should come as little surprise. Rothstein was too shrewd to miss the opportunities inherent in industrial disputes. He would have been aware that both sides hired muscle and that it was becoming increasingly obvious that neither could do that legitimately, or overtly.

These were not the days of the Pinkertons squaring off against the toughest workers in what had all too often happened in the 1890s through the 19-teens. This was not scabs braving rifle fire as at Homestead in 1892. It was not even Wobblies members of the radical Industrial Workers of the World being rounded up, crammed into airless train carriages and dumped without supplies in the middle of the Arizona desert, as had happened at Bisbee in 1917. Even in the union-hostile 1920s, such behavior would have been counterproductive, given the massive increase in media coverage. Similarly, since then the dynamiting of the *Los Angeles Times* building in 1910 and other highly publicized atrocities committed by labor activists had made direct action more covert, especially as the Sacco-Vanzetti trials rumbled on in the background of the 1920s.

Yet, unlike Capone or Benny Fein, Rothstein did not seek to cover his actions with a layer of "ideological" or class justification. He would never have started a soup kitchen for the unemployed like Capone did, nor would he ever have turned down money, *on a principle*! Nor did Rothstein seek to show that his actions in industrial relations represented the "little man" under pressure from the bullying union. It was even more inconceivable that Rothstein would have happily acknowledged any of his business arrangements, let alone allowed the press details of a partnership, as Capone did with his involvement with Becker in the Sanitary Cleaning Company.

Capone relished the semi-legitimate status this deal brought him. Many of the newspapers, and to a certain extent even Hostetter himself, celebrated Capone's potential to end the murky collaboration of City Hall, union bosses and "collusive" business associations. They detailed all the partners in Becker's new enterprise, and even published the value of their shareholding: Capone's share was $25,000 and Curly Humphreys was in for $10,000.[39] Ever the one to bask in the glory of his own achievements, Capone did little if anything to deny the connection with Becker.

It is unthinkable that Rothstein would ever have allowed any of his business connections to be so publicly discussed. Perhaps the best testament to his secrecy and influence are the tales surrounding his involvement in the long-running International Ladies Garment Workers Union strike. According to some versions, a frustrated group of Jewish garment factory owners called on Rothstein's wise and well-connected father. While "Abe the Good"—as he was known in the local Jewish community—had not talked to his son in years, he knew of Arnold's connections in the underworld, and advised them to contact Rothstein. It appears that Rothstein senior gave them sound advice, since his son's influence was such that he finished the strike with two phone calls.[40]

According to this version of events, it was hardly surprising that Arnold could achieve this, since it was he who was issuing orders to the goons. Consistent with this account, it was Rothstein who was funding and drawing the benefit from both the thugs he loaned out to the bosses, as well as those he supplied to the unions.[41] What is far more surprising is that apparently he called them off in an attempt at rapprochement with his father. Rothstein's sentimental action was pretty near unique in the legends surrounding his prosperous but not very long career—which ended suddenly in November 1928 with his assassination in his "office" at Lindy's Diner on Broadway. A fellow gambler, to whom Rothstein owed money he was not going to pay, hired the killer. Rothstein was forty-six years old.

Rothstein was to all intents and purposes both the very embodiment and the vanguard of a new breed of criminal. Perhaps more importantly he was also indicative of a growing fear. Coinciding with the Depression, the fear of racketeering was no longer dominated by ideas that the nation's prosperity was being held back—if not held to ransom—by the unreasonable demands of organized labor. Organized labor's conspiracy to bring down capitalism had been controlled, and yet the apocalypse had still happened. Now the public mood, in sympathy with the hordes of those who had recently been made unemployed, was informed by a growing belief that the threat posed by racketeering came from ruthless criminals like Rothstein, not the corrupt union bosses or business leaders who had tried to drive Becker out of business, employed Fein's thugs or called in Capone.

These career villains were dedicated to the infiltration of legitimate businesses of all types, as well as the transformation of illegitimate enterprises into what looked like legitimate businesses. Not only that, but legitimate business, in the new climate since the economy had collapsed, seemed to be imitating the gangsters, and creating their own rackets. Newspapers exposed crooked dealings in all areas of American life. As well as uncovering racketeering in the traditional industries of laundry, dyeing, dry-cleaning, trucking, construction and clothing manufacture, they added obvious targets like household and business insurance, advertising, tire shops and car repairs.

It was Colonel Robert Insham Randolph, the president of the Chicago Association of Commerce, who summed up what many Americans felt when he told the *Chicago Tribune*'s gangland specialist, "There is scarcely a commodity exposed for sale today that does not cost more because of the racket."[42] Given that feeling, it is hardly surprising that in the increasingly grim years between 1929 and 1932, when many Americans struggled with progressively harder times, the nation had something of a witch-hunt over racketeering. As everything appeared ever more unaffordable to the working man, the press embarked on what seems only a little bit short of a frenzy to expose "rackets." Journalists discovered scams in what appeared very unlikely places.

The Survey "blew the lid off" a cartel of doctors and clinics that undercut the rates paid to private practitioners. To do this these doctors apparently used techniques "reminiscent of the methods of intimidation employed against recalcitrant members and non-members of high-class racketeering organizations."[43] The Woman's Journal told its readers how "innocent" women were being framed on charges of prostitution which required the "right" bondsman to swear to their virtuous nature and get them released. The Literary Digest reported a similar racket, in which landladies, nurses and other women who came into contact with men through their work were threatened with moral impeachment unless they paid inspectors to issue the right permits.

Not to be outdone, Scribner's Magazine showed how the investigative journalists for the big dailies themselves acted like racketeers in order to secure a story. While on the theme of the press as perpetrators rather than simply reporters, the same article argued that the precursor to the rackets of the times were actually the newspaper circulation wars of the early decades of the twentieth century. But perhaps the strangest was the exposé in Popular Science that gave details of a fortune-telling racket that it claimed was costing Americans $125 million a year—and yet no one saw it coming.[44]

Never one to shy away from hyperbole—or simple explanations—the indomitable Hostetter claimed, "Racketeering has been undergoing a considerable change these past two years…. Whereas several years ago organizations of business men and organized labor were principally responsible [for rackets], with the criminal acting merely as a tool or agent, the criminal is now gaining the ascendancy. What is more alarming, organized criminality is directing its efforts toward the control of business and labor as a means of perpetuating itself."[45]

One of the main reasons for this fear was the growing realization that Prohibition was most probably on its way out. There was evidence that the coalition of moral, political and financial pressure groups that had conquered state legislature after state legislature and steamrolled the Volstead Act through Congress was now showing cracks. Leading businesses realized they were paying for the dubious pleasure of trying to enforce a measure that had not brought them the benefits they'd expected. Further, the father of the measure—the irrepressible, peerless and ruthless lobbyist, Wayne Bidwell Wheeler—was now dead. Moral commentators who had envisaged a new world without alcohol now had to admit that the excesses of the flappers, the explosion in teenage petting parties, and the immoral influence of jazz—not to mention bootlegging and unregulated bathtub gin—were at least to some extent the result of Prohibition.

Newspapers, academics and other opinion-formers claimed the nation was suffering from an increase in violent crime as gangsters fought turf wars. They saw a boom in political corruption and alcohol poisoning as well as a huge escalation in the prison population. Even some of those who had previously been the most committed of Prohibition's supporters were coming to the conclusion that all this was the result of a measure that didn't, and couldn't, work. The papers gleefully reported that many of the opportunist supporters and enforcers of Prohibition, like the Grand Dragon of the largest state Klavern of the whiter-than-white Ku Klux Klan, had been either caught drinking, distilling, brewing, smuggling—or worse.

Given these currents in popular opinion, many politicians sensed the changing attitudes and felt they could now justify the repeal of the "Great Experiment." After all, most had only supported the measure as a vote winner anyway. As Franklin Delano Roosevelt was saying, now that the nation was bumping along the bottom of a deep depression, people needed a drink to make life that little bit more bearable. It would also make "the alky racket" a considerable source of revenue for the government, rather than the racketeers.

The nation's politicians were not the only ones who felt a change was coming. According to the press and those who commented on such matters, rumrunners, bootleggers and dive owners were aware the booze-fueled bonanza of the 1920s was probably coming to an end. Many had diversified. Even before the repeal of Prohibition, the attorney general claimed that only some twenty percent of the racketeers' income came from the "Alky Racket."[46] Yet they still needed to find something to invest in, something to keep their men employed.

The situation was succinctly summed up by an exchange reported some years later in the 1950s by the *Chicago Tribune*. The paper reported Capone's sidekick Curly Humphreys explaining the situation to a veteran union activist, Steve Sumner, who in December 1931 was resisting the threats of the Outfit. Humphreys told the aged and recalcitrant secretary of the Milk Wagon Drivers Union that the writing was on the wall for the union's independence. He told Sumner, "We're going to take over this joint ... [because] Prohibition is going out and soon there won't be an 18th Amendment. We've got a big organization and must take care of our boys."[47]

The result was that whether Humphreys's concern for the well-being of his minions was the reality or not, there was a general suspicion that "gangsters" and "racketeers" had infiltrated the day-to-day commerce of the nation. There was a belief in many quarters that the criminal influenced the behavior of a huge proportion of the nation's legitimate businesses. By 1932—a year before the repeal of the Volstead Act—Hostetter reckoned "racketeering" cost "the citizens of Chicago alone more than $145,000,000 a year ... a yearly extortion toll equal to that of the whole City Government ... in a time of industrial depression and economic disaster."[48] Of course, like so many claims made for the extent of organized crime, this is unverifiable, since Hostetter was never one to reveal his sources, or shy away from a dubious statistic for lack of evidence.

Nevertheless, others pointed out that these dire economic consequences were not limited to his findings or to Chicago. The New York State Crime Commission claimed racketeering was costing the nation between twelve and eighteen billion dollars a year.[49] The press broke these figures down to show that racketeering was costing between 5 to 25 cents on every dollar spent by those living in Chicago. It was calculated that every single person living in New York either knowingly or unwittingly paid between $96 and $144 a year to rackets. What was even more alarming was the claim that these figures rose considerably for workers in the garment, trucking and other racketeer-controlled occupations that employed some of the poorest workers in the city.[50]

There was a feeling that racketeering had become a major problem because there hadn't really been any concerted effort to put an end to either the rackets or their causes. Some reasoned that the government was actually condoning racketeering. They argued that by prosecuting the most high-profile racketeer in the country—Capone—for his failure to pay income tax, they were treating him as a legitimate businessman, giving a green light to other racketeers. Others argued that politicians, police, lawyers and union leaders were all so corrupt that it would be impossible to winkle out the racketeers and prosecute them—even if the desire was there to attempt to do it.

This view is clearly expressed by the redoubtable enemy of American hypocrisy, H.L. Mencken, in his review of *New York World* journalist Courtney Terrett's 1930 book, *Only Saps Work*. Mencken argued, "Inasmuch as there seems to be no feasible way, under our laws, to put them [the racketeers] down, it would be futile to get in a rage about them." But even the arch-iconoclast Mencken shied away from supporting the claim that "the current obese development of racketeering began during the Harding administration, and is a product of the gaudy stealing which then went on at Washington."

Mencken also tapped into a popular theme when he argued that some rackets had become so common because they were, if not beneficial, then certainly effective. He told his readers "racketeering, in its higher phases, has ceased to be mere brigandage, for its ostensible victims really get some benefit from it. What they buy, in brief, is relief from excessive and ruinous competition."[51] He was not saying anything which had not already been said. Hostetter had not condemned Capone's taking over Becker's dry cleaning empire. Rather, he saw Capone as a rational and rationalizing alternative to union-mob rule. He agreed with Becker that when the law is powerless to protect business, other guardians needed to be found. After all, "A standing army of hoodlums, handy with submachine guns and easily mobilized in high-powered motor cars, can upon occasion bring a sense of security that statutory law no longer conveys."[52]

While many commentators, particularly those on the left, were opposed to Hostetter's union-bashing position, there were—even among them—those who agreed with his stance on rationalization. Academics and other theorists, including criminologists, argued that it was lack of regulation and rationalization brought about by stifling antitrust laws that had essentially atomized business and enabled racketeers to prosper. John Landesco argued that Chicago, like most major American cities, had "a situation of cut-throat competition among small business enterprises" that fostered "an economic condition in which business is seeking agreements to end ruinous competition but where the Sherman Anti-Trust Act and similar legislation prohibit such agreements."[53] The radical Wisconsin University Professor of Economics, John R. Commons, sent a letter he'd received from a former student for the consideration of the editor and readers of the *New Republic*.

The anonymous ex-student highlighted what Commons called the "economic advantages" inherent in racketeering. He argued, with obvious approval, that in Chicago he'd met part-time workers who had witnessed the racketeers firsthand. Their stories showed that, driven by pure, unrestrained capitalism, the racketeers in the city had created a self-regulating system. In his mind the "racketeers have come in to prevent cutthroat competition. Salesmen and truck drivers are organized, and when a firm is found to be cutting under agreed standards, the racketeers controlling the firm pull off the salesmen of the firm as well as the truck drivers." He argued that just like Fascism in Italy and Communism in Russia, America had its own regulated, command economy, in the shape of "racketeering in Chicago."[54] In essence he approved, although he did not expand on exactly what was entailed in the process of negotiating "agreed standards" or "encouraging" workers to abide by them—under either Mussolini's, Stalin's or Capone's regime.

Such views were not limited to an academic readership. In a series of articles under the title "Invisible Government," the popular journalist Samuel Crowther—who also ghostwrote Henry Ford's autobiography—told the nation's women about racketeering. In one article he claimed that the business conditions created by antitrust legislation were promoting racketeering just as surely as the Volstead Act had promoted bootlegging.[55] Walter Lippmann, spokesman of the liberal left, put racketeering down to "excessively competitive conditions."[56] And the well-known and best-selling sociologist Robert Lynd, co-author of the definitive study of 1920s small-town America, *Middletown*, argued that nothing would change with regard to racketeering until there was genuine and concerted popular pressure.[57]

But it was Raymond Moley, left-wing professor of law at Columbia University and leading early New Deal theorist, who was the most influential. He argued that the archetypal racketeers were not the unions, but the robber barons of the second half of the nineteenth century. But he also went further than simply pointing out the dangers of unregulated, cutthroat competition. Moley was behind the 1933 National Industrial Recovery Act (NIRA), which empowered trade associations by reducing the scope of antitrust legislation, while at the same time protecting labor with legislation on pay and protecting workers' rights to organize.[58] With one side of the act, Moley had neutralized a great deal of business racketeering by simply allowing what would formerly have been viewed as illegal cartels or "rackets." However, in closing this door on the racketeers, the other side of the act inadvertently opened a new door for the labor racketeer.

## New Deal Racketeers

It is a basic premise behind several theories of organized crime that the gangster culture thrives in illicit markets. The argument runs that when something is prohibited, banned or restricted, organized crime will find a way of supplying that product or service. The prohibitions of alcohol, gambling, prostitution or narcotics are the most obvious and frequently quoted examples, and all have been seen as central to the growth of organized crime. Similarly, as has been shown, when a state can no longer, or will no longer, protect its citizens—protect their lives and livelihoods, and those of their families and loved ones—then the criminal can and will step in to provide that protection.

Yet sometimes the opposite can be seen to inspire criminal activity. With this in mind, it is worth considering that one of the most important underlying elements of Raymond Moley's reforms was the idea that by relaxing the laws on the restriction of trade associations, the necessity for businesses to involve organized criminal fixers like Rothstein would be reduced. Hopefully, given the right legislation and enforcement, it could be eliminated. So Moley started a process of liberalization of labor organizing that would later build on the 1935 Wagner Act. Section Seven of Moley's act legally protected unions from hostile forces—in the shape of hostile bosses and organized crime.

The New Deal started a process of evening up, if not actually reversing, the previous balance of power in labor relations. Unsurprisingly, given its proven adaptability, the trajectory of racketeering reflected this seesawing of strength. Perhaps it would be more accurate to claim that this disruption and disequilibrium became central to the perception and reporting of racketeering. A very clear example of this fluctuation and the way in which it was reported is demonstrated in one of the few industries that truly weathered the Great Depression, the Hollywood film industry.

In 1933, the studios were riding high on the huge growth in the movie industry as Hollywood went through its "Golden Age." The industry had benefited from a flood of unemployed migrants pouring into California, eager to escape the ever-worsening reality of Depression life. This migration for work had beneficial effects for the already thriving industry. The booming studios sought to cut costs by drawing on the massive pool of unemployed labor lured by the glamorous image of the movies. This already significant effect was given additional dynamism by the increasingly deep slump in almost every other industry. Nevertheless, as is often the nature of capitalism, those in power in the studios felt they must do all they could to ensure that the tables remained tilted firmly in their favor.

On the other hand, unless they were protected, the unions knew that the studios would be able to ruthlessly exploit the ambition and predicament of the seemingly endless stream of hopefuls eager to work in Hollywood. They were aware the studios sought to introduce contracts that could severely curtail union activity and limit their ability to use industrial action to a minimum. The position became ever more dire for the unions as the decade wore on, and the Depression bit harder. Increasingly the studios felt they were on the verge of breaking the unions, buoyed up by the realization that every unionized worker's job had a queue of others, hopefully less militant drones willing to step in, no matter how rough the conditions, or how poor the pay. The industry teetered on the edge as this precarious situation continued into the early 1930s.

However, by the time FDR entered the White House, the Motion Picture Producers Association had pretty well destroyed the power of the leading stage workers' and theater technicians' union. The triumph of the studios had culminated in the breaking of a strike in 1933 and what was for employees the disastrous renegotiation of the terms of contract within the so-called Studio Basic Agreement of 1923. The new agreement between the studios and the International Alliance of Theatrical Stage Employees (IATSE) essentially made the union agree to cut members' pay and relinquish their closed shop. The result was that overall membership in the Hollywood IATSE locals plummeted from 9,000 to just 200. And it didn't stop there. In January 1936, one often cited source claimed the studios had succeeded in reducing the thousands of members of the once-dominant Local 37 of the IATSE to a mere thirty-three dues-paying members.[59]

But that union impotence did not appear to last long. By the end of 1936 the union was apparently powerful enough to negotiate another Basic Studio Agreement. To outsiders it appeared to reverse the humiliations of the disastrous 1933 agreement. This variant instigated closed-shop deals with the leading studio bosses, including Joe Schenk of 20th Century–Fox, Albert Warner of Warner Brothers, Louis B. Mayer of Metro-Goldwyn-Mayer, and most other major players in the business. What was more, the union negotiators claimed that they were bargaining on behalf of more than 12,000 camera operators, stage carpenters, stage porters, grips, lab and sound technicians, props handlers, lighting operators and—perhaps most importantly, and certainly most numerously—cinema projectionists.

At first glance this new agreement seemed to represent a dramatic and positive improvement in the fortunes of the union. Not only had it recruited vast numbers of new members, but it had used this new clout to great advantage. This development could be seen as a highly positive result of the New Deal's empowering of the American workingman and a major victory for American unionism. In essence it appeared that the union's members had their status recognized by the studios. Achieving their ultimate goal of a closed shop, the union would now be empowered to better protect the rights, the wages and the conditions of its members. It could also exclude nonmembers from making inroads that might erode these benefits. This view is certainly backed up by the timing of these improvements in the status of unionized labor in Hollywood. It coincided with liberalizing of federal labor law under the 1935 Wagner Act.

Yet for some interpreters the reality was quite the opposite of worker empowerment. To those like the actor Robert Montgomery, and Kenneth Thompson, the executive director of the Screen Actors Guild, the deal struck between the studio bosses and the IATSE was anything but enabling for those working within the studios. It was, in fact, the result of backroom negotiations in which the union and its members had been used as pawns. The reality was that it was a deal between organized crime and the studio bosses. The members of the IATSE had been duped, betrayed and traded to give the bosses stability and organized crime a new income stream.

Under the agreement, the union's autonomy and freedom of action were entirely constrained. Little exemplifies this better than the trajectory of wages. In the remaining years of the decade, the average wages for members of the union would decline by anywhere from fifteen to forty percent. What was more, it appeared that anyone who tried to protest or expose the deal for what it really was would likely be beaten up, sacked or perhaps both. In the case of the IATSE's regional boss in Chicago, Tommy Maloy, the consequences were even more dire. He was murdered.[60]

Montgomery and Thompson showed that a brutal, scar-faced, small-time bootlegger, hustler and one-time pimp with the cartoonish name Willie Bioff, had largely been responsible for brokering this poisonous deal. A former gang member, Bioff had moved west to escape from Chicago, where he was wanted on a "pandering" (pimping) charge. Once in California he had taken over the running of the West Coast region's IATSE. He and his partner—the affable, intelligent, alcoholic union activist and IATSE national president, George Browne—essentially sold the IATSE to the bosses. In return for what was seen as a "sweetheart" deal for the studios, guaranteeing that IATSE members would not strike, Bioff and Browne took 2 percent of all IATSE members' salaries, a figure that amounted to some $2 million.

There are questions that are raised by this interpretation. Not the least is mystery of what gave a small-time hood like Bioff the clout to negotiate with some of the most powerful and ruthless men in the country. And, perhaps more baffling, what made these studio bosses willing to meet them in the first place, and then take them seriously? The answer lies in organized crime. It was the knowledge that the pair were backed by the Chicago mob.[61] In essence, Bioff represented the man who was meant to have been Capone's "crown prince" in the "Outfit," Frank Nitti.[62] Nitti was interested in expanding his dealings with unions, particularly those with national reach. Some idea of the ambition, scope and methods of Nitti can be gleaned from the testimony of George B. McLane, the business agent of the Chicago local of the International Bartenders Union.

In September 1939, McLane told a Cook County grand jury that Nitti had told him how he would use his contacts in "various organizations, including the Teamsters" Union, to make sure that "our people out there [on the West Coast] voted for me [McLane] General President" of the International Bartenders Union. When McLane asked how they would do this, Nitti told assured him he had a tried and tested method by which "they had taken over organizations thru the same channels" and then "parcel[ed] out different parts of the country" to their operatives. The operative for "the eastern part of the country" was to be Browne.[63]

The relationship between Bioff, Browne and Nitti went back to 1923, but it did not really come to fruition until nearly ten years later. In 1932, after having negotiated a lucrative scam—ironically, involving maintaining a wage cut for IATSE movie theater workers—Bioff and Browne were flush with cash and went on a very public spending spree.[64]

Natives of Chicago, they both spent much of this money in Club 100, an Outfit-owned casino in Chicago's Loop district. Here the scale of their losses inevitably attracted attention of the management, and the two small-time racketeers began "negotiations" with Nitti. Within weeks the two minor racketeers had been persuaded to let themselves be "absorbed" into Nitti's operation. The deal was understandably very much in Nitti's favor, and initially involved the pair paying over 50 percent of their earnings to the Outfit—a rate which would later rather predictably rise to 75 percent and finally 90 percent.

In return for this cut, and to utilize the pair's proven abilities, the Outfit used its contacts within the labor movement to make sure that Browne was elected as the national president of IATSE. This development made it possible to expand the small-time operation the pair had in Chicago. Backed by the muscle and money of the Outfit, the two could turn their talents to setting up a nationally backed venture. They now felt that they were capable of extorting large sums from some of the most influential men in the entertainment industry. It also gave the rather excitable Bioff the backup and protection to wave guns, threaten mayhem, and shoot his mouth off to studio bosses with what seemed like impunity—until it brought unwanted attention.

These changes illustrate a great deal about the new face of labor racketeering. After all, the IATSE was a national union, with locals all over the country. It was not a small laundry-based operation like those on which Gorman had preyed. Nor was it a garment local like those that had provided the income for Dopey Fein. In taking on the IATSE, the Outfit was not limiting itself to activity in a single city—as with Capone and Rothstein. What is most immediately apparent is the vast increase in the reach and ambition of organized crime.

Much of this was the result of the New Deal's labor reforms. Union leaders, like politicians, had always been seen by many as more or less corruptible, but the scale had never really been seen as that great. After the Wagner Act liberalized union regulation, the powers unions gained in the 1930s were almost entirely governed by the executives of the union. Just as the growth in city size and complexity had triggered greater opportunity for corruption with urban administration, the same was true of the new expansion in union power. What was more, even if local unions were clean, their structure had not evolved to control the increased powers they now found they had. A corrupt national executive could overrule the wishes of the members, and that almost unlimited power was sometimes for sale—as Browne showed.

## Westbrook Pegler "Racket Buster"

Not only does the Bioff-Browne racket show how syndicated crime was using the unions' new status to access new and more ambitious levels of extortion, graft, kickbacks and bribery, but it also clearly demonstrates how, when exposed, the whole process of racketeering polarized opinion. It was not merely the timing of the racket that dictated how it was portrayed, but obviously it was equally dependent on who was exposing the situation.

In Hollywood, the studio bosses claimed that they paid off Bioff because he had been terrorizing them, sabotaging stages and cinemas, threatening strikes and walkouts—and demanding money to prevent further similar occurrences. And there was no doubt he had done this. Yet according to some on the left, the studios had only themselves to blame. They maintained it was the bosses themselves who had called in Bioff, in order to keep their costs down and make sure the work force was totally compliant.[65]

These commentators argued that before Browne became president of IATSE, the union locals had exercised real power. After his accession, that power had been subsumed to the whims of a national body that was now dominated by organized crime. The crusading left-wing politician, journalist and attorney Carey McWilliams perhaps best illustrated this. According to his account, once the deal had been struck, "twelve thousand studio workers were amazed to report to work and find notices on the bulletin board advising them that membership in the IATSE was a first condition of employment.... [As a result,] the producers [bosses] did not have to deal with the membership, but with Browne and Bioff, who ... [already] had begun to receive payoffs from them.... Had the producers not 'paid off' to Willie [Bioff] and George [Browne], even to the tune of $500,000, they might have had to pay ten times that amount in wage adjustments."[66]

Others sympathetic to organized labor saw Browne's tactics as a necessary evil. They saw his establishment of an IATSE closed shop as a victory for the principles of unionism. They were more pragmatic. As Herb Aller, an IATSE stalwart, later recalled: "Our feeling was that Browne could do the job. How and when no one cared."[67]

One person who did care was the journalist Westbook Pegler, and he made sure that many more Americans became aware of this fundamental change in racketeering. Since 1933 Pegler had written a column, "Fair Enough." By the end of the decade it went out six days a week, and was read by an estimated ten million readers, in 174 newspapers all over the nation—and Pegler made Bioff and other corrupt union officials a centerpiece of his reportage. Starting in November 1939, he pointed out Bioff's criminal record, uncovered his mob connections, detailed his dirty tactics, and exposed his personal corruption. What was more, he kept up this pressure, relentlessly publishing details on Bioff and his scams in Hollywood until the authorities had to act. Even then he didn't stop. His final blast came as he condemned the impotence of the legal system when the racketeer walked free in January 1945 after serving a mere two years of his ten-year sentence.[68]

Westbrook Pegler did more than simply bring a bent union official to book. He cemented what would become a persistent idea in the public's mind—that American unions were frequently involved with racketeers. To Pegler, Bioff and other corrupt union officials were representative of "a hundred thieves and gangsters, embezzlers and terrorists who hold office in the unions of the American Federation of Labor."[69] Further, much of the blame for this union corruption he laid at the door of the White House. His argument was that the under huge expansion of unionism encouraged by the policies of the New Deal—union membership expanded from representing 3 million U.S. workers in 1932, to over 7 million by 1940—had speeded up the growing appeal of the organized labor cash cow to post–Prohibition organized crime.

While Pegler was condemned in one account as a "fakir and a one-sided industrial stooge," there was considerable evidence to back his claims in the Bioff case.[70] It was largely as a result of Pegler's persistent accusations about Bioff that the racketeer turned informant shortly after arriving in Alcatraz. The evidence he produced significantly reduced his sentence while at the same time supporting Pegler's claims. It was also strong enough to convict seven members of the Chicago "Outfit." Each of them received ten years for extortion. Dramatically, it led to their boss Frank "The Enforcer" Nitti, who was also incriminated, shooting himself before going to trial. Perhaps more importantly, it was not only Bioff that Pegler condemned as corrupting the cause of organized labor, nor were his investigations limited to Hollywood.

Pegler launched an equally unrelenting and similarly successful campaign high-lighting corruption within construction industries in New York. George "Poker Face" Scalise was the highly successful president of the Building Service Employees International Union (BSEIU). Under his leadership the New York City membership of the union expanded twenty-fold, from 1500 to 30,000 dues-paying unionists. Outwardly it appeared that the smooth, diplomatic Scalise was the opposite of the thuggish Bioff. However, the urbane, snappily dressed, happily married and very well-connected Scalise nonetheless had a similar criminal record to that of Bioff, having been convicted at 18 years old of a pandering charge in 1913.

This had led to his serving four and a half years in Atlanta Penitentiary. Pegler also made assertions that Scalise was closely associated with big-time gangsters like Francesco Ioele and Arthur Flegenheimer. These two characters were gangland royalty. Ioele, more generally know by his anglicized name of Frankie Yale, had been Capone's original employer, and Flegenheimer was the "real" name of the legendary Dutch Schultz. Pegler claimed Scalise had worked as a bodyguard for Yale and used that connection to gain support from Al Capone in his rise up the BSEIU ladder. He also argued that Scalise used Schultz's massive clout to get the Teamsters' recognition of the parking garage work-ers. What was more, Pegler accused the supremely ambitious Scalise of using these con-nections to intimidate employers and to then go on to extort money from them.[71]

What made Pegler's attack on Scalise all the more potent was the decision by the president of the American Federation of Labor, William Green, to defend the embattled union executive. No doubt at the building unionist's request, Green called on Pegler to forgive Scalise's indiscretions. Green argued that Scalise had served his time for the youth-ful offense, which he pointed out had taken place over 20 years before, and for which Scalise had paid the price in prison time. He also advised Pegler to await the court's verdict on the pending extortion charges.[72]

Pegler was never one to shy away from a fight, so these requests merely spurred him to go in for the kill. Instead of backing off, he accused Green and senior AFL officials of complicity in Scalise's crimes. Without citing much hard evidence to support many of his claims, Pegler argued, "They [racketeers] infest the A.F. of L. to such a degree that the organization has negligently lost its right to public respect as a labor movement and has become the front for a privileged terror obviously comparable to the Mafia of Sicily. The Mafia, too, began with high motives, but as it developed power became a terroristic organization.… I don't subscribe to the proposal that the leadership of the AF of L unions is, on the whole, either able or honest. If it were able it would kick out the criminals, and if it were honest it would not co-operate with or even associate with them."[73]

The attacks yielded results. Within months, on the evidence of Pegler's column, that indomitable enemy of the New York racketeer, Thomas Dewey, exposed Scalese. He showed him as having used the union to extort over $100,000 from employers since 1937. Scalese got 10 to 20 years. Pegler got a Pulitzer.

## Reds and Robber Barons

That is not to suggest that racketeering, or even that subset, labor racketeering, were simply the province of those even ostensibly representing the workers. Frequently corporations and bosses would pay racketeers to avoid problems, avoid strikes, or infiltrate and subvert their opponents' organizations. Such tactics were the specialty of two of the most notorious New York City mobsters of the 1920s: Louis "Lepke" Buchalter and Jacob "Gurrah" Shapiro, who took payments at one time or another from most of the bosses with whom Benny Fein did battle in the garment district.[74]

Those corporations that could afford it kept such services "in house." From the mid–1920s, Henry Ford's vast empire controlled its labor relations through the services of the diminutive, ultra-violent psychopath Harry Bennett. Bennett saw it as his duty to terrorize Ford employees into acquiescence with the anti-union stance of Henry Ford by the 1920s. He achieved this by means of his "Service Department" of thugs. Drawn from ex-convicts, athletes and petty criminals, they maintained the "open shop" armed with anything from fists to pistols and whips. They were a considerable force by the late 1930s, described by one commentator as "the world's largest private army" of anywhere between 3,500 and 6,000 men.[75]

Whatever their numbers, their techniques were brutally effective. Bennett's underworld connections and encouragement of extreme violence cowed all but the most reckless of union officials. It was combined with and egged on by Ford's increasing paranoia about the security of both his family and his business. Throughout the 1920s, like most business leaders, the auto magnate was convinced Reds meant to take over his factories. With the New Deal's encouragement of unionization, this fear grew. In the early 1930s Ford lived in constant fear of his children's being kidnapped.

One of the results of these obsessions was that Ford gave ever-greater protection and power to Bennett, in whom he placed increasing trust. In turn Bennett took full advantage of Ford's trust and expanded the activities of his Service Department. The net effect of this freedom and protection was that Bennett and his men could afford to take very little notice of the law, safe in the knowledge that they were supported by one the most powerful men in the country. Since Ford was a huge employer and economic force wherever his plants were constructed, the local authorities turned a blind eye to the escalating brutality, and prosecutions were extraordinarily rare. Whipping, tarring and feathering, Bennett's men maintained what Ford approvingly called the nonunion "citadel of the open shop" in all the company's plants.

At times the violence was little short of breathtaking. United Auto Workers (UAW) activist George Baer was so badly beaten by Bennett's men while trying to organize support in Dallas that he was left permanently blind in one eye. Dallas police had participated in the beating.[76] While trying to unionize autoworkers in Memphis, Tennessee, Norman Smith was dragged from his car by Ford Servicemen. He was then beaten over the head with hammers and pistol butts and left for dead. He survived, and eyewitnesses gave the license plate details of his assailants to the local police. No action was taken.[77] However, such beatings were almost mild when compared with the treatment meted out to a communist-led protest march passed the huge Rouge River Ford plant in 1932. Ordering them to disperse, Bennett was struck on the head by a brick thrown by one of the marchers. In retaliation, the Service Department men, local police and the wounded Bennett shot into the crowd. They killed four marchers and wounded twenty-eight. There were no prosecutions.[78]

In some ways—in many ways—the concept of racketeering can be seen as the residue of the fierce Gilded Age battles between labor and capital. These battle lines were familiar to the American public, the media and politicians by the 1930s. They had been drawn long before Hostetter coined the word in our modern context. When the problem was considered—in all its political, economic, ethnic and racial shades—allegiances fell into one of two camps. Some saw it as industrial problems caused by and resulting from organized criminal activity prompted by predatory capital. Others saw it as organized criminal activity prompted by corrupt labor. Obviously this was predicted and predicated by class and economics, but it also shows how interpretations of what organized crime was changed over time—reacting to, and reflecting back, political, economic and social changes.

To those who used the issue—notably Hostetter, Pegler and Thomas Dewey—the history of racketeering in the 1920s and 1930s is simply a question of the struggles of good against evil. It is the surmounting of simplified obstacles with some of the inherent problems and issues of their times exposed, confronted and overcome. To Hostetter and Pegler, the overweening power of the unions was the essence of the problem. This viewpoint would become increasingly accepted as fact in the years of the Cold War as the belief gained traction that organized crime was as an overarching, omnipotent and omnipresent criminal countergovernment.[79]

Pegler, in particular, had already sowed this seed when he argued that the New Deal reforms had given "organized labor … the powers of government without the responsibility of government … [facilitating] the establishment of an irresponsible invisible government in the hands of union leaders" and their puppet masters in organized crime.[80] This made it the perfect tool for communist activism, and anticommunist rhetoric, an idea that had an impressive pedigree in American thought. As one analyst of the mob's infiltration of the labor movement later pointed out, it is "clear that organized criminal groups, those that resemble the Mafia model, were tolerated [since the turn of the century in the USA] more than radical political groups advocating socialist and communist dogma."[81]

On the other hand, to Dewey the problem lay in the impotence, not the strength, of labor. In this he was in agreement with Raymond Moley. In his 1930 study of racketeering in the New York Times, Moley saw the essence of racketeering lying with protection rackets run by the bosses, not the workforce. In his analysis he harked back to examples of what he saw as weak central government allowing the emergence of robber barons, both in medieval European history and more recent U.S. history. This was an interpretation that had a long pedigree. Many of the most illustrious investigative journalists of the 1890s and 1900s, including many of those Theodore Roosevelt condemned as "muckrakers," saw the accumulation of senselessly massive fortunes as a racket in itself and the perpetrators as racketeers.

Like many of the Progressives, Henry Damarest Lloyd railed against the acceptance of the "great money makers … gluttons of luxury and power," who he claimed ruled the country. The highly influential economist Edward Alsworth Ross agreed. As he saw it, big business was the archetype of organized crime, representing a criminal movement so overwhelming it could simultaneously "pick a thousand pockets, poison a thousand sick, pollute a thousand minds or imperil a thousand lives."[82] Theodore Roosevelt himself saw the original trust, John D. Rockefeller's Standard Oil as being run by, and in the interests of, "the biggest criminals in our country." What was more, as others showed, these ubiquitous "trusts" were protected, supported and enriched by toadies, lobbyists and apologists at all levels of government.[83]

In her attack on Standard Oil, Ida Tarbell provided meticulous evidence to back up

Roosevelt's suspicions. After having investigated his activities in great detail, Tarbell concluded that Rockefeller was the epitome of a new breed of immoral, cruel, ruthless and seemingly unstoppable criminal. Building her case with painstaking research, she came to the same conclusion as Roosevelt, but extended it by arguing that in her opinion, Rockefeller represented a new and malignant spirit in business and the country as a whole.

What Tarbell found even more frightening was that his methods and morality had become normalized, enabling a generalized corruption of some elements of American society:

> He [Rockefeller] is simply the type preëminent in the public mind of the militant business man of the day. From bankers down to street vendors we have in operation the code which he has worked out so perfectly, and to which he has given the sanction of piety. And this code, so repugnant to the sense of fair play and so demoralizing to intellectual honesty, has worked its way into every activity of life, until with a growing element of the country success is the justification of any practice, until no price is too great to pay for winning. In commerce "the interest of the business" justifies breaking the law, bribing legislators, defrauding a competitor of his rights ... he is the founder of a creed charged with poison.[84]

# 8

# Big Business

## Big Business as Organized Crime

*It is proper that railroads and other interests, quasi-public and public, should have the right to appear before legislative committees and present reasons for and against the passage of any bill. They likewise should have the privilege of addressing the individual legislators in a proper way. The maintenance of a professional lobby breeds corruption and should not be permitted. Professional lobbying should be made a crime.*—Governor Jefferson Folk's inaugural speech as Governor of Missouri, January 9, 1905[1]

Eight years before Folk put forward the ideas above, the *New York Tribune* had condemned another Missouri politician, "Mr. McPherson," as a "Vaudeville Legislator" when he tried to "make lobbying a felony." The paper lumped McPherson's "freak bill" in with those of "Mr. Hood [who] introduced a bill prohibiting railway conductors and trainmen from flirting with women passengers," and "Mr. Wamsley [who] has mystified his fellow legislators by introducing a bill prohibiting railroads from using wooden rails and tying them with string." What was striking was that most of these "absurd bills" were connected with the "corporate and industrial concerns of the state," and even if these particular bills were considered farcical, the anxieties that underlay them were considered anything but frivolous at the time.[2]

In contrast to the years before Folk's condemnation of lobbying, two years later, the governors of Wisconsin, Illinois, Texas and Georgia introduced similar measures, and the Democrat presidential candidate for 1908, William Jennings Bryan, was demanding a law prohibiting corporate funding for campaign funds.[3] Over these years at the dawn of the twentieth century, there can be little doubt that in the mind of a growing proportion of the American population, business combinations were seen as the real criminal organizations. To those who opposed them, they were simply there to make larger fortunes for the plutocrats and keep down the rights of the workers, since most Americans working in paid employment now worked in industry.

By 1890, the majority of the U.S. working population was no longer involved in agriculture or the extraction of resources, but was employed in manufacturing, service or financial activities. The upheaval involved in the transition from one form of economy to the other would inevitably create casualties—financial, moral and political—as it had done in Britain, Germany and other European nations.

The industrialization of America was different from that of its leading competitors, Britain and Germany. The Civil War had spurred a technological and organizational boom, and the relative belatedness and compressed time period magnified and exaggerated many of the problems associated with industrialization encountered by other nations. But arguably in America it was the sheer size, the massive resources and the diversity of the country, that played up the negative side of the shifts in the economy. It was ironic that the very industrial and engineering feat that really united the reconstituted Union of 1865 was perhaps the catalyst for greatest, most organized criminal enterprise the nation had seen to that point.

It is not difficult to argue that the transcontinental railway dwarfed the piracy, bootlegging, counterfeiting and gangsterism that had characterized organized crime in the public perception in the period before the Civil War. While some would claim that it is possible to highlight slavery, genocide or land theft as examples of greater crimes before, none of these would be prosecuted like the crimes associated with railroads.[4] In the sheer scale of the fraud, the complexity of organization and levels of amoral ambition, the railroads set the bar for a new level of criminal activity.

Investigative reporters could not resist reporting the shenanigans of the financiers of this wonder of technology as a new nadir reached by American businessmen. They could not help fueling a public suspicion of the railroads as the epitome of the woes that plagued the nation as a result of industrialization. It is difficult to think of another industry that had such a transformative effect on the U.S. in the last quarter of the nineteenth century. The railroads opened up the West, enabling their exploitation of its riches and population of its lands.

The railroads fueled the demand for steel that enabled Carnegie to build his fortune. They demanded financing at a previously unknown level, which boosted Wall Street. They provided jobs, transported manufactured goods and raw materials, as well as people and supplies. However, with all these benefits, it is also difficult to think of another industry that consistently led to demands for control and accusations of corruption and unfair competition. The railroad was the symbol of both U.S. achievement, and of the rottenness of U.S. society.

In April 1871 the *North American Review* exposed that in their attempts to gain control of the Erie Railroad, Jay Gould and "Diamond" Jim Fisk had undertaken to fight their nemesis, Cornelius "The Commodore" Vanderbilt. The ins and outs, comments made, and deals done, entertained first the financial cognoscenti, then, when the popular press got hold of it, shocked the public. The result was "the most remarkable examples of organized lawlessness, under the forms of law, which mankind has yet had an opportunity to study."[5] However, the Erie War, as it was known, could not retain this dubious honor for long.

It was spectacularly toppled when the next year the *New York Sun* revealed the extent of the machinations of Thomas Durant's Credit Mobilier. In a series of articles in September 1872, it emerged that the finance vehicle for the Union Pacific—the company charged with building the westbound half of the continental railroad—had absorbed $70 million in federal government grants, in addition to public funding and other sources of income. This vast sum had been used to construct the $50 million worth of track by the time that it joined the Central Pacific at Promontory Point, Utah, in May 1869.[6]

Durant and his confederates had embezzled; they had defrauded and bribed, grafted and stolen not just federal funds, but the money, reputation and assets of stockholders and even politicians. Paid by the mile, according to the terrain, Durant's team had falsified the surveys to increase their income. They had turned the flat land, which paid the lowest level of grants, into mountains, which maximized their payout. They had deliberately taken circuitous routes to increase the mileage and attract even more funding. They even added miles by deliberately overshooting the meeting place for the eastbound and west-bound construction teams, creating stretches of useless, duplicated line running side by side.

Nor were the perpetrators limited to those working on the project. It was not only the foremen or surveyors who were in on the fraud. Those involved went from Wall Street to Washington, and reached the highest level at both. Alongside bankers and brokers, Durant's fellow criminals included not just the then vice-president of the United States, Schuyler Colefax, but his successor in that office, Henry Wilson, and a serious future contender for the White House, James G. Blaine.[7]

The huge project of linking the two coasts of the continent was considered too much for one single company. As a result, the construction was undertaken by two massive corporations: one working westward, the other working eastward. This somewhat predictably doubled the opportunity for corruption, and graft was not limited to the company charged with building the section from east to west—the Union Pacific. The Central Pacific (CP)—the company building the railroad from west to east—had also played equally fast and just as loose with funding.

Their equivalent of the Credit Mobilier, the prosaic-sounding Contract and Finance Company, had sucked at least double what the Union Pacific had grabbed from the government: somewhere around $150 million. Exceeding the fraud of the Credit Mobilier, it could produce only bills for only $90 million worth of construction. But even that was pretty impressive, since it has been estimated that the actual costs of construction were a little over a third of that figure—a "mere" $32 million.[8]

The railroad bonanza did not stop when the transcontinental line was finished; it really only got going. Once the main route across the nation was complete, and the huge profits exposed, the country underwent what can only be seen as a railway-building fever. It seemed everywhere needed to be connected to everywhere else. Spur lines were needed. Alternative routes became necessary, and rail was the only way to do that. However, it did not seem that necessity was the only driver. Throughout the 1870s, railroads were constructed following the principles of fraud, graft and criminality established by the continental railroad.

One of the best examples of the evolution of this process was cited by the unforgettably nicknamed "Sockless Socrates of the Plains." Jeremiah Simpson was a Kansas populist and unrelenting critic of the railroads. In a statement to Congress, he charged that the 8,000 miles of railroad in the state by 1890 had cost a maximum $100 million to build. He calculated the construction companies involved had raised an initial $300 million, and then sold bonds for a further $300 million. So as he saw it, a $100 million project had cost investors $600 million.[9]

In these boom years, railroads were built from tiny towns that had good "boosters," or men willing to lobby at previously unheard-of rates. In many cases this was simply a question of getting someone influential, or connected, in the railroad's pocket. There was little new in this procedure, although the railroads did have a shabby pedigree by the 1880s. When the two less-than-honest tycoons, Jay Gould and Cornelius Vanderbilt, were fighting each other for the control of the Erie Railroad in the late 1860s, they had established a benchmark for the corruption of politicians. It was alleged that in the New York legislature at Albany an assemblyman cost $5,000, but if he was on a relevant committee he could charge $25,000. Predictably, given the opportunities and nature of this criminality, many of these politicians were not even honest in their graft, frequently taking bribes from both sides. One notorious but influential committeeman took four sets of bribes over the same vote.[10]

If the scale of the bribes is taken as an index for the cost of bribing officials in railroad decisions, then it is possible to see that by the 1890s either politicians had become less dependent on this source of funding, or—more likely—the practice had become so normalized that it cost significantly less. Some rather randomly selected incidents show that there was a decline in the value of bribes over the next twenty years or so.

In 1875, the *New York Times* "special correspondent" estimated that "some rascally member of the lobby pockets $5,000 or $10,000, pretending that it cost them that sum to secure their votes."[11] In New York in 1886, three aldermen were arrested for taking $400,000 in bribes to deliver the Broadway rail franchise.[12] By 1893, the Kansas Railroad Commissioner was accused of taking $15,000 for a decision favorable to the Terminal Railroad Co. of Kansas City.[13] In 1907 the manager of the tenders for the street railroads in Chattanooga, Tennessee, took a bribe of $250 "for his vote and influence."[14] That same year the scale of the perception of bribery had dropped to an even lower level. The newspapers and public were concentrating on free rail passes for politicians in return for influence.[15]

## Hell on Rails

It was not as if the robbery and bribery perpetrated by the railroads ended with the initial construction processes. In many ways that was just the start. The railroads now started to overcharge farmers and other producers dependent on the railroad and based their prices not on a reasonable rate of return, but what the market could stand—often when stretched to its fullest extent. They obeyed the whims of the emerging trusts and chiseled prices for the huge, established conglomerates.

As Henry George predicted in 1868, when he answered his own questions about the implications of the new transcontinental railroad: "It kills little towns and builds up great cities, and in the same way kills little businesses and builds up great ones."[16] It was an essential part of the trusts' playbook to make the rates they charged to them by their pet railroads appear so high that they ruined smaller or less capitalized competitors as the extortionate charges piled up. These actions led to attempts to criminalize such practices by setting maximum rates per mile. By 1907, Ohio, Kansas and Missouri had passed regulation that limited rates to two cents per mile, and New York, Pennsylvania, Michigan, Illinois, Texas and Minnesota were debating similar measures. Wisconsin was debating a two-and-a-half-cent rate limit.[17]

According to critics, this would not entirely stop the crimes of the railroads. Sometimes their technique was entirely the opposite. Railroads frequently gave huge rebates to their largest customers, creating a wildly uneven playing field and making it impossible for new firms to enter a market, or for existing, smaller, less well-capitalized companies to compete. Once the competition was eliminated, companies remaining could be charged an economic rate—if the railroad had the clout to enforce it. Both of these techniques were, incidentally, exposed by none other than Ida Tarbell as a favorite practice of the railroads associated with Standard Oil.

The way the railroads used their power was essentially to be a test of the financial stamina of the customer, but sometimes the customers—or perhaps victims is a better phrase—rebelled, creating that curiously American dilemma relating to who was the actual criminal. One of the best examples of anti-railroad actions can be found in a sensationally violent standoff at Mussel Slough in California's San Joaquin Valley on May 11, 1880. As a group of farmers were being evicted from land that had been granted to the Southern Pacific Railroad, events escalated into a shootout with the U.S. Marshal and the band of deputies charged with removing the farmers. By the end of the shooting, seven men were dead, and one was very badly wounded. But even that high body count is not the most significant element of the incident. It is remembered more as a parable that clearly demonstrated the way in which the corporation had fundamentally altered and led many to question the unalloyed benefit the railroad was meant to bring to the West.

The action summed up the nature of the change in U.S. society that many of the leading technologies of the time had wrought, and the divisions they had created. Some commentators argued that the farmers at Mussel Slough were squatters, illegally making their living off land the railroad had earmarked for a route to southern California. These lawless men had then proved their contempt for property rights by mercilessly attacking those with the legal duty of removing them.[18]

Others pointed to the fact that the farmers had agreed to pay $2.50 an acre and had legal entitlement to the land, and what was more, the railroad had no intention of constructing a route over the region. They also point out that the railroad wanted violence, or was at least prepared for it. They call attention to the fact that the marshal sent to evict the farmers was actually a sharpshooter and his deputies were, in reality, little more than desperados.[19]

According to this view, the railroad was trying to evict them because the company itself had reneged on the deal. The railroaders were aware that the land values in area had risen, and hostile press accounts claimed they now sought to charge the famers between $15 and $100 an acre.[20] Who started the shooting is also hotly debated, but arguably what is important is not who shot at whom first, but the way in which both sides fell neatly into the divisions developing across the nation.

Both sides believed they were in the right. Both sides believed the others were breaking the law. Both sides accused the other of acting with criminal intention—although the laws that were broken may have been more based in morality and ethics than existing legislation. The criminality of the events relied entirely on what the commentator took as a start point—the onward and desirable march of progress, or the idea that this was the Eden of the West that had been interrupted and corrupted.

In many ways railroads became the symbol of the gulf separating views of the evolution of American corporate structure—or at least the labor/capital struggle that would go on to inform the relationship of organized crime and its association with business. This was true not only where what may be considered criminal practices thrived, but also in the way in which they promoted a dog-eat-dog business environment in which lawbreaking became normal practice—if not a necessity. It should come as no surprise that it was a railroad boss who coined what can be seen as a motto for organized business crime from then onwards. Milton H. Smith, president of the Louisville and Nashville Railroad, succinctly noted that the emerging "society, as created, was for the purpose of one man's getting what the other fellow has, if he can, and keep out of the penitentiary."[21]

There is also another lesson to be learned from the animosity and mistrust many felt towards the railroads. While the rail system can be held responsible for the creation of a new scale of organized crime in this period, contemporary newspapers seemed to be curiously reluctant to admit this connection. While there was indubitably a sentiment bubbling under the surface that railroads represented the power of the plutocrats, oligarchs or trusts, this is rarely put into terms of "organized crime" or anything approximating it. Other than headlines reflecting the various investigations into railroad malfeasance—Congress's Poland Committee and Wilson Committee on the Credit Mobilier being the most prominent examples—the phenomenon appears remarkably underreported.

A quick, less than critical search of the leading papers of the time using the keywords "organized crime," "crime" *and* "railroad" reveals very few articles connecting the two. Of the one hundred and thirty-seven headlines this search turned up drawing the connection in the period 1865 to 1941, only one was written in the nineteenth century. That article is perhaps most interesting, since under the headline "Organized Crime," it argues: "The country is in far more danger from plumbers than railway monopolists."[22] To our peril, perhaps, historians and other commentators since have largely ignored this warning. We have continued, blissfully unaware, to see a variety of other criminal elements as more threatening than the plumbers.

In some measure the press's rather striking absence of comment can be seen in the fact that the expression "organized crime" had not really gained the currency it would later achieve. It was not yet the hydra-headed, omnipotent syndicate it would become in the Cold War. But another important clue for an alternative interpretation of the apparent silence can also be found in the comments of a leading newspaperman of the times. E.W. Scripps, the founder of what would become United Press International, claimed: "Out of every dollar expended by newspaper publishers, on the average ninety cents is spent for the purpose of getting advertising revenue, and only ten cents is spent in payment for news, instruction and opinion creating.... The press in this country is so thoroughly dominated by the wealthy few ... [that it no longer acts as protection for] the mass of people ... from the brutal force and chicanery of the ruling and employing classes."[23] This seeming lack of interest was largely true of the main newspapers after the initial flurry of interest in the Credit Mobilier's antics in the early 1870s. With their reliance on mass circulation to generate advertising, the dailies fought shy of taking on big business, and the railroads were big. As one commentator explained: "In the first place the railroads advertise in nearly every newspaper and practically every editor rides on a free pass. This represents a steady, fruitful income and in itself disposes the editor to a friendly treatment of the railroads."[24]

This reticence proved less true of the booming magazine sector at the turn of the century, as Ida Tarbell's exposé of Standard Oil clearly illustrated. The so-called "muckraker" journalists loved to associate business with criminal activity, and leading the trend was *McClure's Magazine*. This was the investigative journal for which Tarbell worked, and it was Tarbell herself who spearheaded the attack on the rail barons. Tarbell demonstrated that the very root of Rockefeller's "monopolistic trust" lay with Standard Oil's ability to gouge prices, obtain rebates, and buy up the opposition in this vital form of transport. In this, other journalists on the staff of *McClure's* backed her.

The veteran muckraker Lincoln Steffens argued that the Southern Pacific had become "the actual sovereign" of California, and the railroads had "seized the government" of

New Jersey. Another colleague, Ray Stannard Baker, went even further. He wrote a six-part, 50,000-word attack on the railroads' criminal record that reiterated Tarbell and Steffens's complaints about the railroads' being in bed with monopolists, buying off newspapers and politicians, riding roughshod over the rights of individuals, and charging exorbitant rates.[25] The year after Baker's attack, another article appeared in *McClure's* that added yet another new criminal aspect to the railroad's already depressing catalogue—murder, or at least manslaughter.

Carl S. Vrooman reckoned that 10,000 had been killed on the American railroads and a further 80,000 left "mangled" in the three years prior to 1907. This carnage, he argued, was the direct result of the failures of the railroads to observe sufficient care, or to invest sufficient money in safety or maintenance. He showed that the railroads were generally careless about upkeep and updating of both rolling stock and the rail network—as well as the signaling system and railroad crossings. Added to this, Vrooman showed how those working for the railroads seemed either oblivious to or unconcerned about this bloodshed. He showed how those at the highest levels seemed to be concerned only with profit, and those lower down were for a variety of reasons unable or unwilling to rectify the situation.

Alongside the now ubiquitous public perception of the stockholder-driven plutocrat heading the rail systems, Vrooman detailed the poor pay, youth, inadequate training and understaffing of those working on the railroads, arguing it contributed to the terrible safety record. With exhaustive examples, Vrooman demonstrated that a passenger on an American train was five times more likely to be killed on a journey as a similar traveler in Germany, and six times more likely to meet a fatal accident than in Belgium. Yet, in spite of regulations introduced in the early years of the twentieth century, the indefatigable Vrooman also produced statistics that showed the situation was getting worse. He pointed out that the average passenger on a U.S. railroad was three times more liable to be killed or injured on his or her travels in 1907 than on the same journey in 1897.[26]

What Tarbell, Baker, Steffens and Vrooman showed was that the association of crime with business was not simply the result of fraud, false accountancy, embezzlement, corruption or other ways of illegally amassing wealth. They, and others, demonstrated that the crimes of the railroads also drew on a more-or-less deliberate record of negligence resulting from bad management, greed, laziness and poor oversight—as well as lax legislation forcing them to attend to such measures. To them and many others, the railroads were not unique: they were actually representative. The idea that the trusts, the factory owners, the bankers, and the bosses all cared nothing for the general public other than as consumers or wage slaves was, to them, criminal. If we take the idea that organized crime was what the papers and public opinion held it to be, then at this stage of American history, many argued that the railroads' behavior certainly put them forward as prime suspects.

# 9

## Organized Crime Fighters

### Hiram Whitley

In the wake of the kidnapping of Charles Lindbergh's baby in 1932, Congressman A. Piatt Andrew (Republican, Massachusetts) told Herbert Hoover's cabinet: "We have in recent years an alarming development of organized crime in this country on a scale never before known and without parallel elsewhere."[1] This version of the so-called "crime-wave" the nation was experiencing played well with J. Edgar Hoover's calls for a unified, federalized police force—under *his* control.

This demand was especially apt during the years when the New Deal was planning to defeat the "fear" represented by the Depression with the centralization of so many other aspects of American life and American governance. But A. Piat Andrew was wrong: the scale of organized crime had been known before, and there was little new in the approach his words evoked. Hoover was not the first to try to federalize law enforcement.

In his history of the Federal Bureau of Investigation, Rhodri Jeffreys-Jones argues that Hiram Whitley, the head of the Treasury Department's U.S. Secret Service, had created a proto–FBI in the 1870s. But in fact, Whitely is interesting for other reasons. In many ways he prefigures J. Edgar Hoover. In background and physical appearance, they were very different. Unlike the rather short and stout but dapper Hoover, Whitley was a larger-than-life character. Legend has it that he was six-foot-ten, with near superhuman stamina and will. Also unlike Hoover, he was a man of action, direct and uncomplicated. In the eyes of the public—at least initially—the Secret Service Department he set up was no less impressive.

In many ways Whitley's methods were similar to Hoover's. He was particularly keen on establishing an effective bureaucracy. He was a stickler for record-keeping, and very keen on the latest technology—using photography and telegraphy to publish images of suspects, and other cutting-edge techniques. He was also adamant about the type of agents the service attracted. Like Hoover, he was also determined that the Department should have demonstrable probity. During his career, Whitley's agents made "1,200 arrests, one-half of which resulted in Penitentiary sentences."

Using a policy of infiltration, he had utilized a large body of informers. They made up just under 30 percent of the Department's employees. However, these unsavory but necessary characters were kept strictly in line by a small elite—a little over 10 percent—of largely former military officers of "good" background.[2] Whitley was also, like the future head of the FBI, very keen on keeping himself and his Department in the headlines. Like Hoover, he made it appear that in the early 1870s America was undergoing a crime wave the likes of which had never been experienced before. An article in the *New York Times*, bragging about Whitley's successes in the first two years of his control of the Department, shows his priorities. It also demonstrates the extent of federal crimes.

Most arrests focused on counterfeiting and smuggling. Over 450 of them were for counterfeiting, passing "queer" currency. These included "cleansing and dealing in cleansed revenue stamps" to fraudulently show that duty had been paid on smuggled goods. The next biggest category of arrests was for smuggling, largely of alcohol, cigars, diamonds, lace and lottery tickets, with a little over 350 arrests. All other arrests combined came to about 85 in total, and included such crimes as perjury in U.S. courts, defrauding those in receipt of federal pensions, desertion from U.S. armed forces, impersonation of U.S. officers, piracy, and illegal voting.[3]

Over the years of Whitley's time in office, smuggling was a huge industry. Import, stamp and other duties made up the lion's share of government revenue, with the result that disproportionate effort was put into policing the enforcement of customs duties. It has been estimated that between 1869 and 1874, Treasury officials collected a little under $1 billion (over $18 billion in today's money). They seized over 3,500 shipments and collected over $4 million in fines. Nevertheless, at this point the vast majority of smuggling was taking place on an opportunistic, ad hoc and small scale.

Most of it involved businessmen trying to avoid duties on raw materials or stock in order to gain a competitive advantage. There were sailors trying to subsidize their pay with a little smuggling on the side. Tourists smuggled in souvenirs and presents. Immigrants tried to bring in a few extra goods to sell to set themselves up. It was hardly organized crime in the accepted sense. Where the real organized criminal networks came in was in the systematic evasion of duties by big business. Most notable among these was the sugar trade coming in from the West Indies. While the figures involved were enormous, and the operation highly organized and systematic, the operations were more connected with the bribery of corrupt politicians and customs officials, and were not investigated by Whitley's Secret Service.[4]

What was more, unlike many other crimes—notably those involving political corruption, or crimes against property—few U.S. citizens saw smuggling as a serious threat to their wealth, health or well-being. Duties were seen as simply one more drain on scarce resources: something to be avoided. In fact, many Americans could either see themselves smuggling, bought smuggled items, or turned a blind eye to the trade. So although these arrests, busts and investigations were hyped as organized crime, in the much of the public eye they were not perhaps the most important organized criminal network Whitley would destroy in his brief period at the head of the Secret Service.

Over the years when the nation was trying to reintegrate, rebuild and reform the post–Civil War South, Whitley's Secret Service had played a major role in the prosecution of so-called White Line activists. Largely lumped together under all-purpose name "Ku Klux Klan," these groups were committed to the reinstatement of the status quo ante. They sought the preservation of a world of clearly defined racial, class and political boundaries of the antebellum South. They wanted to hark back to a world that existed before the Thirteenth, Fourteenth and Fifteenth Amendments had threatened to empower the former slaves of the region, and make them tools of the northern invaders.

Neither his career, nor his apparent ideology, would have singled out Whitley as the natural choice for overseeing such work. Much of his detective experience had involved the capture and return of fugitive slaves in prewar Missouri. What was more, he had joined the Confederate forces in New Orleans during the war, but had opportunistically changed sides when New Orleans fell in 1862. He then cultivated a friendship with General Benjamin "Butcher" Butler, the Union's notorious military governor of the city, and enlisted in his forces.

Butler was recalled in December 1862, largely as a PR move on the Union's part— an act centering on his "uncompromising" treatment of opponents. Although he was closely connected, it appeared at the time that Whitley escaped the associated taint. Now thoroughly committed to the Union and with letters of introduction from Butler, he joined a band of local irregulars and set to hunting down outlaw Confederate guerrillas to pocket the high federal bounties on their heads. As if to add to his commitment to the new regime, after the war he worked briefly for the Internal Revenue Bureau, enforcing the hated liquor and alcohol taxes in the moonshining areas of Virginia, Tennessee and the Carolinas.

Given this history, it would probably be safe to assume that when the war ended, Whitley was not committed—at least not on ideological grounds—to the protection and empowerment of the former slaves. Nor was he a likely leader to choose for the prosecution of those fighting for the ideals of the "Old South" in the struggles of the postwar brave new world of the South. Nevertheless, it was these criminals that Attorney General Amos Akerman—another former Confederate—ordered Whitley's Secret Service to investigate. And Whitley *did* seem effective.

Committing eight agents and numberless local informers, the Secret Service spent three years investigating Klansmen. By the time they had finished their campaign in 1874, they had prosecuted nearly 1,000 terrorists. With a characteristic lack of false modesty, Whitley would claim, towards the end of his life, that the figure was nearer to 2,000. But head counts aside, what is significant is that the operation was truly federal in scale.[5] It was overseen and funded from D.C., organized from New York City, and operating across state lines in the Carolinas, Alabama, Florida, Georgia and Tennessee.

Some idea of the level of threat the depredations and violence of the Klansmen inspired in central government can be gathered from the budget given to Whitley and his fellow Klan-hunters. It rose from a meager $20,000 in fiscal year 1871–1872 to a whopping $1 million in 1872–1873.[6] However, unlike Hoover's campaigns against the organized criminals of the 1930s, in spite of a larger haul of crooks jailed, and arguably the breaking up of a far more real—or at least more tangible—threat to personal safety and the cohesion of the state, Whitley's actions have been largely forgotten.

In part this is the result of a sense that Reconstruction was a failure—both at the time and since. Some Northern commentators at the time saw the expenditure of funds on a region that didn't seem to want peace as a waste of resources. Many did not want to provoke another war for the sake of a group of ex-slaves who, once empowered, would only move north and take jobs. The ambitious were more interested in the fortunes to be had from industrialization and the seemingly unlimited potential of the western lands being opened up.

What was more, commentators from the South had a different set of reasons for ignoring Whitley's achievements. Many felt that the White Liners fought for a reasonable cause. They saw the objectives of those they saw as "vigilantes" as centering on the restoration of Southern pride and Southern virtue. They saw the military occupation, the civil rights legislation and the incorporation of the former slaves imposed by Washington as triumphalist, even prejudiced, and certainly ill-advised. Their view was that the Northerners were the wrongdoers: the true organized crime was committed by these interlopers and opportunists. This view gained currency across the nation, and was prevalent throughout the period of this study, perhaps going some way to explain Whitley's relative historical obscurity. It is perhaps worth investigating this a little further.

## Reconstruction as Organized Crime

The Reconstruction period—generally seen as 1865 to 1877—was a time of lawlessness in much of the former Confederacy: lawlessness which has been interpreted in a variety of ways ever since. Today the emphasis is on the unknown but significant number of blacks who were beaten, raped, hanged and murdered for claiming legal rights granted by postwar Constitutional amendments. The figure for those murdered or otherwise brutalized over these years is certainly in the thousands, maybe even the tens of thousands.[7]

Yet at the time of these crimes the victims and the perpetrators, the criminals and the lawmen, were seen by many contemporaries as entirely different from those who we might place in those roles today. In the mind of many Southerners, the problems essentially focused on the supporters of the recently enfranchised blacks and those who moved into the area for their own profit. At best these incomers moved into the area full of misplaced zeal to improve the lot of the ex-slaves, showing a staggering ignorance of the reality of the situation. At worst, they were downright criminals.

To the less sympathetic, these white northerners apparently poured into the region to take advantage of the economic opportunities presented in the rebuilding and renovating of the devastated South. Known as "carpetbaggers," after the empty cases with which they arrived—bags that would be filled with money swindled from true Southerners—they were violently resented. Along with their Southern "scalawag" sympathizers and aides, they were seen as scavengers and parasites, and were frequently warned off with greater or lesser levels of violence.

Unsurprisingly, Republicans in the region condemned these actions. To them the problem lay with the violent insurgents. South Carolina's Attorney General Daniel Henry Chamberlain—a "moderate Republican"—saw the vigilantes involved in this mayhem as "an evil which had assumed enormous proportions." To him it was an "organized crime," organized in a manner made all the more grotesque by the fact that they had "the partial sympathy at least of the mass of white people."[8] He, and many others, argued that in what appeared like a concerted effort, Republican politicians and organizers of both colors were smeared, attacked or driven out, as the region's conservative whites fought to reinstate the Southern way of life with its Democrat elites, strict color lines, and equally strict race etiquette.[9]

To these white Southerners, the real criminals were the Republican overlords who imposed the misguided policies of Reconstruction on their unfortunate homeland. These ambitious and inhuman mandarins were either politically naïve or downright evil politicians who hoped to use the brutal and bestial, ignorant and vengeful former slaves and unscrupulous northern adventurers to plunder the prostrate South. It seemed obvious to these conservative white Southern observers that these politicians aimed to set up an impregnable political fortress guaranteed to withstand the increasingly enfeebled assaults of disenfranchised and outnumbered Southern Democrats.

Cozying up to the now enfranchised blacks, overseeing them exercise their vote, these unscrupulous Northern pirates could ensure that a Republican majority could be guaranteed in the region, more or less in perpetuity. It was clear to the former elites and their supporters that this catastrophic rearranging of the political and racial balance of the region would result in permanent and irreversible damage to the South.

This was not simply a perspective that dominated the interpretation of those in the former Confederate states, nor was it only held by those commenting at the time. The majority of journalists, historians, playwrights and novelists on both sides of the Mason-Dixon Line, throughout most of the period of this study, argued that the events of these years constituted a misguided and shameful episode in the history of the nation. They saw them as events where organized crime dominated the territory of a defeated, but honorable, enemy.

There were certainly high-profile examples they could point to in order to justify this perspective. The most notorious of these was that of General Adelbert Ames, the New England–born Republican military governor as well as senator for Mississippi. Elected in 1874, some two years later Ames became the first governor to face impeachment proceedings for corruption while in office. The details of the case are instructive, since they clearly demonstrate the way in which criminal accusations and criminal activity had become perceived in Reconstruction as a part of both the rhetoric and reality of politics in the postwar South.

Yankee, Republican and reformist blood ran deep in the veins of Ames, and he'd spilled it for the cause. He was a Union war hero who had been wounded in heroic action at the First Battle of Bull Run. He was also related to one of the most hated figures of the North's occupational forces in the conquered South. His wife was the daughter of Benjamin Butler.

His father-in-law was perhaps the most unpopular Union leader in the South. Pudgy, balding, with drooping eyes, he was not an eye-catching figure in an area which placed great worth in its dashing leaders. He was also a committed advocate of the incorporation of blacks into Southern society. Unsurprisingly, Butler became a particular focus of Southern hate. The Confederate diarist Mary Chesnut called him a "hideous cross-eyed beast." She damned him for his behavior to Southern sympathizers in general, and women in particular, during his highly unpopular, and ultimately unsuccessful, term as military governor of New Orleans.[10]

By contrast with his beastly father-in-law, Ames was young, attractive, well-connected, intelligent, politically well-connected and very ambitious. In 1865, he looked set to have a glittering career as a war hero and committed young exponent of the revolutionary urges that looked set to reform the postwar nation. In fact, he ended up as either an example of the North's cynical and criminal exploitation of the defeated South, or as a martyr to the criminal subversion of the idealistic themes of Reconstruction. Ames chose to launch his post-military career by continuing the objectives that had fired so many in the Union cause of the Civil War. The young crusader chose to attempt to racially integrate his adopted state of Mississippi.

Unsurprisingly, in one of the former centers of slave and cotton culture, he came up against staunch opposition from the state's conservatives. He found himself effectively stymied at every turn. This came to a head in 1875. Ames argued that his enemies, through the use of systematic violence and intimidation, had effectively disenfranchised Republicans and Freedmen in the 1875 state election. He denounced the resulting "Redemptionist"

Democrats who achieved effective legislative control of the state as the being the "product of force and fraud." In return, Ames found himself smeared.

Along with a "gang" of other northern "carpetbaggers," he was accused of having moved to the region to undertake systematic fraud and corruption—for his own advancement. Perhaps even more unforgivably in the eyes of his opponents, Ames's encouraging of the Freedman's Bureau in its work of black voter registration and the education of former slaves was seen as trying "to stir up strife between the white and colored citizens" of Mississippi.[11] While he knew, as he confided to his wife, that his real crime lay simply in his support for integration, he also realized that he would not be able to fight the charges in a state now dominated by his opponents.

Instead, he resigned under the impending threat of an impeachment trial that he knew he could not win. While we might see this as a sensible and pragmatic response to overwhelming odds, at the time it looked like an admission of guilt. The result was that for years to come, Ames's name became a byword for the misguided and corrupt northern interference in the region. Ames was seen as the typical carpetbagger, a spineless opportunist who fled the region when his corruption, greed and perfidy were exposed. But what is interesting and instructive is that his detractors, even at the time, were not simply Southerners, Democrats or white supremacists.

One of his leading accusers was no less a figure than Elisha Benjamin Andrews, the president of that bastion of New England idealism and abolitionism, Brown University. Andrews wrote of Ames as having a "baleful" influence on the history of Mississippi. Strangely Andrews was, like Ames, a New Englander and a Union veteran with the wounds to prove it, but his stance is indicative of the way in which the views of the Southern insurgents spread into mainstream U.S. thought nationwide.

In one of a series of articles in *Scribner's Magazine*, Andrews published a section of what would later become his highly regarded history of the United States. In it Andrews contradicted Ames's account of the 1875 Mississippi election. While firmly on the side of the Republican reformers, his account effectively exonerated the Southern conservatives and, like the versions of events put forward by the hostile Southerners, it accused Ames of abandoning his radical policies when they were no longer practical.

Andrews maintained that Ames had failed to persuade President Grant of the necessity to send federal troops to guard polling stations to allow black voters the ability to cast their ballot in Mississippi. He argued that this meant that Republicans could no longer rely on ignorant and compliant black voters to swamp their white counterparts. Realizing that they could not win without the massive black vote, Andrews claims that Ames's cowardly criminal conspiracy had fallen to bits. He argued that "Ames' party had [sold out] and made an amicable arrangement with the Conservatives, which assured a fair and peaceable election. This resulted in Republican defeat."[12]

He also alleged that in his time as governor, Ames had presided over a corrupt regime that ruthlessly and systematically pillaged the state's coffers. By way of evidence, he pointed out that Ames's governorship had plunged Mississippi's finances from a positive balance deep into the red—to the tune of some $20 million. Although the causes of this are open to debate, Andrews maintained that it was the result of criminal activity. Further, he pointed out that the situation was so dire, the corruption so widespread, that the state was still "beggared" and suffering the consequences of that debt at the time of his writing, over twenty years later, in 1895.[13]

But it was arguably the novel medium of film that really most effectively reinforced this image of Reconstruction as the criminal project of self-serving renegades and political opportunists. In 1915 the son of a Confederate soldier produced the most successful American film to date. David Wark Griffith sold his masterpiece, *The Birth of a Nation*, to the American public as a carefully researched and historically accurate portrayal of the momentous years 1861 to 1867. The film was filled with vivid set-piece images that would have been familiar to the audience, as well as quotations from historical figures and historians—including President Woodrow Wilson.

In the film Reconstruction was portrayed, as a reviewer in the *Miami Herald* put it, as "more of a blot on the history of the country than the war itself."[14] It clearly illustrated to the estimated 18 million viewers who had seen it by 1924 that the political shenanigans of the carpetbaggers and their black allies had only narrowly been prevented from destroying the South, but the cost was enormous. As the *Topeka Plaindealer* put it, the "Republican Party had sacrificed the old Union war veteran ... and [at the same time] wronged the colored race" in their highly organized and criminal ventures.[15]

It is plain to many interpreters that Reconstruction offered one of the most blatant, widespread and damaging instances of organized crime in U.S. history to that date. Carpetbagger or Klansman, conservative Southern Democrat or radical Republican, Confederate veteran or Union veteran, it is a clear example of how the political stance of the commentator is central to the accusation, and not just at the time of comment, but way beyond—into the historical record, for years to come.

Given such contested views, it is clear to see why Whitley's achievements were largely ignored. Add to this Whitley's background and it is easy to see why both sides in the debate may well have, more or less deliberately, failed to acknowledge his achievements. Whitley had betrayed the South. He had worked for that most hated of Northern hypocrites, Butcher Butler, and the Union Army. He had then gone on to work for the "invaders," not only persecuting moonshiners, but also betraying and hounding those defenders of the Lost Cause, the White Liners, and most particularly, the Klan. He was a turncoat and a traitor—worse, he was a scalawag.

Ironically, many in the North saw his background as that of a Southern turncoat too. He had been a slave-catcher and a bounty hunter. His commitment to the Union cause was little more than the pragmatic loyalty of an ambitious and unscrupulous man who had worked out which side was winning, and then joined them. What was more, many questioned his methods. Those who oversaw and worked with him had reservations. His use of informers was seen as questionable and his willingness to challenge, even threaten to prosecute, those in authority made him powerful enemies to add to those in the South who would love to see him fall—and they did not have to wait long.

The reason for his fall from grace was that Whitley found himself tied up with the antics of Grant's right-hand man, Orville E. Babcock, a supreme survivor and serial criminal, whose antics in the era of Grantism have already been detailed. As head of the Secret Service, Whitely was recruited by Babcock to organize a dirty-tricks operation to blacken the name of a group of investigators getting too close to one of his operations. It backfired and proved to be the undoing of both of them when, some years later, as it became increasingly obvious that he was linked with Babcock's dishonesty, Whitely made a scandalous confession of his own part in the operations—in return for his own immunity.

This confession told how, in April 1874, Babcock had commissioned him to have the safe of U.S. District Attorney Richard Harrington blown. From that safe he was to steal documents relating to an investigation of irregularities in the District Board of

Public Works. These papers were of special interest to Babcock, who was Superintendent of Public Buildings for D.C., and needless to say—true to type—he'd used that post to feather his nest. So, in order to protect himself, Babcock's plan was that those documents would then be placed in the house of Columbus Alexander.

Alexander was one of the leading witnesses for the prosecution of the "District Ring," as the corrupt officials were known, and the investigators frequently met at his home. With the "hot" documents from Harrington's safe placed in Alexander's house, the plan was that they would then be discovered there by Whitely's men. These agents would be acting on a tip and searching the house. Once the papers were found, those opposed to the Ring would themselves be exposed as corrupt. As Babcock allegedly put it to Whitely, the discovery of the documents would "blow the whole crowd out of the water," and therefore exonerate him.[16]

However, from start to finish, the entire operation was bungled. The incriminating documents *were* placed in Alexander's house, but far too late. What would have been a credible situation, in which conspirators were surprised, began to look like an increasingly obvious setup. It was only after the meeting of the investigators had ended that the burglars broke into Alexander's house and left the documents. Then, one of the operatives, Walter Brown, a professional burglar well known to the local police, was arrested and quickly turned state's evidence. This originally led to the prosecution of a district attorney, a couple of local lawyers, and others, who were all acquitted for lack of evidence.

However as Brown's evidence began to hit home, it increasingly pointed to the Secret Service's playing a central role. Moving quickly, Whitley allegedly offered to produce the real perpetrators and their backers, in return for his own immunity from prosecution.[17] His statement, according to Solicitor of the Treasury Bluford Wilson, "created considerable amusement," but the evidence against him was such that it was "sufficient to warrant the dismissal, not only of Whitley, but of his associates."[18] He was dismissed, and lived out his days as a successful farmer, real estate developer and hotelier in Emporia, Kansas, where he was held in some esteem as the "retired" head of the Secret Service. Outside Emporia, his legacy was tarnished and the memory of his considerable achievements in Reconstruction have been remarkably short-lived, tainted as they were with the whiff of corruption and "Grantism."

## Counterfeiting and the Greenback

It is also possible that Whitley's reputation for defeating the Klan has suffered because for one reason or another the public was more enthralled by problems other than these thorny troubles of Reconstruction. As the storm of the safe scandal swirled him around, and while his agents worked on the terror in the South, Whitley himself argued that the most important criminal problem facing the nation was counterfeiting. He told a reporter for the *Boston Globe* in 1874, "The crime of counterfeiting, unlike most others, is confederated and national in its character ramifying from one end of the land to the other.... [It is] a power which we cannot control."[19] There is no doubt that in the minds of the administration this was a pretty common view; during the decade it was willing to dedicate resources to attempting to control it.

To the U.S. government, counterfeiting represented a huge problem in the 1870s. The Civil War had been costly in every way. It had taken more American lives than the combined military deaths in all the other conflicts the nation would fight up until the Vietnam War. It had destroyed most of the South's ability to manufacture, trade, travel and transport. It had done away with the biggest single current asset on the national balance sheet in 1861—slaves—and totally ruined the dominant cotton trade. It had also cost a vast sum to the victorious North, a sum many felt it could never afford.

In the first three months of the war, federal expenditure exceeded income by a factor of 4, and it got progressively worse. Huge hikes in customs duties and taxes, massive sales of public lands, and loans of a scale that boggled the imagination, just about enabled the Lincoln administration to remain solvent. But that solvency came at a cost. It was not only crucial that those who supplied the war effort, and those who fought the war, were paid. The fear that that may not be possible became increasingly likely as the Union failed to achieve that "knockout victory" in the years before Gettysburg.

Further, if the Northern public began to feel that the federal government could not afford to prosecute the war, they might refuse to buy war bonds. This would present the government with the danger that they may turn what were presentiments of defeat into an all-too-devastating reality of having to negotiate with the rebels. What was more, as the war dragged on, and victory eluded the Union, the public increasingly demanded payment for all goods in gold, and bankers voted against loaning their ever-decreasing gold reserves to the U.S. government.

All this made it inevitable that the previously sacrosanct idea of hard, gold-backed currency would have to be replaced by the issuing of a national paper currency. What was more, it was issued in values far beyond the ability of the government to settle in gold. The Legal Tender Act of February 1862 authorized $150 million of the new "greenbacks" to stave off a crisis. The gamble paid off. In June that year, Secretary of the Treasury Salmon P. Chase was able to say that he knew of no instances where a Treasury payment in this paper money had been refused.[20]

However, this universal currency soon became a victim of its own success. It was now possible to counterfeit money that would be undisputed legal tender anywhere that was a part of the United States. What was more, the greenback was quickly adopted by many in the Confederate States of America, where their own "grayback" was frequently viewed as less desirable. The result was that, by one estimate, at least half and maybe as much as 80 percent of all of the greenbacks in circulation by 1865 were fake.[21] Counterfeiting was a huge and very worrying business, worrying enough to be the subject of one of the last conversations Lincoln was to have before his assassination, worrying enough that even in the wake of Lincoln's murder, the government responded by creating the nation's first federal police force.

The Treasury Department's Secret Service was launched in July 1865 and headed up by the rather eccentric and questionably honest Mexican War hero, William P. Wood. With a team of three equally shady subordinates, he was left to carry out his investigations in his own fashion. Their methods—if yielding some impressive results—were usually odd, if not actually illegal. But it is an obvious sign of the importance attached to the issue that, in spite of repeated press reports, his handlers and paymasters at the Treasury turned a blind eye to the practices of the Secret Service.

Wood and his men took full advantage of this leeway, and set out to line their own pockets. When a location was raided, there were frequent accusations that Wood and his men were in the habit of confiscating and declaring any obviously fake money. They were less scrupulous about the real currency: it often disappeared. Relying on a team of paid informants, he and his team allegedly offered protection to counterfeiters and used known criminals to pass on what they knew to be fake money.[22] Nevertheless, they made headlines with massive busts of "queer" money and high-profile convictions of "coney men." What was more, financial meltdown seemed to have been avoided, but the problem remained; in fact, it expanded.

As the ambitions and scope of counterfeiters expanded, so did the level of complexity associated with them. When currency was mostly local, so was most of the opportunity. Now with a national banknote, it was possible to have national ambitions. From the 1870s onwards, Secret Service operatives began to report highly sophisticated, vertically integrated networks. They arrested engravers, plate makers, printers, wholesalers and "queer pushers," who often worked in conjunction, if not cahoots, with each other. Most of these networks centered on either New York City or Philadelphia, but their tentacles extended to "every city of importance as a commercial or monetary center in the United States."[23]

In 1870 the Secret Service unraveled the New York network centered on the Exchange Saloon in the Bowery when they convicted the wholesaler, William "Blacksmith Tom" Gurney.[24] They arrested, but failed to convict, Joshua Miner, the head of the infamous Cognac Street network. Nevertheless, the publicity surrounding the trial exposed the setup that had dominated the pre–Civil War counterfeit operations in New York. In addition they managed to secure the conviction of the previously pardoned head of what was actually a counterfeiting empire centered around the Mississippi River, stretching as far north as Indiana and as far west as Missouri.[25]

Some idea of the sophistication of one of the bigger operations can be gathered from the confessions of Charles "Dutch Charlie" Ulrich. A Prussian national, Ulrich was an engraver by trade. He was first picked up for producing a plate for a $100 bill in Cincinnati in 1866. He was taken to New York, where the Secret Service was headquartered. Here he was tried and sentenced to imprisonment in Brooklyn. Within months he had broken out of jail and fled to Toronto. He was rearrested and sent back to Cincinnati, where he served ten years. Leaving prison, he set up in Philadelphia and printed up $200,000 worth of $50 bills. Half of this was distributed in the U.S. by a highly sophisticated and centralized network of "wholesalers," "queer pushers" and "green-goods men" under Ulrich's supervision. The other half was sent over to colleagues in Vienna and Hamburg. These were sold to emigrants who then brought them with them to the U.S.[26]

The Secret Service methods used to capture Ulrich are instructive. Operating on tipoffs from Viennese police who'd arrested two Americans, they detained Ulrich and found him in possession of an incomplete $100 plate. He was taken to D.C., where he professed to make "a clean breast of it." His information, combined with the intelligence gathered from informants and "stool pigeons," enabled the Secret Service to set up a "sting" operation. Agents waited for months in Ulrich's empty house to catch him red-handed passing plates to a fellow criminal. Ulrich was then allowed to walk free, while five of his fellow counterfeiters were sentenced to terms of up to 12 years. Most newspapers heralded the operation as a great success, but some had reservations. As "Potomac," writing in the Washington Post, contemptuously remarked: "A more consummate villain never went unhung."[27]

Nevertheless, the Secret Service felt it had the situation under control. By the end of the 1870s the majority of the older counterfeiting networks had been either decapitated or disrupted, to the extent that they were unable to function at the level at which they had operated in the decades before. The Secret Service was quick to show how effective it had been, but not willing to entirely do away with a threat that guaranteed its existence. As with all law enforcement agencies talking "organized crime," it was performing a balancing act. The threat needed to appear real enough to require the protection of the public and, in this case, the economy. That way the Secret Service guaranteed their own survival. On the other hand, the threat must not be shown as so overwhelming that the efforts of the body combatting that menace were seen as ineffective.

This is illustrated by the reports of the Secret Service, and the comments of the Service head. In 1879 the Annual Report of James J. Brooks warned, "Of the old gangs of counterfeiters of paper money ... only two remain.... But [now] new and more skillful combinations have been formed from the criminal classes ... and these gangs, by the aid of much ill-gotten wealth command talent and skill, and present phases of operation which render their detection ... more difficult, tedious and expensive than heretofore."[28]

A year later, after a suitable injection of resources from the central government, Brooks's Annual Report bragged that the only real counterfeit gangs remaining had been "confined to two or three border states ... [where] they were considered powerless to harm" the national economy.[29] Nevertheless, he still saw a threat present three years later. His report warned against complacency, telling the public that "with a territory of three million square miles to cover, this present low condition of manufacture and circulation of counterfeit paper money is remarkable, and speaks well for the intelligent skill, industry and faithfulness of the operatives of the [Secret] service."[30]

## A Motorized Crime Wave

It is hardly a surprise to learn that the supreme federal lawman, J. Edgar Hoover, expressed considerable concern throughout his career for the issues of organized crime, or that those issues illustrate some of the main themes of this book. In the early 1930s his conception was largely connected with the threat of the kidnappers, "motorized gangsters," and other criminals whom he saw as allying themselves in fluid and more or less short-lived gangs. Sometimes these alliances were simply put in place to pull off "bank jobs" or to kidnap wealthy victims. At other times they were more prolonged, since they offered services to the criminal community—the means to fence stolen goods or provide safe houses. Whatever the structure he saw organized crime taking, there's little doubt he used it as one of the prime reasons for the expansion of federal policing.

There is controversy over why Hoover chose to expand the authority of the Bureau of Investigation at this point. The seeming consensus at the time was that Prohibition had fueled an upsurge in criminal activity. Prohibition had created a disrespect, if not contempt, for the law in much of the public and the press—not to mention those charged with enforcing it. To many, Prohibition had greatly increased the funds and ambitions of career criminals. What was more, as these phenomena continued to have their effects on organized crime, they coincided with the seismic downturn in the economy that followed on from the stock market crash of 1929.

In his own rhetoric, Hoover chose to ascribe the necessity for the expansion of his agency to a shootout at Kansas City Union Station. In June 1933, as escaped prisoner Frank "Jelly" Nash was transported back to Leavenworth, an attempt was made to free him. As he was being transferred from the custody of one group of lawmen to another, he and four lawmen, including one of Hoover's special agents, were killed or fatally wounded by machine gun fire from would-be rescuers of Nash. The "massacre" was so cold-blooded, so blatant and so violent in its execution, that Hoover would go on to use it to demand further powers that might put an end to such incidents. As he would put it to the International Association of Chiefs of Police one month later, "The problems of organized gang warfare and the defiance by desperate armed criminals of the forces of society and civilization may no longer be ignored. A recent illustration of this armed defiance occurred on June 17 last at the Union Station Plaza at Kansas City, Missouri…. It is a challenge to law and order and civilization itself, and those of us who represent the police forces of the country, both state and national, have accepted the challenge."[31]

In this objective he had presidential support. President Franklin D. Roosevelt had frequently condemned the American public's sympathies for the violent but romantic outlaws they read about in the press and saw on the screen. He argued that this disrespect for law and order was in part a manifestation of demoralization and a feeling of hopelessness. Countering such gloom was a central part of the New Deal rhetoric, and FDR was blunt in his aims. Only two weeks before the massacre, the ultra-patriotic United States Flag Association—an organization headed by FDR himself—launched a government-backed anti-crime drive. Its stated aim was "to arouse public opinion to support local efforts to eradicate criminals and racketeers … [and] to build up an attitude of mind tending toward the eradication of lawlessness."[32]

Perhaps more importantly, Hoover already had active backing at the very highest levels of the Justice Department. Attorney General Homer E. Cummings was pushing for the establishment of a "super-police force" to combat organized crime. He called "kidnappers and racketeers" a threat to the entire nation, whose response he depicted in military-style terms. He argued that the nation must "arm" itself to "try to stamp out this underworld army" in what he touted as a War on Crime.[33] Cummings, like Hoover, was fully aware of the need to have specific events on which he could sell his schemes to the public—and the Kansas City Massacre, as it became known, was a good starting place. It was, as the *Literary Digest* put it, "The Machine-Gun Challenge to the Nation."[34]

The massacre set a precedent. The Hoover-Cummings anti-crime war machine carried on giving details of organized criminals to a public swept along by the lawmen, and pretty soon won a much-publicized victory over George "Machine Gun" Kelly's "gang." The rather hopeless gang leader hit the headlines for the kidnapping of the oil millionaire Charles Urschel. Operating with a team of accomplices, including a glamorous and ambitious wife, Kelly was portrayed as a lethal, ruthless and highly intelligent criminal. Nevertheless, after the largest "manhunt" to date, he was swiftly brought to justice by a mixture of the old-fashioned sleuthing of former Texas Ranger Gus Jones, and the near-photographic memory of Urschel.

Other headline-grabbing cases followed very quickly, reinforcing the idea that there was an army of criminals set to take the nation down. The Kelly case had given the agents a catchy name—G-men. The story has it that Kelly had shouted to the armed agents surrounding him in his final moments of freedom, "Don't shoot, G-men." Whether true or not, the phrase stuck, and FBI agents became government men, G-men, with connotations of clean-cut but ruthless masculinity tempered by an educated dependability. A list of criminals quickly followed, adding to the fame of Hoover's Bureau of Investigation as it fought its battle against "Public Enemies."

Hoover realized the vital importance of public relations for the new agency. He himself made radio broadcasts and gave magazine interviews. Hoover also used a ghostwriter.

From 1933 he employed the former circus performer and reporter Courtney Ryland Cooper to produce a stream of racy, popular, and more-or-less factual pieces on the FBI and its leader. By 1940 together they had published over twenty stories in the *American Magazine* and three books; some of this material was later used as the basis of screenplays for films. Hoover's image was honed, airbrushed and controlled. He posed for still photographs like a Hollywood star. He would be pictured grimly aiming a Tommy gun, or studiously poring over fingerprints, reports or photographs of "public enemies."[35]

That phrase captured the public imagination and the press fed growing demand for accounts of the exploits of Hoover's agents. In the year after the introduction of the phrase into common usage by law enforcers in 1933, the American newspapers incorporated the term "public enemy" into headlines an average of around 3 times a day, every day.[36] Nor was it only the newspapers that used the descriptors. Warner Brothers released the blockbuster *G-Men* in 1935, and in the same year 20th Century–Fox followed with the violent *Show Them No Mercy*. These and other films aimed to create a picture of federal law enforcement as honest, decent and brave lawmen, replacing the glamorous gangster of such films as *Scarface* (1931).

Nor was it only Hollywood that promoted what could be seen as the cult of the G-man. NBC's *Radio Crimebusters* issued updates and gave clues about the hunt for public enemies and appealed to the public for information. By the end of the 1930s Hoover's agents were celebrated in the decade's numerous and popular "pulp" magazines, with at least two monthlies dedicated to them. *G-Men* and *The Feds* had "racket of the month" sections and reprints of the FBI director's speeches. They also encouraged readers to join a G-man club, bound together by a promise to "back the efforts of the federal agents in their fight on crime," and recognized by their possession of a bronze badge. The were comic strip G-men, including *Secret Agent X-9*, whose initial adventures were written by Dashiell Hammett, and *War on Crime*, which was syndicated in 45 papers nationwide.

Nor was the propaganda aimed solely at adults. There were children's books with titles like *Junior G-Men and the Counterfeiters* and *G-Men on the Job*, or *G-Men on the Crime Trail*. For those youngsters who wanted to be more involved, there was also a Junior G-Men club organized by the cereal brand Post Toasties, which in return for proof of purchase would send eager potential lawmen paraphernalia like cap pistols and badges. Six bubble-gum manufacturers produced cards related to "G-Man and Heroes of the Law" and "American G-Men," and there were all sorts of FBI-related toys, which ranged from laboratory kits and costumes to handcuffs and replica guns.

The image Hoover cultivated for his agents was one of constant vigilance: a macho, but scientifically based, dependability. It told the public that in Hoover's hands the nation was safe—the G-men of the FBI, and their relentless leader, never let up in their perpetual fight against crime. The result was that by the mid—1930s he had become as famous as his adversaries—and much longer-lived than most of them. His agency—which from 1935 would be known as the FBI—became a byword for modern, scientific and efficient policing, and it expanded extremely rapidly. Some idea of its success can be gathered from the increase in manpower from 1933 to 1941.

When Hoover took over as chief of the "Crime Bureau," he essentially amalgamated the work force of the soon-to-be-defunct Prohibition Bureau with the Bureau of Identification and added them to his Bureau of Investigation. At that point, Hoover had a shade over 350 agents. By the time the Bureau became the FBI, it had over 600 agents, and by

1941 Hoover had nearly 1600 agents. What was more, the Bureau had struggled to get $3 million to finance its activities in 1933. By 1941 it was drawing nearly $15 million of federal funding and its appropriations had doubled over that period to take over 40 percent of the Department of Justice's entire budget.[37]

## Dillinger's Wild Ride

According to Hoover and the federal government, the FBI was highly effective in its fight against organized crime in the 1930s. They had brought to justice—one way or another—the Barker-Karpis Gang, George Kelly and others, effectively putting an end to the wave of kidnapping that threatened the nation's wealthy. By the end of 1934, the proto-FBI's leader was claiming that his agents had investigated thirty-two kidnap cases, and solved all of them. They had halted the rash of bank robberies in the Midwest with the killing or arrest of such high-profile bandits as "Verne Sankey, Harvey Bailey, Dillinger, Floyd, Underhill, Nelson, the Touhys and many of the satellites of these gangster leaders."[38]

To Hoover and the FBI, it was essential that all of these kidnappers, gangsters and bandits were portrayed as ruthless, well-equipped, intelligent and, above all, organized. If they were not, then why would they represent such a serious threat, and in turn, why would the FBI need such powers and resources? Central to Hoover's portrayal of these criminals was the idea that they meticulously planned their operations. This took them out of the run of "ordinary" criminals and made them appear far more of a networked, connected threat. For example, much was made of John Dillinger's use of the so-called Lamm techniques.

This legendary system was named after the renowned bank robber, Herman Karl Lamm. Born in Prussia, "Baron" Lamm left Germany for the USA in 1914, after being fortuitously cashiered from the German army for cheating at cards. In 1917 he was imprisoned in Utah for a botched holdup. Reflecting on his mistakes, so the story goes, during his time in prison he had the time to develop a sophisticated and universal method which could be applied to bank robberies in the future. Lamm's technique was apparently based on his military experience, and its principles have been seen in countless "heist" movies ever since.

The idea centered on meticulous planning, strict demarcation of duties, precise timekeeping and good intelligence. Having selected a target, Lamm would spend considerable time "casing" the bank. He would note the positions of the tellers, the safes and the exits. He would learn the routines of guards and when and where deliveries and collections were made. He would then assemble a team of specialists—gunmen, lookouts, bagmen, safe-blowers and getaway drivers. He would also choose a specific route to and from the target, designate a rendezvous and safe house, and arrange fences for the money.

Lamm would then assign specific duties and run his team through rehearsals to ensure that they were quick, efficient, and operating within a set time limit. When in the raid, they would stick to that limit no matter what distractions or deviations might occur, or how much of the haul they may need to leave behind. On leaving the bank, he'd have a getaway car, engine running—very close by. That car would invariably be up-to-date, high-powered and reliable. What was more, the escape route would be planned and timed—under all possible weather conditions. It appeared nothing was left to chance.

Such planning served him well during the 1920s, when Lamm and his team were effective and successful. Their demise came in 1930, very much as victims of their own success. Alert to the perpetual danger of their own towns being targeted, many Midwestern communities instigated a program of small businessmen protecting their own local bank. When one such local vigilante saw the robbery of a bank in Clinton, Indiana, he rather suicidally took matters—and a shotgun—into his own hands. Coolly walking up to Lamm's car, he panicked the getaway driver, which led to the plan's falling apart. Lamm's gang were chased and surrounded, and Lamm himself was shot near the bank in a gun battle with some 200 vigilantes and policemen.[39]

Yet it was in the aftermath of that seeming disaster that the man seen as the "first modern bank robber" achieved his real legacy. In the wake of the shootout, two surviving members of the gang were imprisoned. They were sent to the Crown Point Prison, Indiana. Here, so legend has it—and more or less reliable sources repeat—these two Lamm gang members met John Dillinger and persuaded him to take them along with him when he famously broke out. In return, Dillinger demanded to know the key to their success. According to this tale, from then onwards, the wild Midwesterner adopted and adapted Lamm's techniques to achieve Public Enemy Number One status with his "wild ride" raiding the banks of the Midwest.[40]

Dillinger's crime spree was impressive—from all angles. He and his gang were known to have carried out twelve lucrative bank robberies, netting themselves hundreds of thousands of dollars. They broke out of jails and broke their confederates out with them. They evaded detection by 5,000 police and FBI agents in five states, and even raided a police arsenal to rearm themselves. They escaped from gun battles and traps unscathed, and they did all this between June 1933 and June 1934. As the *Cleveland Plain Dealer* pointed out, Dillinger made the law look "extraordinarily dumb."[41]

But there was more to it than that. Dillinger's nonchalant swagger, his bravado and daring, gave him a curiously strong appeal to the public. Women wanted to be *with* him, and men simply wanted to *be* him. This appeal was illustrated by some of the events that immediately followed Dillinger's gunning down in Chicago. There were reports that it took "ten patrolmen to clear the way" for Dillinger's father to get in to see the body of his son when it lay in McCready's Funeral Home. Even then, "a group of 50 women attempted to force their way into the rooms." Nor was such seeming adulation limited to women. While this scene was taking place at the funeral home, one reporter discovered a former associate of Dillinger's, Lester Gillis, aka "Baby Face" Nelson, was proudly bragging that he was now dating a girlfriend who had been "Dillinger's little pal."[42]

Here was a man who, as the Depression really started to bite into the increasingly parched and broke heartland of the nation, truly had the power to represent the little man fighting back against the system—and winning. Here was a man who was truly dangerous, truly threatening to Hoover. Hoover had to be careful how he handled Dillinger's image, all the more so because Dillinger's continued evasion of the huge manhunt dominated the headlines, and his shooting had potential to create a martyr. This particular outlaw had the potential to undo all the work of the meticulous press handling inherent in the reporting of the cases of Machine Gun Kelly, Ma Barker, and Bonnie and Clyde. The *New York Tribune* succinctly summed up this view when it said that Hoover's men should spend "less time on publicity and more on marksmanship."[43]

Hoover used a two-pronged approach. On the one hand, he played up the viciousness and untrustworthiness of Dillinger, accentuating the danger he and his type presented to the nation. He repeatedly pointed out that the outlaw had been cashiered from the U.S. Navy for desertion and had been involved in thefts and other petty crimes all his life. He showed that Dillinger had been betrayed by other low-life "ex-pals," including the "woman in red" who betrayed him to the "Feds." He claimed Dillinger was a loser, a thief who had "died penniless" with only $7.70 in his pocket.[44] Hoover's press briefs also reiterated the fact that Dillinger's gang were responsible for the murder of twelve people: federal and local policemen as well as civilians. Hoover also played up the fact that Dillinger had repeatedly abused women, citing a story that he had even used "four girls as shields" in a bank robbery in Sioux Falls.[45]

To bang this untrustworthy and malicious image home, Hoover repeatedly used the terms "rat," "vermin," "crazy killer" and "yellow killer" to describe Dillinger and his confederates. This attitude was neatly summed up in the first of the National Broadcasting Company's *G-Men* radio shows. In it, one of Hoover's agents says to his buddy: "I wish it weren't Dillinger. Sam—I'm game—if you were going to war to face *men*, I could stand it—but he's a *rat*. He'll shoot you behind your back."[46]

However, many sympathetic commentators did not buy this totally negative view of Dillinger. Some saw him as unnaturally intelligent and charismatic for a "hoodlum." One Nevada paper even called him a "misguided genius."[47] Attempting to combat this, Hoover claimed that with this charisma the outlaw had supercharged the careers of other "small-time crooks who would never have been heard of if they hadn't gotten in with Dillinger."[48] According to this line of reasoning, Dillinger made these thugs more ambitious, more ruthless and more effective—which made it all the more imperative to catch him.

It seemed that Hoover—rather perversely—also rather encouraged the media to portray Dillinger as a bright man, in order to make him a suitable enemy for the high-powered agents of the Department of Justice. In keeping with this, a Nebraska paper argued, just after Dillinger had made his daring escape from Crown Point prison, that law enforcement should be a career for the brightest: "Its candidates should be men of high intelligence, men who can match brain power with the John Dillingers and win."[49]

Essentially, if Dillinger was seen simply as a sadistic, amoral, brutal thug, then it would appear that the number of agents and police involved in hunting him down was disproportionate. Of course it may not have been a question of the quantity of these agents, but more one of the quality. Based on their experience as federal Prohibition agents, it may well have been that law enforcers were, as many of the public suspected, simply hopeless or totally corrupt.

If, however, Dillinger was seen as a criminal mastermind, a criminal genius, then the task confronting Hoover and his men seemed all the more daunting. If they could bring such a figure to justice, then the agents' efforts appeared all the more impressive. What was more, given his viciousness and brutality, the tough methods employed—however violent—would be entirely justified and the eventual victory for law and order would be all the more impressive.

Unsurprisingly, given the care he had lavished on the press, Hoover's men received predominantly favorable coverage. When Dillinger was gunned down by federal agents coming out of the Biograph Theater in Chicago, arm in arm with his girlfriend, the vast majority of papers reported it Hoover's way. Papers the following day ran headlines like "Department of Justice Chief Had Promised His Agents Would Get Dillinger"; "Five of Dillinger's Gangsters are Still at Large: Three of Pals Slain, Eight Locked up in Prison";

"Federal Agents to Push Hunt for Dillinger Men"; and "Killing Dillinger Spurs Fight on Organized Crime."[50] Dillinger's death, it would appear, was considered by Hoover to be a major blow to organized crime in America.

## Ma Barker: Criminal Mastermind?

If Dillinger's "wild ride" brought these elements to the fore, then it was the killing of Ma Barker that perhaps really brings Hoover's manipulation of the media image of organized crime into even sharper question. Hoover built up the reputation of Donnie "Ma" Barker into what his ghostwriter would call "The Mother Lode of Crime." According to his depiction of the woman, she provided shelter, security and fencing facilities for "some of the most desparate outlaws of the midwest." In Hoover's press releases, Ma's appearance was cast aside to reveal the true nature and intentions of this innocent-looking fifty-something woman.

She liked to depict herself as "a quiet, demure, round woman who smiled pleasantly and took great interest in quiet, respectable surroundings."[51] In reality, Ma, according to Hoover, was the "she-devil" of organized crime. Hoover painted Ma as the cold-blooded, highly efficient and calculating lynchpin of a ruthless and highly organized gang of bandits. What was more, her "sweet little old lady" image did more than simply put law enforcers off the trail of her gang. It enabled Ma to get into places where her "boys" would have attracted unwanted attention and use her superb organizational skills to plan sophisticated robberies and kidnappings.

Most importantly, her demure appearance meant she could spend considerable time casing target banks. She would enter the bank politely asking assistance by feigning a hopelessly unworldly inability to write checks or deposit money. While chatting amiably with the staff, according to Hoover, she was actually scoping where the safes and security men were positioned. While fumbling with her purse, she was checking what constituted the bank's peak business hours. She was calculating where—when the alarm was raised—the nearest police may come from, and how long it would take them to arrive.

Before this, she would have booked local hotel rooms in a variety of aliases she used. She would produce impeccable references from previous acquaintances, affidavits that fit perfectly with her homely looks and dress. It was a wise precaution using Ma. After all, the arrival in town of the frightening-looking—and recognizable—Alvin Karpis, or the shabby, alcoholic abortionist "Doc" Moran may well have attracted unwanted attention, but who would connect this sweet old lady with the impending "bank job"?

When she was settled close to where the job was planned and felt safe, she would notify her "boys." Together they would create a "getaway chart." This was done by having Ma sit in the getaway car as one of her boys drove to the pre-planned safe house. Sometimes this could be as far as 500 miles from the bank. The route would be meticulously planned, noting "every dangerous curve, every place where it was possible to take a side road and thus defeat pursuit."[52] Maximum speeds would be noted, and predicted weather and traffic conditions taken into consideration. In short, Ma noted anything that could give the bandits an advantage over their pursuers, and anything that could help them evade capture.

According to Hoover, at this point, with the rehearsals complete and the plan mapped out, Ma would give the gang the benefit of her "expert knowledge." She might remind the assembled gang of the vital importance of sticking to the times laid out in the plan and to avoid mentioning names, or she might point out mistakes made in previous "jobs." She also gave advice on how best to control the bank staff. Hoover told his readers that this sweet old lady would now tell her boys how best to terrorize innocent men and women doing their jobs. As he, or actually his ghostwriter, Courtney Riley Cooper, explained, there would be

A smoothing of the hair, a clearing of the throat, and then:
  "I believe you boys would get along better at that place with machine-guns. Flash them the minute you step into the bank. It's close quarters, you know—you could cover everybody easily."[53]

Interestingly, Hoover also details one incident where Ma actually played an active, rather than an organizational, role in a crime. Shortly after her son Fred and Alvin Karpis joined Ma in Minnesota, police in St. Paul received a copy of *True Detective* that showed pictures of the gang. They planned a raid, and on busting the premises in which Ma and her boys had been staying, they found it empty. According to Hoover's account of the incident, the gang suspected they had been informed on by Ma's partner, a 72-year-old itinerant bill-poster and drunk, Arthur Dunlop.

Relations between Dunlop and other members of the gang had been strained for some time. Dunlop had been fractious, objecting to the constant moving and the way the "boys" treated him. According to Hoover—living up to his portrayal of her as a cold-hearted, practical, criminal-mother figure—Ma acted to save the gang. He claims that after a row, Ma herself killed her lover, the snitch. Hoover's evidence for this conclusion is rather unbelievable. It hinges on the account of his ghostwriter who, with melodramatic license worthy of the pulp fiction of the era, told readers "his nude body was found on the shore of a Minnesota lake, pierced by three bullets at close range. Not far away was a blood-stained woman's glove."[54]

Hoover's interest in Ma started when she and her boys had diversified out of bank jobs and moved into kidnapping. They kidnapped St. Paul brewing magnate William A. Hamm in 1933 and banker Edward G. Bremer in 1934. This meant they found themselves liable to investigation under the recently passed Lindbergh Act. Named after the unfortunate kidnapped son of the famous trans–Atlantic aviator, this legislation made kidnapping a federal offense and brought into play the entire mechanism of Hoover's super-crime agency, who were charged with apprehending the gang.

After over a year of hunting them down, in January 1935, one of the gang's hideaways was raided in Chicago. One of Ma's sons was captured with a map and letters detailing the gang's HQ in the Ocala region of Florida. Within hours "the special squad" of twelve picked agents of the newly formed FBI were on a plane from Chicago to Florida. Not much later, they had surrounded Ma's HQ and were calling on the occupants to surrender. In true gangster style, they were answered by machine-gun fire and a four-hour fire-fight.

The agents used tear gas grenades and fired over 2,000 rounds into what had been Ma's rather elegant large white house. When the shooting stopped, they entered the devastated building and found two bodies. Fred Barker, Ma's son, was dead; eleven bullets had hit him, but as Hoover put it, he had his Thompson submachine gun "still clutched in his hands." Next to him lay his dead mother. She'd been struck by three bullets, and her "machine gun still warm, lay across her body."[55]

Unlike the rather celebratory tone that followed Dillinger's shooting, the press were largely more-or-less factual and descriptive about the shooting of Ma. Typical was the *Christian Science Monitor*, which headlined "Federal Men Shoot Down Bremer Kidnaping Gang." Even more bland was the *Los Angeles Times*, which ran "Kidnap Suspect and His Mother Slain in Battle." However, when the dust had settled and Hoover had worked his media magic, the *Chicago Tribune* went with the more dramatic "G-Men's Guns Roar Gangster's Death for Old 'Ma' Barker."[56]

Perhaps this rather muted initial reception was the public reaction to Hoover's men having shot dead a woman who had no criminal record and was already a grandmother. It was hardly what they expected of their law enforcers. As historian Bryan Burrough has argued, "Hoover's demonization of Ma Barker ... went beyond the need to defend the facts of her death."[57] He claims that his motive was less self-justification, and more his visceral hatred of what he saw as the breakdown of home life caused by the failure to discipline children. Whatever reason lay behind Hoover's demonizing Ma Barker, and whether or not he was justified in those accusations, there is no doubt that in late 1934 and early 1935 he saw her gang—and her in particular—as a serious threat. This is apparent in the resources he allocated and the rhetoric he used.

Yet Hoover's War on Crime continued beyond the killing of Fred and Ma Barker. Although the other members of the Barker-Karpis Gang had either been killed or arrested, Alvin Karpis remained at large. It was not until May Day, 1936, that Karpis was caught, but that was a celebrated event. Karpis had become Public Enemy No. 1 and his arrest was played for all it was worth, with Hoover bigging up his own role in the capture in New Orleans.[58] Hoover claimed that this coup represented "an effective blow at the heart of organized crime." He went on to say, "To interrupt that work by denying the FBI sufficient men and equipment ... would be the greatest service that anyone could render to the mobs of the underworld."[59]

What this really shows is one view of what actually constituted organized crime in the minds of law enforcers—and, via the way they transmitted this in the media, the general public. Hoover portrayed the "crime wave" of the first half of the 1930s as being the work of a sophisticated national network of criminals. In his depiction there was a pool of criminals just waiting to be called on to perform a job. These men—for they were largely men—were known to each other, so that anyone planning a bank robbery or kidnapping could draw on a pool of skilled specialists. They could summon artisan crooks—from safecrackers and bagmen to getaway drivers. Hoover argued that these minions were controlled and manipulated by masterminds, gang leaders like Lamm, Dillinger or Ma Barker.

In his mind, the only way to control organized crime was the neutralization, or elimination, of those figures. As he would put it, some months after Dillinger's killing, it was now the federal lawmen who had the upper hand: "The masterminds are being mastered.... The truth is, the masterminds are on the outside bringing them [the federal agents] in, or shooting it out with them."[60] However, in order to maintain his supreme position, he would need to secure further victories, and in order to do that he needed resources—which in turn required publicity.

## Hoover Versus Dewey

*Most racketeering depends on petty acts of intimidation which, repeated many hundreds of times, build up the racket to huge proportions.... I am confident that with your*

*help we can stamp out racketeering in New York. We can make this city too dangerous for*
*organized crime.*—Radio address by Thomas E. Dewey, Special Prosecutor July 30,
1935[61]

As Ma Barker and Alvin Karpis were being hunted and eliminated, in New York the ambitious young public prosecutor Thomas Dewey was busy constructing his own version of the organized criminal mastermind. Dewey was arguably using even more shaky evidence and even more high-handed methods than Hoover. He disguised convicts' histories in order to improve the way that their testimonies played to the jury. He coached witnesses in what to say and he cut deals that ignored their crimes to get them to inform in the first place. Yet such behavior apparently didn't matter, since it appeared that the public were enthusiastic about this "racket-busting" attorney. It was clear that they felt that regardless of his methods, he got results. That said, the Director of the FBI was not so enthusiastic.

The effects of Dewey's rising popularity were particularly damaging for Hoover, all the more so since his self-declared victory of the War on Crime had suddenly left him out of the headlines. In spite of Hoover's statements about "a talking prosecutor" not being "a working prosecutor," historian Jessica Pliley has argued that the focus of newsprint and radio airtime around organized crime was now being generated by Dewey. The young prosecutor's imprisonment of the "underworld boss" Lucky Luciano on pimping charges was changing the public perception of what constituted organized crime's true threat to the nation. To Pliley this change was nothing less than a challenge to the position of Hoover's FBI as the "nation's premier crime-fighting force."[62]

However, it is arguable that the real legacy that attaches to Dewey in the orthodox history of organized crime is more focused on his influence as a potential victim than his achievements as a law-enforcer. Luciano's sentence—for 30 to 50 years—was impressive, and certainly dominated the headlines of the time. But it was apparently Dewey's meticulous research, which led to the gradual dismantling and eventual decapitation of the Jewish mob in New York, that would have the greatest impact in the long run. And this was not necessarily of vital importance for its own sake, but as with so much in organized crime, it related to the way in which the narrative was interpreted and would continue over time to be interpreted.

Yet Dewey's racket-busting was impressive in its own right. By the time Luciano was imprisoned, Dewey had also put bootlegger, numbers racketeer and gangland boss Irving Wexler, better known as Waxey Gordon, in prison for tax evasion in 1933. His relentless pressure on gangland meant Louis "Lepke" Buchalter—the labor racketeer—had effectively ceased activities. Buchalter was being investigated by Dewey for the murder of a union official, and by 1936, the constant scrutiny from the law had proved too much. He had disappeared. In 1935 Lepke's partner Jacob "Gurrah" Shapiro was sentenced to a two-year term for racketeering in New York's fur district, and was also on the run until his surrender to the FBI in 1938.

Nor was it only by direct prosecution that Dewey had silenced mob activity in the nation's largest city. The constant pressure he exerted on the New York City mob had driven long-term Luciano ally Benjamin "Bugsy" Siegel to decamp to California. He would never return. Perhaps even more importantly, in 1938 Luciano's right-hand man—and the reputed brains of the operation—Meyer Lansky, moved to Cuba. He had left the U.S. to set up and run a lucrative gambling operation for the island's recently instated strongman, Fulgencio Batista. However, his exodus was probably just as much the result of the constant stress of operating under the eyes of Dewey's investigators as it was motivated by the financial inducements of Cuba's new regime.

By the early 1940s it appeared Dewey was well on the way to defeating organized crime in one of its most important centers. This was certainly the way it would be portrayed by gangland itself, according to another very ambitious East Coast lawyer. As one paper rather breathlessly reported in January 1941: "Gangdom's fear of District Attorney Thomas E. Dewey was illustrated today by the revelation that Arthur (Dutch Schultz) Flegenheimer was assassinated because he insisted that Dewey be put out of the way. Instead however the czars of New York's underworld, forseeing that Dewey's death would inflame public sentiment, and 'all of us would burn,' decreed the death of Schultz…. All this is the story that has been given to District Attorney William J. O'Dwyer by Albert Tannenbaum … one of O'Dwyer's best witnesses against the Brooklyn murder mob that has been dubbed 'Murder, Inc.'"[63] The story behind this threat to Dewey had had a long gestation in which little elements of the underworld were seemingly uncovered, and an enduring, if perhaps unreliable, picture would be assembled by a variety of politicians, lawyers and journalists.

## The Birth of Murder, Inc.

> *"Murder is safe in Brooklyn."*—Thomas Dewey in 1938 campaign for the New York governorship[64]

The story that would emerge as "Murder, Inc." had been rumbling in the papers since the arrest of "Brooklyn's Public Enemy No. 1" in March 1939. Abe "Kid Twist" Reles had been arrested and charged with the shooting of Robert Vaccerino, a senior aide in the Brooklyn Plasterers' Union, who it was said "would recover."[65] The perpetrator was a rather minor figure, well known in his local area, but certainly not a national player like Capone or Luciano. That would soon change.

By the time of this crime, Reles, the papers reported, had been arrested twenty-seven times. Since 1920 he had been brought in on a series of charges, but according to the stories in New York City papers, he had only been convicted nine times, and these were relatively minor crimes ranging from disorderly conduct to assault. Yet there was also suspicion he was connected with gangland murders, but these more serious charges had never been made to stick. This time there was evidence he was linked to this assault, which bore all the marks of a bungled labor racketeering contract.[66]

While these suspicions may well have been inspiring the arresting officers, some fancy footwork by a gangland-connected lawyer quickly got Reles released on a bail bond. But that was only the beginning. Within a month of Reles's arrest, the papers were reporting that the arrest was linked not only to labor racketeering, but also "bail bond and abortion rackets," as well as a vice syndicate of equal size to the one "which District Attorney Thomas E. Dewey broke up in the borough of Manhattan." There were also rumors that Brooklyn's leading Democrat politicians, lawyers, and Tammany Hall were involved. Reles's rap sheet had grown from 27 arrests to 36, but he'd only been convicted three times—instead of nine. What was more, according to the papers, he was now not simply a Brooklyn criminal, he was one of "New York's toughest hoodlums," with deep mob connections.[67] What was more, and far worse for Reles, was that Vaccerino had died.

Although Vaccerino's death was associated with Reles, it was another murder that had taken place six years earlier that saw him indicted. Reles and two others were charged with the shooting of Alec "Red" Alpert in November 1933. They had been acquitted of the charge the following year. However, using new evidence, Brooklyn DA William O'Dwyer reassured the papers that this time he had an "air-tight case."[68] Much of this confidence relied on the evidence of the 24-year-old, recently married, Abraham "Pretty" Levine, who implicated Reles and eleven other "gangsters" as being members of a "murder syndicate" used by "Louis (Lepke) Buchalter ... Lucky Luciano ... [as well as] upstate gangs and the Purple Gang in Detroit." Telling the papers he "feared that he and his family had been marked for death," he told of their involvement in "at least a dozen murders," including Alpert's.[69]

O'Dwyer, like Dewey, had political office in his sights. He was keen to be Tammany's candidate for mayor in 1941, and like Dewey saw crimefighting as his best ticket. A former policeman, O'Dwyer got into his stride pretty quickly and characterized the subsequent arrests to the *New York Times* as "the most important cleanup of the underworld that I have seen in fifteen years."[70] A couple of days later in late March 1940, the "murder syndicate" had become "Murder, Inc.," and the tally of killings was up to at least fifteen. What was more, Reles agreed to "sing" to "escape from the electric chair."[71] From now on, the body count escalated. By the end of March the murders had reached thirty, and fascinatingly gruesome snippets emerged in the papers of how "Murder, Inc." functioned. Ominously, O'Dwyer told the North American Newspaper Alliance's Ira Wolfert that they had "only scratched the surface of thus far ... [uncovering] a murder business ... [that had] kept pace with modern industrial development."[72]

Yet O'Dwyer put it differently to the *New York Times*' Frank Adams. He told the reporter that the "combination" operated in a very similar way to the rackets of Chicago in the early 1930s. In his reading of how the murder network functioned, young impressionable men were given relatively huge loans "to impress the girls or gamble" by loan sharks, "shylocks," affiliated to the mob. When the youngsters realized they would be unable to repay the loans, they were "furnished with guns and told to go out and commit hold-ups to pay off" the money. After a few robberies, the "new recruits" were "hopelessly in the clutches of the gang." The gang now essentially owned them. They could not go to the police for fear of having their past actions exposed. Should they turn against the gang, they would face a life on the run. They could now be used for "rubbings out," or assassinations of other recalcitrant gang members.[73]

Only days later, O'Dwyer's Homicide Bureau chief, Burton Turkus, reported Reles's detailing the evolution of a far more sophisticated and threatening organization. The way Turkus interpreted what Reles told him, it was an "underworld enterprise" that was national in scope, and that "followed in structure the outline of all giant corporations in that it is a kind of loose federation of units. Each unit operates in a district as a separate enterprise with a hierarchy of employers and managers, all working on a commission basis. While each unit is nominally separate, it is part of the organization of a whole district which, in turn, is part of the organization of a whole territory, which in its own turn, is part of the organization of a whole nation."[74]

He also went on to pass on the details "Mr. O'Dwyer's squealers" had given him about how a killing was commissioned: it was a hierarchical process. Essentially, once a victim was designated, the "boss" would "give the nod" to his underlings. The task was then assigned to a "sub-boss" who would frequently "palm it off on 'the troops' whenever he could." He also maintained that when the "sub-boss was in the unfortunate position of not having enough on any employees to force them to kill, he had to do it himself. This accounts for the murder indictments against Abe Reles."[75]

O'Dwyer backed up this view of the situation, and this strictly hierarchical picture of the organization. He told the *Times* that two of what he termed "the Big Six" New York mobsters had come into New York from out of state. They intended to "direct the intimidation and 'silencing' of witnesses and informers against the Brooklyn murder syndicate." He told reporters that Isidore Berstein and Benjamin "Bugsy" Siegel had come in from California in order to "try to restore order, calm jittery nerves, guide things until the 'heat' is off."[76] The insinuation was clear. It was apparent from this account that this "Brooklyn murder syndicate" was actually a national organization.

## The Evolution of Modern Organized Crime

> *And daily "Murder, Inc.," one of the greatest crime rings ever exposed, moves toward ultimate liquidation—a proceeding punctuated not by a trustee's gavel, but by the jerk of an executioner's hand on a lethal switch.*—Glodwin Hall in the *Atlanta Constitution*, October 20, 1940

In June 1940, the Murder, Inc. body count was up to 57 and it showed no signs of peaking. By October that year it had topped 100.[77] What was perhaps even more worrying than the numbers they had killed was where these victims had met their grisly fates. It appeared, according to the increasingly frequent newspaper stories, that the Brooklyn murder squad was actually only a part of a national syndicate.

The investigators, press and "squealers" maintained that the Brooklyn Murder Syndicate had grown from a local small-time racket that exploited impressionable youngsters to pull off small-time local holdups. It had grown into a corporately structured syndicate in which members could order a hit anywhere in the country—and know it would be carried out, discreetly, reliably and anonymously.

At the heart of the rumors of this national reach and dependability was the way in which it could command extraordinary levels of discipline. The racket's utilization of implicit threats of violence within its original low-life community had been maintained as the organization grew. It stemmed from the idea that the original youngster "troops" would know that they would be charged with killing those who stepped out of line, and failed to carry out an order. In turn they could expect the same treatment if they transgressed. This self-policing cycle of murder and terror enabled the syndicate to provide for the safety and security for those running the racket.

In turn, the extreme violence employed in running the syndicate had a certain simple effectiveness that helped it to expand and at the same time maintain its secrecy. It seemed that this had appealed to bigger fish—Lepke Buchalter, Lucky Luciano and the Purple Gang, among others. They sensed they could rely on Reles and his colleagues, since the latent violence of their regime had the potential to keep those charged with contracts focused on the task at hand, knowing that if they did not, someone in the racket would "rub them out." Drawing on this simple but effective plan, it appeared that the organization grew organically—until Abe Reles started to talk.

At the same time, Dewey's aide Turkus indicated that Reles had told him that there was a supreme boss—a "Mr. Big," as he called him—lurking behind Murder, Inc. He tantalized readers with his comments that claimed, "We know already that there is one boss. We know who he is too.... No, his name has not figured in the newspapers yet. If we ever get enough on him to arrest him, his name will surprise."[78] This claim had obvious parallels with those made by Dewey's assertions about the role of Luciano in the nation's organized criminal hierarchy. However, just as "Gangdom's Singing Master," Reles, appeared ready to reveal all, he died.

Apparently he fell from the sixth-story window of the Half Moon Hotel on Coney Island where he and two other "rats" of Murder, Inc. were being held for their own safety by a whole squad of the NYPD. Reles, it appeared, was about to give evidence naming Louis "Lepke" Buchalter as the "president of Murder, Inc." O'Dwyer speculated that he had been so terrified about the consequences of this action for himself, his wife and two young sons, that he made a bid for freedom. Climbing from his window on a bedsheet-covered wire, he crashed to his death onto the hotel's sun deck below.[79] As one wag put it: the canary could sing, but he could not fly.

Sadly for O'Dwyer, his bid to become mayor of New York did not fly either—at least not this time. It appeared that the success of the Murder, Inc. trials were quickly forgotten in his case. He lost to the sitting mayor, Fiorello H. LaGuardia—although he won in 1946 after what proved for him to be a very successful war. It appeared that he had moved on from his fascination with the nation's underworld. However, in Burton Turkus's case and the history of organized crime, the Murder Syndicate had a much more interesting half-life. Turkus teamed up with an Associated Press sportswriter, Sid Feder, and in 1951 they published the highly influential account of the antics and influence of the Murder Syndicate under the title *Murder, Inc.*

Turkus and Feder set out a saga of an organization that was arguably as important to the development of the orthodox history of organized crime as the initial "exposure" of the American Mafia in New Orleans in 1890, or the mythical Atlantic City Conference of 1929. In his introduction to the book, Feder argued that Murder, Inc. had changed its name in the years between Reles's "accident" and the publication of his book. As he put it, "make no mistake about it: Murder, Inc. was, and is, the national Syndicate." He goes on to argue that Murder, Inc. had evolved to become the death squad that "rubbed out" those who upset the Commission—a shadowy coalition of the most powerful criminals in the nation.

It is now a well-known narrative. The Commission emerged in the wake of the power struggle that modernized and amalgamated New York's leading crime families, the so-called Castellammarese War, which ran from 1930 to 1931. The ultimate victor of that civil war of organized crime—Lucky Luciano—decreed that once the bloodletting had ended, a governing body, a "Commission" would be essential. According to Feder, this was vital to "promote profitable illegitimacy" and "halt indiscriminate killing."

Feder was certain that—at least in terms of these aims—it had been an unqualified success, at least at the time of writing, in 1951. He argued: "Since the origin of the Syndicate, there has been no killing of a gang boss that was not 'okayed'—from Dutch Schultz in 1935 to Charley Binaggio in 1950." He ended his introduction with the statement that with Murder, Inc. "the underworld has organized its government."[80] This account quickly gained popular currency, and in the process grew to be increasingly associated with the Italian Mafia—a connection Turkus had always denied. He preferred the more vague term Syndicate. Yet the same year as Turkus's book came out, the Senate Crime Committee, the so-called Kefauver Committee, explicitly made the connection, arguing, "There is a nationwide crime syndicate known as the Mafia…. Its leaders are usually found in control of the most lucrative rackets in their cities. There are indications of a centralized direction and control of these rackets…. The Mafia is the cement that helps to bind the Costello-Adonis-Lansky syndicate of New York and the Accardo-Guzik-Fischetti syndicate of Chicago."[81]

A decade later, this view was given a particular boost by the confessions of a rather minor foot soldier in the Mafia, Joe "The Rat" Valachi. Valachi very publicly confessed his membership in what he termed the Cosa Nostra ("Our Thing") to the McClellan Committee on Organized Crime in 1963. His history of the evolution of the movement reiterated the Castellammarese War narrative, and tallied with Feder's with regard to the creation of the Commission and the role of Murder Inc.

However, it is certainly possible to question Valachi's credentials and the veracity of his claims. Most importantly, he was still a junior member in the 1960s, and certainly not a party to the organization's decisions at that time, let alone thirty years earlier. Yet Valachi was seen as talking from firsthand knowledge of events that he would almost certainly have heard of only indirectly. Nevertheless, his views reached a massive audience. His confession was televised and his largely rambling memoirs later extended into a best-selling book, *The Valachi Papers*, by a none too fastidiously fact-checking journalist, Peter Maas.[82]

Before long, the Feder-Turkus version of events had become conflated with Valachi's account and was taken as gospel by much of the American public. That is not to say that the acceptance of the interpretation was limited to popular accounts, or nonacademics. This conception of the highly organized, centralized and powerful Commission also gained a very impressive following at the highest levels of criminology. The Cosa Nostra view of organized crime stuck. Even the previously skeptical J. Edgar Hoover came out in favor of Valachi's view, arguing, "La Cosa Nostra is the largest organization of the criminal underworld in this country, very closely organized and strictly disciplined. They have committed almost every crime under the sun."[83] This dogma also fed one of the most influential books on organized crime.

University of California sociologist and criminologist David Cressey came out strongly in favor of the Valachi interpretation, and his opinion was important outside academia. Cressey was one of the leading consultants on the President's Commission on Law Enforcement and Administration of Justice (1966–1967). So when he published his seminal *Theft of a Nation* (1969), based on the testimony he gave that commission, it became an instant best-seller. In this book Cressey acknowledged that his assessment of the formation of the Commission was "based principally on the memoirs of one soldier, Joseph Valachi," which in turn drew from the same narrative sources as the inflated role given to the Syndicate by Turkus and Feder.[84]

Pretty soon the Murder, Inc.-Syndicate-Commission version of the evolution of organized crime had become the accepted view. In the canon of organized crime, Reles's Brooklyn thugs had risen to become the Cosa Nostra's national hit squad. What is more, that tide of opinion has remained high, even into this century. A typical example of the way in which it fed the orthodox narrative of organized crime can be seen in the December 2002 edition of the popular history journal, *American History*. In an article titled "Dewey defeats the Dutchman," Stephen Currie repeats Turkus's version, complete with quotes from Dutch Schultz, Dewey, Dixie Davis and Turkus himself—as well as others. There are no attributions or citations.[85]

Some would say that simply drawing on Turkus, with his knowledge of what went on in the Murder, Inc. courtrooms and his close relationship with Dewey, was enough to guarantee the accuracy of his account. This was certainly true for Virgil Peterson, who reviewed *Murder, Inc.* the year after it was published in 1951. Peterson was one of the leading authorities on organized crime, and a luminary of the Chicago Crime Commission—so his word carried weight. Feder and Turkus's rigorous approach to sifting evidence impressed him. Peterson claimed, "Even if Murder, Inc. were merely the product of the imaginative mind of a writer of detective story thrillers, it would make fascinating reading. But this book is far from fiction. It deals primarily in cold facts—facts that were established in the court room."[86] Not everyone has seen it like that. Perhaps their doubts are best expressed by one of today's foremost historians of organized crime.

After examining the Murder, Inc. trial transcripts, Alan A. Block has argued that Turkus and Feder had an agenda aimed at getting maximum impact for their book. With that in mind, they aimed to magnify the threat posed by Murder, Inc., beyond even what had been attempted by contemporary newspapers. Block argues that to hype the impression their book would make, they systematically exaggerated, wrongly extrapolated and willfully misinterpreted Reles's statements. In his view, they magnified the motives and actions of the Syndicate so much that "everything, no matter how counterfactual, led to the big conspiracy, The Organization" of crime.[87]

It may strike modern readers as rather odd that in spite of the Jewish background of Reles, Buchalter, Siegel and other central figures in the drama of Murder, Inc., orthodoxy via the typewriters of Turkus, Valachi and Cressey linked the hit squad with the Italian Mafia. Drawing on Block's work and that of other historians of organized crime, like Dwight C. Smith and Humbert S. Nelli, Mike Woodiwiss concludes that this counterintuitive move owed much to the times in which the interpretation gained overwhelming credence.

Over these years, as he says, the "Mafia conspiracy became the conventional wisdom." Further, as Woodiwiss points out, this was the post–Holocaust world, and Jews were no longer the scapegoat of choice.[88] But this had certainly not always been the case. In the decades before Murder, Inc. emerged as a national threat, Jewish criminal networks, as we have seen, were central to the white slavers, Prohibition bootleggers, and labor racketeers, as well as other aspects of organized crime. But by the 1940s it appeared their time had passed. The baton that granted control of America's underworld was by this time firmly in the hands of the Italians.

However, by 1991 that primacy was under threat, if not eclipsed. As the FBI director William Sessions told the Congressional Hearing on Asian Crime: "Only a few years ago, Chinese criminal groups operating in the U.S. were small and were disorganized." Two years after his address, with the increasing evidence of Chinese people-smuggling operations and narcotics trafficking, they were seen as significant "new threats to the United States and the international community." Later that year, President Clinton would condemn them as a "national security threat."[89]

# 10

## Chinese Organized Crime: The One That Got Away

*The Murder of Little Pete*

> *Whereas, the influx of large numbers of Chinese into this state are a cause of great complaint to the citizens, and a fruitful source of crime and disease, and offer a continual temptation to the commission of outrage and crime ... be it resolved by the House and Senate concurring, that our senators and representatives in Congress be ... instructed to use their influence with the Executive of the United States and the Senate to cause the existing treaties with China to be so modified as to prevent the immigration of Chinese to this state.*—Oregon Chinese Exclusion Law, 1862[1]

It can hardly be a surprise that organized crime is frequently brought to light by a murder. Most famously, the apparent activity of the Mafia came to the attention of the American public with the killing of David Hennessy in 1890. Nearly twenty years later, the killing of New York's near legendary Italian Squad leader, Joe Petrosino, in Palermo played up the image of the international power of the Black Hand. Similarly, in the years between these two killings, a murder took place in San Francisco that briefly highlighted another threat. This time it was not Italian organized crime: both the victim and the perpetrators were Chinese, and the victim was not a policeman, but a crime boss. However, although the murder shone a light on an aspect of organized crime that had been obscured, the lessons that can be drawn are somewhat different.

While accounts vary about the exact details, the essence of the scene, as it was reported at the time, is familiar from the gangland killings in modern Mafia films—although the European gangsters have been transmuted into Chinese, and Little Italy has been transposed into Chinatown. In a small barbershop on the corner of Washington Street and Waverly Place in the heart of San Francisco's Chinatown, a Chinese man is sitting in a chair with a hot towel covering his face. Three assassins see their chance. One silently blocks the door and keeps lookout for the bodyguard, who's been sent to buy a newspaper. The second assassin silently points his gun at the three barbers standing beside vacant chairs, and also covers a customer who unwittingly walks into the shop. His actions indicate for them to stay silent and no one speaks.

Pushing aside the barber who is about to shave the intended victim, the third assassin creeps up on the man in the chair. The man's face is fully covered by a steaming towel and the assassins are stealthy, deliberate and practiced in their movements. The man in the chair is totally unaware of the proximity of his enemies. Grabbing his ponytail as a cord, the killer pulls back the victim's head and fires several rounds from his revolver down inside the doomed man's shirt collar and into his chest. He dies quickly and silently. Their mission accomplished, the three murderers run out of the shop and disappear.

The victim of this well-planned killing was known by a variety of names including Fong Ching, Fung Wing and Fung Jing Toy. But while his name may have been disputed, his role in San Francisco's Chinatown was not. "Little Pete," as local Europeans knew him, had for some years been acknowledged as the "King of Chinatown." Arriving in San Francisco from mainland China at the age of five, he had started off as an errand boy in a shoe store. Ambitious and intelligent, he had learned English at night classes at the Methodist Mission, and pretty soon became an interpreter/broker for Chinese importers. In this capacity he became associated with the Sam Yup Company—one of the Six Companies, benevolent societies formed to protect Chinese immigrants in San Francisco.[2]

With a knowledge of English and experience of working with U.S. customs and other officials that was unusual in the Chinese-American population, Little Pete was soon meeting and negotiating on behalf of many of Chinatown's most influential merchants. He became the go-between for them with officials, businessmen and politicians outside the Chinese community, a service from which he derived considerable prestige and financial reward from both parties. He also built personal relationships with those outside his own community, including some at the highest level of California politics.

Although only thirty-three years old at the time of his murder, Little Pete was a highly successful businessman and very influential figure in Chinatown. Yet there was a darker, less legitimate side to the ambitious man's activities. In addition to his role as fixer and go-between, Little Pete also ran brothels and gambling houses. Alongside these semi-legitimate enterprises, he was also involved in illegal operations, largely centering on the peculiar position of the Chinese at this time in the United States.

From 1882 until 1943, Chinese immigration to the U.S.—except for a few select groups—was largely illegal. The majority of those Chinese who lived in America inhabited a strange shadowland in which their legal rights were curtailed, and their ability to naturalize as U.S. citizens was essentially negated. Particularly relevant to their status from Little Pete's perspective was the proscription on Chinese residents testifying in court. The ever-resourceful Little Pete exploited the increasingly hostile atmosphere for the Chinese in California by running a very lucrative sideline fixing juries of Europeans sitting in judgment over Chinese defendants—for a considerable fee. He also set up a very profitable business illegally shipping impoverished girls from rural China to the brothels of California and other cities in the West.[3]

All these activities and his friendships with the non–Chinese business and political communities made Little Pete a very wealthy, influential and important man in the city in general, and also meant that he was certainly the most powerful man in Chinatown. Yet his murder made page twenty-seven in the next day's *San Francisco Chronicle*.[4] By contrast, the murder of Hennessy and Petrosino had made the front pages of both the *New Orleans Times-Picayune* and the *New York Times*—and continued to dominate the news for several days, if not weeks, subsequently.

Maybe even more telling than the relegation of the crime to the back pages is the way in which the local press reported the stories that followed in the wake of the murder. Just as the murders of Hennessy and Petrosino led to the papers' highlighting and exposing the criminally alien nature of the Italian communities in New Orleans and New York, so Little Pete's assassination spurred a flurry of interest in the peculiarities and threats associated with crime in Chinatown. The mood of the press with regard to Little Pete's death is perhaps best summed up in an article on page six of the *San Francisco Chronicle* of January 26—three days after the murder took place.

Titled "The Chinese Vendetta," it details how, just like the murder of Hennessy in New Orleans, Little Pete's death "was not a homicide from the Chinese point of view, but an execution." He "had been formally condemned to death by members of an opposing clan," and "friends of the dead magnate, far from calling on the city authorities to punish the assassins, are plotting to make a shambles of Chinatown in the effort to wipe out the score."[5] Nor was the *Chronicle* alone in this assessment. Two days later the *Los Angeles Times* was talking of "A Mongol vendetta ... [which, it claimed, would involve] not less than three thousand [Chinese] ruffians, armed to the teeth, one half to avenge the death of a member of their lodge, and the other half armed to resist the attack."[6]

The *Chronicle* had pointed out that the murder is only "one phase of the present war in Chinatown," which threatened to get even more violent.[7] In this view the *Chronicle* was supported by an article run in the *San Francisco Call* detailing events that took place weeks before Little Pete met his demise. It warned of forthcoming "trouble in Chinatown," spurred by the killing of a Sam Yup Tong member, Lo How, in retaliation for the earlier killing of Chew Ging, a See Yup Tong man. Two weeks later, and a week before his own death, the *Washington Post* linked the killings with Little Pete.[8] The names would have meant little to the readers of the newspaper, but the essence of the article was revealing, in that it showed that killings—including that of Little Pete—were part of the ongoing gang wars linked with the nation's Chinatowns.

According to contemporary newspaper accounts, such turf wars periodically erupted as a result of struggles for control of the lucrative gambling houses, brothels and opium dens of the Chinese ghettoes in San Francisco and other cities. They were reported as full-blown wars, and in keeping with such an interpretation, some form of external mediation was said to be required to end them before there was complete annihilation of one side or the other. As befitted the American view of the Chinese-Americans as non–Americans, mediation in this case did not come from America.

One of the best accounts of how this un–American mediation was seen as being invoked can be found in a magazine produced for young Americans. In the April 8, 1897, edition of *The Great Round World and What Is Going On in It* told the youngsters how the war that resulted from Little Pete's death was resolved. It detailed how the "Chinese Consul [in Washington, D.C.] had got tired of this" war. His annoyance led him to send the Emperor of China a "fatal letter, accusing the See Yups of treason" for refusing to disclose the murderers of Little Pete and hand them over to the authorities in San Francisco.

The dispatch of the letter left mediation of the dispute with the Chinese Emperor, and according to the rather gleeful account in the youngsters' magazine, this had dire consequences for the See Yups. It meant that the unfortunate Tongs were left with a stark set of choices. If they refused to identify the murderers, they could at least stop fighting. If they refused those two options, they could instead decide "between going back to China and having their heads cut off, and allowing their innocent relatives to be punished for them."[9] Unsurprisingly, given these monstrous choices, the gangs abruptly stopped fighting.

## Tong Wars

*Talk of the Italian Mafia! There has never existed such another organization of des-*
*peradoes and villains as the Chinese highbinders, and these maintain their organization*
*and ply their trade more or less openly in every city of the United States which maintains*
*any considerable colony of Chinese.*—Louis J. Beck, 1898[10]

There's a great deal that can be learned from the story of the See Yup Tong and the Emperor. With all the talk of tetchy Consuls, irascible and cruel emperors, and threats of "chopping off heads," the tale clearly demonstrates how the Chinese were portrayed as barbaric and alien. It also shows how the Chinese in San Francisco were viewed as being peculiarly outside, if not actually immune to, the workings of the American justice system. The authorities in San Francisco figure remarkably little in this rendition of the murder of Little Pete. While other accounts—particularly those aimed at a more politically active readership than teenagers—make more of the influence of the SFPD in the case, the story is nonetheless indicative.

There is no doubt the so-called "Tong Wars" worried the authorities. San Francisco's Chinese population had been wracked by these clan feuds since the earliest days of Chinese settlement in the 1850s, and they would continue at least until the second decade of the twentieth century. Denied naturalization and the franchise, the Chinese population had established what was essentially a system of self-government. One commentator of the time saw the situation as essentially mirroring the status of the European "concessions" in China. He argued the nation's Chinatowns constituted a colonial dependency within the United States.[11]

By the turn of the twentieth century, these Chinatowns had what amounted to their own government. They certainly had their own judicial and diplomatic institutions. Voluntary associations played a vital role in this government. Uniting members of the same Chinese family name or those from the same province of China, they provided a level of social cohesion in an alien and often hostile country. They also provided a system of counseling, dispute resolution and patronage. Some went even further and provided services such as English classes, informal day care for children, and ad hoc work exchanges.

Nor were they simply mutual aid organizations. Many of the officials who oversaw the running of the Chinatowns would have risen up through the ranks of such organizations, and would draw much of their support from the membership. They were often those who mediated in financial or matrimonial disputes, and it was these figures who acted as the leaders meeting with the white city officials. In short, these official voluntary networks formed the pool from which Chinatown's elites were drawn.

This inevitably led to a certain partisanship and contributed to feelings of alienation and accusations of corruption and nepotism, with more-or-less physical score settling always following. One of the results was that alongside these recognized organizations, America's Chinatowns evolved shadow institutions, or secret societies. Often founded and populated by disaffected members of the recognized societies, these did not really interact politically with the host community, or with the imperial regime in China. Instead, their political objectives were aimed at activity within the enclave itself or shadow orders in China. That didn't mean they were not influential. For example, the establishment of Sun Yat Sen's anti–Manchu republic in 1911 owed a great deal to the financial and political support of a particularly powerful secret society in the U.S.[12]

This lack of involvement with "American" society enabled the secret societies—known variously as Tongs or Triads—to move into criminal activities within Chinatowns with relative impunity. There were a variety of reasons for this impunity. With the passage of the 1882 Chinese Exclusion Act, many Chinese felt even more unwelcome and slighted, although little probably changed in terms of the day-to-day prejudice they experienced. The Act reinforced a sense of "us and them" between themselves and the "Anglo" population of the city in which they lived. One of the results of this ostracism was an increasing solidarity among the populations of Chinatowns. It is therefore rather unsurprising that from around this time the Tongs are seen as starting to play a role in the government of Chinatowns.[13]

So, by the 1890s and 1900s, when Tong activity was seen as reaching a peak—at least in terms of violence—the Tong leaders were frequently well-connected enough to be able to protect themselves from much of the potential hostility within the Chinese communities. What was more, they were also in a position to bring pressure to bear on those below them. The threat of not just violence, but also political retribution, could be used to control would-be whistleblowers or those with a grudge within Chinatown. Nor was their protection limited to the Chinese community.

Perhaps for the reasons detailed above, police who worked the Chinatown details of San Francisco and other Chinese districts of the nation were meant to be even easier to bribe than those who worked other districts of the cities of the U.S.—and those others were by no means scrupulously honest. What was more, there was no outright prohibition of the main vices with which the Tongs were connected. Prostitution, opium and gambling were all legal—if heavily regulated—in San Francisco and most other major cities that had Chinatowns.

Given that legality, and that regulation, the opportunity to buy off a police raid, or to "disappear" the infraction of a regulation, meant that there were considerable opportunities for corruption, or at least what one historian has called a "tacit cooperation" between the police and lawbreakers in Chinatown.[14] There was also another reason for this cooperation. The majority of Americans outside Chinatown and its borders would not have considered Chinese organized crime of particular interest or relevance to their lives. As the twentieth century progressed, Chinatowns shifted from being seen as a threat to the nation, to more of a tourist attraction.[15] This shift is enlightening.

Although many of those who went to Chinatown "slumming" may have realized that the area's pagodas, temples, dragon and lion statues, and picturesquely costumed residents hid as much poverty, vice and crime as any other immigrant colony, some chose to ignore it. Others may well have been there for the cut-price opium, the colorful courtesans (as they liked to call the district's sex slaves), or the equally exotic gambling.[16] Either way, the result was that most newspapers—and consequently most of the general public—over the years of this study argued that the main way in which the Chinese had an impact on American organized crime was in their seemingly senseless but notoriously bloody inter-Tong warfare.

As if to illustrate this, in the late 1920s Herbert Asbury, in his very popular but none-too-reliable *Gangs of New York*, told his readers that "Americans" visiting Chinatowns may well be treated to a mock "opium crazed Tong battle" over a kidnapped "slave girl."[17] What he describes is just like the reenactment of Custer's Last Stand they could see if they had gone to Buffalo Bill's Wild West Show at the turn of the century. Both scenes would have owed little to the truth. Both were romanticized, stereotypical and patronizing in the extreme, yet both had the connivance of those who played out the rather demeaning roles allotted to them—and there was more than simply money behind that compliance of the Tongs.

## Chinese Criminal Exceptionalism

It suited Chinese criminals to be seen as organized only for the purposes of massacring each other, and it suited them even better if they didn't really have to do even that. Attracting attention is not a trait any seriously organized criminal network really wants to cultivate, as Rothstein so clearly showed in the 1920s. At the time, and for many years afterwards, sophisticated Chinese crime was seen as a contradiction in terms. A relatively recent analysis of the terms used to refer to Chinese organized crime in scholarly texts produced as late as the twenty-first century finds that they commonly include "recent," "emerging," "developing" and "nontraditional." The same analysis finds that the words "old," "established" and even "organized" are specifically deemed unsuitable to describe it.[18]

This meant that to all intents and purposes, until the late 1980s and early 1990s, Chinese crime was not seen as a particularly important threat to the U.S. scholars, law enforcers, politicians and other commentators frequently claimed that like most other non–European-American criminal networks, Chinese-American crime was deemed as being confined to the "ethnic enclaves" of America. It was seen as small-scale and not particularly well-organized. It was seen as dealing with commodities and services that were of interest only to the Chinese community, and because of that, it was not really seen as interacting with other criminal groups.

Such thinking plays to the models of "ethnic succession" as put forward by Daniel Bell in the 1950s. This theory maintains that as immigrant groups become accepted and integrated into American society, so they abandon the need for the "queer ladder" of crime to rise out of poverty and persecution. The trajectory of the Germans, Irish, Jews and even Italians seems to prove this thinking.[19] When applied to Asians, it would appear that as Chinese migration to the U.S. was opened up from 1943 onwards, so it was their turn to use the criminal "ladder" to rise to prominence. The results of this "new" immigrant group leapfrogging to prominence only became apparent to outside observers in the 1980s.

In the 1970s, Alan Block disagreed. He maintained that such thinking ignored the role of wider society and the political economy, favoring instead a view of organized crime that was stuck in an "ethnicity trap."[20] In the early years of the twenty-first century, his student Jeffrey McIllwain extended this thinking. McIllwain convincingly argued that this surprise at the rise of Chinese organized crime was yet another example of the predominance of a type of Eurocentric thinking.

This mindset was, he claimed, so ingrained that those who held it could not even bring themselves to admit that Asians may be able to form organized gangs, let alone produce networks controlled by "criminal masterminds" in the mold of the Irish machine politicians or Jewish white slavers, or extortionists like the Black Hand. As he demonstrated in a study of New York's Chinatown at the turn of the twentieth century, arguably this was a view that was cultivated by Chinese criminals themselves.[21] Yet, while perhaps desirable for a variety of parties, this contained, exclusive and isolated assessment of Chinese criminal networks does not really stand up to closer scrutiny—even as early as the time of Little Pete's demise, and before.

That said, the vices in which Chinese organized crime had traditionally dealt were certainly activities that—although not unique to China—they had brought with them. Opium, prostitution and gambling had a long history in China, and arguably had even greater appeal in Chinese America. Chinatown, and the American-Chinese population in general, were largely male—and often involved in arduous work. They found themselves treated with, at best, ambivalence, and more frequently hostility by the host population. Given this grim, solitary and isolated life, human contact and sex often had to be purchased. In this lonely and mundane existence, it was a natural reaction to obliterate reality with narcotics, and the escapist fantasy of winning the means to a better life was eminently understandable.

While these activities were not generally illegal until the twentieth century, they were frowned on by both "American" and Chinese society. New York and San Francisco—the homes of the largest Chinese populations in the U.S.—both passed local ordinances banning opium smoking, but they were rarely enforced. In fact, as has been discussed, the police charged with their enforcement frequently took money to look the other way. Nevertheless, dealing in these commodities was considered immoral, and a gateway to other, more obviously and more seriously illegal, activities.

The places where drugs, gambling and prostitution took place were considered meeting places for the urban underworld. They were run by crooks and frequented by low-lifes. Opium dens, gambling hells and brothels in Chinatown were seen as hubs in which stolen goods were fenced. They were portrayed as labor exchanges where specialist criminals could be recruited. They were also seen as intrinsically dangerous. A man in a brothel—anywhere, let alone in what was essentially a foreign country—is liable to blackmail, robbery or assault. A man in a "casino" is liable to be ripped off, or mugged if he wins. Further, a man—especially a white man—in an opium-induced stupor was a defenseless target to be robbed, attacked or kidnapped.

There was also a peculiar and unnatural egalitarianism that pervaded Chinatown. It was an area where a white hedonist or escapist—even of the highest rank—would stand a better chance of anonymity than if he practiced those habits elsewhere. But this came at a price. Any colleague, or acquaintance meeting him in the opium den, gambling hell or brothel in the Chinese quarter would have to explain his own presence there, before he could condemn the presence of another. In this area the "sporting type" could experience the exotic without being judged. Being in the area gave a frisson of the prohibited, and that in turn made the experience that much more exciting. What was more, the police were either thin on the ground, or bought off.

Within Chinatowns' vice dens, whites mixed with Chinese and the upper echelons of society rubbed shoulders with their inferiors. As one reporter put it, in the opium den "a Union League Club [one of the most exclusive and prestigious clubs in New York] man will lie with the head of a City Hall Park bunco steerer [a petty con-man's assistant] upon his chest, laughing and joking as if they had been 'comrades, comrades ever since we were boys.'"[22] If this display of unseemly classlessness was worrying to some, it was the mixing of the sexes that demonstrated the real worries for the majority. The hazards and implications of this were perhaps best illustrated in another Chinatown murder, this time in New York.

## Elsie Sigel

*For Chink Lover She Left Home And Was Slain*—Banner headline, *Atlanta Constitution*, June 20, 1909

On June 8, 1909, Elsie Sigel was a relatively unknown, pretty and headstrong nineteen-year-old. If she had any sort of fame at the start of that month, it was as the granddaughter of something of a German immigrant celebrity, Franz Sigel. Franz had served with gallantry—if not much military success—as a general in the Union forces of the Civil War. As one of the few German-Democrat generals, he'd become something of a poster boy for German-American New York during the war and its aftermath. Within years of his death in 1902, there were statues erected of him, and even a park named after him.

Elsie's father, Paul, was less conspicuous, but nonetheless successful. He had gone on to build on his father's success and made a fortune through shrewd and lucky speculation. By the time of Elsie's birth he'd built himself a mansion in Manhattan's then-swanky Washington Heights. Like many wealthy men in New York at the turn of the twentieth century, Paul encouraged his wife, Anne, to spend her time involved in good works. Anne's particular cause was the Sunday school at the rather genteel St. Andrew's Church on Fifth Avenue—which specifically aimed to convert and minister to the "Heathen Chinee" of the district.

Encouraged by her mother, Elsie in turn took on similar charitable works, concentrating her efforts on the Bowery Rescue Settlement and Recreation Room for girls—a flophouse for Chinese prostitutes. This charity meant that Elsie spent increasing amounts of her time in Chinatown, much of it in the company of a 30-year-old Chinese man called Leon Ling (aka Leon Leo Lim, William L. Lion or Willie Ling). In many ways there was nothing untoward about this relationship. Ling was well known to the Sigel family, being a member of the congregation of St. Andrew's.

Not only did the handsome and confident young Leon sit next to the mother and daughter in church, but he frequently escorted the Sigel pair around Chinatown, and eventually started to spend a growing amount of time unchaperoned in the company of Elsie. This was generally seen as acceptable purely because of the unspoken recognition on both sides of Ling's inferior status as a Chinese man, and his apparent dependence on the charity of both Anne and Elsie. In essence this subservient and dependent position reduced him to a status that effectively emasculated him, making him a safe escort for Elsie.

Yet while this androgynous status may have, to some extent, placated Elsie's mother, and very reluctantly came to be accepted by her father, it was certainly not the way in which Elsie saw Ling.[23] Taking advantage of the excuses her charity work gave her, Elsie began to spend more and more time away from home, and more and more time with Ling, and given the headstrong nature of Elsie, it did not take long for their relationship to become physical.

On June 9, Elsie became famous. She was reported to the police as having gone missing, having failed to appear at her grandmother's house.[24] On June 18, the putrefying body of a girl was discovered stuffed into a trunk in Ling's apartment at 782 Eighth Street. Identifying the body by her monogrammed locket as being Elsie, Anne Sigel was so grief-stricken she needed medical attention. The corpse was bloated and stinking. Elsie's body was near naked and the cause of death was obvious. A crude noose had bitten deeply into the skin of her now bloated neck. However, there was no sign of the occupant of the flat, Ling.[25]

Alongside the body of the girl, the police discovered more than 100—some accounts raise this to 1,000—love letters written to the man they christened the "Mongol Don Juan," Ling. On examining the letters, it emerged that thirty-five of them were signed "E.S." The others, the papers announced, "were from young white women, many of whom had been teaching in Chinese Sunday schools."[26] The police commissioner's secretary, Dan Slattery, told the press that all the other letters were "well-written" and addressed Ling by his Chinese name. Many of them, he said, were signed "Nellie." There were also postcards, "all [of which] had some loving message inscribed on the back," indicating that "Ling was doing a land-office [meaning, quick turnover] business with women's affections."[27]

The letters from Elsie detailed a passionate, complex and rather one-sided love, since it quickly emerged that Elsie's passion was not reserved for Ling alone. It appeared she had also had at least one other Chinese lover, Chu Gain, the owner of an upmarket Chinatown restaurant. This, the Port Arthur, was a very successful eatery that catered to an adventurous, middle-class, white clientele. What was more, the letters from Elsie showed that not only did she have two Chinese lovers, but they both knew about each other. Letters to one lover would maintain that she could not wait to see him again, and that the other one was simply a distraction. She would imply the opposite in letters to her other lover.[28]

Yet, in spite of her protestations of true love, it appeared this oriental love triangle had cost Elsie her life. When Chu was brought in for questioning, he admitted crossing the color barrier and having "known Miss Sigel intimately." Further, he also told the police that Ling had threatened him with violence for his relations with the girl and that the threats had been issued both in person and by letter.

A national manhunt for Ling ensued. Papers claimed Ling was sighted in New Orleans, Pittsburgh, Washington, D.C., Vancouver (British Columbia), Philadelphia, San Francisco and other cities. Papers around the country claimed men resembling him had been arrested, only to be released. Some said he had fled to Cuba or China, and others reported he had hanged himself, while others claimed he had been drowned.

## Opium Smuggling

> *Except for its occasional tong-feud outbreaks, Chinatown is not a disorderly quarter. Its occupants are not engaged in Black Hand outrages or in gang raids. The laws they are chiefly occupied in breaking are the laws against gambling and traffic in opium. The attitude of the Chinese themselves toward this exceptional crime [the murder of Elsie Sigel] is favorably shown in the efforts of the Chinese authorities at Washington and the Chinese Masons in bringing the perpetrator to justice.—Washington Post, June 27, 1909*

Whatever happened to Ling, and whether or not he was guilty of the murder, it is interesting, from the perspective of organized crime, that relatively few of the commentators saw the murder as being connected with Chinese organized crime. It is curious that while Americans were informed by the press that Tongs controlled "the life and death of every Chinese resident in this city [New York]," it was not generally considered that a high-profile murder in the heart of the Chinese quarter of New York was connected with the Tongs.

If the same event had taken place in other immigrant colonies, the result would perhaps have been reported with relation to organized crime. The murder of a wealthy heiress in Little Italy would most probably have excited comment about the involvement of the Black Hand. The death under mysterious circumstances of a rich young Gentile girl in a Jewish area would have certainly led to suspicions, if not accusations, of the involvement of white slavers. Yet while it is possible to find claims that Ling was the leader of the Hip Sing Tong, or a member of the Gee Kong Tong, such allegations were not widespread—or frequent.[29] Such accusations just seem to have been considered, at least by the more thoughtful press, as a part of what the *Washington Post* called the "moral hysteria following the Sigel murder."[30]

On the other hand, when Tongs were mentioned in connection with Elsie's murder, they were most frequently portrayed acting as agents alongside the forces trying to bring to justice the renegade Ling. This can be seen in a letter to the editor of the *New York Times* from the Lone Gee Tong that denied Ling was ever a member and instructed its genuine members against "directly or indirectly aiding, abetting, assisting or comforting that dastardly murderer."[31] This instruction fits with popular notions of the time that Chinese organized crime was cowed by the white American population, or just too feckless to indulge in activity that ran the risk of antagonizing the white population, or spilling over the boundaries of Chinatown.

There are, however, good examples of where this assumption can be proved wrong. They usually involve smuggling. Today we are pretty well conditioned to think that Asian smugglers would most probably be importing narcotics. This would initially be to avoid the high tariffs before the essential prohibition of opium for recreational use with the Harrison Narcotics Act of 1915. Yet in spite of widespread condemnation of the Chinese use of opium, that was not the leading concern in the early twentieth century. Periodically opium smuggling would be seen as a severe threat. One 1928 report—at the height of the renewed drive to keep the Prohibition-era nation dry—argued that opium was "far surpassing … rum running in monetary value."[32] Even so, it was certainly not seen as having the same level of threat to national morality, or health, by law enforcers or—perhaps more importantly—the drys among the general population.

This harks back to the central prejudice at the heart of American attitudes to Chinese organized crime. Rightly or wrongly, opium users were seen as either being from, or based in, Chinatown. Since white Americans were essentially insulated from what took place in those regions—unless they chose not to be—opium smuggling did not represent a serious threat to general America. This thinking is illustrated by an incident that made the front page of Boston papers in 1923: a white opium smuggler was arrested in Chinatown.[33] Arrests of Chinese smugglers rarely attracted such notoriety, even though some of the busts made in this period were far larger in scale than that of the lone white man.

It also seemed that opium smuggling was a declining problem—or at least one that was being "managed." One customs official told a reporter that a little over a decade after the Harrison Narcotics Act of 1915, "There is not the great number of opium addicts that many think." The same customs agent also claimed that as a consequence of legislation, opium smuggling—based on the evidence of seizures made—seemed to have decreased by nearly two-thirds from the peak activity at the turn of the century.[34] Others were less confident. A reporter, commenting nearly ten years after the upbeat remarks of the confident agent, argued that U.S. Customs had little real interest in halting the opium trade, and consequently had little impact on it. He called American seizures a "mere trifle" and argued that opium's usage in the U.S. was actually expanding—at a significant rate.[35]

## People Smuggling

> *Owing to the loose interpretation of the laws by sympathetic U.S. Commissioners, and the radical diversity of opinion between the judges of the Federal Courts, the crafty practices and fraudulent devices of the Mongolians themselves, the ready aid of well-paid allies on the border line, perjured witnesses, and the oath-breaking and bribe-taking public officials, the exclusion laws have become more honored in the breach than in the observance. From Tampa Bay at one corner, from Puget Sound at the other, from El Paso at the south, from San Francisco at the west, to New York at the east, to the Vermont, New York, New Hampshire, and Maine line on the north comes the same narrative of betrayed trusts on the part of debauched customs and judicial officials, and of hordes of these barred and branded Mongolians pouring into the United States, each with his bribe-money in one hand, his fraudulent papers in the other, and perjury on his lips.*—J. Thomas Scharf, "The Farce of the Chinese Exclusion Laws," *The North American Review* 166, No. 494 (January 1898): 97

Although opium smuggling was acknowledged as a problem—to a greater or lesser extent—its impact conformed to general consensus about Chinese organized crime: it generally dealt in products for Chinatown, and as such it didn't have that much impact on U.S. society as a whole. What was seen as far more of a threat to the nation was the smuggling of Chinese people themselves. Since the 1882 Exclusion Act, the immigration of Chinese into the U.S. had been severely curtailed, to the extent of virtually halting the arrival of all but a few privileged classes of immigrants from China. Yet, it seemed that even with these "laws as harsh as tigers" forbidding entry to the bulk of Chinese migrants, the populations of Chinatowns seemed to be growing.

In reality, according to the U.S. Census, the overall numbers of Chinese-Americans during the period of exclusion declined from 105,000 to 60,000. However, what was curious was that the Chinese population seemed to have discovered the elixir of life. Rather than aging—as one would expect if there was no replenishment of numbers by migration—the bulk of Chinatowns' populations remained predominantly male and the age range remained largely between 22 and 44 years old.[36]

Ignoring the obvious statistical problems inherent in the question of where the older Chinese went and where the younger ones came from, some put this continued growth down to the fecundity of the "Celestials" (so named because of a former name of China, the "Celestial Empire"). According to the crude logic of race theorizers of the time, as a primitive race, the Asian devoted vast proportions of his or her energies to breeding. Race theorizers argued this gave them an ability to massively increase their numbers—far more quickly than Europeans.[37]

Even allowing for a general belief in this theory, the fertility of the women of Chinatown would have needed to be spectacular. According to a rough estimate, in order to account for the numbers of Chinese in the country by the time of the removal of the exclusion legislation in 1943, each legally resident individual Chinese woman of childbearing age would have had to have given birth to over 200 children.[38] Since that was clearly impossible, a marginally more sophisticated explanation was put forward that rested on subversion of the rules. There was a consensus that the seeming expansion of the nation's Chinatowns must be the result of evasion, or flouting, of the restrictions on Chinese immigration.

Typical of this view were reports that the wily Chinese were bamboozling the authorities by pretending that they were someone else. In this era before photographic passports, the *Baltimore Sun* told its readers that Chinese immigrants "all have one yellow complexion ... the same black almond shaped eyes ... and wear a cue done up in the same style and [of] the same color." These ubiquities meant even the most detailed of descriptions of them were useless for the identification of an individual.[39] One immigration official was, however, capable of seeing through such ruses. Inspector Putnam, based in Los Angeles, told a reporter: "It is a gift I cannot explain. It is somewhat like recognizing an easterner in a throng of Southern California people. The contraband Chinese have a peculiar scared look, so that it is little trouble to tell one once I find him. Even though one's face may look the picture of innocence, there is almost invariably when I put my hand on him, a tremor about his frame that betrays his guilt."[40] Another paper showed how Chinese "coolies" could often produce affidavits from "any number of Chinese witnesses to prove" that they were "merchants" and allowed to travel back and forth to China, free from restriction.[41] This was held to be particularly true after the fire following the 1906 San Francisco earthquake, which destroyed the vast majority of the records relating to Chinese immigration.

More commonly, it was suspected, those illegally entering the country simply evaded detection by immigration officials, and were smuggled into the country by professional gangs. This was largely done via the land borders of Mexico and Canada, since this type of route had two great advantages over the maritime options. Firstly, emigration to those countries was far less regulated than that to the U.S., and secondly, there was a lengthy, inhospitable, sparsely populated and therefore porous border separating the nations.[42] While numbers involved in this trade are obviously difficult to calculate, the feeling at the time was that they were significant.

According to contemporary commentators, the smuggling of undocumented Chinese immigrants got started almost immediately after the Exclusion Act came into law. Established networks dedicated to opium smuggling meant that it was simply a question of adapting an existing expertise to handle a new product. The safe routes, the best stops and safest rendezvous were already known to the smugglers. They knew where customs officers and immigration officials were based, and how they patrolled—and where they did not. Alongside this, the construction of the Canadian Pacific Railroad was using vast numbers of "coolies," often very close to the American border.[43]

This is borne out by the immediate reports of Chinese crossing the Canadian border. Less than a year after the Chinese Exclusion Act of 1882, the customs collector at San Francisco claimed at least 100 Chinese had been smuggled into Washington State in a matter of days, and this was by no means unusual. A couple of months later the *New York Times* told readers it was "a fact well known to the residents of British Columbia that at the present time Chinamen are crossing the [United States] border in batches of 20 or 30" via Puget Sound.[44]

Nevertheless, such figures were known to be a tiny proportion of those smuggled into the States. A customs official told the journalist Julian Ralph, with only a little exaggeration, that patrols were so limited on vast stretches of the Canadian border that "there is no part of it over which a Chinaman may not pass into our country without fear of hindrance; there are scarcely any parts of it where he may not walk boldly across it at high noon."[45] By 1891, that same journalist had put a figure of 1,500 Chinese a year illegally crossing the Canadian border.[46]

Ten years later, the House Committee on Immigration reported that there were over 20,000 Chinese smuggled into America annually.[47] It seemed that later reforms to the federal system of border control around the same time as the San Francisco earthquake served to somewhat reduce this number, but it still remained a problem to the immigration services. By 1928, a statistical review estimated that anywhere between 7,000 and 50,000 Chinese had entered the U.S. in the decade to 1920, with the author finally settling on a total of around 27,000, or just under 3,000 a year—twice the estimate of 1891, but far below the 1901 claim.[48]

The discrepancy in numbers probably had much to do with the way in which the immigrants were smuggled across the border. Chinese workers would be smuggled in batches, never large numbers. This meant those who crossed Puget Sound could be shipped in smaller boats, which could land with greater ease at more isolated locations. Frequently, Chinese immigrants would be "piloted" through the borderlands by resident Chinese. Those who took the purely land routes could be shepherded, sheltered and hidden by resident Chinese miners and woodsmen in the huge expanses of unpopulated borderlands. In one area of Washington State, they were aided and hidden by Chinese who lived on a nearby Indian reservation, having married local women.[49] They may be hidden in Chinese laundries or opium joints along their route, or disappear into the work gangs on the railroad, for as one inspector put it, "They get into the Chinese camp and mix with the balance of the Chinese [and] it is very difficult to tell who the recently arrived Chinese are."[50]

Sometimes the schemes used were sophisticated, sometimes they were more opportunist. Treasury department agents uncovered one extraordinarily refined route in 1890 in Port Huron, Michigan. Described as a sort of "underground railroad scheme" for Chinese laborers, it had agents spanning Asia and the Americas, from Hong Kong to London to Nashville to Ottawa and a host of other cities. Shipping up to 200 Chinese at a time, agents received $20 a head at each of the staging posts as the network essentially shipped laborers, pretty much to order, anywhere in the United States.[51] Others chose to hide the laborers in plain sight. One such network simply put the immigrants in sleeper carriages on their journey from Toronto to New York. The smugglers did this because they knew that the sleepers were not inspected, since the "celestials" would not normally have, or use, the money to travel in such extravagant comfort.[52]

On the southern border, the numbers of hopeful Chinese entering America following exclusion were initially not so great, but after 1900 the numbers of Chinese entering from Mexico climbed dramatically. Chinese workers were employed in farming, mining and railroad construction as well as the nation's nascent manufacturing industries, but not in the Mexican states bordering the U.S. The result was that in these regions in 1890 the population was numbered at less than 500.[53] It would have been very difficult to hide Chinese in such a small population.

Nevertheless, there was a sense that Chinese were moving north. By 1888, Washington was putting pressure on the Mexicans to ban the immigration of Chinese into Mexico, as reports began to circulate in the capital of the illegal entry of "coolies" from the south. Two years later, Treasury Department agents reported Chinese workers from Mexico arriving in San Francisco, developments that were laid out the year afterwards in a detailed report to Congress.[54]

That 1890 report is revealing. It essentially shows the problems of trying to enforce immigration policy—problems that dog the Border Patrol to the present day. A San Diego customs official told of at least 150 different mountain trails used by the smugglers in his region alone. Others told of how understaffed they were. Quite a few detailed the tragic consequences of smuggling operations that went wrong, and left Chinese stranded in the most inhospitable terrain with no water, shade or means of transport. Reports also made much of resident Chinese helping the would-be migrants. Maps were shown to the Committee that showed the "Chinese Underground Railway," and testimony was taken that showed how guiding migrants had become something of a cottage industry for Chinese living in the border regions.[55]

The inspectors made much of the way in which their resources were hopeless against both the huge expanse of border, and the persistence and desperation of those Chinese trying to cross it. They also complained to the Committee that when Chinese were caught trying to sneak into the U.S., the law obliged the Americans to send them back to where they came from. The Chinese inspector at San Diego told the Committee how nonsensical this policy was: "Should an officer take a Chinaman to the State line to-day, he will undoubtedly follow that officer back to the city the first dark night …. they know full well the Mongolian will be in our Chinatown early next morning for breakfast."[56]

The result of the 1891 Committee was an increase in federal powers. Replacing the old emphasis on state-level control of borders, and state-level funding, enabled an expansion of the supervision of immigration and started a process of centralization. However, the changes coincided with an increase in the number of restrictions being placed on immigrants arriving from Europe at the ports of the eastern seaboard. Since this was funded out of the same pot of money, federalization actually had the effect of spreading the resources for border patrol more thinly and negating the supposed advantages of a centralized funding scheme.

Nevertheless, by the early years of the twentieth century, improved targeting of resources and management led to far more effective policing of the Canadian border, especially under the auspices of the American regional immigration commissioner, Robert Watchorn. Further, the Canadians were hardening their own policy towards Chinese immigration. Led by the Vancouver businessman and Conservative MP for Vancouver, Henry Herbert Stevens, Canada moved from a liberal attitude to Asian immigration to an increasingly exclusive regime. In 1901 they doubled the immigrant head tax for Chinese to $100, and then in 1904 they put it up to $500. In 1923, they entirely excluded Chinese immigration.[57] By contrast, in December 1899, Mexico and China signed a treaty giving full freedom of movement and residence as well as full commercial relations to each other's nationals. It was not until 1921, under pressure from the U.S., that this was amended to preclude labor migration.[58]

The result of these changes was that the Chinese smugglers increasingly turned their attention to developing the Mexican routes. Typical of these operations was one that centered on the twin towns of Nogales. In many ways it was the perfect location for people smuggling, straddling as it did the border between the territory of Arizona and the Mexican state of Sonora. One such network was uncovered by Secret Service agents in 1901. Organized by a local Tong boss, Yung Ham, who lived in Nogales's Chinatown on the Mexican side of the border, it was simple in its execution.

Chinese arriving in Mexico would be distributed in small towns along the main railroad line to Nogales. They would then await instructions about where and when they were to congregate to cross the border. On being given instructions, they would gather at the jump-off point, an isolated area where local officials had been paid to make sure there was no border-guard presence. At other times they simply got to the border and presented papers marked with a "cabalistic letter A" to show that they were to be allowed into the U.S. According to the Secret Service, this indicated "the amount demanded had been paid" to corrupt border officials.[59]

Having crossed the border, the Chinese would be split into small groups to meet up with agents for the smugglers. They would then be shepherded off into the U.S., to disappear among the Chinese populations of the mining camps in Phoenix, or the Chinatowns of California. It was estimated that over the years in which he carried out this trade, Yung Ham sent at least six thousand Chinese into the U.S. He charged anywhere between $50 and $250 a head, depending where they were coming from, where they were going and the costs he might incur.[60] Almost half of those smuggled were subsequently caught and returned, but the other half carried on into the United States and disappeared into the Chinese communities.

When the network was broken, several U.S. officials, including U.S. Collector of Customs William Hoey, were arrested, charged with corruption, and sacked. While Hoey protested his innocence and achieved a brief notoriety in the national papers, Yung was not mentioned at all.[61] There is no record in the reports of the time of his being prosecuted. Once again it appeared Chinese organized crime was largely invisible, coming to light only because of the connection with white American government officials.

# 11

## The Slave Trade

### American Siberia

> *A quiet looking citizen enough is Dr. Jin Fuey Moy, who appeared with his American wife, his American frock coat, his almost American daughter and $4,000 worth of American family jewels before the federal Commissioner in Jersey City the other day. With his short, slick hair, his smile and his pearl stickpin, he did not look the least like an agent of a great body whose arms stretch mysteriously from the Orient both ways around the bulge of the world, whose men rob, lie, bribe and kill to get their human contraband undiscovered across our border, whose stinking slavers come sneaking down with doused lights from two oceans on our coasts, a corporation which here, in the United States of America holds hundreds of men in bondage, often little lighter than that of the Southern negroes before the war.—New York Tribune, May 14, 1911*

Less than a month before his dismissal, William Hoey exposed the scale of the smuggling ring operating from Nogales. He pointed out that one of the most troubling aspects of the whole case was the exposure of a "gang of slave dealers" working hand-in-hand with the smugglers. Central to these was a ruthless Chinese middleman, Sing Lee. Although based in Nogales, he sent most of his workers to Phoenix, where he was known to the authorities as "a Celestial experienced in human traffic." It was claimed that he operated a business that smuggled "hundreds of coolies" at a time into the U.S. He drew in unskilled labor from Guaymas, Mexico, and San Francisco to work as what amounted to slave labor in local mines.[1]

Nor was this trade limited to Arizona. Alongside the mines of Phoenix, what amounted to Chinese slaves were put to work in mines all over the West. White farmers and white corporations all over the nation exploited Chinese workers. "Coolies" were put to work for no financial return or other reward. They were kept more or less imprisoned and exploited in all imaginable ways by their own people in the brothels and the laundries of Chinatowns around the nation. In short, many of the Chinese shipped into the U.S. by smugglers fell into the hands of unscrupulous employers.

Chinese men and women entering the U.S. would have no idea of where they would be going, and no idea of where they were once they got there. Undocumented immigrants, with little English and even less knowledge of how America worked, were prime targets for exploitation. They had no way of publicizing their fate, and no means of seeking legal redress even if they could. Smugglers could increase the sums made by trafficking Chinese by taking money from the migrant, while at the same time being paid by those seeking unskilled labor for construction, mining, agriculture, sex work, domestic work or other drudgery.

However, some 1,500 miles east of Nogales, this debt slavery, or peonage as it had become known, was making far greater headlines, and, it seemed, was affecting thousands of people—American citizens. In Alabama it emerged that the law enforcers had been selling "convicts" to a variety of workplaces, including mines, farms, railroads, lumber-yards, turpentine works, lime kilns and steel works. These unfortunates could be charged with minor, if not imaginary, crimes, which might range from gambling to speaking inappropriately to a woman. If they could not prove that they were employed, they could be arrested under the catchall "vagrancy" charge. Perhaps they simply owed money to a storeowner, or landlord.

Whatever the reason for their conviction, they would be "sold" for tens of dollars to local businesses, and worked—often in appalling conditions—to pay back their debt. It may be for one year, it may be for five or even ten years. Sometimes they would be chained at night. They would always be punished for attempting to escape. Often they would be beaten to instill absolute obedience or improve their productivity and output. What united all these "criminals" was that they were generally young, almost universally male, and nearly always black. This was essentially a way of subverting the Thirteenth Amendment's prohibition of slavery, and re-establishing the black man as the low-cost beast of burden in the former Confederacy: the engine of revivified Southern industry and agriculture.

This trade was highly organized and inclusive. It utilized the political and business elites, the judiciary and the local police force with the more-or-less tacit collusion of the vast majority of whites in at least the states of Georgia and Alabama, and arguably more of the Deep South. It was also against the spirit, if not the letter of the law. It relied on the provision of the Thirteenth Amendment that permitted the continuity of "slavery" and "involuntary servitude ... as a punishment for crime whereof the party shall have been duly convicted."[2] But while these wretches were undoubtedly treated as convicts, the illegality of the "crimes" and legality of the processes for which and by which they had been condemned were much less clear.

In fact, a lengthy investigation by federal marshals and the Secret Service in the early years of the twentieth century was predicated on the true crimes of the abduction, imprisonment, sentencing, trading, mistreatment and often murder in the thousands of such convicts. What emerged was essentially the institutionalized and widespread enslave-ment of black Americans. The *Atlanta Constitution* explained how the system worked. Those involved in the scheme would "bring a negro before a magistrate on a flimsy charge. He is convicted, and, having no money to pay a fine, the white man offers to advance him the money provided the negro will make a labor contract with him for a length of time sufficient to reimburse him for the money and trouble he has taken to keep the negro out of jail. He is thereupon taken away and begins what is frequently a long term of cruel servitude, being frequently whipped for failure to perform work to the satisfaction of the employer."[3]

In Alabama and regions of Mississippi, Florida and Georgia there were laws that allowed the sale of such debts, and empowered the purchase of debts in return for unpaid labor. However, many saw this peonage as going beyond the scope of even such inherently dubious laws. Nevertheless, because of the 1901 Alabama Contract Labor Law, those sus-pected of this practice could only be accused of holding black convicts in peonage under an 1867 statute forbidding the sale of workers into forced labor. Ill-educated, impoverished, disenfranchised, often indigent black men and women were easy prey for this "inhuman form of slave-catching and slave-holding."[4]

Presiding over a 1903 case, the federal Judge Thomas Goode Jones told reporters after the defendant's conviction, "The counsel of the defendant spoke of the negro as a so-called citizen. A man is a citizen whether he can vote or not, and nobody loves a government that would not protect him. The Magistrates [who essentially sold slaves for often spurious debts owed by the defendants] have established slavery for debt in this State."[5] In spite of Jones's condemnation, the practice continued throughout the first decade of the twentieth century. Judge Jones had declared Alabama's Contract Labor Law unconstitutional in 1903, calling it "the source of nine-tenths of the peonage now existing in Alabama."[6] Yet, in most similar cases, Southern judges generally found against the enslavers and paid lip-service to condemning the practice. In reality, the punishment was frequently a fairly small fine—around $100—and then the enslavers left the courtroom, free men. Perhaps the most damning indictment and indication of the depth of corruption, inhumanity and racism were the cases of John W. Pace and his partner Fletcher Turner.

If John Pace of Tallapoosa County, Alabama, were a fictional character, the author would have been accused of overplaying his image. Looming over everyone, he was a huge, shambling, scruffy man with missing fingers and deformed feet—the result of gout and frostbite. To add to his sinister appearance, he hid his "florid" face with a wide-brimmed hat, which also served to cover and shade his balding head. A local paper reported his appearance at his indictment in Montgomery as being that of a "typical mountain farmer [who] ... wore a homespun shirt without a collar ... and whose feet are encased in abnormal shoes, evidently of home manufacture."[7] His cruelty and greed matched his unpleasant appearance.

Pace was convicted of eleven counts peonage in 1903. He was sentenced to fifty-five years. In view of his dreadful health, this was reduced to five years and a $1,000 fine. The fine was swiftly paid by his friends in the courtroom, and given his decrepitude, even the five years was suspended. Still alive in 1905, it was discovered that not only was he still trading slaves, but he was holding two black teenage brothers in chains on his own farm. They had been his personal slaves since 1897. All the while he had been pleading his innocence in court, he had been abusing the two boys.

Yet, on April Fools' Day 1906, as a result of an unusually prolonged wave of white-on-black rioting, murder and violence that swept the nation, Theodore Roosevelt abandoned his earlier promise of a "square deal for the negro" and pardoned Pace on grounds of ill health.[8] Pace lived on for several years and returned to his slave dealing. Fletcher Turner's case was even more telling, for it demonstrated how organized, how deeply embedded and accepted the Alabama trade in forced convict labor had become.

A business partner of Pace's in nearby Dadeville, Turner was indicted shortly after Pace in June 1903. Gauging the mood of Judge Jones, the defense that Turner mounted was different from that of Pace. Turner's confessions told a grim tale, what one paper called "a page from the dark ages."[9] He admitted buying convicts' debts from constable Robert N. Franklin for $40 a head. He told the court he had worked them on his land for no pay. He also disclosed that his son, Allen, had shot one convict who attacked him with an axe, but he demanded a retraction of stories that another forced laborer, a black woman, Sarah Oliver, had been beaten to death for trying to escape.[10]

Still, Turner was unrepentant; in fact, his lawyers argued that he was not actually guilty of any crime. They maintained: "Unlawfully and knowingly holding a person forcibly and against his will and requiring such persons to labor for the holder to work out a debt claimed by the holder to be due to him from such person as set up such count, does not constitute holding such person to a condition of peonage under the laws of the United Sates."[11] This defense essentially challenged the validity of the 1867 Peonage statute as well as the spirit of the Thirteenth Amendment. This bold strategy gained Turner his acquittal. On July 17, 1903, the trial ended with a hung jury. Predictably, although rather publicly, it was "roasted" by Judge Jones, who told the jurors that they had "declined to enforce the law for no other reason than the base one that the defendant is a white man and the victim of the law he violated is a negro boy."[12]

To many other Southerners, Jones's accusations did not constitute exposure of a network criminally trading in slaves, but were simply betraying the "race etiquette" of the region and playing to the Northern gallery. This view was very clearly exemplified by James "Cotton Tom" Thomas Heflin, then Secretary of State for Alabama. When Heflin addressed a crowd of around 2,000 Confederate veterans in the wake of Jones's remarks, he left them in no doubt about how they ought to view Jones's attack on the jury. He told them: "Alabama has recently received unjust criticism in the North. A few so-called peonage cases coming from one or two localities in the State has given the agencies of slander in the North an opportunity to accuse the whole State of Alabama. Cartoons of white men whipping negroes (bound hand and foot) with leather straps studded with tacks have been sent broad cast over the country.... The Federal Constitution guarantees the fair right of trial by jury.... A fair and impartial trial by a jury of one's peers ... is a blessed thing in this land of liberty."[13]

There were frequent accusations of Italian, Greek and Syrian laborers being imported en masse for agricultural and industrial projects. While conditions in which these workers toiled were often bad, opposition to this, the so-called "padrone system," tended to come from white workers, rather than the authorities keen to protect the rights of the laborers, or other humanitarian agencies. They were banned by the 1885 Foran Act, but nonetheless there were still fears that white European immigrants were also being tricked into enslavement in regions of the South.

The owner of a lumber camp in Lockhart, Alabama, was prosecuted unsuccessfully for allegedly holding some twenty-five Germans.[14] In 1907, a Pacific Northwest paper claimed a U.S. Civil Service Commissioner, John Avery Mollhenny, "enticed over 1,000 Austro-Hungarian" immigrants to his canning factory on Avery Island in Louisiana, and kept them there "in a state of virtual slavery by armed guards."[15] None of the major local papers reported the accusations at the time.

In one way this was not surprising. During the first two decades of the twentieth century, while thousands, if not tens of thousands of black convicts were enslaved, beaten, tortured and killed under the Southern peonage system, and later the chain gangs that replaced them. Still, few deaths attracted any outside attention, still less enough local disapprobation to halt the enslavement of black convicts. However, when—nearly twenty years after the big peonage trials of the 1900s—a frail young middle-class man from North Dakota ended up being arrested for vagrancy in Alabama, the consequences made national news.

Twenty-one-year-old Martin Talbert was sold to the Putnam Lumber Company for a $25 fine in 1921 by the sheriff of Leon County in north Florida. Working in one of the company's turpentine camps, the already sick young man was whipped so severely by the camp's "whipping boss" that he subsequently died. When the story came to light, the terrible crime was dealt with in what appeared a civilized way: the whipping boss was given a 20-year prison term for murder, and Talbert's parents got $20,000 compensation from the Wisconsin-based lumber company. What was more, Florida agreed to ban the use of the whip in all its prison camps.[16] The insinuation in Southern papers was that the Northern press had martyred Talbert—made him a "modern John Brown"—and that peonage and other forms of sale of convicts for forced labor had been outlawed.[17]

The reality was that it certainly had not, and it took another even more horrific crime, and tragic death, to make the issue resurface. Three years after Talbert's murder, another young white man was killed by the punishment he received in a Southern prison camp. While serving a two-year term for forgery, James Knox was deliberately drowned in a laundry vat as a punishment for "insubordination." Having abandoned the whip, many camps had turned instead to the "water cure" to maintain discipline. In this horrible torture, the victim was held under water until near death, revived, and then reimmersed several more times. In Knox's case this punishment was carried out in water so hot that according to one witness it scalded off all the poor man's fingernails.[18]

As Douglas Blackmon has argued, to those in the North, Knox's murder was an example of prevalent Southern cruelty and lack of respect for humanity. To Southerners, it was shocking because this was known as a punishment used solely on blacks. However, in terms of the prevalence of this sort of crime, Blackmon cites a series of front-page articles run in the wake of the trial of Knox's murderers in March 1926. These essentially show how the organized network of law enforcers, big business and black slaves thrived in Alabama.

This study in the *New York World* showed how in 1925 alone the prison camps and convict labor sales generated over $250,000 profit for the state of Alabama. Selling of 1,300 convicts to big business, farms and local dealers made close on $600,000 for those involved.[19] The following year, the incoming governor of Alabama moved convicts out of the mines and private businesses of the state, and instead instituted the notorious "chain gangs" of the 1930s and 1940s. However, the practice of leasing convicts remained widespread until legislation finally outlawed the practice in 1948 and 1951.

## Berthe Claiche

> *What profit tears? What profit countless hands*
> *Held up in prayer? Or hearts that for her ache?*
> *Is not her sale price known throughout the lands?*
> *What others traffic for shall we not take?*
> *The White Slave of the Nations there she stands*
> *And waits—till we betray her for our honor's sake.*
> —Stuart P. Sherman (1914)[20]

In July 1905, many of the American reading public were engrossed arguing over the implications of a highly controversial murder. On the face of it, it seemed there was little to dispute. The case related to the actions of a pretty twenty-two-year-old French woman living in downtown New York. On July 5, Berthe Claiche had shot her lover dead.

She had fired three bullets at point-blank range into Emile Gerdron, sometimes reported as Emile Gerdon. Within minutes Gerdron was dead and Claiche stood over him, defiantly, outstandingly unrepentant. In part this was because she could not deny having killed him, since the incident took place in front of several witnesses—and those witnesses were three detectives. But there was more to it than a simple killing; it was—as the huge press coverage attested—a crime that defined many of the problems of the age, and, it could be argued, opened up a whole variety of new controversies.

The three policemen had been called, and not for the first time, to arrest Gerdron. They had been called by Claiche, who accused him of trying to beat her to death. This seemed to stack up, since the policemen who witnessed the shooting would later testify that her actions were carried out in self-defense. According to their account, when they arrived Gerdron was beating the unfortunate girl mercilessly. He then said he had a gun, with which he threatened to shoot the girl if the police did not leave. Berthe had grabbed the victim's gun from him. She then turned it on Gerdron and fired.

Justifying her action, she said Gerdron "put his hand to his hip pocket and exclaimed, 'If you have me pinched, when I get out I will kill you.'" Or this was the story, as one Midwestern newspaper told it.[21] And it was a compelling, if controversial tale. Americans were undecided about not only her guilt, but—and perhaps more importantly—they were intrigued by her motive. A section of the reporting that surrounded the case portrayed Berthe's actions as those of a woman whose moral compass had been destroyed by her horrible experiences as a girl "working on the street." They argued that her squalid life had left her a "hellcat," a woman devoid of the usual nurturing feminine virtues. They maintained that her experiences had conditioned her, and had made her a woman whose reaction to any challenge was to use violence.

Perhaps predictably, one of the best examples of this view is shown in the *New York World*. Never slow to come forward when there was a salacious story, Joseph Pulitzer's sensationalist paper published a picture of Berthe alongside that of another young—also foreign—murderess. The other woman was an Italian, and her name was Josefina Terranova. But the *World* found far more important disparities than simply nationality. In the most basic analysis, the article seems to draw on the work of contemporary advocates of criminological anthropology, such as the Italian Cesare Lombroso.

In the late nineteenth and early twentieth centuries, what one historian has called Lombroso's "magnificent tangle of brilliance and nonsense" were often simplified for popular consumption.[22] Many nonexpert commentators concentrated in particular on his studies on the relationship between physical appearance and propensity to criminal behavior. Drawing on this logic, the *World* piece argued that the differences apparent in the faces of the two women showed their true character. The author of the piece claimed that the expressions of the two women could be used to define the genuine nature of their crimes, and why they were committed. To those who understood the signs, the women's faces, according to the *World*, could show their guilt or innocence.

On the other hand, the paper also argued that the differences between the crimes drew on the two women's backgrounds, and the circumstances of the crimes. The paper claimed that the serene-looking Terranova was entirely justified in the murder of her uncle, the crime that had led to her imprisonment in New York's notorious Tombs. It was clear to the author of the report from her very expression and features of her face that the beautiful young Italian was inherently benign. The piece argued that it must have been an event beyond endurance that had made a woman like Josefina kill her uncle. Sure enough, the article revealed that she had been an innocent virgin who was just about to become a bride when her own uncle seduced her and then mercilessly raped her.

The *World* argued that her innocent face demonstrated the whole sordid evolution of the case. It showed how, after the uncle's callous abuse of her, Josefina must have felt ashamed and defiled. It demonstrated how the horrible events of what should have been the most "joyous event" of her life instead left her feeling "unworthy of her husband's love." The author told his readers that her expression showed she was a virtuous woman who, when placed in the near impossible situation of having been violated by a family member, took the only revenge she could see as possible in her position. Her "Mediterranean temperament" made her passionate and proud. The combined influence of all these elements meant that Josefina had reflexively killed the man who had callously and knowingly destroyed her life when he raped her.

By contrast, according to the *World*, Berthe's gaze showed an entirely different set of characteristics. The French woman had a face that radiated an entirely opposite aura. Still pretty, it exhibited a brazen expression that "showed knowledge that understands and chooses." Ignoring those who pointed out the sorry series of events that led to the fatal shooting—who the author condemned as "sentimentalists"—the paper went on to explain that it was clear that Berthe was "simply a little rat of the city's sewers that turned upon one of the other rats." What was unusual was that, in this case, this everyday occurrence "was brought up to the level of those of us who are fortunate enough to live on the sunlit surface of things that we may sit in Judgment upon her."[23]

However, while some of the paper's readers may well have been flattered by their being placed in Olympian arbitration over such figures, there was a significant section of the public who were entirely sympathetic to the young French woman. Although they were dismissed by the *World* as "sentimentalists," it is easy to see why they may have supported the girl's actions. Why wouldn't they have? Quite aside from the fact that she was being beaten and threatened with being shot, her story was reported in other papers as a tale redolent of pure turn-of-the-century melodrama. The story was sadly pretty common, and it seemed to be becoming more so.

From the age of sixteen, when the unfortunate girl had first met the thirty-six-year-old Gerdron in Brittany, the six-foot-two brute had perpetually physically and sexually abused her. It didn't seem that it had taken much for the worldly Gerdron to persuade the lovestruck young girl to leave her job as a lace-maker in a small rural village. Pretty soon the pair had moved to Paris, where, anonymous in the notoriously libertine city, they had set up house together. However, at this point the situation changed. Within weeks of arriving in the city, with her "virtue" now a memory, Gerdron had begun to pimp the pretty young girl out, while at the same time using her sexually himself. He had continued this treatment when they moved some years later to New York.

The accounts detailed how, once the unfortunate Claiche realized the inescapability of her predicament, the love she had felt gave way to fear and hatred. As this became obvious to the brute, Gerdron, her tormentor had been obliged to hold her prisoner. Claiche later told the papers how Gerdron had prevented her from running away by locking her into their squalid flat for weeks on end. When her "work" meant the door needed to be unlocked—in order to enable clients to enter and leave—he had kept her in the apartment by taking away all of her clothes. In addition, he had controlled her by appropriating and spending all her earnings.

As if such humiliation was not enough, Gerdron had regularly raped and cruelly beaten his young slave. The Frenchman had a fierce temper and took out his anger on the young girl, especially when she attempted to escape—which she tried on several occasions.

Nor was this tragic story based simply on the word of an ex-prostitute. Once Berthe's trial for murder was underway, more respectable neighbors emerged who reported hearing the noise and seeing the results of her treatment—treatment that they claimed had frequently culminated in Gerdron's loud threats to kill her.

While Claiche's case was by no means unique, what made it all the more sensational was the bleakness and pathos of the young girl's account. She was happy to recount her miserable existence, ostensibly as a parable to warn and protect other innocent young women who may be vulnerable to predatory beasts similar to Gerdron. She articulately— perhaps suspiciously so, given her lack of English—detailed his relentless cruelty. She articulately justified her actions, explaining how it had reached such a level that the desperate girl had concluded that anything, even prison or death, was better than her wretched existence with Gerdron.

These accounts of abuse reached a crescendo in the press a month after her arrest and indictment on a charge of murder. In a highly moving account dictated to a Texan woman journalist from her prison cell, the French girl told the reporter her tragic life story. She detailed how her six years with Gerdron had been a time of constant humiliation, brutalization and isolation. Eventually, given that relentless pressure, she had snapped. As she explained: "He took my life as I have now taken his. He killed everything in me. I was only 16 years old."[24]

Initially many readers saw this exploitation of a young woman as yet another tragic example of the decline in the morals of the metropolitan areas of the nation. They saw it as one of the inevitable results of the constant flow into the city of a stream of ill-educated, impoverished immigrants. They saw this blight magnified by the dehumanizing effects of big-city commercialization that was also so much a feature of their age. To them Berthe's fate was indicative of the replacement of genuine values by the relentless commodification of almost everything—a development that now appeared to include women.

By the time Berthe was sentenced in April, the mood of the press—and the majority of those absorbed in the case—had veered from hostility to sympathy for the poor French woman. Unsurprisingly, given the public outrage and shock the case evoked, she avoided the electric chair. Instead she got a lenient five years from a sympathetic court. It is perhaps equally unsurprising that she behaved as a model prisoner and was released after serving only two years of her time.

## The White Slave Trade

As the Claiche case had unfolded, the press increasingly began to shift the emphasis of their investigation away from portraying the fate of the French woman as the tragic story of an individual's downfall. Instead she was pictured as just one victim, a single casualty, of something far more exploitative, even more objectifying and a lot more sinister. Claiche was portrayed as the prey not just of the brutality and callousness of an individual thug, but as yet another pawn of a far more organized, wide-ranging and terrifyingly cynical and callous phenomenon. To reinforce the commercial and wide-ranging nature of her fate, as the case wore on, rather than referring to Berthe by her name in headlines, she increasingly became referred to as *the* "White Slave."

It appeared a new phrase entered the popular lexicon, or at least that expression now had a physical manifestation. In fact the expression and, of course, the phenomenon had already been around for some years. British and French sources had used the expression for nearly three decades, and as early as 1886 the *New York Times* had announced details of "An Infamous Traffic" linking Europe, via Canada, to New York, Chicago, Boston, and other cities in a trade based around the exploitation, degradation and destruction of innocent girls.[25]

The year after the *Times'* exposé, the *New York Herald* reported the enslavement of white American women for prostitution in the Menominee Iron Range region of Michigan. It told of how women of "sixteen, seventeen, eighteen and twenty, respectable and honest but poor … and haggard from a life of misery" were subjected to "horror upon horror." The linkage with slavery was enforced by the treatment the girls had been subjected to. To make the tales even more shocking, it emerged that some had decided they could no longer face captivity and shame. Those who didn't take their own lives tried to run away, only to find they would be "pursued by bloodhounds if they attempt to make [an] escape." What was more, like the plantation slaves of the Old South, the runaways would be whipped when they were inevitably caught.

What made these stories all the more shocking was that these were *white girls*, unlike those subjected to coolie labor in the West or to peonage in the South. The author pointed out that there was also a new dimension to this enslavement. Unlike their predecessors in the cotton and tobacco fields of the past, these unfortunates had to interact with the public. These girls would always be punished in a way that was "severe enough," yet at the same time careful enough "not to injure their [the pimp's] property." This treatment ended up, according to the investigation, leaving "the wretches" with only two options—"the grave and the brothel."[26]

Nor was such treatment unique. In one of the nearby lumber camps of Wisconsin, a year later, a Women's Christian Temperance Union (WCTU) investigator told the story of a woman running from a brothel. She was carrying a weighty ball attached by a length of chain to a shackle on her ankle. Her pimp soon caught her and dragged her back to the brothel, as she screamed at the top of her voice.[27] These and many other tales indicate that there was indubitably a level of coercion inherent in the abduction of many young ladies, and that was surely tantamount to enslavement in the vice industry. Yet it was not until the first decade of the twentieth century that "white slavery" really came to the attention of the public.

What was more, once identified, the phenomenon seemed to be present everywhere. While the Claiche case had created a storm of interest over the months of the trial, it was perhaps more important as a catalyst to further investigations. These soon turned up evidence that her fate was only too common. There were stories of white slaves emerging in cities all over the country. Some idea of the nature of this explosion of interest can be gauged by a quick survey of newspaper headlines for the year from July 1905. This reveals nearly 5,000 headlines that highlight the words "white slave." This represents significantly more citations than can be found for the same expression for all the headlines used in the same newspapers for the years from 1886 to 1905.[28]

These sensational and horrifying cases detailed horrific tales of women imprisoned and enslaved. They emerged from cities as widespread as Chicago; Philadelphia; Seattle; Denver; Wilmington, Delaware; Butte, Montana; Portland (both Oregon and Maine); Helena, Arkansas; and El Paso, Texas, as well as many other less sizeable or significant places. Some of them detailed confessional accounts of the duping, seduction, brutalization and degradation of formerly enslaved girls. Other journals, magazines and newspapers carried stories telling of the auctions of young white women. These often stressed their former girlish innocence and described their beauty in more or less salacious detail, all the while concentrating on their tender youth and complete vulnerability.

The details of the accounts varied. Some described the processes of kidnapping and enslavement—drumming in the details of the extent of their exploitation, they told readers of the paltry prices these innocents attained. Sometimes the papers carried the heartening accounts of the prosecutions of "slave masters." Often these upbeat accounts stressed the growing levels of international cooperation being brought to bear on those carrying out the trade and gave details of the new international agreements designed to eliminate, or at least limit, the trade.

Nevertheless, even in the face of repeated and increasingly concerted efforts to stamp it out, statistics all seemed to indicate that the already horrifying numbers involved were on the increase. The news grew worse as each investigation published its findings. A certain Alice Wilson, who claimed that she was a former white slave herself, was convinced that "there were more than three thousand white slaves in Chicago [alone], and almost every saloon where women congregate, is [in reality] a slave den."[29]

While most sources agreed the problem was pressing both in terms of the numbers involved and the geographic spread, they were not as unanimous about who it was that actually controlled what was increasingly being shown as a complex network of very organized criminals. A step toward identifying the network bosses seemed to have come in November 1905, when the nation's syndicated papers published the confessions of another Frenchman—Anatola Harchaux. A white slave dealer, or "pander," Harchaux was arrested in Pueblo, Colorado, having shipped in several girls via Canada for prostitution.

To many commentators his arrest was a highly important breakthrough. It proved—if anyone still needed proof—the strongly suspected organized nature and the ruthless commercial connection between French panders and the white slave trade in the United States. This view was not only based on the increasingly salacious tales emerging about the brutality of the "vampire" Gerdron, but also a strong conviction that *Belle Epoch* Paris with its permissive, debauched and promiscuous reputation must also be the epicenter of any such trade.

With what appeared at best their pragmatic attitude towards sex, French morals were seen as being, at the very least, questionable. To those who were less forgiving, as a nationality the French—of both sexes—were portrayed as both shameless and perverted in their sexual habits. It was not by chance that oral sex was known as "French sex" or that the condom referred to as a "French letter." Nor was it simply coincidence that brothels were frequently given redolently risqué French names like the *Bon Ton* or the *Sans Souci*. Essentially, many believed that if sex was sold, then it was very often French men—like Gerdron and Harchaux—who sold French women—like Claiche.

Given this association with impropriety, immorality and promiscuity, many of those investigating the "bartering in human souls" were convinced that the French were key players in the white slave trade. Unsurprisingly, it was not long before a sound basis for this French connection had been uncovered and, to many, proved. Nor was it simply newsmen who led the way in showing who was responsible for the hideous traffic. One of the leading players in uncovering this proof was the U.S. Attorney in Chicago, Edwin W. Sims.

After several years of investigation, Sims uncovered what appeared conclusive evidence to support the accusation that the French were at the forefront of a syndicate operating "from the Atlantic seaboard to the Pacific ocean, with 'clearing houses' or 'distribution centers' in all of the large cities…. The syndicate is a definite organization sending its hunters regularly to scour France, Germany, Hungary, Italy and Canada for victims."[30] Nor, it appeared, was this simply speculation or prejudice. Sims had made it his mission to break the white slave trade in one of its main hubs.

For years the city of Chicago had possessed one of the nation's most infamous red-light districts. Catering to all tastes and all pockets, it had even played host—as legend would have it—to the Crown Prince of Prussia. Prince Henry had toasted his uncle, the Kaiser, with champagne. He poured it into the shoe of a high-class escort and drank to him in the nation's most salubrious house of ill repute.

But not all of the Levee District's working girls entertained such esteemed clients with such decadently lavish tastes. Many were brutalized, humiliated and degraded, and few doubted that they had been sold into slavery. These girls would have been lucky to have had any shoes at all, let alone ones from which anyone, let alone a prince, might contemplate drinking anything—especially the finest champagne—with anything other than abject disgust mingled with a fear of infection. What was more, the pimps controlling most of the area would have almost certainly robbed, beaten and then blackmailed any crowned head that entered most of the joints in the district.

The man who had set it as his mission to clean up this vice-ridden area was no naïve idealist. Utterly single-minded, Sims had already risen up the ladder of the legal profession. When he launched his campaign against white slavery, he was attorney for the Northern District of Illinois with a proven record behind him. He had been the one of the leading lawyers involved in the team that had brought down the Rockefeller empire in the protracted but ultimately victorious—if not ultimately entirely successful—series of cases brought against the behemoth that was Standard Oil. He was now determined he would build on this success and propel himself to further success with another equally high-profile cause. With this in mind he saw the increasing furor surrounding the city's unfortunate girls as the perfect vehicle. Ever the crusader, Sims had decided would now clean up the Levee.

## Edwin Sims' Investigations

Although used to reformers, the vice district of Chicago had really never seen anything quite like it. Calling in favors and using connections he'd made in Washington over the years of his Standard Oil work, the determined Sims managed to gather a dedicated team of Secret Service agents supported by some twenty-five federal marshals. He immediately put them to work to—as he put it—"break up this traffic in foreign women." He was nothing if not ambitious in his goals.

Sims was determined to remain in the headlines, and he used language that would keep him there. Shortly after he started his crusade, he told the press—with whom he regularly met—that he was going to rid America of this foul "contamination." According to his own publicity, the results of his raids justified his hyperbole. Simms maintained that the haul of pimps and prostitutes netted by his operation were just as impressive as the scale of the forces he had brought to bear. By the end of his forays in June, Sims had secured twenty-seven indictments against white slavers. These had yielded seventeen convictions and led to the collection of over $125,000 in fines.[31]

As a part of this campaign, on June 23, 1908, Sims sent federal marshals to raid 2021 Armour Avenue in the Chicago Levee District. Here they arrested three working girls and later the brothel owners, Eva and Alphonse Dufour, aka Dufaur. The couple were charged on six indictments centered on the harboring of six "alien" women. This would subsequently rise to over twenty indictments and the discovery of sixteen girls. The Dufours were significant in the evolution of the history of the white slave trade, since they clearly demonstrated the power of those running the operations.

It pretty soon emerged that the notoriety of the Dufours did not depend on what they did to get indicted—although the scale and interconnectedness of their business with that of other panders was shocking. Rather, their importance would stem more from how ineffective those indictments were to prove in the fight to contain white slavery. The events that followed their arrests would show that the existing laws could not contain wealthy, cunning, ruthless and well-connected criminals like the leading panders and brothel owners.

In essence it was this seeming powerlessness that added to the fear surrounding the white slave issue. Truly organized networks of panders, pimps, slavers and madams seemed to be above the law, and those they victimized seemed, perversely, to be beneath it. In the case of Alphonse and Eva, a total of sixteen French girls from their brothel were arrested and held. No bail was set for them, and, given their status, it was unlikely any would have been paid. Essentially, girls like these were expendable. The brothel owners would not pay for them to be released from custody, and their own funds would not cover the costs. What was more, they had no representation to plead their cases.

On the other hand, the Dufours were granted $25,000 bail, which was to be put up by a rather mysterious bondsman called O'Malley—known only as a saloon-owner acquaintance of theirs. Yet, powerful as they were, things did not all go as planned. Rightfully dubious about the trustworthiness of the Dufours, in the event the shadowy O'Malley refused to post bail. Seeing the danger signs, Sims subsequently demanded that bail was doubled. However, it is indicative of the ruthlessness, resourcefulness, connections and disregard for the law that the Dufours still managed to evade imprisonment.

Nevertheless, with the bail now set at a record $50,000, the couple found the money, paid it over and were released. They then skipped the country—a move that it was estimated cost them around $100,000. They headed back to France, where they were later arrested.[32] It was an irony that was not missed by the anti-vice campaigners that the couple were apprehended for trying to sell an American girl to a brothel in Paris. Sims was quick to tell the press that his raids had been successful and "hit the vice trade hard."

Despite the way in which the Dufours escaped justice, in one important regard Sims's bragging to the press was justified. Although at this point he did not mention it, there was far more important evidence that had emerged as a result of the raids he launched in the Levee District. The marshals confiscated a cache of documents and accounts relating to a network of "houses of ill-repute" being run throughout the Levee District and other red-light areas around the country.[33] In turn these documents apparently led to the subsequent arrest of over 2,000 French-born "white slaves" in Minneapolis, New York, Kansas City, New Orleans and St. Louis. It appeared that all of these girls could be traced back to the network centered on Chicago.[34]

Sims's agents were not alone in their discoveries. There were others working on uncovering similar networks in other parts of the country. The same year as Sims made his discoveries about the complexity and international nature of the networks, a truly indefatigable investigator called Marcus Braun disclosed further transnational connections. Braun once again linked the "traffic in human flesh" with the ubiquitous French pimps, and also reinforced what Sims had revealed: there was a strong connection between Chicago and brothels in the rest of the country, especially the West.

Braun was a very different man from Sims. A Hungarian-born Jew of modest origins, he had emigrated to the U.S. as a child. A man of action, he had a history of hands-on investigations in his wide-ranging career. A man of real presence, he had cultivated an aura of macho indifference and bravery bordering on the downright stupid. A famous example of the legend he cultivated about himself was that he relished people knowing he had won a bet by eating his lunch with the lions in their cage while reporting for the *New York Herald* at the Chicago World's Fair in 1893. Quickly bored by simple reporting, he had gone on to bring his unique style of work to the Bureau of Immigration. By the time of the white slave investigations, he had risen to become the Bureau's chief undercover agent, a job that he seemed to revel in because of its inherent dangers. Initially charged with investigating illegal contract laborers entering the U.S., he soon shifted his emphasis to looking into prostitution and trafficking in Europe and the U.S.

In this capacity he uncovered a very well-connected procurer called Paul Heudiard. Offering Heudiard $100 a week, he persuaded him to tell his story, and expose details of how the white slave trade worked out of the hub of Chicago and the West. In many ways Heudiard was an ideal informant. From his own "resort" in Chicago's Dearborn Street, he would prove a vital source of information. The story he told unfolded an interlinked chain that tied in the procuring, transporting, marketing and operating of young girls as prostitutes. His information would reveal to Braun in quite some detail how the "French Rings" operated.

The system that Heudiard exposed showed the methods by which imported French girls entered the New World through Canada. He showed how these innocent and gullible young girls were rapidly disabused of any hopes that their guides and agents were benevolent or honest when they reached the next stage of the process. Arriving at one of the houses in the Levee District of Chicago owned by the slavers, the terrified girls were now readied for their future lives, or as Heudiard put it, "processed."

Having been abducted, the poor wretches now needed to be made compliant. In a culture that prized virginity, this obedience was achieved by making sure that they were rendered unsuitable for any life but vice—in their own eyes and that of society at large. The girls were, as the times dictated unmarried women should be, usually virgins. Once that "virtue" was taken from the girls, polite society dictated that they could not return to their previous lives. With these cultural norms in mind, the girls were then "broken" through repeated and frequent brutalizing, degrading and pitiless sessions of gang rape, often lasting several days.

According to Heudiard's testimony, this also had other advantages for the slavers. Unsurprisingly, the deliberate brutality and mercilessness of the treatment they had received from the "breakers" and their associates put the girls into a state of shock. Horrified, physically battered and abused, often distraught to the point of suicide, they were nursed and consoled by other girls in the employ of the slavers who had already been through the process. These experienced girls were advised for their own safety and well-being to be resigned and compliant. They indoctrinated the newcomers with this readiness to comply with the demands of their captors in order gain even a little respite. In this tender state, the ruined ingénues were then exported to other "sporting houses" as far afield as Washington State, Montana, California, Nebraska, Colorado, Utah, Nevada and Oregon, where they would themselves frequently induct more girls into the system.[35]

What also emerged, clearly, from Braun's investigations was that the French panders operated in conjunction with other groups, and sometimes these appear rather unlikely to our modern ears. For instance, it was claimed that in Colorado the French had partnered up with the Church of the Latter Day Saints. It was this coalition, it was claimed, that was behind one of the most important vice networks in the West, and it was centered on using French connections and French girls. Nor was Braun alone in uncovering this association. Speaking at a conference in Chicago, the well-connected German campaigner, Maria Lydia Winkler, agreed with his findings.

Winkler was associated with the Knights of Love, a French organization dedicated to the stamping out of the trade in young girls. Central to her investigations was the claim that it was the Mormons who controlled one of the most powerful and sophisticated white-slaving operations. She saw the Latter Day Saints as a rather poorly hidden "octopus with its tentacles all around the world." She went on to explain that the Mormons, through their international connections, ran a network dedicated to kidnapping young girls in Hungary and shipping them over to the work in the fleshpots of Utah, via France.[36] Nevertheless, to many investigators it was not the French, or even the Mormons, who were really running this immoral network—nor, it emerged, were they even considered the most important of the white slavers within it.

Even as the Claiche case was being tried, Commissioner of Immigration Robert Watchorn warned reporters that to his mind—and in the opinion of many other experts—there were other foreigners at work in the abhorrent industry. Unsurprisingly, given their reputation for criminality, venality and immorality, there was a suspicion that it was the "New Immigration" that lay at the heart of this trade. Made up of the hordes of arrivals from the Mediterranean and Slavic regions of the Old World, the New Immigrants were coming in their hundreds of thousands each month.

These European savages, it was pronounced, were men and women who would never have had the American's distaste for making money off these poor girls. They would have thought little about the trading away of the innocence of these helpless victims purely for money. Watchorn was certainly not a voice in the wilderness when he argued that other, more hungry immigrant groups than the French were now running the increasingly well-organized trans–Atlantic trade in "human flesh."[37]

Sure enough, within a couple of years, Watchorn's reassessment would lay a basis for the thinking of most other commentators who were by now moving the issue of white slavery to center stage in the public debate. White slavery had all the necessary prerequisites to make it the prime activity of organized criminality. It was international in its scope. It threatened some of the most vulnerable and vital elements of society, and it was about to be linked in with more dangerous threats than the promiscuous and amoral French. It was now about to emerge as one of the most pressing of the nation's problems.

## From Maquereaux to Kaftan

When *McClure's Magazine's* resident expert on urban affairs, George Kibbe Turner, published an article on the subject of the white slave trade in 1909, it both fashioned and coincided with the marked upsurge of interest in the nature of the so-called "Social Evil" in the U.S.[38] Prostitution had a range of elements that made it the perfect issue for the reform-minded, morally driven Progressives who were ascendant in the U.S. With Turner's analysis, the matter of prostitution, the "trade in human souls," essentially evolved from being *a* subject of interest to being *the* subject of interest in the minds of many American Progressives.

To a considerable extent, Turner was the catalyst for this change. His exposure of the white slave trade steered investigations away from being dominated by a shocked moral outrage. Instead he attempted to show how the trade worked, who controlled it and who benefitted from it. In doing so, he demonstrated a new attitude towards morality, social change and their connection with organized crime.[39] Turner was an experienced, successful journalist of what Theodore Roosevelt famously called the "muckraker" school. He was a dedicated investigator, and he had considerable expertise in this particular subject.

This was not Turner's first work on urban vice. He had published an article on the topic in 1907, and it had been a great success. "The City of Chicago: A Study of the Great Immoralities" had been the most commercially successful article for the leading muckraking journal, *McClure's*, that year. The 1909 article was in some measure an attempt to replicate that success. In keeping with this ambition, the second article, titled "The Daughters of the Poor," was hyped as being "the most startling and important article published in years—a plain story ... of how the White Slave Trade in American girls developed in New York ... and has spread to every large city of the United States."[40]

However, it was not simply the hype that differentiated this article from those that had gone before. In his previous work, Turner had shown that prostitution and the importing of prostitutes was often a business controlled by individuals working for themselves. Two years later, he seemed convinced that as the numbers of victims involved expanded in the late nineteenth century, these men, and they were according to him largely men, had often formed a loose, but nonetheless connected, network of criminals. In keeping with current thinking of the time, he maintained that this network had been centered in France, but he didn't see Frenchmen as the most important movers in the trade.

According to Turner, in order to meet expanding demand, the French panders had increasingly pulled in a ready supply of young, poor and gullible girls from the slums, ghettoes and shtetls of Eastern Europe. In "Daughters of the Poor," while admitting their role and stressing the organized nature of their setup, Turner moved the problem away from being rooted in the rather *ad hoc* activities of a group of depraved, cruel and chauvinistic Frenchmen. In his analysis, this group were essentially men on the make, seizing every opportunity to make money, and paying little attention to either the laws of the land or common humanity. In essence they were men like Berthe Claiche's pimp/lover, Emile Gerdron.

However, in the years since the turn of the twentieth century, Turner saw a change in those who led this hideous trade. He argued that things had moved on. The little cruel and heartless pimp running a few girls had been replaced by true white slavery—a genuinely global phenomenon, and one with truly threatening implications and connotations for America.

These were problems that chimed with the specter of the "grosser manifestations of industrial America." These were problems that the Progressive reformers saw as their duty to analyze, publicize and—hopefully—eliminate.[41] What had shocked and outraged

Turner's middle-class American readership in his 1907 article was the development and alteration of themes with which they were already familiar from the tragic story of Berthe Claiche. To some readers, the tale of the French girl was one that excited outrage. The real disgust was aimed at the deception and cruelty meted out to an innocent young immigrant, a girl who was herself little more than a child. To other readers the problem was more one highlighted by the nature of Sims's raid on the brothels of Chicago, and the subsequent connections they had uncovered. To them the social evil largely involved the mechanics of a network of organized criminals associated with the importing of already depraved French girls.

What was significant was that in most early accounts, like that of Berthe herself, these were girls who—while often duped into their "original sin"—probably would have intended to continue to practice, or previously had plied, their immoral trade before leaving their native country. Nor was Turner alone in reaching such conclusions. Similar findings and similar conclusions were clearly demonstrated by the reports given to the undercover investigator, Marcus Braun—and those he, in turn, forwarded to his bosses in Washington. In at least one set of his reports he argued that many, particularly French, prostitutes were shipped into the U.S. with the full knowledge of what they were getting into.

What was more, unlike the more self-conscious working girls of most other nationalities, according to some of Braun's reports, they did not even attempt to deny their intention to work as prostitutes. In one of his reports, the girls in question entered the U.S. from Canada through Sweetwater, Montana. No doubt this rather obscure crossing point was chosen in part because the rough and masculine "frontier" nature of the state and its border guards would make it more sympathetic to importing of "working girls." If the border guards were unusually vigilant or peculiarly unsympathetic, the girls would say they were traveling via the Santa Fe Railroad to Mexico. They would argue that they were simply in transiting through America. This meant that they were not an American problem, for it was not for those guarding the borders of the U.S. to dictate the morals of Mexicans.[42]

In other words, according to Turner, it appeared that before his later revelations, the objections to the so-called panders were largely based on moral grounds. The outrage and interest they excited was mainly concerned with the seeming inability to control the problems of immorality. They centered on the threat posed to the localities,' as well as the nation's, decency by the existence—and in many cases the more-or-less tacit tolerance—of whores, panders, streetwalkers, brothels, pimps and madams.

But in his second, 1909 article, what Turner was showing was that the flood of unfortunate women now being discovered were the victims of a new form of organized crime. The picture he now drew was one of a highly sophisticated and very well-organized network of crime. This more complex form of sex trafficking was far more worrying. It was linked with irresponsible political power, exploitative big money, and unregulated immigration—three of the obsessions of the Progressive Era reformers. It was a threat of an entirely different magnitude, and what was more, Turner was not alone in having claimed to have uncovered what amounted to this new threat: a "vice trust."[43]

In his brief introductory history of the vice industry, Turner indulges the love of categorization and progression that is such a feature of the turn of the century in both Britain and the U.S. He also imbued the life of the prostitute in the mid- to late nineteenth century American cities with what can only be seen as a certain nostalgia. The veteran journalist created a picture of the evolution of the business of prostitution as organized crime. He shows how under the French pimps—*les maquereaux* (mackerels), as they were known—there was a relatively benign and "haphazard" regime. Going back on his original depiction, what he describes under the Frenchmen was essentially a casual, almost paternal, cottage industry of prostitution, rather than the brutal, dehumanized and entirely venal white slavery—as it would later emerge.

According to Turner, in the years of their dominance the maquereaux had ensured that the girls they "ran" were well-presented, clean and sober. Under this regime, Turner claimed that the pimps maintained the morale of the working girls by arguing that prostitution was simply a means to an end. However grim, dangerous and demeaning the life of the working girl may have been under the French pimps, the maquereaux induced them to believe that if they worked hard, they could make enough money to quit prostitution. They even held out the hope that the girls would be able to return to France, and live there, if not as wealthy women, then at least with enough money to allow a good chance of anonymity about their previous life and perhaps sidestep questions of their activities in America.

Be that as it may, and somewhat predictably, given the apocalyptic nature of his revelations, the relatively benign system of the maquereaux that Turner alluded to could not last. Although they operated in "exclusive boarding-houses and clubs," the maquereaux never achieved the requisite political protection essential to give them either safety or stability. Turner does not go into a great deal of detail as to why this was, simply arguing that those who succeeded them were more attuned to the importance of political protection.

According to Turner, the somewhat amateurish French pimps frequently found themselves blackmailed. They were liable to extortion. They were prey to protection rackets and corrupt officials. They were raided, investigated and prosecuted by the authorities. Turner claimed that these pressures meant that eventually the flamboyantly macho, but actually rather ineffectual, French pimps were driven out of the prime vice areas of the city centers and into the less lucrative areas of the small towns and suburbs. Here making their girls pay was often so tricky that many took to cutting their losses and returning to France.

Most of these claims built on evidence produced in his 1907 study of Chicago's underworld. In the section dealing with prostitution, Turner estimated that there were at least 10,000 prostitutes in the city in 1906. He went on to claim that the number was growing, and largely as a result of a new phenomenon. He claimed that white slaves who were being brought in from abroad were rapidly replacing the French and English-speaking working girls of the city. He detailed how over the years leading up to the article, the brothels in the city's notorious Levee District were purchasing new, younger, mainly Polish and Russian-Jewish girls, at the rate of ten to a dozen girls per week.

In his analysis, the growth of this type of business was hardly surprising. To the pimps, the new girls were superior in many ways to the older women they replaced. Most obviously the pimps were in no doubt that they could charge the city's "sporting types" more for these younger, often more attractive, girls. Many customers would not need to be convinced that these younger girls would also be less likely to be diseased.

Further, usually brutally "broken" by multiple rapes, frequent beatings and constant humiliation before they arrived for sale, these girls were often in a compliant, or at least submissive, state of shock. Pimps must have relished the idea of dealing with more innocent, more malleable and gullible girls who, in spite of their lack of English, were reputed to be more acquiescent and easier to control than many of the hard-bitten and cynical older whores they were replacing. But perhaps the main reason for this escalating rate of replacement was simply the purchase price. The costs to the owner of the "resorts" for these younger, more saleable and more manageable girls were pretty well negligible.

## The Vice Trade

According to most accounts of the period, prostitution was a highly lucrative trade in these years, and as such it attracted increasingly organized networks of criminals. Just how much money it could make is open to question, but some idea of just how profitable it could be can be gathered from a study of the prostitution industry in the Pennsylvania city of Lancaster. The investigation by the historian Philip Jenkins shows that a well-run "sporting house" in this small city cleared an average of $400 a week with only a couple of working girls. If that was the case for a small operation in the backwoods, it can only be expected that the opportunities and turnover increased in the larger houses of the larger cities.[44]

This perspective is backed up by the investigations of a New York district attorney who looked into the matter in the early twentieth century. He focused on the prices paid by brothel owners for new girls, and he found it to be remarkably little. According to him, newly arrived girls changed hands in the city "wholesale" for as little as $5 or $10 each.[45] Turner's research claimed the upfront sum paid to the "agent" by the resort was usually a more realistic $50 a head—very exceptionally it may have reached up to $75.[46] Of course the price fluctuated, region by region, with supply and demand.

The comments of one "dealer" illustrate something of the complexities and variables affecting the "market" for enslaved girls. He was quoted as saying that when the reformers and investigators were active in an area, the price shot up. He said that his usual price was less than $10, but when a full-scale vice campaign was underway in New York, he would not risk selling his girls there for as much as $1,000.[47] Whatever price was paid, it was remarkably low, even when compared with that paid for convicts in the South over the same years, or that paid for chattel slaves before the Thirteenth Amendment.

It is even more surprising if the cost is judged against potential earning. In the years leading up to the Civil War, average black chattel slave values, for both sexes and of all ages, reached a peak of $800 around 1858. By this yardstick, the prices apparently paid for these wretched girls were very low. This is especially true when it is considered that they would probably earn the purchaser that outlay in weeks—compared with the ten years the antebellum plantation slave would take to cover his purchase price. It is also important to note that the black slave's $800 was in 1858 dollars, a figure which neglected half a century of inflation.[48]

If the profits and costs of the business were disputed, so estimates of the scale of the trade were also open to speculation. Theodore Bingham, New York's retired police commissioner, argued 2,000 girls a year were "brought in like cattle, used far worse than cattle, and disposed of for money like cattle."[49] Chicago's crusading attorney, Edwin Sims, extrapolated from his raids in the Levee District that there must have been at least 15,000 slaves a year entering the nation.[50] Another contemporary account of the trade had "thirty thousand public women" working in 2,700 "houses of ill fame" in Chicago alone.[51]

It was the chief of the Justice Department's Bureau of Investigation (which would become the FBI), Stanley W. Finch, who had the most shocking statistics. What was more, these were the ones that formed the most frequently quoted basis for the calculations of other commentators. Finch estimated that 25,000 girls were procured for prostitution in the U.S. each year. By his appraisal, in 1912, there were a total of a quarter of a million enslaved girls in the country.[52]

Extrapolating from Finch's figures, another leading anti-vice activist—Clifford Roe—claimed that considerable numbers were needed in order for the trade to stand still and meet the existing demands of the nation's vice industry. Roe estimated that there was a need for 5,000 new girl-victims each and every month, since he startlingly estimated that some 60,000 slaves died and were replaced every year.[53]

There is little doubt that the modern observer should use such figures for "slaves" with caution. Not only are the total numbers of those involved in prostitution pretty near impossible to estimate, but there are various gradations of coercion within the sex trade, even in these years. What is more, in times when women were expected to have no sexual agency, and to prize their modesty above all, the social stigma attached to prostitution was even greater than today. To claim that they had been forced into sexual slavery was perhaps the last fig-leaf, the last scrap of dignity, available to women who had lost, or traded, everything else.

This highlighted another aspect of what was so terrifying in Turner's second article. It is starkly outlined in disclosures made to the Rockefeller grand jury, set up to investigate New York City prostitution. The commission was told by two female undercover agents that four white slaves had been sold, for a collective price of just $160. As might be anticipated, the value was in some measure dictated by the race and age of the victims. The two youngest girls were "American." They were being sold for $60 each. The other two were "foreign" and they changed hands for a mere $20 each.[54] This essentially proved what Turner indicated: that it was not only poor Europeans who were being imported for the sex industry, but girls born and raised in America were also being shipped around the nation for immoral purposes.

In his 1909 article Turner argued that girls were being imported into the vice hub of New York for re-exportation to other cities in the country. These girls, he pointed out, were not all fresh-off-the-boat immigrants. Many were American-born daughters of immigrants from the working-class textile towns of New England and Pennsylvania.[55] What he didn't mention, but other sources did, was that there was also a growing trade in "true American" girls from rural areas, duped, kidnapped and "broken" in identical ways to the victims coming out of Europe.

In part this was seen as a result of the empowering of American women over these years. Others saw it as the result of a less rigid and constrained system of American courtship, which involved suitors treating girls to outings and events in the expectation of some physical reward. No doubt these were ideas fueled by the fears of the seemingly unstoppable course towards an urban industrial society, and away from the small-town, morally based values associated with a bygone age that powered so many of the dilemmas of modernity in this age of change.

Whatever the motive, there was a whole genre of pamphlets and articles warning the rural girl to take care in the big city. Some came from expected quarters. One religiously based "social purity" journal ran articles with titles like "What are the dangers of city life for a country girl?" or "Commercialized vice and the farm. Are our farm girls in imminent danger from this foe?" Other warnings came from less likely sources and seem slightly odd from our perspective today. For instance, the social worker and educator, Jane Addams, argued that the demands made on girls as machine operators in factories of the 1900s so addled their minds they lost their sense of morality. In this state they represented easy prey for the procurers.

While her reasoning is peculiar from our perspective, she was highlighting a genuine worry. To many reformers, the problem of white slavery was intrinsically linked to perceived changes that followed on from "modernity," industrialization and urbanization. According to this reading, the pander/procurer/slaver was enabled by the isolation and dislocation of "modern" urban industrial communities. He was also a product of the immorality resulting from the relativism and self-centeredness of "modern" beliefs and the new opportunities offered by the increase in public spaces that were a central feature of modern cities.

This is well illustrated by another account, with a rather racy picture on its cover. *The Tragedies of the White Slave* quoted Sims detailing a variety of different ways in which "literally thousands of girls from country districts are every year entrapped into a life of hopeless slavery and degradation." It went on to show how girls were abducted from theaters, dance and music halls, railroad stations and ice cream parlors—even shops. It demonstrated how "cadets," "panders," pimps and procurers all preyed on these innocents, luring them with adverts for domestic servants, hotel staff and shop assistants.[56]

The problem was considered so prevalent by the outbreak of the First World War that most major American cities had instituted investigations into the sex trade. The findings varied, but most agreed with the Philadelphia commission, which argued panders utilized almost any public space to proposition, dupe or kidnap innocent young women. It explained how girls would be solicited and approached in "saloons, cafes, restaurants, hotels, clubs, and dance halls…. Many public dance halls, moving picture shows, and other amusement centers are the breeding places of vice…. The public parks are among the worst."[57]

Nowhere was safe, and readers of the reports were shocked by how widespread the threat seemed to be. They were horrified by tales of how apparently sensible and usually high-minded—but romantically inclined—girls were frequently duped into assignations with those they considered to be the man of their dreams, only to be abducted. In short, a host of more or less salacious, sentimental, titillating, factual accounts told American parents, guardians, brothers and teachers that should they "shut their eyes to this canker that is feeding on the flower of our nation they may continue to expect their daughters to be kidnapped, lost or mysteriously [go] missing."[58]

Set against this coercion and enslavement, as historians like Ruth Rosen have argued, it is apparent that many women took to prostitution as a rational choice. Given the often dire circumstances in which they found themselves and the total lack of any other opportunity available for supporting themselves, prostitution was sometimes a sensible option. Obviously the reasons women entered the "oldest profession" varied from person to person, but what is certain that a great many did enter it. One estimate argued that between 1850 and 1900 in New York, between five and ten percent of *all* women had worked as prostitutes between the ages of fifteen and thirty.[59]

Given the vast numbers involved, it is probably safe to assume that not all were coerced into the vice industry, but given the stigma, few would admit to being working girls, let alone give the reasons why they had become prostitutes. Nevertheless, Rosen has estimated that—based on contemporary vice report interviews with arrested prostitutes—less than ten percent could truly be defined as "white slaves" in any meaningful way. This is instructive when contrasted with the authorities' claims at the time that the figure for "enslaved" women in the prostitute population was around sixty percent.[60]

Rosen's findings are upheld by the claims of some writers at the time. While most accounts were written by middle-class white men with a fundamentally conservative or liberal agenda, there were others. The notorious anarchist and feminist Emma Goldman pointed out that as long as factory workers and shop girls continued to be paid less than a viable living wage, prostitution would remain a real temptation. The economics of desperation trumped society's prevalent middle-class Progressive morals. A girl who would earn $10 a week, at best, in a textile mill could earn at least double that on the streets— often she would make considerably more.

Goldman was also convinced that the hypocrisy inherent in Victorian-era sexual relations encouraged prostitution. Young girls were expected to surrender to their husband's sexual desires, while suppressing any hint of desire within themselves. Such submission to sex as a duty/chore was not a million miles away from the concept of money for sex. What was more, Goldman's streetwalkers were not white slaves as depicted in most other accounts. They were not the strikingly lovely young angelic country innocents tricked into losing their virtue by sly foreign types.

Goldman's account omitted the voyeurism and titillation so characteristic of many of the other accounts. The victims she portrayed were girls who had snatched some degree of agency for their lives; they were women who had assumed some control. What Goldman railed against was less the ubiquitous foreign pander, and more the uncaring mill and shop owners whose exploitation forced girls to sell their bodies to make ends meet. She also condemned as the true villains the "johns." In a peculiarly modern argument, she attacked the men, who had daughters and wives, yet who continued to use and then discard these girls like vessels for their own pleasure.

Goldman repeatedly spoke out against what she saw at the root of problem: the hypocritical standards that allowed men to have sexual experience, but condemned the women who gave it to them. She cites the sexologist and progressive intellectual Henry Havelock Ellis, agreeing with him when he condemns the "wife who married for money" far more than the prostitute. She agreed with his assessment that this "respectable" woman was in a worse position than the prostitute, since, according to him, "The prostitute never signs away the right over her own person, she retains her freedom and personal rights, nor is she always compelled to submit to man's embrace."[61]

Whoever made up the true victims of the sex mores of the period, even "Red Emma" Goldman agreed with the fact that there had been an increase in the number of "working girls." Such claims are always difficult to assess, but there is at least one piece of evidence that supports the contention that there was a surge in the numbers of prostitutes in these years. Elementary laws of supply and demand would indicate that the decreasing prices that the resort owners seemed to be paying in the early twentieth century, compared with the years before, were at least partly the result of increased supply—assuming that demand remained relatively constant, which there is no reason to dispute. This bargain price was an even better deal for the pimps and madams, since in the vast majority of cases that charge would then be passed on to the girl herself.

In some measure the girl was encouraged to conform to this repayment through work, having been told the quicker she repaid the money, the faster she would eventually be enabled to leave the profession. However, this glimpse of freedom was often cruelly illusory, since additional charges would be constantly added onto her settlement figure. Ostensibly to cover the unfortunate inmate's expenses, she would find herself paying extortionate charges for rent, or perhaps board or even, most ironically, clothing.[62] Not only were these charges another useful income stream for the owners of the brothels, but they also had other advantages. It kept the girls in a form of semivoluntary slavery, as well as preventing their movement. As an assistant district attorney in Chicago argued, "White slavers ... submerge fresh recruits into hopeless slavery ... [via] a system of indebtedness ... in which their costumes reach as high a figure as $1,200 and even $1,500. This indebtedness is mutually recognized and enforced between the keepers of all houses: in other words, no girl can leave one house and enter another unless she is able to show that she leaves no indebtedness behind her."[63]

## The Cadet System

As with so many aspects of the history of organized crime, it is not the accurate or "true" scope of the problem that is the issue. Rather, it is how the contemporary media reported and exploited the problem. Perhaps most importantly, it was a matter of how the population at large perceived the problem. Whatever the true extent of white slavery, there can be little doubt that, by the time of Turner's second article in 1909—with some notable exceptions—most commentators, law enforcers and activists felt that the numbers of white slaves entering the nation were rising dramatically. Alongside this, the commentators—alive to the language and impact of hyperbole—also convinced their readers that the conditions in which these unfortunate women were being kept and the way they were being treated were deteriorating. All of which implied a more ruthless, efficient and organized operation was now running the trade.

As the prescient Inspector of Immigration Robert Watchorn had predicted, the French were not alone in their involvement in the white slave trade. The place of what Turner saw as the rather unprofessional French pimps was taken by an altogether more sinister and commercially minded group—those he labels the "Kaftans." What was more, the change was well underway when Turner was writing. It had begun to emerge "twenty-five years [earlier with] the third great flush of immigration, consisting of Austrian, Russian, and Hungarian Jews." Over these years the ruthless Jewish "Kaftans" had made their bid for control of the American trade "in innocent flesh." Having already taken over the trade in "South America, Africa and Asia," they were quickly exposed as operating "in half a dozen great American cities."[64]

However, it was not the organization or the scale of the operation that Turner found so distressing. It was more the way in which the Kaftans were rapidly, effectively and unstoppably embedding themselves into the vice districts of America's cities. Just as worrying was that they were doing this with new levels of venality, ambition, and an equally shocking and callous disregard for their poor victims. Where the French had not understood the importance of what gangsters called the "fix"—the crucial connections with well-positioned politicians capable of reversing setbacks and oiling the bureaucratic machine—their Jewish successors were, it seemed, supremely and fully aware of how vital such friends could be.

According to Turner, this was because the maquereaux had been tolerated in sexually liberated conditions of their native France. In fact, as Turner claimed, the pimping "trade became to all intents and purposes a recognized calling, with a distinguishing costume of its own, consisting of black velvet trousers, a blouse, and a peculiar silk cap known as the bijou. These maquereaux start in the business—and most of them remain in it—as the manager of one girl of the poorer classes, whom they place to the best possible advantage…. The French maquereau was not the type finally adapted to conduct the business in the self-governing American municipalities…. He failed to identify himself with any political organization. He consequently had no direct political influence, and obtained his right to break the law simply by payments of money."[65]

Compared with the new breed of pimps—Italians, Irish and, most notably, Jews—the old fashioned, small-time maquereaux—men like Berthe's tormentor Gerdron—were essentially amateurs. They were destined to be replaced, for unlike them, businessmen like Martin Engle and Mordke Goldberg had much higher ambitions, and the drive, ruthlessness and *chutzpa* to achieve them.

The indomitable spirit, dependency on political protection, national network and international connections of the Kaftan slaver were clearly demonstrated in the criminal careers of the Sovinger brothers, Max and Louis. Emigrating from Russia to New York City as children, working as market stall traders, the two boys had hung around brothels from an early age. Soon they had graduated to running small-scale vice operations of their own, in notorious Allen Street on the Lower East Side. When a sudden realization of a newly reformist mood in the electorate made their previous protectors in Tammany turn on them and dismantle the old red-light districts in 1901, the two brothers left town.

Unbowed, the two brothers repeated their winning formula for procuring and "breaking" girls and brothel running in more amenable vice districts. As they had done in New York, the brothers moved on whenever the climate changed. And it frequently did. They set up operations first in Boston, then in Buffalo, St. Louis and Pittsburgh. When the U.S. as a whole looked hostile, they moved abroad and set up shop first in Havana and then Johannesburg. After this national and world tour, they returned to their original stating point—New York. Once home, they put their now near unrivaled experience into a highly successful alliance with Mordke "The King" Goldberg. Between them they ran an empire of vice that owned several large "sporting houses" and oversaw many of the city's smaller operations with only one or two working girls.[66]

Nor were the brothers unusual. In his examination of the "Girl That Disappears," former New York City police commissioner General Theodore Bingham draws a portrait of the typical American "cadet," or procurer, and his victims. Of Irish, Italian or Jewish extraction, he grew up in poverty. Nevertheless he had "street smarts" and an almost limitless ambition—no doubt fired by a perversion of the American Dream ideal that fueled so many over these years. Also like many ambitious young men in the immigrant "colonies" of the turn of the century, the cadet is associated with a street gang from a "pathetically early age."

Similarly, his victims were often drawn from those other, equally ubiquitous figures of the slums of the turn-of-the-century city: the sassy, rebellious adolescent girl. Most of these teenagers could look forward to nothing better than a low-wage, drab and insecure job. This brief spell in employment would often be followed by marriage to a husband with equally low prospects and then a life dominated by poverty, disease, childbirth and squalor. By contrast, teaming up with gang members—with their braggadocio, money to burn and seeming independence—offered a far more exciting and lucrative life.

It was relatively easy for the young cadet to gain sexual supremacy over a young girl who was seduced by these attributes. Two or three others would often follow the first unfortunate victim—relatively quickly. Pretty soon the young pimp would have developed a strategy for recruiting. Some of the potential victims were offered jobs, often promising unfeasibly high pay, for relatively little work. They may well be taken to theaters and amusement parks were they were shown wealthy, well-dressed women to induce "another moth to singe its wings." Bingham sees this technique as particularly effective with chorus girls, factory workers and department store clerks earning as little as $5 a week, and more often than not naïve, alone and lonely. These girls could be induced by the unscrupulous cadet to become yet another one of the "thirty thousand women engaged in the social evil in New York City."

But the real step change in the fortune of Bingham's hypothetical cadet comes when the young pimp is inducted into "a district political club." The political bosses see him as possessing the attributes of a "faithful henchman." Pretty soon they offer him and his "business interests" the full protection of the political machine. In return for strong-arm work at election time and errand running, his organization is allowed to prosper, hiring agents to hunt out ever-increasing numbers of suitable girls.

According to Bingham, the methods of these underlings went far beyond the crude techniques of their precursors who employed them. Not only would they check out theaters for ambitious and gullible chorus girls, they would lurk in the dark nickelodeons and "hang around evening schools, recreation centers, playgrounds and parks." Some even went as far as to set up bogus employment agencies, specializing in the shop assistant, clerical and secretarial jobs that tended to attract young women.[67]

According to Bingham, by offering the potential for good money, the whole process spawned a new generation of procurers, which in turn vastly increased demand and consequently added to the numbers of girls involved. As the industry expanded, the panders, pimps or cadets, as they were variously known, began to employ or pay off not just recruiters, but landlords, madams, runners, "collectors" (who paid off police and court officials), bondsmen, doctors and abortionists—what amounted to a whole band of middlemen. Yet, in order for such an operation to function on such a scale, they needed to be relatively open, since underworld businesses, by their very nature, can only grow to a limited size before their secrecy becomes a hindrance rather than an advantage. This conundrum, and its solution, is apparent in the career of the mysterious "Silver Dollar" Smith.

In spite of his high profile in the underworld, few things are certain about Mr. Smith. In 1885 he had arrived in the U.S. from Lemberg in Poland, or perhaps from Germany, under the name of either Charles Finkelstein or Meyer Salloway (aka Soloman). What was certain was that he was Jewish when he arrived at Ellis Island.[68] What was only slightly less certain was that he ran New York's Eighth District, Essex Market Court gang, which dominated the local police court. The gang was essentially a collective of bent lawyers, bought witnesses and bribable officials that operated out of the Silver Dollar Saloon, opposite the courthouse. Both the saloon and the mysterious Mr. Smith had earned their names from the silver dollars embedded in the concrete floor of the bar, but the titles could have equally well been connected with the sums expended to buy or sell justice.

The extent, level, costs and implications of the machinations centering on the Silver Dollar were brought to light by the thorough investigation into police corruption, the

Lexow Committee. From its report in 1895 until Turner's exposés a dozen years later and beyond, the Committee's findings were used as fuel for sometimes spurious claims of corruption. These were often anti–Semitic, and more often than not involved allegations made against the city's highly corrupt Democrat political machine.[69] What the Republican-led Lexow Committee confirmed was a close connection between the Jewish-led gangs, like that centered on Essex Market, and Tammany Hall—the city's dominant political machine. Lexow shone a light onto this growing phenomenon, but it was Turner who argued that white slavery was one of its main sources of income and power.

Progressive Era clampdowns on gambling had closed most of the city's gambling "hells" and race tracks and enforced stricter policing of street gambling. Since gambling had been a major source of graft income for politicians and policemen on the take, the simultaneous expansion of white slavery was not coincidental. As one "observant old time politician" asked Turner, "Where's a district policeman goin' to get a bit of money nowadays? The poolrooms are all shut down; policy's [illegal lotteries] gone. There ain't no place at all but the women."[70] Nor was such graft limited to the beat cop; it seemed that the corruption often went far higher in the police force. A shocking case illustrated the way in which the police at the highest level not only did nothing to prevent the trade, but in fact in many cases colluded and profited from it themselves.

## Municipal Government Involvement in Vice

At more or less the same time as Berthe Claiche shot her pimp-tormentor, a fifteen-year-old Austrian girl, Rosa Bognar, was hired to work as a nurse through an agency owned by a wealthy Irishman named William J. Ryan. The agency was simply a front for a sophisticated white slavery operation. A particularly ruthless pimp had in fact bought her. Instead of going to work in a house near her home in New York's Washington Street, the unfortunate girl was drugged, gang-raped and sent to a brothel in Allentown, Pennsylvania. However, the young girl was more resilient and resourceful than her captors had assumed. Not only did she escape from the brothel, but once free she marched into Allentown's City Hall and told her story to the city's mayor.

Dr. Albert J. Yost was shocked and, perhaps more importantly, put on the spot to act. He immediately ordered his police chief to prosecute those Rosa detailed as being the men who kidnapped and raped her. Instead, the corrupt city police chief, George L. Smith, took $440 from the pimp who had originally sold the young woman and set out to quash the case. He then paid to have Rosa shipped back to New York. After pocketing the considerable change from the pimp's bribe, he left her at Grand Central Station with a warning not to make trouble ringing in her ears. This time it was the police chief who had underestimated the teenager. Ignoring Smith's warning, Rosa got straight back to Mayor Yost. Smith was sacked and prosecuted. History doesn't record what happened to Rosa.[71]

The story is notable, not only because it illustrates the callous nature and considerable reach of the slaver networks, but also because, according to George K. Turner's assessment of the situation, such a happy outcome would almost certainly not have happened in New York. He argued that protection afforded to the white slavers by the authorities at all levels in the country's metropolitan areas was generally far more effective than the situation in the smaller cities like Allentown.

As Turner pointed out, in the racially stereotyped language of the times, "the acute and intelligent Jew" was now allied with "brutal, saloon-keeping Irish politician."[72] The Essex Market Gang was typical of "the organization of political bodies among cadets … [which were] becoming part and parcel of Tammany and towers of strength at election times…. The red light district was paying some of these [Tammany] men $20,000 and $30,000 a year for this [white slave] traffic and minor politicians began to find it more profitable than gambling and saloon businesses."[73] Bingham nailed that connection home, showing that it was Tammany lawyers who had defended in court all three of the most high-profile trials for keeping disorderly houses. He also argued that it was Tammany tool Judge Thomas C. O'Sullivan who effectively undermined the so-called Rockefeller grand jury, set up to investigate Turner's claims in 1910.

O'Sullivan strongly insisted that the jury focus on formal networks to prove the existence of an organized criminal network at work in the white slave trade. Bingham disagreed with this approach. He thought it was informal networks that were absolutely central to the trade. Bingham knew it would be very difficult, if not impossible to uncover evidence that would prove the existence of formal ties between politicians and pimps.

As if the task were not already difficult enough, Bingham charged that Tammany only instigated the inquiry to buoy up its flagging popularity. As a result, not only did Tammany put the obstructionist O'Sullivan in charge, but even before it started its investigations, it had already done everything it could to sabotage the grand jury's work. As he saw it, "The inquiry had been instituted by friends and near relatives of the traffickers in women's shame [who] were fairly megaphoned that they were in immediate danger of apprehension … every edition of the daily papers shouted threats and warnings of what the grand jury was about to do." The result was, he argued, that O'Sullivan's direction was simply a smoke screen designed to hide the extent of Tammany involvement.[74]

Turner himself had already outlined the reasoning for this nexus when he argued, "Not only was some [Tammany] participation in the sale of women necessary, the use of the gangs of young procurers who had their beginnings in the red light days, became almost indispensible if the politicians were to secure the vote upon which their power rests."[75] According to at least one source, the relationship had an even more tidy symbiosis than the cadets' simply getting protection and the politicians' getting money and votes.

Some accounts claimed that the pimps even used the machine's "grand civic balls" as both recruiting grounds and a means to show off their "wares." Turner gave details of Tammany boss Tim Sullivan's "Summer Picnic" and the Lawrence Mulligan Civic Ball. The latter event, he alleged, culminated in a "grand march of a thousand pimps and prostitutes."[76]All of these events were lavish and debauched affairs, but the First Ward Ball held by Chicago's "kings of slum politics," "Bath House" John Coughlin and "Hinky Dink" Kenna, was legendary.

The 1907 First Ward Ball was held in the Chicago Coliseum. Some 20,000 guests, including 100 policemen and many of the city's leading politicians, reputedly attended it. The revelers drank an estimated 10,000 quarts of champagne and 35,000 of beer, served by 200 waiters. The building was apparently so densely packed that women fainting in the heat caused by the lack of ventilation remained upright in the crush.

The following day, the Rev. R. Keene Ryan condemned Bath House John and Hinky Dink's "Saturnalia" as a procurer's dream. The morning after the party, Ryan told reporters, "Last night's exhibition, with its attendant evil influences, should be suppressed. Never again should the people of this city permit such an orgy to disgrace and befoul its name, carrying as it does sorrow to countless numbers of innocent and unsuspecting girls and boys who, through idle curiosity, are attracted there and forever dishonored by associations made."[77]

It appeared that there was plenty of evidence to back up these suspicions. A year after Turner wrote his second article, the Canadian-born missionary Ernest A. Bell revealed the findings of his eight years of research and missionary work in Chicago's Levee District. Looked at from one angle, Bell showed the situation was even worse in the Second City than in New York. His findings showed that in Chicago it was not simply the French and the Jews involved in the "brothel slavery." He had discovered that safe in "the bath of immunity" provided by Coughlin and Kenna, the Irish, Italians and "Mongolians" all contributed to make the city's red-light district "worse than Paris" in terms of its debauchery.[78]

Even more worrying was the way in which it seemed that, under the protection afforded by corrupt politicians, the cadet system was spreading. According to Bell, "If the pulpit and press are ignorant or cowardly, and sworn officers of the law make void the law," it was not only Chicago but all "other American cities" which would soon "become dumps for the outcast filth of Paris" and centers for "Mongolian brothel slavery, the Black Death in morals."[79] According to Turner, it was already too late. He felt that Bell's dire warnings had now reached a critical level. He argued that since 1901 the system linking politicians and pimps had expanded all over the U.S.: "The New York Jewish cadets were found present in hundreds in San Francisco ... they were strong in Los Angeles [and] ... two of the most notorious [white slave] dealers of New York's East Side were prominent figures uncovered in the political underworld by [Circuit Attorney Joseph] Folk in St. Louis. Today [1909] they are strong in all the greater cities: they swarm at the gateway of the Alaska frontier at Seattle; they infest the streets and restaurants of Boston; they flock for the winter to New Orleans; they fatten on the wages of the government laborers in Panama; and they abound in the South and Southwest and in the mining regions of the West."[80]

By 1910 white slavery, cadets, panders, procurers and all the other language used by the muckrakers and tabloids to describe the "trade in human misery" had become recognizable in the conversation of the affluent, educated, Progressive and socially aware middle class across America. How could they avoid it? The newspapers of the day, novels, plays and magazine articles seemed to have become obsessed with the "social evil." Even those commentators who doubted the extent of the plague seemed to be changing their views.

A good example is the *New York Times*, which up until this point had stolidly gone against the tide of muckraking exposés. Drawing on a variety of drivers, including political allegiances and the wish to distinguish themselves as superior to the competition while demonstrating a sensitivity to their readership, the *Times* insisted on placing itself above the hullabaloo excited by white slavery in the tabloids. The result was that the paper remained skeptical about claims that America was undergoing an epidemic of vice.

Yet in the wake of Turner's article it started seeking empirical proof that could validate or disprove the existence of the trade in New York. The *Times* found this in the evidence produced by two "college women" investigators hired to uncover the reality of white slavery in New York's notorious Tenderloin district by newly appointed and ambitious District Attorney Charles S. Whitman.

The probe found no verifiable connection between Tammany and the panders.

Instead the two intrepid reporters drew a picture of a different vice plague, but one which had "existed for years." The investigations centered on the activities of a "light mulatto" procurer with a Jewish-sounding name: Harry Levinson, aka Harry Shapiro or Harry Druckman. He worked in conjunction with accomplice, Belle Moore—a "negro woman" whose stated occupation was "manicurist." The two undercover investigators exposed that the two worked as a team, dealing in trading "the freedom" of young girls for between twenty and sixty dollars apiece.

Working on the concept that white slavery could only be proved if a trade took place, the two "college women" investigators bought four young white girls from Levinson and Moore. Similar techniques had been used, with a great deal of hardly surprising controversy, by the man who had exposed the whole trade. William Stead had famously bought Lily, a thirteen-year-old girl, on the London streets in 1881 for a mere £5.[81] The girls the agents bought from the mulatto and his partner aged were slightly older, anywhere between fifteen and eighteen years old. The prices they paid were considerably higher. Nevertheless, the bargain was no less shocking, and the *Times* made sure that no reader was left in any doubt about the horrific nature of the deal. When the two undercover agents turned this evidence over to the DA, the *Times* ran a front-page headline that told horrified readers that "Two [of the slaves] Were Children of Fifteen Who Played With a Doll and a Teddy Bear."[82]

Given this shocking evidence, provided by sources which the editorial staff chose to consider as rigorous in their methods as the *Times* itself, the paper was persuaded. They changed their position. Although the forces behind the traffic seemed different from those uncovered by *McClure's* and other "yellow" journals, by 1909 the *Times* began running headlines that indicated there was an organized, criminal conspiracy at work. The *Times* told readers that "There Is a White Slave Traffic" and that "White Slave Traffic [was] Shown to Be Real."[83] The *Times'* quiescence in the exposé was just the start of an escalation of journalistic and public interest in the subject.

Between 1910 and 1914, as one historian has calculated, the word "prostitution" appears five times as often in the *Readers' Guide to Periodical Literature* as in the previous twenty-year period, and three times as often as the ten-year period after 1914.[84] But perhaps the best demonstration of how the fear of prostitution, white slavery and predatory pimps played out to the American public can be gauged from the response in the relatively new medium of the movies.

Often adapted from novels and plays, films reached a wider, often younger and less affluent audience than most other media. What was more, in an ironic twist, it was the very titillating nature of films themselves and the places in which they were shown that contributed to the scare associated with their content. It was not coincidence that over these years the movies became a part of courting for many young Americans. Movie theaters became one of the places where unchaperoned girls could meet the opposite sex for dates. Some moralizers used these changes, coupled with the rather shabby nature of "nickelodeons," as an indication of the increasing promiscuity of American youth. Others simply said that they were yet one more place where "procurers," "cadets" or "panders" could lure young girls into the vice trade.

Nevertheless, in spite of this fear—or maybe because of it—a whole new genre of films dedicated to the "social problem" emerged. These would reach such large audiences that they would alter cinema-going, in both small-town America and the larger cities. To some the appeal of the white slave film was a vaguely masked sexual thrill. To others it was a warning of the perils of promiscuity. To yet another group it was a reinforcement of the dangers of unchecked immigration. Whatever fear or thrill the film played on, those going to the movies would have little doubt about what they were going to see. The films had unambiguous titles like *Inside of the White Slave Traffic* and *Traffic in Souls* (1913); *Smashing the Vice Trust* (1914); *House of Bondage* (1914); and *Is Any Girl Safe?* (1916).

Such was the public interest in the topic that these films fueled new levels of box-office takings of an entirely unheard-of scale. For example, it was estimated that shortly after their release in 1913, the two box office hits *Traffic in Souls* and *Inside of the White Slave Traffic* together were attracting what was then an almost unheard-of audience of 15,000 viewers in New York City each week. Demand was so great that even the massive Park Theatre on Columbus Circle, capable of seating 1800—at a time when the norm was 100 to 500 seats—was turning hundreds of disappointed viewers away for each show.

What was more, in spite of a drop in ticket prices from $2 to 25 cents, the hugely popular *Traffic in Souls* was still generating weekly takings of up to $5,000 in the larger theaters. In fact, the film was so popular that it would go on to become the first movie in U.S. film history to come close to netting a million dollars in its general release. Aside from that record, its appeal becomes more meaningful if it is compared with the previous top-grossing film in the U.S.—a short comedy, *A Bird in the Hand*, made in 1911. That film had brought in a little over $800 nationally in its first week, and the total earnings it had made over its entire release were somewhere in excess of $10,000.[85]

## The International Connections

All these spurs to public awareness, combined with their interest and concern over the threat to the young women of America, were made greater by a growing suspicion amongst the American public that the whole grisly situation was as a result of inefficient government. Campaigners against the vice industry claimed that the "trade in human souls" flourished as the result of a signal failure to implement an effective policy and legislate accordingly. Thanks to gaps in policy and legislation, the brutes responsible were profiting from the brazen defiling of innocent girls. What was even worse was that the vast majority were then going on to escape punishment.

This was seen as especially galling since there were already international procedures to deal with the trade. Starting with the 1904 International Agreement for the Suppression of White Slave Traffic, the leading nations had agreed to a treaty. That treaty was reinforced by another agreement in 1908. This promise of international cooperation signed by the French, Italians, Russians and most other leading European nations. Shocked by the emerging reports at home, in 1907 President Theodore Roosevelt had signed up the U.S. to the agreements, and American delegates were key players in the 1908 treaty.

All this seemed to indicate that there was an international will to make the revolting trade a thing of the past. With transnational agreements, deportation treaties and promises of cooperation between law enforcers on both sides of the Atlantic, it appeared that trading young girls for sexual slavery could be exposed, controlled and hopefully eradicated. However, it soon emerged that it was more window dressing than a serious and concerted campaign. None of the nations seemed committed to act to stop the trade, despite their protestations.

It appeared that even after the agreements were signed it was still possible to utilize the disparity between the growing ease, frequency and cheapness of international transport, and the inability of nations to police their borders—in terms of both entry into and exit from their sovereign territory. For example, Eva and Alphonse Dufour's trafficking operations had been exposed by Sims and formed the basis for many people's knowledge of the French dominance of the trade. It would have been surprising if they had not. The case was splashed all over the local and national papers. Yet in spite of this notoriety, the pair still managed skip their bail and run back to France, where they apparently became invisible to the authorities of both nations for some considerable time.

Nor were the American government's own attempts to deal with the problem unilaterally marked by any great success. The leading forces charged with investigating and prosecuting the trade were given crucial federal powers through the supervision of the Department of Labor's Immigration Bureau. Nevertheless, while this gave them powers to operate across state borders, essentially the efforts to halt the trade were to some degree held back by the association of the problem with immigration. Again this was seen to some degree as a result of policy failure.

The Immigration Bureau relied on increased powers granted under clauses of the 1875 Page Act and 1903 and 1907 Immigration Acts, and this legislation reinforced the notion that the white slave traffic was an imported problem. This near universally held conception was reinforced by the work of the Bureau's chief investigating agent, the almost legendary Marcus Braun. Braun's findings seemed to show that the traffic was a trade among, and of, foreign-born nationals. However, aside from that similarity, Braun saw the "victims" of the traffic in a different light from that of many of his fellow vice-campaigners.

Vitally, in spite of his connections with the exposés of the white slaver Heudiard, Braun's findings showed that most of the "slaves" were actually "hardened" and experienced sex prostitutes before they entered the United States. The girls were not, in his view, forced into the "vice" industry. They may not have chosen to go into prostitution, but many could see no alternative profession. By the time they entered the country, they were more or less voluntary sex-workers rather than kidnapped ingénues.

Unlike the public's image of a virginal white slave, corrupted and seeking only to return to her loving family, these women wanted to earn money. Many did not want to be "freed" from the brothels. Instead they relied on their pimps to maintain their ability to facilitate their entry into the U.S. and continue to earn money through vice. This did not play well with a public driven by feelings that legislation must be aimed at saving corrupted innocents and kidnapped children, not foreign streetwalkers and hard-bitten whores. It also meant that not just the pimps but the girls themselves would be opposed to the authorities as well.[86]

This vision of the nature of imported vice presented a new type of conundrum. Congress could legitimately claim that existing laws were sufficient to control the entry of career prostitutes into the U.S.—they just needed better enforcement. The 1875 Page Act had banned the entry of Asian prostitutes. The Immigration Act of 1903 had given the power to the Bureau of Immigration to exclude people involved in prostitution, as well as to deport prostitutes, pimps and procurers, if they were not already naturalized Americans. Those on the ground charged with investigating, prosecuting and controlling prostitution could argue the age-old plea of policing: they needed more resources. So it was not surprising that Braun's investigations were generally well-received by law enforcers, since they helped them argue that the problem was one of resource allocation. While disputing the nature of the problem, Braun had certainly showed that there was a problem—and a huge one at that.

After years of probing, Braun concluded that there were some fifty thousand foreign prostitutes working in the U.S. for ten thousand predominantly Jewish, French and Belgian pimps. He also discovered that there were considerable numbers of additional Japanese and Koreans prostitutes and procurers operating on the Pacific Coast. However, while this dominance by despicable foreigners complied with, and reinforced, the smugness about the superior morals of native-born, white, American womanhood, it also created terrible problems. When it came to the detection, deterrence and control of white slavery networks, the fact that the perpetrators were foreign gave them considerable advantages.

Effectively, putting the problem into the hands of the Immigration Bureau, while giving investigators federal powers, meant that punishment was essentially limited to deportation. Although the 1903 Act enabled anything up to five years and a $5,000 fine for those convicted of prostitution, the provisions for deportation introduced by the 1907 Act meant that this apparently cheaper, more conclusive option became the favored solution. However, this logic did not stack up in reality. While in theory, making deportation the solution was efficacious—in that it removed both prostitutes and pimps from American territory—as a long-term solution to the problem, it was riven with deep flaws.

At an operational level, it was difficult and time-consuming to prove the involvement of foreign procurers, and to some extent the problem was one of how to prove white slavery was going on at all. Tight-knit "colonies" of impoverished, excluded, ostracized sex workers and other "untouchables" would never take kindly to investigation of their activities at the best of times. The nature and legality of prostitution in general, as well as the degree of coercion and extent of agency involved, would be difficult to investigate at any time. Such investigations were especially problematic in the semi-legal red-light districts of the cities within which prostitution was largely contained in early Progressive Era America.

In addition to these problems, overcoming or penetrating the political and police protection, as well as the gross venality and potential brutality of others connected with stopping the traffic, put serious barriers in the way of investigators. All this meant that investigations needed to pay special attention to local conditions. If they were unfamiliar with the locality, if they were unaware of who was who, who worked for whom and who protected whom, they could easily be sidelined, exposed—or worse. Agents also needed to have a working knowledge of foreign languages, and needed to be able to move within the immigrant communities with ease. The result of these dangers and difficulties was that most Immigration Bureau operatives investigated their subjects by simply frequenting the saloons and cafes suspected of operating as part of the networks.

In this rather arbitrary fashion they gathered information by immersion. They tried to prove their suspicions by casually chatting with clientele over more-or-less lengthy periods of time. While this rather low-key approach had the advantage of keeping their "cover" intact, it was not going to be the most effective way of uncovering the intricacies and extent of the subtle and insidious webs of the white slavers. While Braun took a characteristically direct approach, picking up working girls and driving them directly to Immigration Bureau officials—thereby negating law enforcement intervention or press interference—he still found his efforts hampered by local conditions.

Braun complained about obstructions at almost all levels of law enforcement that severely hampered his investigations in most of the major cities from Montana westward. He claimed that police frequently tipped off vice operations, from which they took protection money, that the Immigration Bureau planned to raid. He also argued that law enforcers at all levels had become so reliant on kickbacks and other forms of income from brothels that they frequently stood in the way of local bylaws outlawing prostitution for fear that they would lose this considerable, more-or-less legally sanctioned source of revenue.[87]

Given these problems, it was perhaps inevitable that the numbers actually arrested for white slaving could not have represented anything more than the tip of the iceberg. What was more, even when suspects were identified and brought in, the subsequent prosecutions were not always successful. The total numbers actually deported under the 1907 legislation for prostitution and procuring were unimpressive. By 1909 a total of two hundred and sixty-one women had been deported, and a mere thirty white slavers identified and deported.

Attempting to stop the traffic at the source proved little more successful. The annual numbers of foreign prostitutes barred from entry by the immigration services clearly demonstrate the consequences and flaws of this rather laid-back approach. They were minimal, climbing from a very measly nine in the wake of the 1903 Act to a hardly shocking one hundred and twenty-four after the 1907 Act. The tally for procurers was little better, rising from three to forty-three over the same period. Such figures hardly demonstrated a plague of vice, and they are even more of a damp squib when seen in a wider context.[88]

These years saw the largest numbers of proportionate legal immigration in American history. Over this period an average of over a million immigrants were recorded entering the nation each year. The signal failure to identify and deport significant numbers of those involved in the trade also brought into question whether Braun's estimates were anywhere near accurate. It seemed to many that there were huge problems with the immigration-based approach. Either the system of investigation and prosecution was woefully inadequate and the problem exaggerated, or the problem was not one of foreign-born nationals in the first place.

What was even more aggravating for the authorities was that even when the system worked and the agents gained a conviction, the problems did not stop and the criminals often walked away from punishment. The inherent and obvious flaw was that deportation admitted a possibility of re-entry at a future date, perhaps under false identity. While records proving the frequency of this are necessarily difficult to find or verify, the cursory nature of checks, the porous land borders of the USA, and the sheer volume of immigrants, would mean that detection of recidivists would be just as unlikely as their detection in the first place. As if that was not enough, the deportation system also had another equally gaping problem.

Those girls unlucky enough to be caught by the relatively few, and not very effective, Immigration Bureau agents could simply marry a local, naturalized American. Marrying during this period effectively trumped the threat of deportation. This was because under the existing legislation—as long as the potential deportee was not Chinese—the marriage immediately made them U.S. citizens. Being an American citizen meant the girl was ineligible, of course, for deportation.

The deportation process itself also helped facilitate this loophole. Clear evidence of solicitation—let alone proof of any illicit sexual act that followed—that would stand up in court was difficult enough, if not impossible, to obtain. In addition, getting and collating the documents and investigating the background for deportation in these years of massive immigration was frequently painfully slow. Then there was a legal procedure that positively creaked along. All this meant that while being held and processed for deportation, the prostitute would often be released on bail—giving scope for her to find a man susceptible to her charms, or failing that, her pimp's money, marry him and eventually go back to work.

The essential problem, as Braun discovered in his investigations in Europe in late 1909, was that most European countries tolerated prostitution. They saw it as a necessary vice that should be regulated, medically controlled and contained. The attitudes of most officials to sex workers, procurers and brothels were pragmatic in the extreme. They saw no reason for America to bar prostitutes, and to them it was clear that the vast majority of those leaving Europe to practice prostitution in the U.S. did so of their own accord. What was more, this pragmatism was similarly evident those who left Europe to work in the U.S. sex industry.

In his informal interviews with prostitutes in France, Belgium and other European nations, Braun learned that these women regarded working in the vice industry in America as a lucrative and relatively easy option. They were aware that they could earn far more in better conditions and for less work in the U.S. than in Europe, although most seemed fully aware of the laws aimed at excluding and deporting them. What was worrying to Braun was that none of those girls he interviewed knew of any of their fellow sex workers who had been barred form entry, or deported from the U.S. for prostitution. That said, he was convinced that there was no organized criminal network overseeing the trade. There were, to his mind, no gangs of panders or procurers operating across and between the Old and New Worlds. Instead, as he detailed in his reports to his boss at the Immigration Bureau, there was simply what he termed an "esprit de corps" that created a mutual aid element that pervaded those Europeans who chose this course of making a living in America.[89]

Nevertheless, driven by what seemed like the near-constant exposures of a white slave traffic in innocent young girls, an enraged American public insisted that Congress do something to halt it. Reformers, journalists and law enforcers demanded that legislation be put in place that would tackle the problem from another angle. That was what they did, and the approach they adopted would have major repercussions for the whole idea of organized crime, over the years of this study and since. Opting to essentially expand the powers of the existing interstate commerce laws, they introduced what amounted to a federally enforced, morally based set of proscriptions on the behavior, habits, relations and commerce of individuals.

## The Mann Act

What is interesting about the Mann Act of 1910 is that while it was called the White Slave Act, and although the sponsors of the legislation saw it as a means of prosecuting the importation, distribution and exploitation of vulnerable girls and women, it has rarely been seen in that light since. The act is largely portrayed by historians as a draconian solution to the policing of the morals of "tomcat" men and runaway daughters and wives.

It has been condemned as a means of enforcing miscegenation ideals forbidding racial intimacy—being invoked most famously to put a stop to the string of white girlfriends flaunted by the black heavyweight champion, Jack Johnson.

A consensus seems to argue that the Act was a failure with regard to stopping "the traffic in human flesh," yet with considerable amending accretions and tweaking, it would continue to form the basis of American anti-trafficking law until beyond the turn of the twenty-first century. Recent scholarly studies of the impact of the Mann Act give credit to many of these views, but also add considerably more depth. For example, Jessica Pliley's study sees it as an act that is invoked to reinforce contemporary attitudes towards sexual/racial/gender transgressions.[90] She also argues that there were different phases that can be detected in the enforcement of the Act in the period of this study, each concentrating on different strands of investigation.

Based on extensive examination of the prosecutions under the act, she finds that the first few years after its enactment the prosecutions *were* of white slave panders. Then the emphasis changed to an effort to stamp out the "social evil" of prostitution as a whole. This campaign stepped up when America joined the Allies in the Great War, and the War Department famously targeted the contaminated prostitute as being more dangerous to American servicemen than a "Hun bullet." Throughout the 1920s the cases focused on the strand that had inspired most prosecutions since the inception of the Act. These largely centered around controlling and containing extramarital and unconventional—although exclusively heterosexual, and nearly always white, or mixed-race—sexual intimacy.

These may have involved runaway daughters or wives. The prosecutions followed because it was maintained that they had been snatched by, or tempted into sin by, a man of another race, usually black, but sometimes Asian or Latino. There were sometimes implicit or explicit allegations that one or both of the partners were notoriously promiscuous. The man may have been significantly older, poorer, or maybe a bigamist. The permutations available for prosecution under the scope of the act were wide. It targeted the transportation of women across state borders "for immoral purposes," and in an era that was characterized by both conformity and experimentation, this vague category was given a broad interpretation by many charged with enforcing it.

Whatever the reason for the prosecution—and J. Edgar Hoover claimed that in his time at the Bureau of Investigation (BOI), from 1922 to 1933, there were over 47,500 investigations under the Mann Act—the legislation was interpreted as being designed to maintain the sanctity of the Anglo-Saxon concept of the male-dominated marital home as the correct place in which white women may have sexual relations. To Hoover it protected vulnerable girls from venal, lust-crazed and perverted men. It could be held that these radicalized and chauvinistically prurient ideas may have constituted an organized criminal, or at least unconstitutional, assault on the human rights of women, nonwhites and even sex workers. Leaving these aside, the Mann Act did tie in with the activities that were viewed as the more conventional provinces of organized crime.

However, in the late 1910s there was an identifiable trend towards using the Mann Act's targeting of those who transported the vulnerable girls to enable the blackmailing of "johns." Wealthy victims were selected by working girls, and set up to be caught in the age-old "badger game" racket. In the traditional version of this scam, while the couple were *in flagrante delicto,* the door of the hotel room would burst open and the pimp would storm in. He would be playing the furious, cuckolded husband looking like he meant serious harm to the unfortunate lover and the errant wife. Often waving a weapon, he would demand that the normally terrified john pay him off.

This rip-off usually worked, and the pimp and his girl would frequently make considerably more than they might from a simple, more conventional "trick." In the Mann Act version, this scam could be varied, with the pimp or an associate playing a law enforcer and accepting a bribe to make the bust go away. The opportunities apparently attracted organized gangs of blackmailers, since the victim was often too terrified of the consequences to make enough fuss to take the blackmailers to law. Further, if he did, there was a chance that he might find himself more than humiliated for his lust, but— at least in his mind—he might also be prosecuted for attempting to bribe a law officer.

While the Mann Act was certainly flawed, and definitely abused, it was nonetheless extensively used, keeping the idea of white slavery fresh in the minds of the public. As late as 1936, playing to the tried and tested technique of using a threat of organized crime to boost his career, J. Edgar Hoover revived the specter of the white slave—this time in small-town Connecticut. As the *Hartford Courant* rather breathlessly put it: "As a matter of fact, with the last of the big kidnapping rings—the Karpis-Barker gang—effectively smashed and with bank robberies steadily declining, the G-Men are finding more time to give to such non-emergency cases as white slavery.... Hoover's agents accumulated a mass of collateral evidence which is now being used to good advantage against nationwide rings of racketeers who are trafficking in women."[91]

After ten weeks of investigations, Hoover's G-men had arrested 80 people, and it was reported they were extending the "Federal vice hunt across the entire land."[92] According to Hoover's depiction, there were strings of "inns and other joints," particularly in Connecticut, that were really disorderly houses, and they were connected in a network "luring young girls into lives of degradation and crime."[93] It was argued that the pimps took the vast majority of the up to "$400 a week these unfortunates earned," leaving the girls with "little except food and clothing."[94] Not that it was a small-time organization. The network uncovered in Connecticut, Hoover claimed, not only had links to, and supplied, brothels in New York, Rhode Island and Massachusetts, but also transported girls south in the winter to "resorts" in Florida. The truth was almost certainly more prosaic.

The FBI played up the role of force and coercion in the working lives of the prostitutes, and downplayed the voluntary nature of the girls' career choices. What is more, according to the files associated with the arrests, it is plain that the network of brothels was loose, informal and competitive. The network was not, as the FBI tried to argue at the time, highly organized and centralized. If the brothels were linked, it was through a group of "girls" on an informal circuit, who rotated on loose weekly contracts around New England and New York. They may have moved South, as many Americans did, but they were not "strong-armed" into degradation—at least not at this stage of their careers. The network was more of an information exchange. The girls, for the most part, voluntarily followed where the "johns" with the money went.[95]

However, as Hoover knew, if he was to compete against the growing popularity of Thomas Dewey, busting a few madams in the backwoods of Connecticut could not compete with his rival's exposure of Luciano's sophisticated and highly organized call-girl network. What Hoover tried to pass off as a network of vice was actually more a sorority of "working girls," but such groups had a long history and central role to play in organized crime. In fact, it is probably fair to say they constitute what can be seen as the very essence of organized crime—a fraternity.

# 12

## The Criminal Fraternity

### Antonio Comito's Confession

On June 30, 1907, thirty-year-old Antonio Viola Comito disembarked from the SS *Europe* at Ellis Island after a seventeen-day Atlantic crossing from Naples.[1] Like so many other dirt-poor Southern Italians, he was in search of the fortune which had so far evaded him in life. In Antonio's case, his failure was not for lack of trying. A native of Catozarro in Calabria, he was well-educated. A grammar school graduate, he had gone on to study printing for four years at the local Institute of Technology in Catanzara. Known to his friends as "professor," he had also trained as a teacher in arithmetic and Italian. Yet, in spite of these trades, he had been unable to find permanent work, and had moved from menial job to more menial job at home in Italy and during a seven-year stay in Brazil and Argentina. As he arrived in New York with little English and no real savings, in the midst of a slump, Antonio's luck did not change—in fact, it got worse.

Six months after his arrival, he was still unable to find permanent work. Whenever he did find a job, the pay was terrible and the employment never seemed to last. The result was that by June 1908 he was still living with his brother, Ernesto, in cramped conditions in Manhattan. Inevitably his relations with his brother deteriorated, and like so many other immigrants before him, Antonio must have concluded that even in the land of opportunity, no one cared if you were down and out. However, by August 1908, the unfortunate Italian had managed to make those all-important contacts within the local community, contacts that enabled him to rise up out of his miserable situation.

One of the catalysts for this change in fortune came in the shape of a "domestically inclined, honest and laborious" thirty-year-old Italian woman. Although Antonio already had a wife in Italy, after meeting Katrina Pascuzzo, he pretty soon pooled resources with her. The relationship was largely pragmatic. Two lonely people in a foreign city, they had "no desire to contract a marriage" and continued, as he put it, to make "an honest front with friends."

Nevertheless, the two moved as a couple into a two-room rented apartment of their own at 68 James Street. In doing this, Antonio was breaking with his disapproving brother and his family, but that did not mean that the couple would have face the New World alone. Alongside Katrina, Antonio had also found a new family. He now had a whole new set of brothers—brothers who came in the form of members of two fraternal societies. Antonio had joined the Ancient Order of Foresters and the Order of the Sons of Italy.

Antonio's adoption of a new set of brothers was not as peculiar as it may sound.

One contemporary estimate argued that some twenty percent of all adult American males belonged to fraternities of one sort or another.[2] Lacking any real state-provided welfare provisions in the early 1900s—at least any comparable to those evolving at this time in Germany, France and Britain—instead Americans embraced the idea of fraternity in a way unmatched in any other nation. In a country that seemed wedded to principles of self-reliance, self-help and individualism, American fraternities could provide a safety net for the workingman without trespassing on the sacrosanct male self-respect. They could be used in a variety of ways. They could offer credit and burial benefits, health and employment insurance, or they could simply be social clubs.

To others they provided a sign of shared purpose. They could link members of a common nationality—like the Sons of Italy—or those in the same trade—as the with the Foresters. They could provide a common political agenda, as with the Knights of Labor, who grew rapidly in the 1870s and 1880s with their crusade to implement a nationwide eight-hour day. They might have a spiritual mission, as with the freethinking Masons, or a charitable mission, as with the Knight of Pythias. In short, in the last quarter of the nineteenth century and the early decades of the twentieth century, whatever their motivation, fraternities ranged from the supremely practical to the absurdly altruistic. They incorporated almost all points of the political, spiritual and class compass and attracted almost all characters in between.[3]

At an individual level, many men chose to join fraternities not only to demonstrate that they belonged to, or believed in, something, but also in order to prove to others that they *were* something. Antonio claimed that he joined both the Sons of Italy and the Foresters to "derive the privileges as well as the regards a gentleman can have." In this respect, Antonio was being more frank than many of his contemporaries. He was shamelessly admitting that he thought that membership of these associations would help further his career.

Perhaps more interestingly, Antonio claimed that he chose the two associations because they were "well thought of in New York ... because they had a significance equal to Masonry."[4] In associating his choice with the Freemasons, he was comparing them with the oldest, most prestigious and most universally respected of fraternities—the very gold standard of fraternal organizations. Masons had been at the center of the American establishment since the founding of the Republic, and would remain there. George Washington had been a Freemason, as, by 1908, had eight other U.S. presidents—including the incumbent, Theodore Roosevelt. However, in spite of rising up the ranks of both fraternities within months, Antonio was wrong in his belief in their powers.

## The Golden Age of Fraternalism

By November 5, 1908, Antonio was out of work again, having lost his job first in an Italian-owned print shop and then in a Spanish-owned one. But it seemed that night that his luck was going to change. Attending a Sons of Italy lodge meeting, he was introduced to a large, dapper Sicilian—a certain Don Pasquale. The seemingly affluent and gracious stranger offered him work in a print shop owned by another brother in the Sons of Italy, who lived in Philadelphia. He took Antonio's address and told him he would call on him.

Sure enough, two days later the Sicilian turned up at 68 James Street with his friend. The two offered Antonio a great deal. They told him they would pay his rent in New

York for the next month to enable him to retain his lease. They offered him the use of a house that they claimed they already owned in Philadelphia. What was more, they said they would pay both his and Katrina's fares to the City of Brotherly Love—and back if he found the work was unsuitable. They also agreed to pay him $20 a week while he was there—twice what he earned in New York. They told him he needed to be ready to travel in two days. The deal sounded too good to turn down, and Antonio agreed there and then. In fact it was simply too good to be true.

It did not take Antonio long to realize he had been duped. He, like many other desperate strangers in America over these years, had found himself wrapped up in crime. Rather than making their fortune in Philadelphia, he and Katrina ended up working for a gang of counterfeiters in a house in the middle of nowhere, in upstate New York. Although they both returned safely to New York, Antonio was soon arrested for his part in the ring and within a short time had given a highly informative, detailed and—to the historian—fascinating account of his adventures.

Fraternalism played a central role in Antonio's confession. Arguably, it was at least partly his commitment to fraternity that had fueled his impressive gullibility with the two Sicilians. After all, hadn't he believed the offer of Don Pasquale and the alleged owner of the print shop in Philadelphia, based almost solely on their membership of "his" fraternity? To him, any member of the order had given his word to aid other brothers in any way that he could; they had sworn to be honest and helpful. Why wouldn't he trust them? But that was not the end of fraternity in the confession.

According to Antonio, it was fraternity that lay behind the entire operation of the counterfeit ring. It was fraternity that enabled them not simply to recruit staff, but to acquire the means of production and distribution. Fraternity, it transpired, was behind the entire operation—or so Antonio believed. Curious about how the counterfeiters could operate what was obviously a large-scale operation, Antonio had tried to discover more. When they were alone one morning, he questioned one of the gang holding him in the upstate house.

The man seemed happy to tell him mysterious details of who they were. According to the man—a Sicilian thug known as Uncle Vincent—they were all members of a "secret society" that, through a mix of terror, loyalty and shared purpose, drove the gang members onward. He told him how he had been recruited after a cattle-rustling operation had gone wrong. When he and his gang had ended up killing two men, Uncle Vincent claimed that the nameless society had spirited him out of Sicily and then set him up in America. It appeared this treatment had given Uncle Vincent infinite faith in the power and prestige of this secret society, as he went on to tell Antonio with awe that it was a "society which never ends, and is bigger than the Masons."[5]

Uncle Vincent may have used hyperbole when he described the "society," but he was not alone in his belief in their powers. He was addressing a phenomenon that was already well-known and had a great deal of credence—and not only in the Italian communities of America. By the time of Antonio's kidnapping, the threat of a huge, more-or-less omnipresent criminal fraternity was taken seriously, even at the highest levels of American society.

This is apparent from the notes accompanying Comito's confession. These claim that the document was little short of revolutionary, saying it "places in the hands of the Government the most damaging statement ever obtained in the prosecution of criminals, here or abroad." They go on to say that with Comito's story "it has at last been established beyond all doubt that such a society exists; that it thrives particularly well in America and in a horrible way. [This society is] the Black Hand, the Mafia, the Camorra—call it what you will."[6]

## The Purpose of Criminal Fraternities

Today the whole idea of criminal fraternities existing in anything other than name seems faintly absurd. It now seems almost quaint that murderous organizations of hardened criminals should touch their eyeteeth as a greeting. It seems pointless for men to go through a meaningless series of long and arcane, scripted conversations to show that they are allies. Yet at the turn of the twentieth century, that is exactly what the Mafia and Molly Maguires were held to have done. This behavior appears at best impractical and puerile, but it seems that in many ways these curious and outlandish signs were the very elements that made the criminal fraternities all the more frightening, sinister and powerful over the late nineteenth and early twentieth centuries.

These absurd rituals demonstrated to those who could understand them that here was an organization that had existed in a secret space, alongside legitimate society—probably for years. These organizations frequently claimed histories and pedigrees. It was argued that their passwords, their greetings and their signals went back so long that they had become sacred texts to those who uttered them and meant nothing to those who had not been inducted. Their very unintelligibility leant them a sinister authority and added to the myths of their international, perhaps supernatural, if not diabolical potency. It was held that these elements were key to the success and longevity of the orders. It was these rituals that had secured their secrecy and, with that, ensured their longevity. It is telling that even those with less antiquity had adopted similar rituals in imitation.

One of the most extreme, but nevertheless illustrative, examples of this phenomenon is found in a supposedly "true" contemporary account of the 1860s Ku Klux Klan. Writing under the name of "Scalpel," Edward H. Dixon claimed to have found himself personally caught up in the terrors of the Reconstruction South and dragged into the very heartland of the insurgent Klan. In his account of events in an unnamed region of East Tennessee, the Klan were figures in "pure white robes" who rode horses that appeared like "jet black monsters."

The local population of superstitious freed black slaves lived in a constant fear of these nightriders, and with good reason. Whenever the Klan appeared, "loud the thunder rolled! More fearful flashed the lightning!" Wherever they turned up, the letters KKK would mysteriously appear on the soil, or on the walls of buildings. These letters were written in blood. If these specters spoke, it would be in twisted rhymes of doggerel, telling the quaking blacks, "No meat we eat but Raw Freedman—Bloody Black meat for the Ku Klux Klan."[7]

Even allowing for Dixon's wild flights of fancy, his account has elements that are drawn from verifiable accounts of contemporary Klan rituals and behavior. The genuine Klan did use what appears to us now as an absurd vocabulary of "doom" and "blood," "terrors," "night hawks" and "goblins." Klansmen also carried out their grisly beatings, rapes and murders dressed in a ridiculously impractical costume. They frequently wore hoods—although not necessarily the familiar distinctive pointed hood which has become their symbol. There is no doubt that while these costumes hid their identity, they also—

as so clearly shown in Quentin Tarantino's film *Django Unchained* (2012)—served to obscure vision and greatly restrict maneuverability.

Is this acceptance of the inconveniences and spectacle of fraternal theatricality simply a sign of a bygone age of innocence? Maybe these are elements that present-day cynics have come to regard as foolish because our world is so much more violent and brutal that it forces the criminals of today to be that much more pragmatic and practical. Whatever the reason, in the twenty-first century, it is almost inconceivable that the cold-blooded businessmen of the Sinoloa Cartel, the zealots of ISIS or the ruthless gangsters of Los Zetos would conduct their business in such a quixotic way, relying on superstition and crude disguise.

That said, we still talk of "criminal fraternities." More tellingly, we continue to picture some criminal organizations—notably the Cosa Nostra and the Triads—as being bound by oaths, observing rituals and adopting pseudo-familial structures. Nor are all these organizations that claim roots in the mists of time imported into America from foreign lands. America has given birth to the Klan, who still value their rituals and ceremonies and continue to wear their hoods. And, if that is too ancient, then consider the outlaw biker gangs—most notably the Hells Angels, Mongols and Banditos.

All of these groups have been founded since the end of the Second World War and are still very much alive. Even so, they all still value the traditional fraternal traits of ciphers, uniforms, symbols, initiations and lodge houses. Yet even in these cases, the peculiar world of the fraternity still seems an odd choice for ruthless criminals. What do they gain from its arcane ceremonies, curious language, and ritual mumbo-jumbo? Delving deeper, other obvious questions come to the surface. Why would a gang, a mob or a syndicate choose to mutate into a fraternity? Why would organizations choose such a structure—what would they gain? What is the history of this connection, and what are the examples in the period of this study?

In order to address these questions it is pretty obvious that it would be an immense help to discover what makes a criminal organization a *fraternity* and at least make an effort to establish some sort of a working definition of what constitutes a fraternity. Here things start to get tricky. Historians, anthropologists and sociologists have struggled with this problem, and found that any simple, all-purpose definition is slippery. Is a fraternity simply—as its name implies—a "brotherhood"?

If so, then what distinguishes it from any other gathering of men, like, say, a club or a society, or even an army? Is it the mysticism and the unintelligible ritual? Or perhaps the distinction lies in the oaths, the threats to do untold evil to those who betray the order, which would imply that the core of such behavior involves retaining secrecy. That in turn raises the question, why the uniforms? Fraternity seems to be a mass of contradictions.

One of the most successful, or at least most thoughtful, definitions comes from the Australian fraternal historian, Bob James. He has come up with a set of rules that can determine the difference between a fraternity and, for instance, an association—or in the case of criminal fraternities, a gang, a mob or a band. According to Dr. James, in order to be a fraternity, the organization must have:

> a gathering point, often designated "a lodge," usually indoor and usually secured against the uninitiated; a ceremony investing initiates with membership; an oath of acceptance sworn by the incoming member; a structure of internal advancement, each level marked by further ceremony, or by a coded token, and each marked by increased levels of discipline and of responsibility related to the internal workings of

the organization and to the organization's wider "message" which necessarily binds each member to the whole, as both contributor and recipient, that whole represented physically, financially, symbolically and/or socially, in positive, "family" terms for the individual, the group and the group's community.[8]

It could be argued that the essence of James's fraternal analysis hinges on three pairs of elements—initiation and loyalty; hierarchy and discipline; and mythology and continuity. Boiled down to these essentials, the peculiarities of fraternalism no longer seem to be simply mumbo-jumbo and play-acting. Given these very practical purposes, the defining features of fraternity become desirable traits—assets that could make vital contributions to the formation, expansion and prosperity of any criminal organization, at any time. Working from this assumption, fraternity becomes a sensible and logical course for criminal organizations to take.

## Criminal Fraternities in Late Nineteenth Century America

At a purely practical level, sooner or later in their history most successful organizations need to recruit in order to survive. They may need additional operatives in order to handle increased workload, or require new skills to either diversify or adapt to changing demands. This is as true of organized crime as it is of any other organization, but it goes without saying that those intent on breaking the law obviously need to recruit more surreptitiously. Of course in the late nineteenth century, as now, it was hardly feasible for a gang to advertise in the public arena for members, making word of mouth recommendation and familial contacts crucial recruitment tools.

It is therefore not really surprising that in many cases authentic blood relatives—family—were favored above all other recruits. American gang history has many more-or-less genuine, more-or-less successful examples. From the James-Younger Gang of the Western border states in the 1870s, through to the Morello family of 1900s New York City, to Ma Barker's sons in Kansas and Oklahoma in the mid–1930s—criminal families, even criminal dynasties, are a feature of the legend and, sometimes, even the reality of the nation's historical crime-scape.

These close familial relationships had obvious benefits. Not only did family connections supposedly negate many of the problems of ascertaining and proving questions of trustworthiness and ability, but also through their imposition of a natural hierarchy, they engendered discipline. Sometimes the family was extended, as in the Mafia "families," which were more associated with regional origins than actual blood ties. Nevertheless the principle was the same. For example, in 1899–1900, Giuseppe Morello employed operatives from outside his wider "family" of Sicilians from his hometown of Corleone. He blamed this deviation for subsequent troubles endured by his gang.

As his business expanded, Morello, or the "Clutch Hand" as he was known, had used Irish "queer-pushers"—small-time crooks paid on percentage to spend counterfeit dollars in order to get genuine currency in their change. Through carelessness and bad luck, these men had attracted the attention of the Secret Service, and were pretty soon caught, grilled and imprisoned—and very nearly led to Morello's own arrest. To the cautious Morello, the advantage of "family" connections was clearly demonstrated by the way in which the Irish queer pushers "sang" when they were arrested and interrogated. By contrast, those Sicilians implicated—all local to Morello's home town of Corleone— even under the notorious "third degree," stuck to their familiar code of silence.[9]

However, drawing from such a small pool had obvious limitations, not the least of which were the natural brakes imposed on expansion and diversification by family numbers and family ability. Fraternity, as demonstrated by the techniques already described in the Mafia's recruitment of Antonio Comito, could provide one answer. Fraternity created a new family, a family by an induction or initiation process, by which the recruit could be cowed into an unswerving loyalty to the existing members of the fraternity. According to early accounts of the rituals of the Sicilian Mafia, it appears that the initiation's primary concern was to inculcate the vaunted virtues of courage, manliness, obedience, loyalty and, most importantly, discretion.

Of course, given the nature of the organization, the history of the induction processes are necessarily shadowy and not entirely reliable. According to the most recent studies, it was the chief of the Palermo police who first recorded initiation rites, in February 1876. The first recordings of "American" Mafia rituals appeared in the 1890s, and show a remarkable similarity in both their structure and language to those from which were recorded in Sicily. Such parallels suggest a commonality and continuity, which would indicate at least some level of formal structure within the organization, a structure capable of surviving transoceanic shifts. This structure was worth preserving in what might be considered a totally different environment from that of the suburbs and villages of Sicily.

The essentials of this ritual initiation are well known. It involves a "godfather" explaining the ideals and regulations of the organization to the initiate, who has been called upon to become a "man of honor." The hopeful's index finger is pricked and his blood dripped onto a holy image—frequently a print or lithograph of the Madonna or perhaps the local patron saint. The image is then set on fire and the ashes dropped into the neophyte's open palms as he repeats an oath. Although there are varieties of the oath, it contains three essential elements—loyalty to the society above all, obedience to the will of the society, and the expectation of harsh retribution for any betrayal of the society.

The oath itself is related to, and reinforced by, the ritual. As with most other fraternal rituals it is laden with symbolism and portent—and as with most criminal fraternities, in the Mafia's case these are not particularly subtle. The inferences of the blood, the burned picture and the ashes are significant. In essence they indicated that the ties now undertaken to the organization were made with more than words. By surrendering his finger to be cut by the godfather, the initiate was surrendering his free will to the honored society. The implication was that he was no longer able to determine his own destiny. His future was now in the hands of the Honored Society. This was reinforced by another element of the ritual. Having broken a taboo by participating in the destruction of a sacred image, for the outcast initiate the Mafia was now his only refuge. His fellow Men of Honor were now his family, and this tie is reinforced by the blood and the oaths.

The Mafia is not unique in this matter. The Camorra, the Mafia's Neapolitan equivalent, used a variation of the Sicilians' bloodletting in their induction ceremony. What was more, such rituals definitely crossed the Atlantic. In one account given to the New York Court of Appeals in 1922, a ceremony is detailed in which the gang's elder ordered the neophyte to cut his own arm. He is then instructed to show the wound to all members of the gang, who in turn put their mouths to the cut and suck blood from the wound. After having done this, they simply utter to the new member: "You have gained." This presumably refers to the recruit's having found a new family.[10]

What is more, details of one New Jersey Italian-American criminal gang's ritual indicate that they had yet another variation. In their ceremony the blood of a new member was mixed with that of others. This was done while a knife was held to the initiate's chest as he swore to uphold the secrecy of the order under all circumstances. This gang was a "Black Hand" order, which according to current scholarship had less to do with fraternity, and more to do with the kind of brand awareness and gravity that a sinister name could give a band of petty crooks. It also shows how ritual was adopted, adapted and incorporated into group formation amongst criminals in this period. It is typical of the pragmatism of Black Handers that the account also claimed the initiate should give the name of a wealthy target for their extortion activities—"as a guarantee of good faith."[11]

This concentration on the familial is not confined simply to the Italian or even the European-American criminal fraternal tradition. Other regions have similar strategies regarding "blood" relations. For example, alongside reports of the fear, spectacle and drama of the Chinese Triad initiation ceremony, it was frequently recorded that the initiate was expected swear that all his blood relatives were dead. This was taken not so much as a literal statement. As brutal as these gangs were, the initiate was not expected to kill off all of his family. It was a metaphorical ideal. As in Italian tradition, the neophyte was expected to now have loyalty simply to the society and to no one else.[12] This was clearly illustrated in documents captured by the Sacramento police in 1892. According to one report, the Bang Kong Tong, or Highbinder, oath was "one of the most terrible that the Chinese are able to devise," and it included a "promise to regard each member as a brother and the closest relative I know. [The initiate was to swear that] if called upon by our society on necessary business I will not inquire whether it is concerning a relative of mine, or whether he be my brother, but I promise to go out in the street and fight and fire pistols."[13] However, it is undeniable that ideas of blood relations and the extended family are considered especially vital to the Italian criminal fraternities. Mafia families, in particular, have become something of a cliché. For example, it is held that Italians in general, especially Sicilians, have traditionally placed an emphasis on the extended family, and not simply in its criminal sense.

Current research questions this, claiming that the nuclear family was far more important than the extended family, but that other business and social networks outside blood relatives played a vital role.[14] Nevertheless, the concept of the *comparatico*—literally cofather, but more commonly translated as Godfather—plays a vital role in many ways. This figure, part mentor, part guardian, part father figure, was particularly important in extending the "spiritual kinship" of the clan. What is more, his presence and influence fits in well with the idea of the family as business unit.

These tribalist ties brought the fraternity back to potent Christian beliefs about hierarchy, respect and loyalty. Arguably more importantly, it also played upon, and up to, the folk traditions of the region. As will be elaborated, these were vital to the fraternal aspects of the Mafia and other fraternities. This familial element has remained constant across all the main criminal secret societies—at least certainly within the Italian setting—right up to the present day. It is a trend that is clearly demonstrated in a transcription of a 'Ndrangheta (Calabrian "Mafia") oath as it was given in evidence in a trial as recently as 1995. The oath spoke of putting "the interests and honour of the association before those of your family, parents, sisters, and brothers. The association is your family from now on and, if you commit infamità [betrayal], you will be punished with death. As you are faithful to the society, in the same way the society will be faithful to you and will help you in times of need. This oath can be broken only with death."[15]

That is not to say that all criminal fraternal initiation oaths or ceremonies stressed longevity, or aimed for global reach. Some were simply founded for a single act, in one specific place. In his account of the famous feud that ended in the legendary shootout at the OK Corral, one contemporary witness claimed that the conspirators formed a fraternity, which had a single and very defined aim—revenge. The fraternity had a suitably theatrical initiation ceremony in which "a death list had been prepared with the most spectacular and dramatic ceremonials, enacted at midnight within the recesses of a deep canyon, during which the names of the elect [those to be killed in revenge] had been written in the blood drawn from the veins of a murderer."[16]

New York city's notorious Whyo Gang took the initiation ritual to its limits. The gang, which ruled over New York's Lower East Side, was reputed to have demanded that all potential members must prove that they had committed at least one murder in order to become a full member. What was more, the act needed to be witnessed by other gang members.[17] While the veracity of this claim is disputed, its roots can be seen as lying in the fraternal structure and show more than simple bravado.

Like so many rituals, it had at its origins a vital practicality designed to guarantee group membership, dependability and discretion. After all, since his fellow gang members had witnessed him carry out a murder, the new gangster had an interest in showing loyalty. As an organization with its whole existence founded on terror and fear, rumors of such mindless violence could be no bad thing: as word of this horrific test got out— which it certainly did—the Whyo's reputation for brutality and ruthlessness spread, and not only among competing gangs, but also with potential victims.

## Barrel Murders and Other Punishments

As the Whyos' consideration of the blackmailing of its own members demonstrated, it was one thing to filter and recruit new members, but it was a totally different issue retaining and disciplining men whose entire lives were dedicated to disobeying the constraints imposed on them by society. In this the world of legitimate fraternity could again provide valuable lessons. The clear hierarchical—patriarchal—structure of domestic life, which dominated the idealized family life in the English-speaking world of the late nineteenth and early twentieth century, was often replicated in the lodge house.

Similarly, the lodge house was often seen as an extension, if not idealization, of the home. It was a place of retreat: a haven of stability, peace and cooperation. It oozed what Masonic shorthand terms "harmony." As the British social reformer Lord Shaftesbury explained, the home was the familial refuge, with its disciplined calm. It was the root of all successful societies. As he saw it, there could "be no security to society, no honor, no prosperity, no dignity at home, no nobleness of attitude towards foreign nations, unless the strength of the people rests upon the purity and firmness of the domestic system.... At home the principles of subordination are first implanted and the man is trained to be a good citizen."[18]

This quest for good citizenship is illustrated in the rituals and structure of three of the most popular American fraternities—the Masons, the Odd Fellows and the Knights of Pythias. All of these see the task of the masters of their "crafts" as being the education, guidance and protection of those lower down the ranks. However, this quest for spiritual maturity is perhaps clearest in the Order of the Knights of Honor (OKH), which has three degrees, called simply "Infancy, Youth and Manhood."[19]

In the shadow world of the criminal fraternities, some groups imitated this domestic structure. The three degrees of the Neapolitan camorra were just as forthright as the OKH in their language. Novices were *giovanotti* (boys) who graduated to become *piccotti* (youths) before emerging as fully-blown *camorrista*. The term *piccotti* is particularly interesting since, according to Mafia scholar John Dickie, it can be translated from the Sicilian dialect as a "lad with attitude."[20] This translation reinforces the patriarchal and disciplinary structure of the fraternity. In part it highlights the adolescence of the middle-grade *camorrista*. It shows him as being motivated by the same hormone-charged bravado and sense of youthful exploration inherent in teenage gang members in all societies over all times—before and since. What is more, the familial structure also implies that those at the top of the pile were charged with disciplining these young tearaways.

Tony Notaro, a neophyte *camorrista*, joining the order in the 1910s in New York, was left in no doubt about the fact that the fraternity expected total obedience. The language was no longer arcane—it was New World clear—but the implications of betrayal were for the time being left terrifyingly vague. Tony claimed he was told at his initiation: "Whatever is done between us [his fellow *camorra*], not a word should be breathed on the outside. You have to respect the bosses. When you are ordered to do a job or kill anybody, whatever it is, even if you are arrested, never say a word and do not talk at all, and do not be afraid and never speak to the police. If you speak to the police, you are discharged from this society, and you have to pay attention to what the bosses—those that have been here before you—will say … in whatever town you might find yourself, Boston, Philadelphia, Pittsburg [*sic*], Chicago, Buffalo—in any town." This rather veiled threat was later explained to Notoro by the head of the fraternity, who told him that now he was a *camorrista*, "when you are ordered to do something, you have to go: and if you don't go, you will get killed."[21]

Regardless of such threats—in fact, because of their apparent authenticity—the American public was aware of the punishments meted out by criminal fraternities in U.S. cities. In 1903, a "trend" that had been developing in the American criminal fraternities came to public attention. It started with the discovery of a medium-sized, iron-bound, wooden-stave barrel on the sidewalk on New York's East 11th Street. The barrel itself was not unusual; it was simply the kind used at the time for transporting and storing sugar. It was its contents that were remarkable. The barrel contained the body of a man whose throat had been cut with such force that it had been almost completely severed the head from the body. In addition the unfortunate victim had been stabbed.

Bodies frequently turned up in the poorer districts of New York. Many of them were the victims of stabbings, but there were several elements about this killing that made the observers suspect that the cadaver had been the victim of a ritual murder. The knife wounds were excessive. The police counted some eighteen stabbings. This made some sense if the victim was seen as having been murdered as a result of a fraternal punishment.

Rumors began to circulate that in many criminal fraternities each member of a gang present at a punishment murder would play a physical part in the deed. This, it was claimed, would have the double advantage of tying the murderers to each other through a shared act in fraternal brotherhood, as well as making sure that each participant had a reason to keep the deed a secret. There were also other signs that something more than the usual sinister forces were at play. It was pointed out that the body had then been bent double and forced into the barrel. As if to illustrate the contempt for the victim, the barrel still contained the detritus of previous use. In the bottom of it, amid the sugar and blood-soaked sawdust were Italian cigar butts and onion rinds, leaving little doubt in the minds of the investigators as to the nationality of the murderer(s).

The case may have remained a rather unimportant, if particularly gruesome, incident in the slums of New York had it not been for the ambitions of the nation's leading news-paperman. Engaged in a seemingly perpetual circulation war with his mentor and rival, Joseph Pulitzer, William Randolph Hearst through his salacious *New York Journal* quickly pointed out the significance of some other aspects of the evidence. Most Americans would have known of the punishments fraternities threatened in their initiation oaths. Here was evidence of these being put into practice by the criminal fraternities.

The paper began by telling its readers the murder was almost certainly the work of a "secret society." To reinforce this: to show that these atrocities were more common than previously thought, and to indicate the reach and cruelty of the orders, the *Journal* pointed out the similarities between this case and two other, as yet unsolved, murders. The first took place in 1901 when the Jewish peddler Meyer Weisbard's remains had been recovered from the shoreline by Pier 11 on New York's East River. His throat had also been slashed and the body wedged into a steamer trunk.[22] The next year, the body of Joe "The Grocer" Catania had been found under the Bay Bridge on Seventy-Third Street. Again, his throat had been cut with such force that the victim was nearly decapitated, and the body was again bent double in order to force it into a sack.[23]

In the view of the *Journal*, the complete disregard for the bodies—their unceremonious bundling into containers, which had not even been cleaned—showed a callous disregard for the victims, typical of ritual punishment killings. Leaving onionskins, cigar butts, and even a receipt in the barrel demonstrated that the perpetrators were not worried about providing obvious and vital clues for the police. To the newspaper, this behavior seemed to demonstrate a high-handed feeling of immunity in the minds of the perpetrators. To support the idea that these traits were connected with secret societies and fraternal punishment, the paper went on to claim that in all three cases "the body [was] put in a place where discovery was certain, as though to ensure publicity and to convey a warning to those who would best understand."[24]

Nevertheless the panic about "ritual murders"—if that is what they can be realistically called—was really remarkably short-lived. It occasionally resurfaced, but although arguably remaining just as ritualistic, as with the later account of the Secret Service agent charged with the initial investigation of the "Barrel Murder," the fraternal element had largely been replaced. The concentration had shifted from the secret society to the gangster. As William Flynn claimed, "You [the American public] are now familiar with the kind of punishment meted out to one whom the gang suspects of having betrayed a member. You have also been acquainted with the Sicilian custom of revenge by way of an actual example ... the man in the barrel."[25]

Perhaps this was because the idea of fraternity in criminal enterprises was being overtaken by a business ethos. By the end of the period, the newspapers certainly seemed to feel that regulation and discipline of criminal gangs had been syndicated. This was clearly evident in their headline-grabbing creation of a national "hit squad" they dubbed "Murder, Inc." Maybe it was because by the 1930s the idea of fraternity had been largely played out as a news item by the sudden growth and equally impressive implosion of the KKK.

It could simply have been that it no longer suited the criminal gangs to be portrayed as fraternities. Yet, if this reticence to be regarded as fraternities was visible by the end of the period, it certainly was not the case at the beginning. In some instances it served the criminal orders very well to be regarded as fraternities. Nowhere is this clearer than in the propaganda of the Ku Klux Klan. From its inception to its outlawing in the early 1870s and into the present day, the Klan has played up its fraternal roots and status.

## The KKK as a Fraternity

The foundation myth of the Klan centered around a group of six ex–Confederate soldiers in the small, sleepy Tennessee town of Pulaski at the end of 1865. Of these men, the so-called "Jolly Six," four had been Freemasons before the War and two had been members of college "frat" houses. As such, at least some of them would have been familiar with the workings of fraternal association, and receptive to the fraternal ideal. Therefore the claim made by founding members that the six simply created the order to stave off boredom after the excitement and action of the war years not only makes the Klan seem harmless, but it is also entirely reasonable.

According to these accounts, here was an organization of jaded young men in a backwater of a defeated and broken region, men who decided to entertain themselves by creating a club, dressing up and creating bizarre rituals. Nothing more.[26] In this version of events, the violence and racial harassment now so synonymous with the Klan only entered the equation after the order spread from Tennessee into neighboring Alabama. Further, although the original "den" had often amused themselves by posing as the ghosts of dead Confederate soldiers and frightening local blacks, they had apparently had no racial or political agenda.

This trait only appeared when members of the Athens, Alabama, den saw a black man riding out with a white school teacher—a fact made all the more appalling by the fact she was a white *woman*. Incensed by this blatant breach of Southern "race etiquette," Klansmen in full costume rode out at night, kidnapped the man, beat him and threw him into a nearby river—instructing him never to repeat his indiscretion again on pain of death.[27] There is no reason to dispute this tale. Such behavior was all too commonplace. It was repeated all across the former Confederacy, seen as simply one of the results of the region's rising race tensions in the wake of abolition.

As the mayhem of Reconstruction faded into history in the late 1870s, the South completed its process of effectively returning to the racial and political *status quo ante*. Disbanded and inactive, the Klan moved from being a seen as a brutal, reactionary insurgent group to being the very embodiment of Southern chivalry. These were knights who defended and promoted the sanitized vision of the slave-owning South as a romantic plantation society. Essentially, in the historiography of Reconstruction over the next three quarters of a century—if not longer—the Knights of the Ku Klux Klan became the Knights of the Lost Cause.

Leading historians, politicians, novelists, dramatists, filmmakers and academics upheld the conceit that the order had fought to prevent the destruction of a unique society where more-or-less happy slaves toiled under more-or-less benevolent masters in a more-or-less rural idyll. Apologists claimed that under the terms of the draconian Third Enforcement Act of 1871, the Klan was essentially outlawed as an organization. Persecution drove it underground. Nevertheless, the order had continued their mission at the cost of their own imprisonment, injury and even death. In these accounts, Klansmen had defended a society that understood and contained the rapacious urges and childlike gullibility of the black. They had staved off the dangers of racial integration and essentially saved the South from ruin.

Fraternity formed a central part of this rehabilitation from criminal insurgency to sanctified organization. From its very inception the Klan had flaunted its ties with Freemasonry. As the organization expanded, these bonds were seen as desirable if not essential. The draw of the lodge house; the familiarity with ritual; the obedience to vows—all were seen as a part of Freemasonry, which would prove essential to the Klan in its vital but secretive mission. But perhaps more important in the long term was the pedigree resulting from connection with the older organization.

This served an important function. Association with Masons gave pedigree and legitimacy to the young organization, virtues made all the more potent when linked with respected and celebrated individuals. Typical of these claims are the connections with Nathan Bedford Forrest. The very model of the dashing, cavalier Confederate cavalry general, he became the Klan's first Imperial Wizard—its national figurehead. Much has been made of Forrest's interest in Masonry. Yet as with so much fraternal history—and especially when in connection with more controversial orders like the Klan—secrecy, deliberate obfuscation and ignorant misinformation play a large role. Although it is certain that he was a Mason, there is evidence to suggest that Forrest never graduated beyond the first of 33 degrees, so the craft's influence on him could not have been seen as life-altering, or even particularly serious.[28]

What was more, Forrest steadfastly refused to publicly acknowledge his position within the Klan, especially after the 1871 Force Act declared the organization criminal. This coyness about affiliation was replicated throughout the higher echelons of the Klan. The bases of these fraternal affiliations are largely histories, predominantly favorable, if not downright celebratory or hagiographic accounts, written around the turn of the twentieth century, years when the myth of the "Lost Cause" gained traction.[29] Many of these interpretations claim that the majority of Grand Dragons (state-level leaders) of the Klan during these years were drawn from the ranks of the Masons. Secrecy makes such claims difficult to justify or deny.

Arguably the most controversial and enduring of these claims to direct connections has centered on the leading Masonic figure of the day. It is claimed that Albert Pike played a pivotal role in the rise of both organizations.[30] The investigation of this claim highlights the shared objectives of the Klan and many Masons in the South. Pike not only supported slavery, he had risked his life to defend it. He was a former brigadier general in the Confederate Army, albeit a rather idiosyncratic and erratic one. What also makes the connection more likely is that Pike was certainly a member of those elites drawn to the new purposes of the Klan—most importantly "home rule" for the South. Even after the military demise of the Confederacy, Pike's allegiance remained steadfast to the defeated South, and his opinion of the increasingly radical racial integration policy of the early 1870s was clearly obvious and frequently stated. He was against it. As he himself put it: "The disenfranchised people of the South, robbed of all the guarantees of the Constitution ... can find no protection for property, liberty or life, except in secret association.... If it were in our power, if it could be effected, we would unite every white man, who is opposed to Negro suffrage, into one great Order of Southern Brotherhood."[31]

Pike was the master of Masonic ritual, and an expert in the esoteric, archaic and romantic elements that contributed so clearly to the appeal of the Masons in post–Civil War America. Association with a man like Pike reinforced a direct link between the Klan and an illustrious roll call of former Masons, which included six former presidents of the United States. However, it is probably not from the Masons that the Klan drew most of its original ritual, ideals and purpose. The most likely influence is the Sons of Malta, an order which, in spite of its Mediterranean name, emerged in the prewar South.

The Sons of Malta were a short-lived society that preyed off the craze for secret societies in the mid–1850s. Originating in New Orleans in 1854, they rapidly spread across the South, then edged up the eastern seaboard before spreading west and all but dying out by the late 1860s. The object of the order was simply the fun of hazing a seemingly endless number of gullible new recruits. Those initiated would then go on to repeat the process in a new area. Alongside being made to recite complex and senseless oaths, the usual initiation would consist of the neophyte's being blindfolded, put into a large basket, and hauled to the ceiling of the lodge while the Sons of Malta ate dinner beneath him. There was also the Boston branch's notoriously terrifying "shooting the chute," in which the candidate was sent careening down a shaft that dropped a full three stories. If he survived, it became his task to perform no other fraternal duties than to recruit further members and take their money. Judging by the fraternity's rapid growth, most initiates were happy to go out and find more unfortunate victims to terrorize.[32]

In this respect the Ku Klux Klan was in its earliest days very similar to the Sons of Malta, especially in its objectives. One historian of the organization's first five years goes as far as to say, "The perpetuation of the initiation was really the principle object of the order."[33] What was more, the limited number of surviving firsthand accounts indicate that the Pulaski Klan's initiation rite draws more on the Sons of Malta's prankish tradition than the solemnity of the more established and serious organizations like the Masons. The ghoulish titles, the alliterative "K"s, the outlandish costumes—all point to this ancestry.

Similarly, the initiation ceremony bears many of the hallmarks of the Sons of Malta. According to Stanley Horn, a historian of the early Klan, even this was simply the result of the placing of random objects in order to increase the difficulty for initiates to negotiate the den blindfolded. The obstacles were designed to confuse and frighten the neophyte, while amusing the fraternalists conducting the ceremony. This prankish interpretation is backed up by the account, given some years later, of two of the founders. It showed that the ritual involved little more than the hooded initiate's hearing some threatening incantations from the "Grand Cyclops" and the "Grand Turk." He would then take a pretty well meaningless set of oaths. On completion he was shown his reflection in a mirror on the den's "royal altar." To the "hilarity" of the fraternity, it revealed that he was wearing a "regal crown" with donkey's ears and his face had been smeared with soot.[34]

This analysis of the fatuousness of the Klan ritual is important since it flags up a central issue of fraternity in criminal associations. It is undeniably possible to argue that at the more complex and sophisticated levels, the ideals of fraternity within these groups should be seen as being little more than simplistic and vestigial, a nod to an imagined ancestry. But then that was not their purpose. Their essentially ersatz ceremonies were not devised to mimic the passage from ignorance to enlightenment, or boyhood to manhood. Nor did they seek to inspire pride in the members' status as workers, artisans or craftsmen. None of this, however, negates their importance. In essence fraternal status endorsed, justified, systematized and disguised their criminal activities. In the case of the Klan it contributed to its rehabilitation; in another case it essentially enabled invisibility.

However the fraternal roots of the Mafia are slanted, there is little doubt that their foundation myths have served them well. They essentially enabled them to hide in plain sight, on and off, on both sides of the Atlantic until the 1990s. Increasingly, research has shown how the continuous repetition of the chivalrous origins of the Mafia made the name synonymous with a form of Sicilian peasant exceptionalism. To those outside Sicily, on mainland Italy and elsewhere, "Mafia" was not so much a fraternity as an attitude. The Honorable Society encouraged this perception of Mafia as a fundamentally Sicilian culture of exaggerated personal prestige, swagger and rustic braggadocio that manifested itself in a picaresque cycle of blood feud and vendetta.[35]

## The Molly Maguires

While the Mafia drew on and cultivated an ancient yearning for Sicilian nationhood and Sicilian virtues, the origins of the Molly Maguires date back to a wave of nationalism that was no less powerful and only slightly less ancient.[36] However, whereas the Mafia managed to utilize the regional stereotypes associated with their foundation myth to their distinct advantage, the Mollys' supposed origins proved to be their undoing.

While the tales of its origins had some veracity in the Old Country, its New World manifestation was at best tenuous, but like a mirror image of the Mafia, contemporary commentators saw it as far more than a name, transported to a new setting. To them it was a secretive and violent manifestation of an old problem. Present-day scholars are not so sure of that pedigree. That is not to say that any American group calling itself the Mollys would not have had a heritage to draw on. Emerging from the religious and class sectarianism, accusations and counterclaims of terrorism and atrocity of British colonial rule in Ireland, the original Mollys certainly existed.[37]

Legend has it that Molly Maguire was an Irish peasant mother evicted from her smallholding around the time of the famine. According to the various tales surrounding her, the tragically heroic woman either fought back against the English and their lackeys trying to evict her from her home and died in the process, and/or founded an eponymous resistance movement. In the account of the Pinkerton undercover agent who infiltrated the Pennsylvania Mollys, the insurgents in Ireland took the name out of respect for the universal Irish mother. He maintained that it was taken to "represent the Irish mother begging bread for her children."[38]

Whatever the truth of the matter, the legendary Molly would lend her name to an infamous band of violent vigilantes, who like the Rebecca rioters in Wales would disguise themselves in women's clothes and wreak bloody revenge on their oppressors under the cover of night. In the American context, they would surface most notoriously as a militant organization representing the hard-pressed Irish immigrant miners of the anthracite coal on what was then a wild frontier region of Pennsylvania.

In this incarnation, the Molly Maguires were associated with an ultraviolent spate of industrial disorder in the anthracite region of Pennsylvania in the 1870s. Over these years some sixteen mine-owners and their foremen were murdered, making the region— and most notably its Irish immigrant workforce—synonymous with Irish terrorism and mayhem. At the center of this disruption was a secretive and bloodthirsty import—the Molly Maguires.

It was the owner of the eponymous detective agency and implacable enemy of the order, Allan Pinkerton, who described them as a "noxious weed transplanted from its native soil—that of Ireland—sometime in the last twenty years.... [It was simply a] midnight, dark-lantern, murderous-minded fraternity."[39] More importantly for this study, they were usually viewed as a subgroup, a "side order" in fraternal terms, of the largest ethnically based fraternity in America—the Ancient Order of Hibernians. In this version of their history they had arrived fully formed, battle-tested from Ireland, and ready for violent action in regions where the Irish were oppressed.

Although this explanation of their organization was first propagated with remarkably little evidence and a clearly hostile agenda in the anti–Catholic press, it quickly spread and remained extraordinarily persistent both within and outside the region. Such ideas persisted, and the Mollys were soon to be condemned as a widespread and highly dangerous Irish secret society. The name often emerged when violence connected with Irish immigrants broke out. For instance, the *New York Times*, which took a consistently hostile view of the "fugitive murderers and conspirators" of the "oath-bound brotherhood," would relentlessly depict them as that "Irish secret society" during the period of their famous trials in the 1870s and beyond.[40] However, there is evidence that questions this generally held assumption.

If the American Mollys were not really a secret society, if they were not a genuine fraternity, then why was this myth put forward, by whom, and why did it persist? The initial source seems to have been the *Miners' Journal*, a Republican, Whig, nativist and "free labor" newspaper published in Pottsville, Schuylkill County, in the heart of Pennsylvania's anthracite region. The editor of the *Journal* was a native of Pennsylvania, born to Welsh Presbyterian parents who inculcated in him a culture of self-discipline, sobriety and self-sufficiency. Benjamin Bannan loathed Catholicism, and the Irish Catholics who represented it. He was raised to see them as drunken, lazy and immoral.

To Bannan, as proof of this immorality, they were also Democrat. Holding the views of that party and their consequent support of the abomination that was slavery, they were willing to condone privilege and cruelty as long as their own jobs were protected. Given his background and beliefs, it is no wonder that under Bannan the *Journal* was the mouthpiece of small-scale entrepreneurial enterprise. It made complete sense that it advocated a form of aspirant, trickle-down capitalism that precluded any understanding of the labor activism of the hard-pressed Irish immigrant laborers who made up nearly a half of the region's workforce and almost all of the propertyless wage slaves.[41]

Bannan's fears of malign Catholic influence came to a head with the election of an overwhelmingly Democrat administration in Schuylkill County in 1856. He became convinced that the election was rigged and that throughout Pennsylvania the Irish vote had been controlled by "a secret Roman Catholic association which the Democracy [sic] is using for political purposes. The Philadelphia *Transcript* says this Association commenced in Boston and now extends all over the country, controlling all the nominations of the Democratic Party in our cities and in some parts of the country."[42] He called this organization the Molly Maguires, although similar accusations elsewhere held the corruption to be the work of the Ancient Order of Hibernians.

By the opening of the 1860s this implication of the Mollys with corruption had expanded into accusations of violence. Inter-ethnic violence had been a feature of the anthracite region since the 1840s. The murder of an Irishman by a Welshman, who was subsequently acquitted and then murdered in turn, had kindled fears of a latent Irish vigilantism among the miners. Nevertheless accusations of organized and systematic violence had remained largely dormant until the Civil War. In the war years, displays of patriotism and political solidarity took on a new significance.

The result was that Bannan's continuing accusations that the increasing level of violence in the region was the work of the highly organized and secret brotherhood took firm root in a receptive national press. For example, when in 1862 and 1863, respectively, a mine foreman and a mine owner were murdered, the *New York Times* was quick to blame organized Molly Maguires and compare their violence and secrecy with the ritual murders committed by the notorious Thuggee cult in India.[43] The result was that by the time that the trials for fourteen other murders took place in the late 1870s, the idea of a violent and secretive fraternity—the Molly Maguires—had taken firm root in the Pennsylvania anthracite fields and elsewhere.

The idea that the Mollys were a fraternity was vital to the purpose of its enemies. It helped them explain why the powers of righteousness could not find hard evidence to reveal the full depth of the association's depravity. They could argue that its code of secrecy was so impenetrable that its evil nature was only visible in its actions. Some would claim this was, like the Mafia, a result of grievous penalties threatened for breaking oaths of secrecy—but again little evidence of this exists. Although it is claimed that they had initiation rites, which would no doubt have sworn initiates to secrecy and loyalty, little is known of the actual ritual of the Molly Maguires. In the not altogether reliable testimony of the Pinkerton agent, James McParlan, posing as a co-conspirator and renegade Irish nationalist, James McKenna, details his induction after an Ancient Order of Hibernians (AOH) meeting. He describes in very vague terms a simple ceremony in which he found himself "ordered to go to my knees, and take my hat off, and there was a document read to me by the [AOH] Division Master, Mr. Lawler ... the substance of which [was] that I obey my superiors in everything connected with the organization, in things lawful and not.... It also contained a clause that I should keep everything secret pertaining to this organization."[44]

This close relationship between the AOH and the Mollys was upheld by the testimony of prosecution witness Manus Cull in the murder trial of Molly Maguire Patrick Hester. A member of both the AOH and the Mollys, Cull saw the two as essentially interchangeable.[45] Other contemporary commentators see the one as a subdivision of the other—a "side order," in fraternal terms. They claim that membership of the Hibernians was an essential prerequisite test of the eligibility for joining the Molly Maguires.[46] That is not to say that the "murderous activities" of the Mollys would have been condoned by the vast majority of the 6,000 or so lodges of the AOH throughout America. Rather, as one source claimed, the national convention of the AOH, meeting in April 1877, "denounced them [the Molly Maguires] in the strongest terms ... [and cut] off from membership the entire territory [the Mollys' stronghold of Schuylkill County, Pennsylvania] in which they were operating."[47]

This connection, or lack of it, is more than simply a question of pedigree. The most notable scholar of the organization maintains that the close association of the Molly Maguires with the Ancient Order of Hibernians was essentially a fabrication that emerged as a result of the trial of some forty members of the group for the murder of sixteen mine owners, foremen and scab laborers. Implying that the two organizations were synonymous, the court was treated to descriptions of the Hibernians' secret signs, a handbook of membership rules and details of their initiation oaths.[48] It was an essential part of the prosecution's case since the depiction of the Mollys as a fraternity enabled their prosecution under conspiracy laws rather than the more difficult charges of murder.

Nowhere is this clearer than in prosecution lawyer Franklin B. Gowen's summing up to the jury. He argued that the accused were all members of "a secret organization, banded together for the commission of crime … [and] securing the escape of any its members" via mutual alibis.[49] This not only made the Irishmen appear far more sinister, it would also imply that each of the killings of the bosses and their employees was connected to the other, and made their execution appear all the more premeditated. Given this slant, these murders were not random acts of violence or retaliation for perceived slights or spites; they became part of an international Irish-Catholic conspiracy.[50] And Gowen had a major interest in securing the convictions. He was the self-made president of the Philadelphia and Reading Railroad—the holding company for the mines in which the majority of industrial action was taking place.

Gowen is also interesting in the context of the Molly Myth from another perspective. He was, like many of his Welsh and English foremen and senior miners, Protestant. However, unlike them he was also an immigrant from Ulster and would have been familiar with—and no doubt hostile to—the Catholic Irish Molly Maguires of the earlier nineteenth century. The same was true of James McParlan, the Pinkerton agent, and the most influential witness for the prosecution. He was also an Ulsterman and an immigrant. As such, both would have been aware of the genre of hostile literature on Irish peasant lawlessness and violence.

One, or both, may well also have been familiar with a rather obscure novel by the well-known Irish writer William Carleton. In *Rody the Rover* (1845), striking Molly Maguires in an Irish mine are exposed by an *agent provocateur*. Although hostile to Rody, the infiltrator, the story is remarkably similar to both Gowen's description of the Mollys and that of McParlan as the agent's boss—Alan Pinkerton. Given the claim and counterclaim, the interpretation and reinterpretation and the controversy surrounding the Mollys that has continued even to today, it is near impossible to know how much of the myth of a mysterious fraternity is actually based on this fictional account.[51]

In the case of the Molly Maguires, fraternity created the myth of an effective, recognizable and terrifying organization that gained notoriety on both sides of the Atlantic. Set against this, there is increasing evidence that could indicate that they never really existed in America—at least not in the form in which has inspired newspapers, journal articles and book-length "true accounts" of terrorism or proto-trade unionism. Moreover, their legacy has lived on in the fiction of Sir Arthur Conan Doyle and the on-screen presence of Sean Connery, not to mention countless historical investigations—some rigorous and scholarly, others less so.[52]

Nor are they alone in this fame. Sherlock Holmes also tangled with the Klan.[53] The Klan's secrecy and brotherly loyalty played a pivotal role in the "redemption" of the region's prewar, caste-based system of government—albeit often more in the way in which the name Klan became the generic term for white supremacist organizations of the period. Nor does it end there. Fraternity, as the work of Miguel Hernandez and Craig Fox is showing, would be one of the chief motives for anywhere from four to ten million American men and women to join the Klan's "Invisible Empire" in the 1920s, making it perhaps proportionately the largest fraternity in U.S. history.[54]

But it is the Mafia that has been the most successful of all three fraternities—in all respects. It has become a staple in both film and fiction, even creating its own genre. Its fraternal structure largely enabled the spread of the Sicilian model of organized crime. Its fraternal secrecy has enabled it to become simultaneously ubiquitous and invisible. At times its very existence has been in question, and yet it is suspected that it controls a significant proportion of the U.S. economy and greater shares of the economies of many other nations. Moreover, it has entered the popular vocabulary in a way unlike any other fraternity—criminal or otherwise. The result is that the largest of the criminal organizations, from the contemporaneous Neapolitan camorra, to today's Russian gangs, tend to be called a "Mafia," making organized crime still appear to be peppered with fraternities.[55]

# Epilogue: Organized Crime, Then and Now

History is obviously never a complete picture of the past. It can't be. It is always a question of selection: it is a focus, an emphasis and a judgment. It is a best fit of what might have happened, and those ideas shift over time. This study cannot lay claim to being any better than that. It has probably ignored what many may consider to be important elements of organized crime. For example, there is little, if any, mention of narcotics, terrorism or gambling. African Americans tend to feature as victims rather than perpetrators.

Characters like Meyer Lansky or Bugsy Siegel play relatively minor roles by comparison with other accounts of the same years. In part this is an editorial decision—the subject is so vast, some things had to be excluded. Other important elements might be missing—and this may well be an oversight, and I have no doubt that when my peers read this, I will learn of many others.

In my own defense, I would like to think that the differences between our vision of organized crime, and those of the period of this study are, for the most part, due to the differences in what those two words meant to readers then, and what they mean now. This depends on what criminal activities were considered the most threatening, immoral or costly to society, then and now.

Nevertheless, there are themes that run through this book. They are themes that are as important for us to notice today as they were at the time when they happened. The common thread of politically motivated accusations may perhaps not have excited as much interest as we might expect. Yet we need to question whether that motivation is as prevalent today—and there is no reason why it should not be.

Even in the short term, we can see how seemingly outrageous theories can gain traction, especially if they are of enough political value. Given sufficient time, vociferous enough advocates and a critical mass of public interest, even the most outrageous claims—for example, criminal fraternities with national and international reach—can become accepted to the point of normality. Organized crime in many guises has sufficient support, public interest and advocacy—and it has certainly been around for long enough.

However, as I hope this book has shown, not all that is *taken* as historical fact *is necessarily* historical fact. Perhaps this is the fault of the historians themselves. It is difficult to imagine that popular perceptions of the history of any phenomenon would, by necessity, draw so heavily on uncorroborated sources. What other histories rely on the evidence of convicted or suspected killers, pimps, bandits, kidnappers and other sociopaths—all keen to settle scores, or clear their names—in the way that has been the case with the history of organized crime? What other histories would, again of necessity, utilize the obviously politically and ethnically partisan accounts of figures like Joseph A. Shakespeare or J. Edgar Hoover without very clearly emphasizing the context in which they were given? What histories of other phenomena would apparently unquestioningly accept the opinions of commercially interested parties like Harrison Gray Otis or Hickman Powell without explaining their relationship to those whom they accused in advance? Historians of World War I, or the Cold War, may well argue they face similar opposition when they try to show a different or at least more nuanced picture, but it appears they are winning the struggle. I am not so sure historians of organized crime are getting as close to victory.

It is perhaps by rehabilitating characters or raising unfamiliar accusations that this study seeks to challenge terms with which we have essentially become far too comfortable to question. New histories enable us to re-examine familiar views that we have about some of the origins of what is an all-too-frequently misunderstood history. By examining the commentary of the times—accurate or not—we can better understand what the public thought represented organized crime, and that is certainly not what I thought would have been the case when I started work on this book.

Another theme that the book hopefully makes clear is the idea that there is not *one* public opinion, any more than there is *one* history. Public opinion in relation to organized crime was, of course, dependent on who said what about it, how that was disseminated and who read or heard it, let alone who it happened to. What was the most threatening aspect of crime in New Orleans in 1890 was not the same as that in New York in 1940. It was not the same for a male black ex-slave in Reconstruction Alabama as it was for a white shop girl in 1900s Chicago or a wealthy investor in 1920s Los Angeles. Of course commentators had their interests, prejudices and personalities; no one would have taken any notice of them if they had not.

Perhaps, given the nature of this account, the last word should go to a gangster. In his terrifyingly fascinating account of post-communist Russian gangster-capitalism, Peter Pomerantsev interviews Vitaly Djomochka. Vitaly is a present-day gangster-turned-film producer who made frighteningly real, but personally glorifying, action films based on his own exploits as a gang boss in Siberia. Facing imminent tragedy as his star waned, he talked to the author about his two careers.

Musing on the fickleness of his former allies and his inevitable fate, he commented to Pomerantsev: "I often think now I should have gone into politics … [but] I just thought it boring. I didn't realise they used the same methods as us. It's too late now, though. I've dedicated myself to art."[1] How many notorious gangsters and politicians in America during the late nineteenth and early twentieth centuries might have had similar regrets, and loved to have remained anonymous to history and be remembered instead for their artistic contributions?

# Chapter Notes

## Prologue

1. Stark cited in the *Oregonian*, July 14, 1939.

2. Justus D. Doenecke, "Harry Elmer Barnes: Prophet of a 'Usable' Past," *The History Teacher* 8:2 (Feb. 1975): pp. 265–276.

3. According to one of today's leading economic historians, the war debt was some $9.8 billion owed by Britain, France and Italy. Adam Tooze, *The Deluge: The Great War and the Remaking of Global Order, 1916–1931* (New York, 2014), p. 12.

4. U.S. Congress, Senate, Subcommittee of Commerce, *Hearings: Investigation of Racketeering*, vol. 1 (Washington, D.C.: U.S. Government Printing Office, 1933), pp. 252, 710.

5. Figures taken from The Tax Foundation, *Facts and Figures on Government Finance*, vols. 17–18 (Baltimore: Johns Hopkins University Press, 1973), pp. 75, 99.

6. Figures taken from Goldthwaite Dorr and Sidney Simpson, *Report on the Cost of Crime and Criminal Justice in the United States* (Washington, D.C.: U.S. Government Printing Office, 1931), and cited in Clayton J. Ettinger, *The Problem of Crime* (New York: Ray Long and Richard R. Smith, 1932), p. 11.

7. For an in-depth analysis of the accuracy of these figures, see E.R. Hawkins and Willard Waller, "Critical Notes on the Cost of Crime," *Journal of Criminal Law and Criminology* 26:5 (Jan.-Feb. 1936): pp. 679–681.

8. In fact, the figure appears to have come from J. Edgar Hoover, who used it in a speech made to the Boy Scouts of America in Tulsa, Oklahoma, in June 1939, cited in *Christian Science Monitor*, June 29, 1939.

9. Max Singer, "The Vitality of Mythical Numbers," *The Public Interest* 23 (Spring 1971): pp. 3–9.

10. Figures extrapolated from a search using the term "Organized Crime" on Proquest.

11. For the origins of Stark's role in Pendergast's demise, see Rudolph H. Hartmann and Robert H. Ferrell, eds., *The Kansas City Investigation: Pendergast's Downfall 1938–1939* (Columbia: University of Missouri Press, 1999), p. 176, and John S. Matlin, *Political Party Machines of the 1920s and 1930s: Tom Pendergast and the Kansas City Democratic Machine* (Ph.D. diss., University of Birmingham, 2009), pp. 219–251.

12. Gordon Hamilton, "Missouri's 'Molly' Stark," *Current History* 50:4 (June 1, 1939): p. 18.

13. *Missouri Democrat*, July 29, 1938.

14. The best examples of this are in the *Kansas City Star*, March 17–18, 1938, and the *Independence Examiner*, January 4, 1938, and January 10, 1939.

15. For details of how the Pendergast machine operated, see Lyle W. Dorsett, "Kansas City Politics: A Study of Boss Pendergast's Machine." *Journal of the Southwest* 8:2 (Summer 1966): pp. 107–118.

16. For a brief account of Pendergast's *modus operandi* in the national context and his importance to the Democrat election campaign of 1936, see the *Seattle Times*, September 30, 1936.

17. For details see Claire Bond Potter, *War on Crime: Bandits, G-men, and the Politics of Mass Culture* (New Brunswick, NJ: Rutgers University Press, 1998); Bryan Burrough, *Public Enemies*, rev. ed. (New York: Penguin, 2009); and Richard Gid Powers, "J. Edgar Hoover and the Detective Hero," *Journal of Popular Culture* 9 (Fall 1975): pp. 257–278.

18. Stephen M. Underhill, "J. Edgar Hoover's Domestic Propaganda: Narrating the Spectacle of the Karpis Arrest," *Western Journal of Communication* 76:4 (2012): pp. 438–457.

19. *Boston Globe*, March 12, 1939.

20. *Boston Globe*, March 12, 1939.

21. For some idea of the extent of coverage as well as its nature, see *Cleveland Plain Dealer*, March 12 and July 9, 1939; *New York Socialist Call*, June 10, 1939; *Boston Herald*, June 25, 1939; and *New Orleans Times-Picayune*, June 25, 1939.

22. Stark in *Baltimore Sun*, June 20, 1939.

23. http://www.organized-crime.de/OCDEF1.htm.

24. Mike Woodiwiss, "Organized Crime: The Dumbing of Discourse," *British Criminology Conference; Selected Proceedings* (July 1999), pp. 3–4.

25. See Mark H. Haller, "Illegal Enterprise: A Theoretical and Historical Interpretation," *Criminology* 28:2 (1990): pp. 207–235.

26. Howard Abadinsky recommending Matthew G. Yeager, *Illegal Enterprise: The Work of Historian Mark Haller* (New York: United Press of America, 2013), back cover.

27. Reported in *New York Herald*, June 19, 1877.

28. Reported in the *Boston Journal*, May 14, 1897.

29. *Chicago Tribune*, April 7, 1911.

30. *Rockford (Illinois) Daily Gazette*, June 5, 1926.

31. *San Diego Evening Tribune*, July 29, 1930.

32. Timothy Gilfoyle, *A Pickpocket's Tale* (New York: W.W. Norton, 1992), pp. 251–269.

33. *New York Tribune*, September 21, 1893, and November 12, 1894; *New York Herald*, May 27, 1892.

34. See Edwin H. Sutherland, ed., *The Professional Thief* (Chicago: University of Chicago Press, 1937).

35. A reasonable assessment of these changes in the nineteenth century is available in David R. Johnson, *Policing the Urban Underworld: The Impact of Crime on the Development of the American Police, 1800–1887* (Philadelphia: Temple University Press, 1979), pp. 41–67.

36. Reported in the *San Diego Union*, October 6, 1937.

37. One of the best researched of these accounts can be found in Mike Dash, *The First Family: Terror, Extortion, Revenge, Murder and the Birth of the American Mafia* (New York: Ballantine Books, 2010). A more challenging, meticulously researched and nuanced interpretation is available in David Critchley, *The Origin of Organized Crime in America: The New York City Mafia, 1891–1931* (New York: Routledge, 2008).

38. Some of the most prominent works that support this view include Ed Reid, *Mafia: The History of the Ruthless Gang That Rules the Nationwide Crime Syndicate* (New York: Random House, 1952); Donald R. Cressey, *Theft of the Nation: The Structure and Operations of Organized Crime in America* (New York: Harper & Row, 1969); Claire Sterling, *Octopus: The Long Reach of the International Sicilian Mafia* (New York: W.W. Norton, 1990); Stephen Fox, *Blood and Power: Organized Crime in 20th-Century America* (New York: Penguin Books, 1990); Thomas Reppetto, *American Mafia: A History of Its Rise to Power* (New York: Henry Holt, 2004); Selwyn Raab, *Five Families: The Rise, Decline, and Resurgence of America's Most Powerful Mafia Empires* (New York: Thomas Dunne Books, 2006). The most thorough revision of the role of the Castellammarese War is David Critchley, "Buster, Maranzano and the Castellammare War, 1930–1931," *Global Crime* 7:1 (2006): pp. 43–78.

39. Peter Maas, *The Valachi Papers* (New York: Putnam, 1968).

40. *Rockford (Illinois) Republic*, December 12, 1927.

## Chapter 1

1. Raymond Chandler, "The Simple Art of Murder," *Saturday Review of Literature* (April 15, 1950): p. 13.

2. For a reasonable overview, see George S. Larke, "Organized Crime: Mafia Myth in Film and Television," in Paul Mason, ed., *Criminal Visions: Media Representations of Crime and Justice* (Cullompton, UK: Willan, 2003), pp. 116–130.

3. Dwight C. Smith, *The Mafia Mystique* (New York: Basic Books, 1974).

4. The most explicit examples of this view of the Mafia's origins tend to be rather old, such as those found in Herbert Asbury, *The French Quarter: An Informal History of the New Orleans Underworld* (New York: 1936); John E. Coxe, "The New Orleans Mafia Incident," *Louisiana Historical Quarterly* 20 (1937): pp. 1067–1110; John S. Kendall, "Who Killa de Chief?" *Louisiana Historical Quarterly* 22 (1939): pp. 492–530. But the essence of their interpretation lives on, not least in the bulk of Internet articles and popular television programs connected with the American Mafia's origins.

5. *Daily Picayune*, November 12, 1890.

6. See Rick Halpern, "Solving the 'Labor Problem': Race, Work and the State in the Sugar Industries of Louisiana and Natal, 1870–1910," *Journal of Southern African Studies*, 30:1 (2004): pp. 36–38.

7. Figures taken from Joseph Masselli and Dominic Candeloro, *Italians in New Orleans* (Mount Pleasant, SC: 2004); Louise Reynes Edwards-Simpson, "Sicilian Immigration to New Orleans, 1870–1910: Ethnicity, Race and Social Position in the New South" (Ph.D. diss., University of Minnesota, 1996); Robert L. Brandfon, "The End of Immigration to the Cotton Fields," *Mississippi Valley Historical Review* 50 (March 1964); and Mary Ann Riviere, *From Palermo to New Orleans* (Lake Charles, LA: 1991).

8. G. Cunningham, "The Italian, a Hindrance to White Solidarity in Louisiana, 1890–1898," *Journal of Negro History* 50:1 (January 1965): pp. 22–36.

9. *Congressional Record* 48th Congress, Session II, February 26, 1885, p. 332.

10. Annie Proulx, *Accordion Crimes* (New York: 2009), p. 49.

11. Appleton Morgan, "What Shall We Do With the Dago?" *Popular Science Monthly* 38 (Dec. 1890), p. 173.

12. *Daily Picayune*, November 12, 1890.

13. For details of Raffo's killing and the Geraci trial, see the *Times-Picayune*, July 27, 1890.

14. *New Orleans Times-Democrat*, October 21, 1890.

15. For examples of the variety and spread of coverage immediately after the murder, see the *Times Picayune*, October 17, 1890; *New York Herald*, October 19, 1890; *San Francisco Bulletin*, October 21, 1890; *Bismarck (North Dakota) Tribune*, October 31, 1890.

16. The position of the reformers over the influence of the Lottery is described in the *Daily Picayune*, July 1, 1890.

17. For details of Louisiana politics in these years, see Joy Jackson, "Bosses and Businessmen in Gilded Age New Orleans Politics," *Louisiana History* 5:4 (Autumn 1964): pp. 387–400.

18. For Macheca's own account, see the *New Orleans Bulletin*, September 17, 1874.

19. Joseph Shakespeare cited in the *Daily Picayune*, October 18, 1890.

20. *New York Herald*, May 15, 1891.

21. David Leon Chandler, *Brothers in Blood* (Toronto: 1975), n p. 81, probably tops the body count with a claim that there were ninety such murders between 1869 and 1889.

22. The list is reproduced in full in United States Department of State, "The Executive Documents of the House of Representatives for the First Session of the Fifty-Second Congress," *Foreign Relations of the United States* (Washington, D.C., 1892), pp. 706–711.

23. See Humbert S. Nelli, *The Business of Crime* (Chicago: University of Chicago Press, 1976), pp. 31–34.

24. Some of the best accounts of the scope of Hennessy's inquiries can be found in the *Times-Picayune*, March 18, 1891, and *New Orleans Item*, May 15, 1891.

25. William Pinkerton to the *Baton Rouge Daily Advocate*, March 17, 1891.

26. For details of Corte's statement, see the *Times-Picayune*, March 17, 1891.

27. This theory is discussed in Thomas Hunt and Martha Macheca Sheldon, *Deep Water* (New York: 2007), pp. 53–58. The frustratingly sparse primary sources that relate details to Carvanna's life and fate are pretty well limited to a statement made by Hennessy's secretary, George Washington Vandervoort, in the papers of the time; for example, see the *New Orleans Daily States*, March 17, 1891.

28. For details, see the coroner's report in *Times-Picayune*, October 19, 1881.

29. The trial is detailed in the *Times-Picayune*, April 24 through April 28.

30. George Washington Vandervoort cited in the *Times-Picayune*, March 18, 1891.

31. Grand jury report cited in the *Times-Picayune*, May 6, 1891, and *New Orleans Item*, May 6, 1891.

32. Details of O'Malley's departure and claim can be found in the *Philadelphia Inquirer*, March 17, 1891.

33. See *New Orleans Item*, March 22, 1891, and the grand jury report, May 6, 1891.

34. *New Orleans Item*, March 23, 1891.

35. Interview with O'Malley in the *New Orleans Item*, April 4, 1891.

36. *Highland Beacon News* cited in the *Times-Picayune*, March 25, 1891.

37. *New York Times*, March 17, 1891.

38. Grand jury report cited in the *New York Tribune*, May 6, 1891, and *New Orleans Item*, May 6, 1891.

39. *New York Times* cited in the *Baltimore Sun*, March 21, 1891. For an assessment of national press reaction, see Christine DeLucia, "Getting the Story Straight: Press Coverage of Italian-American Lynchings from 1856–1910," *Italian Americana* 21:2 (Summer 2003): pp. 212–221.

40. *Texas Siftings*, April 4, 1891.

41. *Daily Picayune*, July 22, 1899.

42. *Philadelphia Inquirer*, March 17, 1891, and *New York Herald*, March 17, 1891.

43. Figures extrapolated from Daniel T. Williams, "The Lynching Records at the Tuskegee Institute," in Kidada E. Williams, *Eight Negro Biographies* (New York: 1970), pp. 3–7, and W. Fitzhugh Brundage, ed., *Under Sentence of Death: Lynching in the South* (Chapel Hill: University of North Carolina Press, 1997), p. 15.

44. *London Times*, March 25, 1891.

45. *St. Albans (Vermont) Messenger*, March 19, 1891.

46. *New York Herald*, March 17, 1891.

47. See, for example, *San Francisco Chronicle*, April 5, 1891; *Los Angeles Times*, April 2, 1891; *Baltimore Sun*, April 2, 1891; *Atlanta Constitution*, April 2, 1891; *Boston Globe*, March 17, 1891; *New York Tribune*, April 16, 1891; *Washington Post*, April 2, 1891; and *Chicago Tribune*, March 18, 1891.

48. *Atlanta Constitution*, April 2, 1891.

49. See *New Orleans Times-Democrat* and *Times Picayune*, August 9, 1896.

50. Cited in Salvatore J. LaGumina, *Wop!: A Documentary History of Anti-Italian Discrimination* (Toronto: 1999), p. 87.

51. Cited in John Higham, *Strangers in the Land: Patterns of American Nativism 1860–1925* (New Brunswick, NJ: 1955), p. 90.

52. Cited in Cristogianni Borsella, *On Persecution, Identity and Activism: Aspects of the Italian-American Experience from the Late 19th Century to Today* (Boston: 2005), p. 59.

53. *Tacoma Daily News*, January 13, 1892.

54. *San Francisco Chronicle*, January 3, 1892.

55. *New York Herald*, January 24, 1892.

## Chapter 2

1. *Boston Journal*, April 14, 1876.

2. Y. Gilinsky and Y. Kostjukovsky, "From Thievish Cartel to Criminal Corporation: The History of Organized Crime in Russia," in C. Fijnaut and L. Paoli, eds., *Organized Crime in Europe* (New York: Springer, 2004), p. 189.

3. John Dickie, *Blood Brotherhoods*.

4. O.M. Ismael, "Illegal Bunkering in Nigeria: A Background and Analysis," *Strategic Insights* 23 (April 2010): p. 8.

5. Allan Nevins, *Hamilton Fish: The Inner History of the Grant Administration*, vol. 2 (New York: Fredrick Unger, 1936), p. 766.

6. Figures taken from David P. Dyer, *Autobiography and Reminiscences* (St. Louis: William Harvey Miner and Co., 1922), p. 154.

7. For details of duty policies, see William F. Shughart, *Taxing Choice: The Predatory Politics of Fiscal Discrimination* (New Brunswick, NJ: The Independent Institute, 1997), pp. 54–65.

8. *New York Evening Post*, December 17, 1867.

9. John McDonald, *Secrets of the Great Whiskey Ring* (St. Louis: W.S. Bryan, 1880), pp. 17–18.

10. Timothy Rives, "Grant, Babcock and the Whiskey Ring," *Prologue Magazine* 32:3 (Fall 2000).

11. James Ford Rhodes, *History of the United States from the Compromise of 1850 to the Final Restoration of Home Rule at the South in 1877* (New York: Macmillan, 1912), p. 187.

12. H.V. Boynton, "The Whiskey Ring," *North American Review* 123:253 (Oct. 1876): p. 327.

13. *New York Times*, February 13, 1876.

14. Julian P. Boyd et al., eds., *The Papers of Thomas Jefferson*, vol. 12 (Princeton: Princeton University Press, 1950), p. 442.

15. The Rev. Royal H. Pullman cited in *Baltimore Sun*, October 5, 1885.

16. Searches carried out using the keyword "bossism" in the *New York Times* Proquest archive and the Library of Congress's *Chronicling America*.

17. William Stead, "Mr. Richard Croker and Greater New York," *Review of Reviews* 16 (October 1897): p. 351.

18. "The Deadly Danger of the Boss and the Gang" in *Colorado Springs Gazette*, January 16, 1903.

19. Joseph B. Bishop, "Are the Bosses Stronger than the People?" *The Century Magazine* (July 1897): p. 465.

20. *New York Times*, March 11, 1894.

21. James Bryce, *The American Commonwealth*, vol. 2 (New York: Macmillan, 1888), p. 106.

22. Moisei Ostrogorski, *Democracy and the Organization of Political Parties*, vol. 2: *The United States* (New York: Macmillan, 1902), p. 161.

23. Figures taken from John J. Lalor, *Cyclopedia of Political Science*, vol. 3, rev. ed. (New York: Maynard, Merrill and Co., 1899), p. 239; New York City Board of Aldermen, *Report of the Special Committee to Investigate the Ring Frauds* (New York: M.B. Brown, 1878), p. 136, and John I. Davenport, *The Election Frauds of New York City and Their Prevention*, vol. 1: *Eleven Years of Fraud, 1860–1870* (New York: J.I. Davenport, 1881), pp. 268–270.

24. *New York Times*, April 13, 1878.

25. For historiography see David R. Colburn and George E Pozzetta, "Bosses and Machines: Changing Interpretations in American History," *The History Teacher* 9:3 (May 1976): pp. 445–463. More current is Terry Golway, *Machine Made: Tammany Hall and the Creation of Modern American Politics* (New York: Liveright, 2014), pp. i–xiv.

26. H. Boulay and A. DiGaetano, "Why Did Political Machines Disappear?" *Journal of Urban History* (November 1985): pp. 25–41.

27. M. Craig Brown and Barbara D. Warner, "Immigrants, Urban Politics and Policing in 1900," *American Sociological Review* 57:3 (June 1992): p. 294.

28. Figures taken from *New York Times*, July 18, 1880, and Oliver E. Allen, *The Tiger: The Rise and Fall of Tammany Hall* (Reading, MA: Da Capo Press, 1993), pp. 105.

29. Mark H. Haller, "Organized Crime in Urban Society: Chicago in the Twentieth Century," *Journal of Social History* (Winter 1972): p. 211.

30. Stephen P. Erie, *Rainbow's End: Irish-Americans and the Dilemmas of Urban Machine Politics, 1840–1985* (Berkeley: University of California Press, 1988), p. 64; Tomasz Inglot and John P Pelissero, "Ethnic Politics in a Machine City: Chicago's Poles at Rainbow's End," *Urban Affairs Quarterly* 28 (June 1993): pp. 526–543; and Thomas M. Henderson, *Tammany Hall and the New Immigrants: The Progressive Years* (New York: Arno Press, 1976), passim.

31. *San Francisco Bulletin*, October 2, 1871.

32. *New York Herald-Tribune*, October 4, 1894.

33. David C. Hammack, *Power and Society: Greater New York at the Turn of the Century* (New York: Russell Sage Foundation, 1982), p. 187.

34. Cited in Ostrogorski, op. cit., p. 408.

35. Henry Champernowne, *The Boss: An Essay upon the Art of Governing American Cities* (New York: George H Richmond and Co., 1894), pp. 113–115.

36. William L. Riordan, *Plunkitt of Tammany Hall* (New York: McClure, Phillips, & Co., 1905), passim.

37. *Chicago Daily Tribune*, April 1, 1893.

38. William T. Stead, *If Christ Came to Chicago: A Plea for the Union of All Who Love in the Service of All Who Suffer* (London: Review of Reviews, 1894), p. 222.

39. Orville D. Menard, *Political Bossism in Mid-America: Tom Dennison's Omaha, 1900–1933* (Lanham, MD: University Press of America, 1989).

40. See Joy Jackson, "Bosses and Businessmen in Gilded Age New Orleans Politics," *Louisiana History* 5:4 (Autumn 1964): pp. 387–400.

41. Most of these accounts draw, to a greater or lesser extent, on the "firsthand" account of the settlement John S. McClintock, *Pioneer Days in the Black Hills*, rev. ed. (Norman: University of Oklahoma Press, 2000), in Swearengen's case especially pp. 69–70 and 164. See also Richard White, *It is Your Fault and None of My Own: A New History of the American West* (Norman: University of Oklahoma Press, 1991), pp. 353–389.

## Chapter 3

1. *Chicago Tribune*, September 6, 1920, and *Boston Globe*, September 8, 1920.

2. *New York Times*, September 7, 1920; Kim Long, *The Almanac of Political Corruption, Scandals and Dirty Politics* (New York: Delacorte Press, 2007), p. 143.

3. *New York Times*, January 20, 1930.

4. Chicago gang members and gangs are listed in the Al Capone section of the *FBI Records*, file 9: "Memorandum for the File July 28, 1936."

5. Richard T. Enright, *Capone's Chicago* (Lakeville, MN: Northstar Maschek Books: 1931).

6. Walter Noble Burns, *The One-Way Ride: The Red Trail of Chicago Gangland from Prohibition to Jake Lingle* (Garden City, NY: Doubleday, Doran, 1931).

7. For a good example of this school, see Fred D. Pasley, *Al Capone: The Biography of a Self-Made Man* (New York: Washburn, 1930).

8. *Chicago Tribune*, May 13, 1931.

9. Robin F. Bachin, *Building the South Side: Urban Space and Civic Culture in Chicago, 1890–1919* (Chicago: University of Chicago Press, 2004), p. 303.

10. Frank J. Loesch in the *Chicago Tribune*, March 25, 1931.

11. John Landesco, "Organized Crime in Chicago," in Illinois Association for Criminal Justice, *The Illinois Crime Survey* (Chicago: Blakely, 1929), p. 902.

12. Herbert Asbury, *The Gangs of Chicago* (New York: Alfred Knopf, 1940), p. 337.

13. Kenneth Allsop, *The Bootleggers: The Story of Chicago's Prohibition Era* (New York: Doubleday, 1961), p. 204.

14. Robert M. Lombardo, *Organized Crime in Chicago: Beyond the Mafia* (Urbana: University of Illinois Press, 2013), p. 88.

15. William Allen White, *Masks in a Pageant* (New York: Macmillan, 1928), p. 484.

16. John Bright, *Hizzoner Big Bill Thompson: An Idyll of Chicago* (New York: J. Cape and H. Smith, 1930), pp. 282–283.

17. Lloyd Wendt and Herman Kogan, *Big Bill of Chicago* (Indianapolis: Bobbs-Merrill, 1953).

18. Douglas Bukowski, *Big Bill Thompson, Chicago and the Politics of Image* (Chicago: University of Illinois Press, 1998).

19. Gerald Leinwand, *Mackerels in the Moonlight: Four Corrupt American Mayors* (Jefferson, NC: McFarland, 2004), pp. 63–64.

20. *Chicago Tribune*, June 2, 2009.

21. George Schottenhamel, "How Big Bill Thompson Won Control of Chicago," *Journal of the Illinois State Historical Society* 45 (Spring 1952), pp. 30–49.

22. John Kobler, *Capone: The Life and World of Al Capone* (Cambridge, MA: Da Capo Press, 1971), p. 62.

23. Edward R. Kantowicz, *Polish-American Politics in Chicago, 1880–1940* (Chicago: University of Chicago Press, 1975), pp. 152–153.

24. *Chicago Tribune*, December 9, 1921.

25. *Chicago Tribune*, December 19, 1921.

26. Kobler, op. cit., p. 62.

27. *Daily Illinois State Register*, November 4, 1922.

28. Cited in Bryan B. Sterling and Francis N. Sterling, *Will Rogers' World: America's Foremost Political Humorist Comments on the '20s and '30s and '80s and '90s* (New York: M. Evans, 1993), p. 42.

29. *Washington Post*, May 14, 1923, and *New York Times*, November 18, 1923.

30. *New York Times*, May 22, 1928, and *Augusta (Georgia) Chronicle*, June 11, 1930.

31. *Chicago Daily News*, March 24, 1928.

32. *New York Times*, June 5, 1926.

33. Carl Schurz Lowden, "Chicago, The Nation's Crime Center," *Current History* 28:6 (Sept. 1, 1928): p. 892.

34. Illinois Association for Criminal Justice, *The Illinois Crime Survey* (Chicago: Blakely, 1929), p. 923.

35. *New York Times*, November 22, 1927.

36. Examples can be found in the *Seattle Daily Times*, April 29, 1926; *Baltimore Sun*, February 22, 1927; and *Chicago Daily Tribune*, May 29, 1927.

37. *Montreal Star* cited in *Hyde Park (Illinois) Herald*, May 14, 1926.

38. *Daily Illinois State Journal*, April 4, 1928.

39. J. Anne Funderburg, *Bootleggers and Beer Barons of the Prohibition Era* (Jefferson, NC: McFarland, 2014), p. 336.

40. *Bellingham (Washington) Herald*, July 18, 1927.

41. Cited in Fred D. Pasley, *Al Capone: The Biography of a Self-made Man* (Garden City, NY: 1930), pp. 202–203.

42. William Allen White, "They Can't Beat My Big Boy," *Collier's* 79 (June 18, 1927): p. 8.

43. *Daily Register Gazette* (Rockford, IL), August 5, 1927.

44. James Fentress, *Eminent Gangsters: Immigrants and the Birth of Organized Crime in America* (Lanham, MD: University Press of America, 2010), p. 258.

45. Quotation taken from Illinois Association for Criminal Justice, *The Illinois Crime Survey* (Chicago: Blakely, 1929), p. 902. For contemporary comment, see *Cleveland Plain Dealer*, April 5, 1927.

46. *Chicago Daily News*, April 3, 1928.

47. *New York Times*, February 4, 1931.

48. *Chicago Tribune*, February 17, 1931.

49. For example Reinhard H. Luthin and Allan Nevins, *American Demagogues: Twentieth Century* (Boston: Beacon Press, 1954), p. 96; Kenneth Allsop, *The Bootleggers: The Story of Chicago's Prohibition Era* (London: Hutchinson, 1961), p. 204; Luciano Iorizzo, *Al Capone: A Biography* (Westport, CT: Greenwood, 2003), p. 59.

50. Herbert Asbury, *The Gangs of Chicago* (New York: Alfred Knopf, 1940), p. 340.

51. William Allen White, *Masks in a Pageant* (New York: Macmillan, 1928), pp. 497–499.

52. Illinois Association for Criminal Justice, *The Illinois Crime Survey* (Chicago: Blakely, 1929), p. 902.

53. Matthew G. Yeager, *Illegal Enterprise: The Work of Historian Mark Haller* (Lanham, MD: University Press of America, 2013), pp. 30–33.

54. Herbert Asbury, *The Gangs of Chicago* (New York: Alfred Knopf, 1940), p. 337.

55. Robert G. Folsom, *The Money Trail: How Elmer Irey and his T-Men Brought Down America's Criminal Elite* (Washington, D.C.: Potomac Books, 2010), p. 53, and Bill Bryson, *One Summer: America 1927* (London: Doubleday, 2013), p. 532.

56. John H. Lyle, *The Dry and Lawless Years* (London: Prentice Hall, 1960), p. 256.

57. David E. Ruth, *Inventing the Public Enemy: The Gangster in American Culture, 1918–1934* (Chicago: University of Chicago Press, 1996).

58. *Springfield Republican*, April 12, 1931.

59. *Chicago Daily Tribune*, December 20, 1932.

60. *Chicago Daily Tribune*, December 20, 21 and 22, 1932, and January 1, 1933.

61. *Chicago Daily Tribune*, September 28, 1933.

62. *Chicago Tribune*, February 16, 1933.

63. *Chicago Tribune*, March 7, 2013; Edward M. Burke, "Lunatics and Anarchists: Political Homicide," *Chicago Journal of Criminal Law and Criminology* 92:3 (Spring 2002): p. 798; and John H. Lyle, *The Dry and Lawless Years* (London: Prentice-Hall, 1960), pp. 258–268.

64. Gus Russo, *The Outfit: The Role of Chicago's Underworld in the Shaping of America* (London: Bloomsbury, 2001), pp. 86–98.

65. Robert M. Lombardo, *Organized Crime in Chicago: Beyond the Mafia* (Urbana: University of Illinois Press, 2013), pp. 97–98.

## Chapter 4

1. Henry F. Pringle, "Jimmy Walker," *The American Mercury* (November 1926): p. 272.

2. See Enright's obituary in the *New York Times*, September 5, 1953.

3. *Time*, August 23, 1926.

4. Michael A. Lerner, *Dry Manhattan: Prohibition in New York City* (Cambridge, MA: Harvard University Press, 2007), pp. 160–170.

5. A detailed account of the murder and Vivian Gordon's threats to expose the NYPD can be had in the *New York Times*, February 27, 1931.

6. Letter from Vivian Gordon to John E.C. Bischoff, dated January 19, 1931, cited in the *New York Times*, February 28, 1931.

7. Herbert Mitgang, *Once Upon a Time in New York: Jimmy Walker, Franklin Roosevelt and the Last Great Battle of the Jazz Age* (New York: Cooper Square Press, 2000), p. 105.

8. See *New York Tribune*, February 27, 1931.

9. *New York Times*, February 28, 1931.

10. *Baltimore Sun*, March 18, 1931.

11. *New York Times*, May 1, 1931.

12. *New York Times*, June 19, 1931.

13. *New York Times*, July 1, 1931.

14. *Los Angeles Times*, June 9, 1932.

15. *New York Tribune*, December 3, 1893.

16. New York State Senate, *Report and Proceedings of the Senate Committee Appointed to Investigate the Police Department of the City of New York* (Albany: J.B. Lyon, 1895), pp. 2752–2754, 2843, 3136, 3253, and 3548–3549.

17. Michael P. Roth et al., *Historical Dictionary of Law Enforcement* (New Haven, CT: Greenwood, 2000), p. 93.

18. *New York Times* obituary of William S. Devery, June 21, 1919.

## Chapter 5

1. Dennis Lehane in *New York Times*, September 4, 2014.

2. *New York Times*, September 4, 2014.

3. Guy W. Finney, *The Great Los Angeles Bubble: A Present Day Story of Colossal Financial Jugglery and the Penalties Paid* (Los Angeles: Forbes, 1929).

4. Richard Rayner, *A Bright and Guilty Place: Murder, Corruption and LA's Scandalous Coming of Age* (New York: Doubleday, 2009).

5. John Buntin, *LA Noir: The Struggle for the Soul of America's Most Seductive City* (London: Orion Books, 2014).

6. Albert Atwood, "Money From Everywhere," *Saturday Evening Post* (May 12, 1923): p. 10.

7. Kevin Starr, *The Dream Endures: California Enters the 1940s* (New York: Oxford University Press, 1997), p. 159, Rayner, p. 3.

8. Remi Nadeau, *Los Angeles: From Mission to Modern City* (New York: Longmans, Green and Co., 1960), p. 214.

9. Anne Marie Kooistra, "Angels for Sale: The History of Prostitution in Los Angeles, 1880–1940" (Ph.D. diss., University of Southern California, 2003), pp. 181–189.

10. Carey McWilliams, "Los Angeles," *Overland Monthly and Out West Magazine* (May 1927): pp. 135–136.

11. Kenneth Anger, *Hollywood Babylon* (San Francisco: Straight Arrow Press, 1975).

12. Carey McWilliams, *Southern California: An Island on the Land* (Salt Lake City: Gibbs Smith, 1948), p. 243.

13. Guy W. Finney, *The Great Los Angeles Bubble*, p. 186.

14. Finney, pp. 11–12.

15. McWilliams, *Southern California*, p. 136.

16. Details of Chandler's fortune taken from his obituary in *Chicago Tribune*, September 24, 1944.

17. *Saturday Evening Post*, June 5, 1926.

18. "Harry Chandler and Harrison Gray Otis," *California Journal* 30:11 (1999): p. 24.

19. *Los Angeles Times*, April 26 and May 31, 1921.

20. *Los Angeles Times*, July 29, August 1, 16, 18, 1923, and July 23, 1924.

21. *Los Angeles Times*, April 17, 1925.

22. *Los Angeles Times*, April 13, 1926, and John Buntin, *LA Noir*, p. 28.

23. *Los Angeles Times*, May 21, 1931, and Buntin, op. cit., pp. 29–30.

24. Jules Tygiel, *The Great Los Angeles Swindle: Oil, Stocks and Scandal During the Roaring Twenties* (Berkeley: University of California Press, 1994), p. 177.

25. *Los Angeles Evening Express*, February 19, 1928.

26. See, for example, *Los Angeles Times*, December 22, 1929; *Washington Post*, December 22, 1929; and *San Francisco Chronicle*, December 22, 1929.

27. Duncan Aikman, "Savonarola in Los Angeles," *American Mercury* (December 1930): pp. 423–430.

28. *Los Angeles Times*, April 1, 1930.

29. *Los Angeles Times*, November 19, 1930.

30. *Los Angeles Times*, August 2 and October 28, 1928; July 1 and 11, August 22, October 17 and 25, 1929; and January 1 and 3, 1930. Quote from *Los Angeles Times*, October 25, 1929.

31. *Los Angeles Times*, December 2, 1931.

32. *Los Angeles Times*, August 11, 1932.

33. Kevin Starr, *The Dream Endures: California Enters the 1940s* (Oxford: Oxford University Press, 1997), pp. 166–167.

34. Joseph Gerald Woods, "The Progressives and the Police: Urban Reform and the Professionalization of the Los Angeles Police" (Ph.D. diss., University of California at Los Angeles, 1973); and Fred Viehe, "The Recall of Mayor Frank L Shaw: A Revision," *California Historical Quarterly* 59 (Winter 1980/1981): pp. 290–305.

35. Buntin, *LA Noir*, pp. 56–58.

36. For example, *Los Angeles Times*, February 28, 1932.

37. Sharon Elaine Sekhon, "Exposing Sin City: Southern California Sense of Place and the Los Angeles Anti-Myth" (Ph.D. diss., University of Southern California, 2002); and Thomas Sitton, "Urban Politics and Reform in New Deal Los Angeles: The Recall of Mayor Frank Shaw" (Ph.D. diss., University of California, Riverside, 1983), pp. 3–5.

38. Sitton, op. cit., pp. 59–61.

39. Sitton, pp. 113–114.

40. See C.K. Allen, "Crime Inc.," *The Spectator* (August 31, 1951): pp. 262–263.

41. Matt Weinstock, *My LA* (New York: Current Books, 1947), p. 54.

42. James H. Richardson, *For the Life of Me: Memoirs of a City Editor* (New York: Putnam's, 1954), p. 213.

43. Weinstock, *My LA*, pp. 55–56.

44. Theodore J. Lowi, *The End of Liberalism: The Second Republic of the United States* (New York: W.W. Norton, 1979), p. 3.

45. Robert Gottlieb and Irene Wolt, *Thinking Big: A History of The Los Angeles Times* (New York: Putnam's, 1977), p. 224.

46. Sitton, pp. 85–117.

47. *Los Angeles Record*, April 22, 1927.

48. Joe Domanick, *To Protect and to Serve: The LAPD's Century of War in the City of Dreams* (New York: Pocket Books, 1994), pp. 40–44.

49. *Hollywood Citizen-News*, November 29, 1933.

50. *Los Angeles Times*, July 9, 11, and August 8, 1937; and Fred W. Viehe, "The Recall of Mayor Frank Shaw," pp. 296–297.

51. *Los Angeles Times*, September 27, 1936, and September 9, 10 and 17, 1937.

52. *Los Angeles Times*, September 11 and 15, 1937.

53. *Los Angeles Examiner*, March 10, 1938.

54. Viehe, pp. 291–293.

55. Chandler, *The Long Goodbye*, p. 213.

## *Chapter 6*

1. Timothy Gilfoyle, *City of Eros* (New York: 1992).

2. Jeffrey Adler, *First in Violence, Deepest in Dirt* (Cambridge, MA: 2006).

3. Federico Varese, *Mafias on the Move* (Princeton: 2011).

4. See Michael Woodiwiss, *Organized Crime and American Power* (Toronto: 2001), and Michael Woodiwiss and Dick Hobbs, "Organized Evil and the Atlantic Alliance: Moral Panics and the Rhetoric of Organized Crime Policing in America and Britain," *The British Journal of Criminology* 49 (2011).

5. This idea of "frozen images" is taken from Robert Wiebe, *The Search for Order, 1877–1920* (New York: 1967), p. 96, and expounded in Woodiwiss (2001), op. cit., p. 173.

6. U.S. Senate, *Hearings Before the Subcommittee of the Judiciary on The National Prohibition Law* 69th Congress (Washington, D.C., 1926), p. 154.

7. *Ibid.*, p. 79.

8. See *New York Times*, December 4, 5 and 13, 1925.

9. See *New York Times*, July 4, 1920, and C. Stout, *The Eighteenth Amendment and the Part Played by Organized Medicine* (New York: 1921), p. 48.

10. For details of Dwyer's career, methods and demise, see Herbert Asbury, *The Great Illusion: An Informal History of Prohibition* (New York: 1950), pp. 253–254, and Fred J. Cook, *The Secret Rulers: Criminal Syndicates and How They Control the U.S. Underworld* (New York: 1966), pp. 72–74.

11. Figures and quote taken from M.R. Werner, *Privileged Characters* (New York: 1935), p. 275, and William A. Cook, *King of the Bootleggers: A Biography of George Remus* (London: 2008), pp. 49–50.

12. Herbert Asbury, *The Great Illusion*, p. 221.

13. Writers Program of the Work Projects Administration in the State of Ohio, *Cincinnati: A Guide to the Queen City and Its Neighbors* (Cincinnati: 1943), p. 126.

14. Remus cited in Edward Behr, *Prohibition: Thirteen Years That Changed America* (New York: 1996), p. 102.

15. F. LaGuardia in *Congressional Record*, August 20, 1919, p. 4071.

16. F. LaGuardia in *Congressional Record*, March 24, 1926, pp. 6174–76; July 3, 1926, pp. 13012–15; and *New York Times*, October 7, 1927; *New York World*, December 9, 1927; *New York World*, December 11, 1927; and *New York Times*, December 20, 1927.

17. F. LaGuardia in *Congressional Record*, February 7, 1925, p. 3276.

18. F. LaGuardia in *Congressional Record*, March 24, 1926, p. 6175.

19. F. LaGuardia in *Congressional Record*, March 24, 1926, p. 6175.

20. Cook, *King of the Bootleggers*, p. 45.

21. Duff Gilfond, "LaGuardia of Harlem," *American Mercury* (June 1927): p. 153.

22. U.S. Senate, *Hearings Before the Subcommittee of the Judiciary on The National Prohibition Law* 69th Congress (Washington, D.C., 1926), p. 222.

23. See Michael A. Lerner, *Dry Manhattan: Prohibition in New York City* (Cambridge, MA: 2007), pp. 106–107.

24. Cited in Richard C. Lindberg, *To Serve and Collect: Chicago Politics and Police Corruption from the Lager Beer Riot to the Summerdale Scandal 1855–1960* (New York: Praeger Press, 1991), p. 161.

25. *New York Times*, January 12, 1920.

26. Imogen B. Oakley, "The American People vs. the Alien Bootlegger," *The Outlook* (May 5, 1926): p. 18.

27. *New York Times*, December 21, 1920.

28. Billy Sunday cited in Andrew Sinclair, *Prohibition: The Era of Excess* (New York: 1962), p. 248.

29. For an analysis of the ethnicity and nationality of the leading bootleggers of the era, see Alan Block, *East Side-West Side: Organizing Crime in New York 1930–1950* (New Brunswick, NJ: 1983), pp. 131–141.

30. See, for example, Claire Stirling, *The Mafia* (London: Hamish Hamilton, 1990), pp. 61–62.

31. For example, see Carl Sifakis, *The Encyclopedia of American Crime* (New York: 1982), p. 589.

32. See Varese, op. cit., pp. 106–121, and David Critchley, *The Origins of Organized Crime in America* (London: 2009).

33. See Daniel Fuchs, "Where Al Capone Grew Up," *The New Republic* (September 9, 1931): pp. 95–97.

34. Lewis W. Hunt, "The Rise of a Racketeer: A Portrait of Alphonse Capone," *The Outlook* (December 10, 1930): pp. 574–576.

35. Katherine Fullerton Gerould, "Jessica and Al Capone," *Harper's* (June 1931): p. 93.

36. Pasley, *Al Capone*, p. 352.

37. Ed Reid, *Mafia* (New York: 1952), p. 41.

38. Peter Bart, "The G-Men's Propaganda Machine," *Variety* 387:3 (June 3, 2002): p. 3, 54.

39. Mario Puzo, *The Godfather* (New York: 1969), pp. 285–288.

40. Puzo cited in George De Stefano, *An Offer We Can't Refuse: The Mafia in the Mind of America* (New York: Faber and Faber, 2006), p. 113.

41. Lydia Miranda Oram, "Sentimental Mafia, This Invisible Thing of Ours: The Mafia and Politics in American and Italian Film and Media" (Ph.D. diss., University of New York, 2011), pp. 44–63.

42. U.S. Congress, Select Committee on Improper Activities in the Labor or Management Field, 1958 cited in David Critchley, *The Origins of Organized Crime in America* (New York: 2009), p. 138.

43. For example, see Michael Woodiwiss, *Crime Crusades and Corruption: Prohibitions in the United States 1900–1987* (London: 1988), pp. 105–107.

44. *New York Times*, May 26, 1930.

45. See Ralph Bushnell Potts, *Seattle Heritage* (Seattle: 1955), pp. 79–83.

46. Taken from *Baltimore Sun*, August 30, 1930.

47. *Seattle Times*, March 8, 1926.

48. *Seattle Times*, November 17, 1927.

49. *Baltimore Sun*, August 30, 1930.

50. Mabel Walker Willebrandt, *The Inside of Prohibition* (Indianapolis: 1929), p. 237.

51. *Baltimore Sun*, August 30, 1930.

52. Cited in *Literary Digest* (June 16, 1928): p. 10; and "New Dred Scott Decision," *Outlook* (June 1928): p. 293.

53. Isidor Einstein, *Prohibition Agent No. 1* (New York: Frederick A. Stokes, 1932).

54. Franklin Adams, "Conning Tower," published in the *New York World* and cited in David Kyvig, *Repealing National Prohibition* (Chicago: 1979), p. 114.

55. Figures taken from Daniel Okrent, *Last Call: The Rise and Fall of Prohibition* (New York: Scribner's, 2011), pp. 360–362; and T.Y. Hu, *The Liquor Tax in the United States* (New York: Columbia Business School, 1950), pp. 160 and 164.

56. Cited in the *New York Times*, December 29, 1926.

57. "Dr. Norris's Poison Liquor Report," *Literary Digest* (February 26, 1927): p. 14.

58. Figures taken from Deborah Blum, *The Poisoner's Handbook* (London: 2010), pp. 152–155; and "New York's Liquor-Poison Epidemic," *Literary Digest* (October 27, 1928): p. 16.

59. Quotations and statistics taken from "Murder by Poison Bootleg Liquor," *Literary Digest* (January 15, 1927): pp. 7–9.

60. "Dr. Norris's Poison Liquor Report," *Literary Digest* (February 26, 1927): p. 14.

61. Chief Justice William Howard Taft cited in "Wiretapping Held Legal," *Literary Digest* (June 16, 1928): p. 10.

## Chapter 7

1. Cited in James B. Jacobs, *Mobsters, Unions, and Feds: The Mafia and the American Labor Movement* (New York: New York University Press, 2006), p. xvi.

2. Harry Millis and Royal Montgomery, *Organized Labor* (New York: McGraw-Hill, 1945), p. 670.

3. Craig M. Bradley, "Anti-Racketeering Legislation in America," *The American Journal of Comparative Law* (Fall 2006): pp. 677–678; United States Senate, *Investigation of So-Called Rackets: Hearings Before a Subcommittee of the Committee On Commerce* 73rd Congress, 2nd Session (1933), pp. 80–86.

4. Michael Woodiwiss, *Organized Crime and American Power* (London: University of Toronto Press, 2001), p. 10.

5. Carl Sifakis, *The Mafia File: The A–Z of Organized Crime in America* (New York: Equation Books, 1988), p. 21.

6. *Chicago Tribune*, May 18, 1929.

7. Walter Nobel Burns, *The One-Way Ride: The Red Trail of Chicago Gangland from Prohibition to Jake Lingle* (New York: Doubleday, 1931).

8. For an idea of the support for the account, see Michael Woodiwiss, "Fifty Years Investigating Institutional Corruption and Organized Crime: An Interview with Selwyn Raab," *Trends in Organized Crime* 18.1–2 (June 2015): pp. 78–79.

9. *New York Times*, March 23, 1939.

10. Mike Woodiwiss in unpublished manuscript *Lies about Criminals: The Construction of an Acceptable "History" of Organized Crime* (2016). Quotations taken from J. Richard "Dixie" Davis, "Things I Couldn't Tell Till Now," *Collier's*, July 22, July 29, August 5, August 12, August 19, August 26, 1939.

11. See details of "Dewey Brain Trust" in *San Francisco*

*Chronicle*, October 28, 1939, and *Evansville (Indiana) Courier and Press*, August 23, 1939.

12. *Uniontown (Pennsylvania) Evening Standard*, August 25, 1939.

13. Andrew Wander Cohen, "The Transformation of 'Racketeering,' 1927–35: Crime, Market Regulation, and the Rise of the New Deal Order." Paper given at the Social Science History Association Annual Meeting, November 1995. Available on the Web as faculty.maxwell.syr.edu/awcohen/Research/Writing/ssha2.pdf.

14. Gordon L. Hostetter and Thomas Quinn Beesley, *It's a Racket!* (Chicago: Les Quin Books, 1929), p. 4.

15. *Chicago Tribune*, November 13, 1927.

16. Chicago *Daily News*, June 13, 1930.

17. John Landesco, "Organized Crime in Chicago," in *The 1929 Illinois Crime Survey* (Chicago: Illinois Association for Criminal Justice, 1929), p. 997.

18. Landesco, p. 975.

19. *Chicago Tribune*, May 27, 1928.

20. Harold Seidman, *Labor Czars: A History of Labor Racketeering* (New York: Liveright, 1938), p. 107.

21. *Chicago Tribune*, May 27, 1928.

22. Cited in *Chicago Tribune*, June 6, 1928.

23. *Chicago Tribune*, November 14, 1928.

24. Morrison Handsaker, "The Chicago Cleaning and Dyeing Industry: A Case Study in 'Controlled' Competition" (Ph.D. diss., University of Chicago, 1939), p. 357.

25. Seidman, *Labor Czars*, pp. 112–114.

26. Bill Bryson, *One Summer: America 1927* (London: Transworld, 2014), p. 534.

27. See Robert M. Lombardo, *Organized Crime in Chicago: Beyond the Mafia* (Urbana: University of Illinois Press, 2013), p. 94.

28. *Chicago Journal of Commerce*, December 17, 1927.

29. Hostetter and Beesley, *It's a Racket!* pp. 50–59.

30. Andrew W. Cohen, "The Racketeer's Progress: Commerce, Crime and the Law in Chicago 1900–1940," *Journal of Urban History* 29:5 (July 2003): pp. 587–589.

31. *Rockford (Illinois) Republic*, May 9, 1934.

32. *New York Times*, January 18, 1931.

33. *Rockford (Illinois) Republic*, May 9, 1934.

34. Victor A. Olander, Secretary-Treasurer of the Illinois State Federation of Labor, in a letter to Senator William E. Borah cited in *Rockford (Illinois) Morning Star*, March 29, 1932.

35. "Seeks to Expose Racketeer Bodies," *Federation News*, July 7, 1928, cited in Cohen, "The Transformation of 'Racketeering.'"

36. Irving Bernstein, *The Lean Years: A History of the American Worker, 1920–1933* (Boston: Houghton Mifflin, 1960), p. 84.

37. *Boston Globe*, November 17, 1928.

38. *New York Times*, January 12 and 16, 1914; July 12 and September 24, 1915; John Hutchinson, *Imperfect Union: A History of Corruption in American Unions* (New York: E.P. Dutton, 1970), pp. 69–71; and Rose Keefe, *The Starker: Big Jack Zelig, The Becker-Rosenthal Case and the Rise of Advent of the Jewish Gangster* (Nashville TN: Cumberland House, 2008), pp. 287–294; and Cornelius Willemse, *Behind the Green Lights* (New York: Alfred A. Knopf, 1931), p. 289.

39. "Chicago's New Use for Gunmen," *Literary Digest* 97 (June 16, 1928): p. 9.

40. Benjamin Stolberg, *Tailor's Progress: The Story of a Famous Union and the Men Who Made It* (New York: Doubleday, Doran, 1944), p. 140.

41. Mary M. Stolberg, *Fighting Organized Crime: Politics, Justice and the Legacy of Thomas E. Dewey* (Boston: Northeastern University Press, 1995), p. 163.

42. Fred F. Pasley, *Muscling In* (New York: Charles H. Bohn, 1931), frontispiece.

43. Mary Ross, "Where Doctors Racketeer," *The Survey* 62:4 (May 15, 1929): pp. 227–228.

44. Katherine O'Shea McCarthy, "Briefer Contributions: Racketeering—A Contribution to a Bibliography," *Journal of Criminal Law and Criminology* 22:4 (Fall 1931): pp. 578–585.

45. Gordon L. Hostetter, "The Growing Menace of the Racketeer," *New York Times Magazine* (October 30, 1932): p. 3.

46. "Gangsters and Prohibition," *Literary Digest* 109 (May 30, 1931): p. 10.

47. *Chicago Tribune*, May 11, 1953.

48. Hostetter, "Growing Menace," p. 3.

49. "High Costs of Rackets Ruining Business," *Literary Digest* (April 18, 1931): p. 9.

50. Samuel Crowther, "Invisible Government: What Racketeering Costs the Home," *Ladies Home Journal* 48 (February 1931): p. 3; and John Gunther and J.W. Mulroy, "The High Cost of Hoodlums," *Harper's* 159 (October 1929): pp. 529–540; and "High Costs of Rackets Ruining Business," p. 9.

51. H.L. Mencken, "The Land of Rackets," *American Mercury* (October 1930): p. 255.

52. Hostetter and Beesley, *It's a Racket!* pp. 38–39.

53. Landesco, "Organized Crime in Chicago," pp. 997, 1093.

54. "Stabilization through Racketeering" *The New Republic*, September 30, 1931.

55. Crowther, "Invisible Government," p. 20.

56. Walter Lippmann, "The Underworld: Our Secret Servant," *Forum* 85 (January 1931): pp. 1–4.

57. Robert Lynd, "Businessman a Hero," *New Statesman* 35 (August 23, 1930): pp. 616–617.

58. Raymond Moley, "Behind the Menacing Racket," *New York Times Magazine* (Nov. 23, 1930): pp. 1–2; and Raymond Moley, *After Seven Years* (New York: Harper Bros., 1939), pp. 184–185.

59. Jack Wilson, "Movie Moguls Imported Willie Bioff," *Labor Action* 5:45 (November 10, 1941): p. 2.

60. Gene Mailes and Mike Nielsen, *Hollywood's Other Blacklist: Union Struggles in the Studio System* (London: British Film Institute, 1995), pp. 16–17.

61. Sidney Lens, *Left, Right and Center: Conflicting Forces in American Labor* (Hinsdale, IL: H. Regnery, 1949), p. 89.

62. For contemporary details of Nitti's rise to power in the "Outfit," see *Los Angeles Times*, March 28, 1932.

63. *Chicago Tribune*, December 5, 1940.

64. *Chicago Tribune*, August 10, 1941.

65. Wilson, "Movie Moguls," p. 2; and Oliver Pilat, *Pegler: Angry Man of the Press* (Westport, CT: Greenwood Press, 1973), p. 167.

66. Carey McWilliams, "Racketeers and Movie Magnates," *New Republic* (October 27, 1941): pp. 533–535.

67. Herb Aller, *The Extortionists* (Beverly Hills, CA: Guild Hartford, 1972), p. 55.

68. David Witwer, *Shadow of the Racketeer: Scandal in Organized Labor* (Chicago: Illinois University Press, 2009).

69. Pegler cited in *Life Magazine* (May 6, 1940): p. 34.

70. *Hartford Courant*, September 17, 1942.

71. David Witwer, "The Scandal of George Scalise: A Case Study in the Rise of Labor Racketeering in the

1930s," *Journal of Social History* 36:4 (Summer 2003): pp. 917–940.

72. *New York Times*, February 10, 1940.

73. Westbrook Pegler, "Fair Enough," cited in the *(Boise) Idaho Statesman*, February 5, 1940. However, "Pegler did more to assert these connections than to explain them," Witwer, op. cit., p. 917.

74. *New York Times*, October 16, 1935.

75. Eleanor R. Hunter, "The Labor Policy of the Ford Motor Company" (master's thesis, Wayne State University, 1942), p. 47.

76. George Lambert, "Dallas Tries Terror," *The Nation* (October 9, 1937): p. 377.

77. Michael K. Honey, *Southern Labor and Black Civil Rights: Organizing Memphis Workers* (Urbana: University of Illinois Press, 1993), pp. 87–89.

78. *Detroit Times*, March 8, 1932.

79. For a discussion of this phenomenon, see James B. Jacobs, *Mobsters, Unions, and Feds: The Mafia and the American Labor Movement* (New York: New York University Press, 2006).

80. "Fair Enough," August 15, 1939.

81. Robert J. Kelly, *The Upperworld and the Underworld: Case Studies of Racketeering and Business Infiltrations in the United States* (New York: Kluwer, 1999), p. 48.

82. Edward Alsworth Ross, *Sin and Society: An Analysis of Latter-Day Iniquity* (Boston: Houghton Mifflin, 1907), p. 30.

83. Henry Demarest Lloyd, *Wealth Against Commonwealth* (Boston: Harper Brothers, 1894), p. 169; Lincoln Steffens, *The Shame of the Cities* (New York: McClure, Philips and Co., 1904); and David Graham Phillips, "The Treason of the Senate," *Cosmopolitan* (April 1906), pp. 628–638.

84. Ida M. Tarbell, "John D. Rockefeller: A Character Study, Part Two," *McClure's Magazine* 25:4 (August 1905): p. 399.

## Chapter 8

1. *New York Tribune*, January 10, 1905.

2. *New York Tribune*, February 24, 1897.

3. *Wall Street Journal*, March 19, 1907.

4. Michael Woodiwiss, *Organized Crime and American Power* (Toronto: University of Toronto Press, 2001), pp. 15–67.

5. Charles Francis Adams, *Chapters of Eyrie* (New York: Holt, 1871), pp. 135–136.

6. *New York Sun*, September 4, 1872.

7. Kristofer Allerfeldt, *Crime and the Rise of Modern America* (New York: Routledge, 2011), pp. 40, 168–169.

8. Richard Rayner, *The Associates: Four Capitalists Who Created California* (New York: W.W. Norton, 2008), pp. 159–162.

9. Michael Woodiwiss, *Organized Crime and American Power* (Toronto: University of Toronto Press, 2001), pp. 111–112.

10. Charles F Adams, "A Chapter of Erie," *North American Review* 109 (July 1869): pp. 70–72.

11. *New York Times*, January 11, 1875.

12. *New York Herald*, April 6, 1886.

13. *Omaha World Herald*, April 21, 1893.

14. *New Orleans Times-Picayune*, October 3, 1907.

15. *Wall Street Journal*, March 19, 1907.

16. Henry George, "What the Railroad Will Bring Us," *Overland Monthly* 1 (October 1868): p. 303.

17. *Wall Street Journal*, March 19, 1907.

18. James L. Brown, *Mussel Slough Tragedy* (n.p., 1958), pp. 17–20.

19. Richard Maxwell Brown, *No Duty to Retreat: Violence and Values in American History and Society* (Norman: University of Oklahoma Press, 1991), pp. 108–110; and Richard J. Orsi, *Sunset Limited: The Southern Pacific Railroad and the Development of the American West, 1850–1930* (Berkeley: University of California Press, 2005), pp. 102–103.

20. *San Francisco Chronicle*, December 8, 1878, and March 31, 1879; and *San Francisco Examiner*, March 31, 1900.

21. Ray Ginger, *The Age of Excess: The United States From 1877 to 1914* (London: Macmillan, 1971), p. 20.

22. *New York Times*, September 18, 1883.

23. Charles R. McCabe, ed., *Damned Old Crank: A Self-Portrait of E.W. Scripps Drawn from His Unpublished Writings* (New York: 1951), pp. 141 and 144.

24. Ray Stannard Baker, "Railroads on Trial, Part V: How Railroads Make Public Opinion," *McClure's Magazine* (March 1906): p. 548.

25. Doris Kearns Goodwin, *The Bully Pulpit: Theodore Roosevelt, William Howard Taft and the Golden Age of Journalism* (New York: Simon & Schuster, 2013), pp. 644–652.

26. Carl S. Vrooman, "Can Americans Afford Safety in Railroad Travel?" *McClure's Magazine* (August 1907): pp. 421–427.

## Chapter 9

1. Cited in *New York Times*, March 5, 1932.

2. See Rhodri Jeffreys-Jones, *The FBI: A History* (New Haven, CT: Yale University Press, 2007), pp. 20–22.

3. *New York Times*, March 9, 1876.

4. Figures taken from Andrew Wender Cohen, "Smuggling, Globalization and America's Outward State," *Journal of American History* 97:2 (September 2010): p. 372.

5. Philip H. Melanson, *The Secret Service: The Hidden History of an Enigmatic Agency* (New York: Basic Books, 2005), pp. 13–16; and Allen W. Trelease, *White Terror* (Baton Rouge: Louisiana State University Press, 1995), pp. 409–416; and William F. Connelley, *A Standard History of Kansas and Kansans*, vol. 2 (Chicago: Lewis, 1918), p. 2217.

6. Jeffreys-Jones, *The FBI*, p. 25.

7. Dorothy Sterling, ed., *The Trouble They Seen: Black People Tell the Story of Reconstruction* (Garden City, NY: Doubleday, 1976), puts the figure at 20,000 (p. 393), whereas Philip Dray, *At the Hands of Persons Unknown: The Lynching of Black America* (New York: Random House, 2002), cites contemporary sources giving 3,500 from General Philip Sheridan and 10,000 from the anti-lynching campaigner Ida Wells-Barnett.

8. Chamberlain quoted in the *Cincinnati Tribune*, November 1, 1871.

9. See Nicholas Lemman, *Redemption: The Last Battle of the Civil War* (New York: Farrar, Straus and Giroux, 2006).

10. Mary B. Chesnut in C. Vann Woodward, ed., *Mary Chesnut's Civil War* (New Haven, CT: Yale University Press, 1981), p. 343. See also Michael D. Pierson, "'He Helped the Poor and Snubbed the Rich': Benjamin F. Butler and Class Politics in Lowell and New Orleans," *Massachusetts Historical Review* 7 (2005): pp. 36–68.

11. *The Testimony in the Impeachment of Adelbert*

*Ames, as Governor of Mississippi* (Jackson, MS: Jackson, Power and Barksdale, 1877), p. 46.

12. E. Benjamin Andrews, "History of the Last Quarter Century in the United States III: Downfall of the Carpet-Bag Regime," *Scribner's Magazine* 17:5 (May 1895): p. 569.

13. *Ibid.*, pp. 576–578.

14. *Miami Herald*, February 19, 1917.

15. *Topeka Plaindealer*, February 14, 1924.

16. Cited in the *Chicago Tribune*, April 10, 1876.

17. For details of the conspiracy, see *Cincinnati Commercial*, April 21, 1876. For Whitley's confession, see *New York Times*, April 5, 1876.

18. Solicitor Wilson cited in *Boston Daily Globe*, September 11, 1874.

19. *Boston Globe*, September 11, 1874.

20. For details of the process, the chronology and levels of funding as well as Chase's full statement, see Bray Hammond, *Sovereignty and an Empty Purse: Banks and Politics in the Civil War* (Princeton, NJ: Princeton University Press, 1970), especially pp. 244–247.

21. *National Police Gazette*, November 26, 1867.

22. See for example *New York Times*, October 16, 1866, and *New York Tribune*, April 15, 1867.

23. Louis Bagger, "The Secret Service of the United States," *Appleton's Journal* 20 (September 1873): p. 360.

24. *New York Times*, September 20; October 5 and November 30, 1876.

25. See Stephen Mihn, *A Nation of Counterfeiters: Capitalists, Con Men and the Making of the United States* (Cambridge, MA: Harvard University Press, 2007), pp. 351–353.

26. *New York Times*, January 18, 1879.

27. For the opposing views, see *New York Times*, June 20, 1880, and *Washington Post*, August 24, 1880.

28. *New York Times*, November 27, 1879.

29. *Baltimore Sun*, December 2, 1880.

30. *Hartford Daily Courant*, November 21, 1883.

31. Cited in *New York Times* and *Chicago Tribune*, August 1, 1933.

32. *New York Times*, June 3, 1933.

33. *New York Times*, July 2, 1933.

34. *Literary Digest* (July 1, 1933): p. 34.

35. Richard Gid Powers, "The FBI in American Popular Culture," in Athan Theodoris, ed., *The FBI: A Comprehensive Reference Guide* (Phoenix, AZ: Oryx Press, 1999), pp. 270–278.

36. Tapping in the words "public enemy" to Proquest Historical Newspapers yielded 1,034 headlines between 1933 and 1934.

37. Figures taken from Theodoris, pp. 4–5.

38. *Baltimore Sun*, December 9, 1934.

39. For details of Lamm, see Walter Mittelstaedt, *Herman "Baron" Lamm: The Father of Modern Bank Robbery* (Jefferson, NC: McFarland, 2012).

40. For an example of a source that reiterates the legend, see Carl Sifakis, *The Encyclopedia of American Crime* (New York: Facts on File, 1982), pp. 410–411.

41. "Dillinger Case Stirs Nation's Press to Sarcasm," *Literary Digest* (May 5, 1934): p. 9.

42. *Hartford Courant*, July 24, 1934.

43. "Dillinger Case Stirs Nation's Press to Sarcasm," p. 9.

44. *Washington Post*, April 29, 1934, and *Los Angeles Times*, July 24, 1934.

45. *Baltimore Sun*, March 7, 1934.

46. "The Life and Death of John Dillinger," *G-Men* aired July 20, 1935.

47. *Nevada State Journal*, March 5, 1934.

48. *Washington Post*, July 24, 1934.

49. *Omaha World-Herald*, March 6, 1934.

50. *Daily Boston Globe*, July 23, 1934; *Chicago Tribune*, July 1934; *Los Angeles Times*, July 23, 1934; and *Christian Science Monitor*, July 23, 1934.

51. J. Edgar Hoover, *Persons in Hiding* (Boston: Little, Brown, 1938), pp. 23–25.

52. Hoover, *Persons in Hiding*, p. 25.

53. Hoover, *Persons in Hiding*, p. 26.

54. Hoover, *Persons in Hiding*, p. 26; and Chris Evans and Howard Kazanijian, *Ma Barker: America's Most Wanted Mother* (Lanham, MD: Rowman and Littlefield, 2017), pp. 78–80.

55. Hoover, *Persons in Hiding*, p. 37.

56. *Christian Science Monitor*, January 16, 1935; *Los Angeles Times*, January 17, 1935; and *Chicago Tribune*, October 19, 1935.

57. Bryan Burrough, *Public Enemies* (London: Penguin Books, 2004), pp. 508–509.

58. See *Washington Post* and *New York Times*, May 2, 1936. For details of the controversy surrounding Hoover's, role see Stephen M. Underhill, "J. Edgar Hoover's Domestic Propaganda: Narrating the Spectacle of the Karpis Arrest," *Western Journal of Communication* 76:4 (July–September 2012): pp. 438–457.

59. *Washington Post*, May 3, 1936.

60. *Los Angeles Times*, October 1, 1934.

61. Cited in full in *New York Times*, July 31, 1935.

62. Jessica R. Pliley, *Policing Sexuality: The Mann Act and the Making of the FBI* (Cambridge, MA: Harvard University Press, 2014), pp. 185–186; and *New York Times*, July 31, 1935.

63. *Chicago Tribune*, January 26, 1941.

64. Cited in *Chicago Tribune*, April 15, 1940.

65. *New York Tribune*, March 17, 1939.

66. *New York Times*, March 17, 1939.

67. *Chicago Tribune*, April 17, 1939.

68. *New York Times*, February 3, 1940.

69. *Atlanta Constitution* and *New York Times*, March 18, 1940.

70. *New York Times*, March 18, 1940.

71. *New York Times*, March 24, 1940.

72. *New York Times*, March 27, 1940, and *Boston Globe*, March 31, 1940.

73. *New York Times*, March 31, 1940.

74. Burton Turkis cited in the *Atlanta Constitution*, April 5, 1940.

75. *Atlanta Constitution*, April 5, 1940; *Christian Science Monitor*, April 9, 1940.

76. *New York Times*, April 5, 1940.

77. *New York Times*, June 4, 1940, and *Atlanta Constitution*, October 20, 1940.

78. *Atlanta Constitution*, April 5, 1940.

79. *Atlanta Constitution*, November 13, 1941.

80. Sid Feder in his introduction to Burton B. Turkus and Sid Feder, *Murder Inc: The Story of the Syndicate* (New York: 1951), pp. xiii–xiv.

81. Senate Crime Committee, 1951, cited in Daniel Bell, "Crime as an American Way of Life," *The Antioch Review* 13:2 (Summer 1953): p. 143.

82. Peter Maas, *The Valachi Papers* (New York: Bantam Books, 1968).

83. The President's Commission on Law Enforcement and Administration of Justice, *Task Force Report: Organized Crime* (Washington, D.C.: U.S. Government Printing Office, 1967), p. 6.

84. Donald R. Cressey, *Theft of a Nation: The Structure*

*of Crime in America* (New York: Harper and Row, 1969), pp. 36–37.

85. Stephen Currie, "Dewey Defeats the Dutchman," *American History* 37:5 (December 2002): pp. 38–46.

86. Virgil Peterson reviewing *Murder, Inc.* in *Journal of Criminal Law, Criminology and Police Science* 43:2 (July–August 1952): p. 229.

87. Alan A. Block, *Perspectives on Organizing Crime: Essays in Opposition* (Boston: Kluwer, 1991), pp. 4–9.

88. See Mike Woodiwiss's as yet unpublished manuscript *Double Crossed: The Failure of American Organized Crime Control*, pp. 128–131.

89. Taken from Jeffrey Scott McIllwain, *Organizing Crime in Chinatown: Race and Racketeering in New York City 1890–1910* (Jefferson, NC: McFarland, 2003), pp. 6–7.

## Chapter 10

1. Charles A. Tracy, "Race, Crime and Social Policy: The Chinese in Oregon, 1871–1885," *Crime and Social Justice* 14 (Winter 1980): pp. 14–15.

2. See the entry for "Ching, Fong" in Xiaojian Zhao and J.W. Park, eds., *Asian Americans: An Encyclopaedia of Social, Cultural, Economic and Political History* (New Haven, CT: Greenwood, 2013), pp. 310–311.

3. Richard H. Dillon, "Little Pete, King of Chinatown," *California Monthly* 79 (December 1968): pp. 42–58.

4. *San Francisco Chronicle*, January 24, 1897.

5. *San Francisco Chronicle*, January 26, 1897.

6. *Los Angeles Times*, January 28, 1897.

7. *San Francisco Chronicle*, January 26, 1897.

8. *San Francisco Call*, December 30, 1896, and *Washington Post*, January 17, 1897.

9. *The Great Round World And What Is Going On In It* 1:22 (April 8, 1897): pp. 24–31.

10. Louis J. Beck, *New York's Chinatown: An Historical Presentation of its Places and People* (New York: Bohemia, 1898), p. 133.

11. Stewart Culin, "Customs of the Chinese in America," *Journal of American Folk- Lore* 3 (July–September 1890): p. 193.

12. James Cantlie and Sheridan Jones, *Sun Yat-Sen and the Awakening of China* (New York: Fleming H. Revell, 1912), pp. 26–27, 132–134.

13. William Hoy, *The Chinese Six Companies* (San Francisco: Chinese Consolidated Benevolent Association, 1942), pp. 23–24.

14. Robert Wells Ritchie, "The Wars of the Tongs," *Harper's Weekly* 54 (August 27, 1910): p. 8; and Stanford M. Lyman, "Conflict and the Web of Group Affiliation in San Francisco's Chinatown, 1850–1910," *Pacific Historical Review* 43:4 (November 1974): p. 489.

15. Ivan Light, "From Vice District to Tourist Attraction: The Moral Career of he American Chinatown, 1880–1940," *Pacific Historical Review* 43:3 (August 1974): pp. 367–394.

16. Herman Scheffaner, "The Old Chinese Quarter in San Francisco," *Living Age* (August 10, 1907): p. 361.

17. Herbert Asbury, *The Gangs of New York: An Informal History of the Underworld* (New York: Garden City, 1927), pp. 315–316; and Light, "From Vice District to Tourist Attraction," pp. 388–391.

18. Taken from Jeffrey Scott McIllwain, *Organizing Crime in Chinatown: Race and Racketeering in New York City, 1890–1910* (Jefferson, NC: McFarland, 2004), p. 7.

19. Daniel Bell, "Crime as an American Way of Life: A Queer Ladder of Social Mobility," *The Antioch Review* 13:2 (Summer 1953): pp. 131–154.

20. Alan A. Block, "History and the Study of Organized Crime," *Urban Life* 6 (January 1978): p. 455.

21. McIllwain, *Organizing Crime in Chinatown.*

22. Unknown reporter in New York, 1891, cited in Timothy Gilfolye, *A Pickpocket's Tale: The Underworld of Nineteenth-Century New York* (New York: Norton, 2006), p. 89.

23. For details of the family knowledge, see statement of Police Commissioner Theodore Bingham's secretary, Dan Slattery, in the *Boston Globe*, June 20, 1909.

24. Taken from statement of cousin Macel Sigel, published in the *Boston Globe*, June 20, 1909.

25. *Chicago Tribune*, June 20, 1909.

26. The details of the letters can be found in the *Boston Globe*, the *New York Tribune, New York Times*, and other papers, June 20, 1909.

27. *Boston Globe*, June 20, 1909.

28. For examples of Elsie's letters to the two men, see *Washington Post*, June 25, 1909.

29. *San Francisco Chronicle*, June 23, 1909, and *Baltimore Sun*, June 23, 1909.

30. *Washington Post*, June 27, 1909.

31. *New York Times*, July 4, 1909.

32. *Washington Post*, April 8, 1928.

33. *Boston Globe*, April 10, 1923.

34. *New York Times*, July 21, 1929, and *Washington Post*, April 8, 1928.

35. *New York Times*, March 14, 1937.

36. Kenneth Chew, et al., "The Revolving Door to Gold Mountain: How Chinese Immigrants Got Around U.S. Exclusion and Replenished the Chinese American Labor Pool, 1900–1910," *International Migration Review* 43:2 (Summer 2009): p. 412.

37. Robert McClellan, *The Heathen Chinese: A Study of American Attitudes Toward China, 1890–1905* (Columbus: Ohio State University Press, 1971).

38. Helen Chen, "Chinese Immigration into the United States: An Analysis of Changes in Immigration Policies" (Ph.D. diss., Brandeis University, 1980), p. 177.

39. *Baltimore Sun*, June 21, 1882.

40. *Los Angeles Times*, January 21, 1903.

41. *San Francisco Chronicle*, October 2, 1899.

42. Erika Lee, "Orientalisms in the Americas: A Hemispheric Approach to Asian American History," *Journal of Asian American Studies* 8:3 (2005): pp. 235–56.

43. *New York Times*, October 22, 1883, and July 7, 1884.

44. *New York Times*, August 9 and October 22, 1883.

45. Julian Ralph, "The Chinese Leak," *Harper's New Monthly Magazine* 82 (March 1891): p. 520.

46. Ralph, "The Chinese Leak," p. 520.

47. Roger Daniels, *Guarding the Golden Door: American Immigration Policy and Immigrants Since 1882* (New York: Hill and Wang, 2004), p. 24.

48. Luther Fry, "Illegal Entry of Orientals into the United States Between 1910 and 1920," *Journal of the American Statistical Association* 23:162 (June 1928): pp. 173–177.

49. Patrick W. Ettinger, "Imaginary Lines: Border Enforcement and the Origins of Undocumented Immigration 1882–1930" (Ph.D. diss., University of Indiana, 2000), p. 87.

50. *New York Times*, August 26, 1885.

51. *New York Times*, March 7, 1890.

52. *New York Times*, June 10, 1891.

53. Raymond B. Craib, "Chinese Immigrants in Porfirian Mexico: A Preliminary Study of Settlement, Economic Activity, and Anti-Chinese Sentiment" (master's thesis, University of New Mexico, 1994), p. 8.

54. Kenneth Cott, "Mexican Diplomacy and the Chinese Issue, 1876–1910," *Hispanic American Historical Review* 67:1 (1987): p. 74.

55. Ralph, "The Chinese Leak," pp. 523–524; and Patrick W. Ettinger, "Imaginary Lines: Border Enforcement and the Origins of Undocumented Immigration 1882–1930," Ph.D. diss., University of Indiana, 2000, pp. 96–99.

56. Statement of Dade E. Coon, Chinese Inspector San Diego cited in Ettinger, "Imaginary Lines," pp. 99–100.

57. Julie F. Gilmour, "H.H. Stevens and the Chinese: The Transition to Conservative Government and the Management of Controls on Chinese Immigration to Canada, 1900–1914," *Journal of the American East-Asian Relations* 2:3 (2013): pp. 175–189.

58. Evelyn Hu DeHart, "Coolies, Shopkeepers, Pioneers: The Chinese of Mexico and Peru (1849–1930)," *Amerasia Journal* 15:2 (1989): pp. 91–116.

59. *Washington Post*, August 25, 1901.

60. *San Francisco Chronicle*, August 25, 1901.

61. George E. Paulsen, "The Yellow Peril at Nogales: The Ordeal of Collector William M. Hoey," *Arizona and the West* 13:2 (Summer 1971): pp. 113–128.

## Chapter 11

1. *San Francisco Chronicle*, July 20, 1901.

2. Christian G. Samito, ed., *Changes in Law and Society During the Civil War and Reconstruction: A Legal History Documentary Reader* (Carbondale: Southern Illinois University Press, 2009), p. 189.

3. *Atlanta Constitution*, May 27, 1903.

4. "Peonage in the South," *Outlook* 74 (June 13, 1903): p. 391.

5. *New York Times*, July 25, 1903.

6. Cited in the *New York Daily People*, June 21, 1903.

7. *Montgomery Advertiser*, May 30, 1903.

8. *New York Tribune*, July 28, 1903; *Atlanta Constitution*, March 30, 1905; and *Baltimore Sun*, April 1, 1906.

9. *New York Daily People*, June 21, 1903.

10. *New Orleans Times-Picayune*, June 22, 1903.

11. *Montgomery Advertiser*, July 3, 1903.

12. *Savannah Tribune*, July 18, 1903.

13. *Montgomery Advertiser*, July 19, 1903.

14. *Montgomery Advertiser*, November 22, 1906.

15. *Portland Oregonian*, December 10, 1907.

16. For details of the case and its repercussions see, for example, the *Idaho Statesman*, November 29, 1923; *San Diego Union*, September 13, 1923; *St. Paul Appeal*, April 21, 1923; *Morning Olympian* (Washington), April 13, 1923; *New Orleans States*, April 4, 1923; and the *Manatee River Journal* (Florida), April 5, 1923.

17. See for example the *Winston-Salem Journal*, May 9, 1923.

18. *Biloxi Herald* (Mississippi), January 28, 1926; *Bellingham Herald* (Washington), November 3, 1926; and *Augusta Chronicle* (Georgia), November 5, 1926.

19. Douglas A. Blackmon, *Slavery By Another Name* (New York: Anchor Books, 2008), pp. 368–369.

20. Stuart P. Sherman, "The White Slave," *The Nation* (May 28, 1914): p. 628.

21. *Duluth News-Tribune*, July 15, 1905.

22. Nicole Hahn Rafter in her introduction to a translation of Cesare Lombroso and Guigielmo Ferrero, *Criminal Woman, The Prostitute and the Normal Woman* (Durham, NC: Duke University Press, 2004), p. 32.

23. *The New York World*, February 28, 1906.

24. *Fort Wayne News*, August 17, 1905.

25. *New York Times*, April 17, 1886.

26. *New York Herald*, January 30, 1887.

27. Kate C. Bushnell, "Working in Northern Wisconsin," *WCTU State Work* 3:7 (November 1888): p. 7.

28. The survey was carried out using http://www.genealogybank.com/gbnk/newspapers/ and Proquest.com's *New York Times, Washington Post, Chicago Tribune* and *Los Angeles Times* archives.

29. *Belleville* (Illinois) *News Democrat*, March 9, 1906.

30. Edwin W. Sims, *The White Slave Trade Today* (Chicago: unknown publisher, 1910), p. 57.

31. Sims quote and figures taken from Jessica R. Pliley, *Policing Sexuality: The Mann Act and the Making of the FBI* (Cambridge, MA: Harvard University Press, 2014), p. 66.

32. *Chicago Tribune*, June 24 and 26, 1908, and January 15, 1909.

33. For details of French involvement in Chicago white slavery over these years see letter from Marcus Braun to Daniel J. Keefe (Commissioner General of Immigration), January 23, 1909, in *Marcus Braun Report: Prostitution and White Slavery Immigration Investigations*, Sept. 1, 1908–Jan. 31, 1909, Records of the Immigration and Naturalization Service, Series A: Subject Correspondence Files, Part 5: Prostitution and White Slavery, 1902–1933 (hereafter *Braun Reports*).

34. William P. Dillingham, *Importing Women for Immoral Purposes* (Washington, D.C.: 1909), p. 7; *Chicago Tribune*, June 24 and July 1, 1908; and Karen Abbott, *Sex in the Second City* (New York: Random House, 2007), p. 156.

35. Letter from P.L. Prentis (Inspector in Charge, Vancouver, BC) to Commissioner of Immigration, Montreal, January 4, 1909, in *Braun Reports*, Part 5: Sept. 1, 1908–Jan. 31, 1909.

36. *Denver Post*, September 6, 1906, and *Daily Illinois State Register*, October 11, 1906.

37. *New York Times*, December 24, 1905.

38. George Kibbe Turner, "The Daughters of the Poor: A Plain Story of the Development of New York City as a Leading Center of the White Slave Trade of the World, under Tammany Hall," *McClure's Magazine* 34 (November 1909): pp. 45–61.

39. Egal Feldman, "Prostitution, the Alien Woman and the Progressive Imagination, 1910–1915," *American Quarterly* 19:2 (Summer 1967): pp. 192–206.

40. Advert run in *Collier's Magazine*, October 23, 1909.

41. Mark Thomas Connelly, *The Response to Prostitution in the Progressive Era* (Chapel Hill: University of North Carolina Press, 1980), p. 6; and Feldman, op. cit., pp. 192–193.

42. Letter from P.L. Prentis (Inspector in Charge, Vancouver, BC) to Commissioner of Immigration, Montreal, December 23, 1908, *Braun Reports*, Part 5: Sept. 1, 1908–Jan. 31, 1909.

43. See Mara L. Keire, "The Vice Trust: A Reinterpretation of the White Slavery Scare in the United States, 1907–1917," *Journal of Social History* 35:1 (2001): pp. 5–41.

44. Philip Jenkins, "'A Wide-Open City': Prostitution in Progressive Era Lancaster," *Pennsylvania History* 65:4 (Autumn 1998): pp. 516.

45. *Washington Post*, April 30, 1910.

46. Turner (1909), op. cit., p. 47.

47. Jean Turner-Zimmermann, *Chicago's Black Traffic in White Girls* (Chicago: Chicago Rescue Mission, 1912), p. 14.

48. Figures taken from http://www.measuringworth.com/slavery.php.

49. Theodore Bingham, *The Girl That Disappears: The Real Facts About the White Slave Traffic* (Boston: Gorham Press, 1911), p. 15.

50. Edwin S. Sims, "The White Slave Trade of Today," in Ernest A. Bell, ed., *Fighting the Traffic in Young Girls* (Chicago: G.S. Ball, 1910), p. 49.

51. Turner-Zimmerman, p. 7.

52. Stanley Finch, *The White Slave Traffic: Address by Stanley W. Finch, Chief of the Bureau of Investigation of the Department of Justice, before World's Purity Congress, Louisville. KY, May 7, 1912* (Washington, D.C.: International Reform Bureau, n.d.), p. 2.

53. Clifford George Roe, *The Great War on White Slavery, Or Fighting for the Protection of our Girls* (Philadelphia: P.W. Ziegler, 1915), p. 15.

54. *New York Times*, May 3, 1910.

55. Turner, "The Daughters of the Poor," p. 47.

56. Hal McLeod Lytle, *Tragedies of the White Slave* (New York: Padell, 1910), p. 8.

57. *Report of the Vice Commission of Philadelphia* (Philadelphia: 1913), p. 21.

58. Lytle, p. 8.

59. Timothy Gilfoyle, *City of Eros: New York, Prostitution and the Commercialization of Sex, 1790–1920* (New York: Norton, 1992), pp. 57, 59.

60. Ruth Rosen, *The Lost Sisterhood: Prostitution in America, 1900–1918* (Baltimore: Johns Hopkins University Press, 1982), pp. 38–50.

61. Emma Goldman, *Anarchism and Other Essays* (New York: Mother Earth, 1911), pp. 184–186.

62. George Kibbe Turner, "The City of Chicago: A Study of the Great Immoralities," *McClure's Magazine* 28:6 (April 1907): pp. 580–582; and Clifford G. Roe, *Panders and Their White Slaves* (Chicago: Fleming H. Revell, 1910), pp. 13–14.

63. Assistant District Attorney Parker to the Illinois Vigilance Association cited in the *Atlanta Constitution*, March 7, 1909.

64. Turner (1909), op. cit., p. 45.

65. Turner (1909), op. cit., pp. 46–47.

66. George Kibbe Turner, "Tammany's Control of New York By Professional Criminals: A Study of a New Period of Decadence in the Popular Government of Great Cities," *McClure's Magazine* 33 (June 1909): pp. 120–122; Edward J. Bristow, *Prostitution and Prejudice: The Jewish Fight Against White Slavery, 1870–1939* (New York: Schocken Books, 1983), pp. 152–153; and Bell, "Crime as an American Way of Life," pp. 131–154.

67. Bingham, *The Girl That Disappears*, pp. 39–51.

68. For contradictory biographical details, see *New York Times*, March 6, 1889; and Rose Keefe, *The Starker: Big Jack Zelig, The Becker-Rosenthal Case and the Advent of the Jewish Gangster* (Nashville: Cumberland House, 2008), p. 68.

69. New York State Senate, *Report and Proceedings of the Senate Committee Appointed to Investigate the Police Department of New York City*, vol. 3 (Albany: J.B. Lyon, 1895), pp. 2989; 3105; 3181 and 3283.

70. George Kibbe Turner cited in *Chicago Tribune*, October 24, 1909.

71. *New York Tribune*, July 25, 1905.

72. Turner, "Tammany's Control of New York," p. 119.

73. George Kibbe Turner cited in the *New York Tribune*, October 22, 1909.

74. Bingham, *The Girl That Disappears*, pp. 23–28.

75. George Kibbe Turner cited in *Chicago Tribune*, October 24, 1909.

76. Turner, "Tammany's Control of New York," p. 132.

77. *Chicago Examiner*, December 15, 1908.

78. Ernest Albert Bell, *Fighting the Traffic in Young Girls* (Chicago: G.S. Ball, 1910), pp. 260–261.

79. Bell, *Fighting the Traffic in Young Girls*, pp. 261–262.

80. *New York Tribune*, October 22, 1909.

81. W.T. Stead, "The Maiden Tribute of Modern Babylon," *Pall Mall Gazette*, July 7, 1885.

82. *New York Times*, April 30, 1910.

83. *New York Times*, December 9, 1909, and April 30, 1910; Gretchen Soderlund, *Sex Trafficking, Scandal and the Transformation of Journalism 1885–1917* (Chicago: University of Chicago Press, 2013), pp. 124–147.

84. David J. Langum, *Crossing Over the Line: Legislating Morality and the Mann Act* (Chicago: Chicago University Press, 2006), p. 15.

85. *Variety*, December 19, 1913; Shelley Stamp Lindsey, "'Oil Upon the Flames of Vice': The Battle over White Slave Films in New York City," *Film History* 9:4 (1997): 352–353; worldwideboxoffice.com.

86. See Jessica R. Pliley, *Policing Sexuality: The Mann Act and the Making of the FBI* (Cambridge, MA: Harvard University Press, 2014), pp. 37–38.

87. See for example Ann R. Gabbert, "Prostitution and Moral Reform in the Borderlands: El Paso, 1890–1920," *Journal of the History of Sexuality* 12:4 (October 2003), pp. 575–604, which claims that corrupt law enforcers in the town effectively blocked vice laws until the 1930s.

88. Figures from U.S. Senate, *Report on Importation and Harboring* (Washington, D.C., 1910), pp. 60–61.

89. See Pliley, *Policing Sexuality*, pp. 45–51.

90. Pliley, *Policing Sexuality*.

91. *Hartford Courant*, October 26, 1936.

92. *Boston Globe*, November 13, 1936.

93. *Hartford Courant*, October 26, 1936.

94. *Atlanta Constitution*, August 25, 1936.

95. See Pliley, *Policing Sexuality*, pp. 186–204.

## Chapter 12

1. Details taken from "Black Hand Confessions 1910," Box 1, Lawrence Richey Papers, Herbert Hoover Presidential Library, West Branch, Iowa (hereafter referred to as "Comito Confession"), pp. 1–6; Transcript of Case 56: Circuit Court of the United States: Southern District of NY, *The United States of America against Giuseppe Calicchio, Giuseppe Morrello et al.* (March 6, 1911): Cross-examination of Antonio Comito, pp. 89–95; and Mike Dash, *The First Family: Terror, Extortion and the Birth of the American Mafia* (London: 2009), pp. 184–187.

2. W.S. Harwood, "Secret Societies in America," *The North American Review* 164:485 (1897): p. 617.

3. See Harriet W. McBride, "The Golden Age of Fraternalism: 1870–1910," *Heredom* 13 (2005): pp. 117–166.

4. "Comito Confession," pp. 5–6.

5. "Comito Confession," pp. 10–12, 29–34 and 45–46.

6. *Ibid.*, "Notes."

7. Edward H. Dixon, *The Terrible Mysteries of the Ku-Klux Klan* (New York: 1868), pp. 18–19, 53–55.

8. Bob James, *The Australian Centre for Fraternalism, Secret Societies and Mateship*, cited on the Web site http://www.fraternalsecrets.org/fraternalism.htm.

9. For details of the counterfeit and Secret Service operation, see *New York Tribune*, June 12, 1900. For the effects on Morello, see Dash, op. cit., pp. 109–110.

10. New York State Court of Appeals, *The People of New York against Pellegrino Marano*, New York 569 Testimony of Tony Notaro, pp. 52–53.

11. For details of these rituals and their significance, see David Critchley, *The Origin of Organized Crime in America: The New York City Mafia, 1891–1931* (New York: 2009), pp. 25–26, 49, 63, 119, 105–106. See also *New York Sun*, December 26, for the "39 Articles of the Black Hand."

12. For further details, see B.J. Ter Haar, *Ritual & Mythology of the Chinese Triads: Creating an Identity* (London: 2000), especially pp. 104–105.

13. *Sacramento Bee*, June 1, 1892.

14. See Ida Fazio, "The family, honour and gender in Sicily: Models and New Research," *Modern Italy* 9:2 (November 2004): pp. 263–280.

15. Translated and cited in Letizia Paoli, *Mafia Brotherhoods: Organized Crime, Italian Style* (New York: 2003), p. 101.

16. Taken from the memoir of Tombstone mayor John Clum, cited in Jeff Guinn, *The Last Gunfight* (New York: 2011), pp. 259–260.

17. See *New York Times*, January 6, 1884; *New York World*, August 7, 1885; and Ashbury, *Gangs of New York*, pp. 206–227.

18. Lord Shaftesbury cited in Anthony S. Wohl, ed., *The Victorian Family: Structure and Stresses* (London: 1978), p. 9.

19. See Mark C. Carnes. *Secret Ritual and Manhood in Victorian America* (New Haven: 1989), p. 120. For details of the Knights of Honor, see Frank W. Blackmar, ed., *Kansas: A Cyclopedia of State History*, vol. 2 (Chicago: 1912), p. 79.

20. Dickie, op. cit., p. 168.

21. Tony Notoro giving evidence at the trial of Pellegrino Marano for the murder of Nick Morello, New York State Court of Appeals, *People of New York against Pellegrino Marano*, pp. 52–53 and 74.

22. For details see *New York Times*, January 19, 1901.

23. See *Brooklyn Standard Union*, July 24, 1902.

24. *New York Journal*, April 13, 1903.

25. William J. Flynn, *The Barrel Mystery* (New York: 1919), p. 22.

26. For example, see D.L. Wilson, "The Ku Klux Klan, Its Origin, Growth, and Disbandment," *Century Illustrated Magazine* 28 (July 1884), p. 401.

27. For details of the incident, see Stanley F. Horn, *The Invisible Empire: The Story of the Ku Klux Klan, 1866–1871* (Boston: 1939), p. 14.

28. For details of Forrest and the Masons, see Brian Steel Wills, "Bedford Forrest" (Ph.D. diss., University of Georgia, 1991), p. 507.

29. See David W. Blight, *Race and Reunion: The Civil War in American Memory* (Cambridge, MA: 2001), and Nicholas Lemann, *Redemption: The Last Battle of the Civil War* (New York: 2006).

30. See Walter Lee Brown, *A Life of Albert Pike* (Fayetteville, AR: 1997), pp. 439–442; Sarah Lawrence Davis,

*Authentic History of the Ku Klux Klan, 1865–1877* (New York: 1924), p. 276; Horn, op. cit., pp. 245–262, 335–337; John C. Lester and D.L. Wilson, *Ku Klux Klan: Its Origins, Growth and Disbandment* (New York: 1905), p. 27.

31. Albert Pike, "The Ku Klux Klan," *Memphis Daily Appeal*, April 16, 1868.

32. For details of the Sons of Malta, see Albert Clarke Stephens, *The Cyclopeadia of Fraternities*, rev. ed. (New York: 1907), p. 284–285; and *Baltimore Sun*, March 31, 1868.

33. Horn, *The Invisible Empire*, p. 14.

34. Lester and Wilson, *Ku Klux Klan*, pp. 63–65.

35. See John Dickie, *Cosa Nostra*, rev. ed. (London: 2007), especially pp. 148–150.

36. Probably the most comprehensive account of the Molly Maguires and the basis of the background for this paper is Kevin Kenny, *Making Sense of the Molly Maguires* (New York: 1998).

37. For details of the purposes and the mutation of the Mollys and other organizations, see Tom Garvin, "Defenders, Ribbonmen and Others: Underground Political Networks in Pre-Famine Ireland," *Past and Present* 96 (August 1982): pp. 133–155.

38. Cited in Kenny, op. cit., p. 24.

39. Allan Pinkerton, *The Mollie Maguires and the Detectives* (New York: 1877), p. 8.

40. *New York Times*, March 25, 1884.

41. See Kevin Kenny, "Nativism, Labor, and Slavery: The Political Odyssey of Benjamin Bannan, 1850–1860," *The Pennsylvania Magazine of History and Biography* 118:4 (October 1994): pp. 325–361.

42. *Miners Journal*, October 3, 1857, cited in Anthony F.C. Wallace, *St. Clair: A Nineteenth Century Coal Town's Experience with a Disaster-Prone Industry* (Ithaca, NY: 1988), p. 323.

43. *New York Times*, November 7, 1863.

44. Cited in Joseph H. Bloom, "Undermining the Molly Maguires," *American History* 34:3 (August 1999), p. 54.

45. See Argument of F.W. Hughes in *Commonwealth versus Patrick Hester, Patrick Tully, and Peter McHugh* (Philadelphia: 1877), p. 7.

46. A contemporary evaluation of the connection can be found in *The Molly Maguires: Cut-Throats of Modern Times* (Tamaqua, PA: 1969), p. 5.

47. Cited in Adolf W. Schalck and David C. Henning, *The History of Schuylkill County, Pa.*, vol. 1 (Philadelphia: 1907), p. 164.

48. For details, see Francis P. Dewees, *The Molly Maguires: The Origin, Growth and Character of the Organization* (Philadelphia: 1877), pp. 98–102.

49. R.A. West, *Argument of Franklin B. Gowen* (Pottsville, PA: 1876), cited in Toni Arriola, "Ethnic Bias, Irish Literature, and the Molly Maguires: The Making of a Legend" (master's thesis, California State University, 1997), p. 59.

50. See Kenny, op. cit., pp. 231–235.

51. This thesis comes from Arriola, op. cit., especially pp. 74–91, and William H. Burke, *Anthracite Lads: A True Story of the Fabled Molly Maguires* (Erie: 2005).

52. See Kevin Kenny, "The Molly Maguires in Popular Culture," *Journal of American Ethnic History* 14:4 (Summer 1995): pp. 27–46.

53. See "The Five Orange Pips" in Sir Arthur Conan Doyle, *The Adventures of Sherlock Holmes* (London: 1891).

54. See Craig Fox, *Everyday Klansfolk: White Protestant Life and the KKK in 1920s Michigan* (East Lansing, MI: 2011); and Miguel Hernandez, "Animosity and Broth-

erhood: The Ku Klux Klan and the Freemasons in 1920s Indiana" (master's thesis, University of Exeter, 2011).

55. For a good example of this phenomenon, and one of the most interesting accounts of modern organized crime, see Misha Glenny, *McMafia: Seriously Organized Crime* (London: 2009).

## *Epilogue*

1. Peter Pomerantsev, *Nothing is True and Everything is Possible: Adventures in Modern Russia* (London: Faber and Faber, 2015), pp. 39–40.

# Bibliography

## Newspapers

Atlanta Constitution
Augusta Chronicle (Georgia)
Baltimore Sun
Baton Rouge Daily Advocate
Belleville News Democrat (Illinois)
Bellingham Herald (Washington State)
Biloxi Herald (Mississippi)
Bismarck Tribune (North Dakota)
Boise Idaho Statesman
Boston Globe
Boston Herald
Boston Journal
Chicago Daily News
Chicago Journal of Commerce
Chicago Tribune
Christian Science Monitor
Cincinnati Tribune
Cleveland Plain Dealer
Colorado Springs Gazette
Congressional Record
Daily Illinois State Journal
Daily Illinois State Register
Daily Picayune
Denver Post
Detroit Times
Duluth News-Tribune (Minnesota)
Evansville Courier and Press (Indiana)
Evening Standard (Uniontown, Pennsylvania)
Fort Wayne News (Indiana)
Hartford Daily Courant
Hyde Park Herald (Illinois)
Independence Examiner (Missouri)
Kansas City Star
London Times
Los Angeles Examiner
Los Angeles Times
Manatee River Journal (Florida)
Miami Herald
Missouri Democrat
Montgomery Advertiser (Alabama)
Montreal Star
Morning Olympian (Washington)
Morning Star (Rockford, Illinois)
New Orleans Bulletin
New Orleans Daily States
New Orleans Item
New Orleans Times-Democrat
New Orleans Times-Picayune
The New Republic
New York Daily News
New York Daily People
New York Evening Post
New York Herald
New York Herald-Tribune
New York Sun
New York Times
New York Tribune
New York World
Omaha World Herald
The Oregonian
Rockford Daily Gazette (Illinois)
Rockford Republic (Illinois)
Sacramento Bee
St. Albans Messenger (Vermont)
St. Paul Appeal (Minnesota)
San Diego Evening Tribune
San Diego Union
San Francisco Call
San Francisco Chronicle
San Francisco Examiner
Savannah Tribune
Seattle Times
Socialist Call (New York)
Springfield Republican (Illinois)
Tacoma Daily News
Topeka Plaindealer
Wall Street Journal
Washington Post
Winston-Salem Journal (North Carolina)

## Magazines

Appleton's Journal
The Century
Collier's Magazine
Cosmopolitan
The Great Round World and What Is Going On in It
Literary Digest
The Living Age
McClure's Magazine
The Nation
National Police Gazette
North American Review
Overland Monthly
Pall Mall Gazette (London)

*Saturday Evening Post*
*Scribner's*
*Time*
*True Detective*

## Unpublished Works

Arritola, Toni. "Ethnic Bias, Irish Literature, and the Molly Maguires: The Making of a Legend." Master's thesis, California State University, 1997.

Chen, Helen. "Chinese Immigration into the United States: An Analysis of Changes in Immigration Policies." Ph.D. diss., Brandeis University, 1980.

Craib, Raymond B. "Chinese Immigrants in Porfirian Mexico: A Preliminary Study of Settlement, Economic Activity, and Anti-Chinese Sentiment." Master's thesis, University of New Mexico, 1994.

Edwards-Simpson, Louise Reynes. "Sicilian Immigration to New Orleans, 1870–1910: Ethnicity, Race and Social Position in the New South." Ph.D. diss., University of Minnesota, 1996.

Ettinger, Patrick W. "Imaginary Lines: Border Enforcement and the Origins of Undocumented Immigration 1882–1930." Ph.D. diss., University of Indiana, 2000.

Handsaker, Morrison. "The Chicago Cleaning and Dyeing Industry: A Case Study in 'Controlled' Competition." Ph.D. diss., University of Chicago, 1939.

Hernandez, Miguel. "Animosity and Brotherhood: The Ku Klux Klan and the Freemasons in 1920s Indiana." Master's thesis, University of Exeter, 2011.

Hunter, Eleanor R. "The Labor Policy of the Ford Motor Company." Master's thesis, Wayne State University, 1942.

Kooistra, Anne Marie. "Angels for Sale: The History of Prostitution in Los Angeles, 1880–1940." Ph.D. diss., University of Southern California, 2003.

Matlin, John S. "Political Party Machines of the 1920s and 1930s: Tom Pendergast and the Kansas City Democratic Machine." Ph.D. diss., University of Birmingham, 2009.

Oram, Lydia Miranda. "Sentimental Mafia, This Invisible Thing of Ours: The Mafia and Politics in American and Italian Film and Media." Ph.D. diss., University of New York, 2011.

Sekhon, Sharon Elaine. "Exposing Sin City: Southern California Sense of Place and the Los Angeles Anti–Myth." Ph.D. diss., University of Southern California, 2002.

Sitton, Thomas. "Urban Politics and Reform in New Deal Los Angeles: The Recall of Mayor Frank Shaw." Ph.D. diss., University of California Riverside, 1983.

Wills, Brian Steel. "Bedford Forrest." Ph.D. diss., University of Georgia, 1991.

Woods, Joseph Gerald. "The Progressives and the Police: Urban Reform and the Professionalization of the Los Angeles Police." Ph.D. diss., University of California at Los Angeles, 1973.

## Articles

Aikman, Duncan. "Savonarola in Los Angeles." *American Mercury* (December 1930).

Allen, C.K. "Crime Inc." *The Spectator* (August 31, 1951).

Bart, Peter. "The G-Men's Propaganda Machine." *Variety* 387:3 (June 3, 2002).

Bell, Daniel. "Crime as an American Way of Life." *Antioch Review* 13:2 (Summer 1953).

Block, Alan A. "History and the Study of Organized Crime." *Urban Life* 6 (January 1978).

Bloom, Joseph H. "Undermining the Molly Maguires." *American History* 34: 3 (August 1999).

Boulay, H., and A. DiGaetano. "Why Did Political Machines Disappear?" *Journal of Urban History* (November 1985).

Bradley, Craig M. "Anti-Racketeering Legislation in America." *American Journal of Comparative Law* (Fall 2006).

Brandfon, Robert L. "The End of Immigration to the Cotton Fields." *Mississippi Valley Historical Review* 50 (March 1964).

Brown, M. Craig, and Barbara D. Warner. "Immigrants, Urban Politics and Policing in 1900." *American Sociological Review* 57:3 (June 1992).

Burke, Edward M. "Lunatics and Anarchists: Political Homicide." *Chicago Journal of Criminal Law and Criminology* 92: 3 (Spring 2002).

Bushnell, Kate C. "Working in Northern Wisconsin." *Women's Christian Temperance Union State Work* 3:7 (November 1888).

Chandler, Raymond. "The Simple Art of Murder." *Saturday Review of Literature* (April 15, 1950).

Chew, Kenneth, et al. "The Revolving Door to Gold Mountain: How Chinese Immigrants Got Around U.S. Exclusion and Replenished the Chinese American Labor Pool, 1900–1910." *International Migration Review* 43:2 (Summer 2009).

Cohen, Andrew Wender. "The Racketeer's Progress: Commerce, Crime and the Law in Chicago 1900–1940." *Journal of Urban History* 29:5 (July 2003).

_____. "Smuggling, Globalization and America's Outward State." *Journal of American History* 97:2 (September 2010).

Colburn, David R., and George E. Pozzetta, "Bosses and Machines: Changing Interpretations in American History." *The History Teacher* 9:3 (May 1976).

Cott, Kenneth. "Mexican Diplomacy and the Chinese Issue, 1876–1910." *Hispanic American Historical Review* 67:1 (1987).

Coxe, John E. "The New Orleans Mafia Incident." *Louisiana Historical Quarterly* 20 (1937).

Critchley, David. "Buster, Maranzano and the Castellammare War, 1930–1931." *Global Crime* 7:1 (2006).

Crowther, Samuel. "Invisible Government: What Racketeering Costs the Home." *Ladies Home Journal* 48 (February 1931).

Culin, Stewart. "Customs of the Chinese in America." *Journal of American Folk-Lore* 3 (July–September 1890).

Cunningham, G. "The Italian, a Hindrance to White Solidarity in Louisiana, 1890–1898." *Journal of Negro History* 50:1 (January 1965).

Currie, Stephen. "Dewey Defeats the Dutchman." *American History* 37:5 (December 2002).

DeHart, Evelyn Hu. "Coolies, Shopkeepers, Pioneers: The Chinese of Mexico and Peru (1849–1930)." *Amerasia Journal* 15:2 (1989).

Dillon, Richard H. "Little Pete, King of Chinatown." *California Monthly* 79 (December 1968).

Doenecke, Justus D. "Harry Elmer Barnes: Prophet of a 'Usable' Past." *The History Teacher* 8:2 (February 1975).

Dorsett, Lyle W. "Kansas City Politics: A Study of Boss Pendergast's Machine." *Journal of the Southwest* 8:2 (Summer 1966).

Fazio, Ida. "The family, honour and gender in Sicily: Models and New Research." *Modern Italy* 9:2 (November 2004).

Feldman, Egal. "Prostitution, the Alien Woman and the Progressive Imagination, 1910–1915." *American Quarterly* 19:2 (Summer 1967).

Fry, Luther. "Illegal Entry of Orientals into the United States Between 1910 and 1920." *Journal of the American Statistical Association* 23:162 (June 1928).

Fuchs, Daniel. "Where Al Capone Grew Up." *The New Republic* (September 9, 1931).

Gabbert, Ann R. "Prostitution and Moral Reform in the Borderlands: El Paso, 1890–1920." *Journal of the History of Sexuality* 12:4 (October 2003).

Garvin, Tom. "Defenders, Ribbonmen and Others: Underground Political Networks in Pre-Famine Ireland." *Past and Present* 96 (August 1982).

Gerould, Katherine Fullerton. "Jessica and Al Capone." *Harper's* (June 1931).

Gilfond, Duff. "LaGuardia of Harlem." *American Mercury* (June 1927).

Gilmour, Julie F. "H.H. Stevens and the Chinese: The Transition to Conservative Government and the Management of Controls on Chinese Immigration to Canada, 1900–1914." *Journal of the American East-Asian Relations* 2:3 (2013).

Haller, Mark H. "Illegal Enterprise: A Theoretical and Historical Interpretation." *Criminology* 28:2 (1990).

_____. "Organized Crime in Urban Society: Chicago in the Twentieth Century." *Journal of Social History* (Winter 1972).

Halpern, Rick. "Solving the 'Labor Problem': Race, Work and the State in the Sugar Industries of Louisiana and Natal, 1870–1910." *Journal of Southern African Studies* 30:1 (2004).

Harwood, W.S. "Secret Societies in America." *North American Review* 164:485 (1897).

Hawkins, E.R., and Willard Waller. "Critical Notes on the Cost of Crime." *Journal of Criminal Law and Criminology* 26:5 (January–February 1936).

Inglot, Tomasz, and John P. Pelissero. "Ethnic Politics in a Machine City: Chicago's Poles at Rainbow's End." *Urban Affairs Quarterly* 28 (June 1993).

Ismael, O.M. "Illegal Bunkering in Nigeria: A Background and Analysis." *Strategic Insights* 23 (April 2010).

Jackson, Joy. "Bosses and Businessmen in Gilded Age New Orleans Politics." *Louisiana History* 5:4 (Autumn 1964).

Jenkins, Philip. "'A Wide-Open City': Prostitution in Progressive Era Lancaster." *Pennsylvania History* 65:4 (Autumn 1998).

Keire, Mara L. "The Vice Trust: A Reinterpretation of the White Slavery Scare in the United States, 1907–1917." *Journal of Social History* 35:1 (2001).

Kendall, John S. "Who Killa de Chief?" *Louisiana Historical Quarterly* 22 (1939).

Kenny, Kevin. "The Molly Maguires in Popular Culture." *Journal of American Ethnic History* 144 (Summer 1995).

_____. "Nativism, Labor, and Slavery: The Political Odyssey of Benjamin Bannan, 1850–1860." *The Pennsylvania Magazine of History and Biography* 118:4 (October 1994).

Lee, Erika. "Orientalisms in the Americas: A Hemispheric Approach to Asian American History." *Journal of Asian American Studies* 8:3 (2005).

Light, Ivan. "From Vice District to Tourist Attraction: The Moral Career of the American Chinatown, 1880–1940." *Pacific Historical Review* 43:3 (August 1974).

Lindsey, Shelley Stamp. "'Oil Upon the Flames of Vice': The Battle Over White Slave Films in New York City." *Film History* 9:4 (1997).

Lippmann, Walter. "The Underworld: Our Secret Servant." *Forum* 85 (January 1931).

Lowden, Carl Schurz. "Chicago, The Nation's Crime Center." *Current History* 28:6 (September 1, 1928).

Lyman, Stanford M. "Conflict and the Web of Group Affiliation in San Francisco's Chinatown, 1850–1910." *Pacific Historical Review* 43:4 (November 1974).

Lynd, Robert. "Businessman a Hero." *New Statesman* 35 (August 23, 1930).

McBride, Harriet W. "The Golden Age of Fraternalism: 1870–1910." *Heredom* 13 (2005).

McCarthy, Katherine O'Shea. "Briefer Contributions: Racketeering—A Contribution to a Bibliography." *Journal of Criminal Law and Criminology* 22:4 (Fall 1931).

McWilliams, Carey. "Los Angeles." *Overland Monthly and Out West Magazine* (May 1927).

_____. "Racketeers and Movie Magnates." *New Republic* (October 27, 1941).

Mencken, H.L. "The Land of Rackets." *The American Mercury* (October 1930).

Morgan, Appleton. "What Shall We Do with the Dago?" *Popular Science Monthly* 38 (December 1890).

Oakley, Imogen B. "The American People vs. the Alien Bootlegger." *The Outlook* (May 5, 1926).

Paulsen, George E. "The Yellow Peril at Nogales: The Ordeal of Collector William M. Hoey." *Arizona and the West* 13:2 (Summer 1971).

Pierson, Michael D. "'He Helped the Poor and Snubbed the Rich': Benjamin F. Butler and Class Politics in Lowell and New Orleans." *Massachusetts Historical Review* 7 (2005).

Powers, Richard Gid. "J. Edgar Hoover and the Detective Hero." *Journal of Popular Culture* 9 (Fall 1975).

Pringle, Henry F. "Jimmy Walker." *The American Mercury* (November 1926).

Ross, Mary. "Where Doctors Racketeer." *The Survey* 62:4 (May 15, 1929).

Schottenhamel, George. "How Big Bill Thompson Won Control of Chicago." *Journal of the Illinois State Historical Society* 45 (Spring 1952).

Singer, Max. "The Vitality of Mythical Numbers." *The Public Interest* 23 (Spring 1971).

Stead, William T. "Mr. Richard Croker and Greater New York." *Review of Reviews* 16 (October 1897).

Tracy, Charles A. "Race, Crime and Social Policy: The Chinese in Oregon, 1871–1885." *Crime and Social Justice* 14 (Winter 1980).

Underhill, Stephen M. "J. Edgar Hoover's Domestic Propaganda: Narrating the Spectacle of the Karpis Arrest." *Western Journal of Communication* 76:4 (2012).

Viehe, Fred. "The Recall of Mayor Frank L. Shaw: A Revision." *California Historical Quarterly* 59 (Winter 1980/1981).

Wilson, Jack. "Movie Moguls Imported Willie Bioff." *Labor Action* 5:45 (November 10, 1941).

Witwer, David. "The Scandal of George Scalise: A Case Study in the Rise of Labor Racketeering in the 1930s." *Journal of Social History* 36:4 (Summer 2003).

Woodiwiss, Michael. "Fifty Years Investigating Institutional Corruption and Organized Crime: An Interview with Selwyn Raab." *Trends in Organized Crime* 18.1–2 (June 2015).

_____. "Organized Crime: The Dumbing of Discourse." *British Criminology Conference: Selected Proceedings* (July 1999).

Woodiwiss, Michael, and Dick Hobbs. "Organized Evil and the Atlantic Alliance: Moral Panics and the Rhetoric of Organized Crime Policing in America and Britain." *The British Journal of Criminology* 49 (2011).

## Official Sources

Federal Bureau of Investigation. FBI Records.

Illinois Association for Criminal Justice. *The Illinois Crime Survey.* Chicago: Blakely, 1929.

New York City Board of Aldermen. *Report of the Special Committee to Investigate the Ring Frauds.* New York: M.B. Brown, 1878.

New York State Senate. *Report and Proceedings of the Senate Committee Appointed to Investigate the Police Department of the City of New York.* Albany: J.B. Lyon, 1895.

The President's Commission on Law Enforcement and Administration of Justice. *Task Force Report: Organized Crime.* Washington, D.C.: U.S. Government Printing Office, 1967.

Senate of the State of Mississippi. *The Testimony in the Impeachment of Adelbert Ames, as Governor of Mississippi.* Jackson, MS: Jackson, Power and Barksdale, 1877.

U.S. Department of State. "The Executive Documents of the House of Representatives for the First Session of the Fifty-Second Congress." *Foreign Relations of the United States.* Washington, D.C., 1892.

U.S. Department of the Treasury. *Records of the Immigration and Naturalization Service, Series A: Subject Correspondence Files, Part 5: Prostitution and White Slavery, 1902–1933.* Washington, D.C.: U.S. Government Printing Office, 1933.

U.S. Senate. *Hearings Before the Subcommittee of the Judiciary on The National Prohibition Law.* 69th Congress. Washington, D.C., 1926.

U.S. Senate. *Investigation of So-Called Rackets: Hearings Before a Subcommittee of the Committee on Commerce.* 73rd Congress, 2nd Session, 1933.

U.S. Senate. *Report on Importation and Harboring.* Washington, D.C., 1910.

U.S. Senate, Subcommittee on Commerce. *Hearings: Investigation of Racketeering,* vol. 1. Washington, D.C.: U.S. Government Printing Office, 1933.

## Books

Abbott, Karen. *Sex in the Second City.* New York: Random House, 2007.

Adams, Charles Francis. *Chapters of Eyrie.* New York: Holt and Co., 1871.

Adler, Jeffrey. *First in Violence, Deepest in Dirt.* Cambridge, MA: Harvard University Press, 2006.

Allen, Oliver E. *The Tiger: The Rise and Fall of Tammany Hall.* Reading, MA: Da Capo Press, 1993.

Aller, Herb. *The Extortionists.* Beverly Hills, CA: Guild Hartford, 1972.

Allerfeldt, Kristofer. *Crime and the Rise of Modern America.* New York: Routledge, 2011.

Allsop, Kenneth. *The Bootleggers: The Story of Chicago's Prohibition Era.* New York: Doubleday, 1961.

Anger, Kenneth. *Hollywood Babylon.* San Francisco: Straight Arrow Press, 1975.

Asbury, Herbert. *The French Quarter: An Informal History of the New Orleans Underworld.* New York: Alfred A. Knopf, 1936.

_____. *The Gangs of Chicago.* New York: Alfred Knopf, 1940.

_____. *The Gangs of New York: An Informal History of the Underworld.* New York: Garden City, 1927.

_____. *The Great Illusion: An Informal History of Prohibition.* Garden City, NY: Doubleday, 1950.

Beck, Louis J. *New York's Chinatown: An Historical Presentation of its Places and People.* New York: Bohemia, 1898.

Behr, Edward. *Prohibition: Thirteen Years That Changed America.* New York: Arcade, 1996.

Bell, Ernest A., ed. *Fighting the Traffic in Young Girls.* Chicago: G.S. Ball, 1910.

Bernstein, Irving. *The Lean Years: A History of the American Worker, 1920–1933.* Boston: Houghton Mifflin, 1960.

Bingham, Theodore. *The Girl That Disappears: The Real Facts About the White Slave Traffic.* Boston: Gorham Press, 1911.

Blackmon, Douglas A. *Slavery By Another Name.* New York: Anchor Books, 2008.

Blight, David W. *Race and Reunion: The Civil War in American Memory.* Cambridge, MA: Harvard University Press, 2001.

Block, Alan A. *East Side-West Side: Organizing Crime in New York 1930–1950.* New Brunswick, NJ: Transaction, 1983.

_____. *Perspectives on Organizing Crime: Essays in Opposition.* Boston: Kluwer, 1991.

Blum, Deborah. *The Poisoner's Handbook.* London: Thorndike Press, 2010.

Borsella, Cristogianni. *On Persecution, Identity and Activism: Aspects of the Italian-American Experience from the Late 19th Century to Today.* Boston: Dante University of America Press, 2005.

Boyd, Julian P. et al., eds. *The Papers of Thomas Jefferson,* 12 vols. Princeton: Princeton University Press, 1950.

Bright, John. *Hizzoner Big Bill Thompson: An Idyll of Chicago.* New York: J. Cape and H. Smith, 1930.

Bristow, Edward J. *Prostitution and Prejudice: The Jewish Fight Against White Slavery, 1870–1939.* New York: Schocken Books, 1983.

Brown, James L. *Mussel Slough Tragedy.* N.p., 1958.

Brown, Richard Maxwell. *No Duty to Retreat: Violence and Values in American History and Society.* Norman: University of Oklahoma Press, 1991.

Brown, Walter Lee. *A Life of Albert Pike.* Fayetteville: University of Arkansas Press, 1997.

Brundage, W. Fitzhugh, ed. *Under Sentence of Death: Lynching in the South.* Chapel Hill: University of North Carolina Press, 1997.

Bryce, James. *The American Commonwealth,* 2 vols. New York: Macmillan, 1888.

Bryson, Bill. *One Summer: America 1927.* London: Doubleday, 2013.

Bukowski, Douglas. *Big Bill Thompson, Chicago and the Politics of Image.* Chicago: University of Illinois Press, 1998.

Buntin, John. *LA Noir: The Struggle for the Soul of America's Most Seductive City.* London: Orion Books, 2014.

Burke, William H. *Anthracite Lads: A True Story of the Fabled Molly Maguires.* Erie County Historical Society, 2005.

Burns, Walter Noble. *The One-Way Ride: The Red Trail*

*of Chicago Gangland from Prohibition to Jake Lingle.* Garden City, NY: Doubleday, Doran, 1931.

Burrough, Bryan. *Public Enemies*, rev. ed. New York: Penguin, 2009.

Cantlie, James, and Sheridan Jones. *Sun Yat-Sen and the Awakening of China.* New York: Fleming H. Revell, 1912.

Champernowne, Henry. *The Boss: An Essay upon the Art of Governing American Cities.* New York: George H. Richmond, 1894.

Chandler, David Leon. *Brothers in Blood.* New York: E.P. Dutton, 1975.

Chandler, Raymond. *The Long Goodbye.* London: Hamish Hamilton, 1954.

Conan Doyle, Sir Arthur. *The Adventures of Sherlock Holmes.* London: Smith Elder, 1891.

Connelley, William E. *A Standard History of Kansas and Kansans*, vol. 2, Chicago: Lewis, 1918.

Connelly, Mark Thomas. *The Response to Prostitution in the Progressive Era.* Chapel Hill: University of North Carolina Press, 1980.

Cook, William A. *King of the Bootleggers: A Biography of George Remus.* Jefferson, NC: McFarland, 2008.

Cressey, Donald R. *Theft of the Nation: The Structure and Operations of Organized Crime in America.* New York: Harper & Row, 1969.

Critchley, David. *The Origin of Organized Crime in America: The New York City Mafia, 1891–1931.* New York: Routledge, 2008.

Daniels, Roger. *Guarding the Golden Door: American Immigration Policy and Immigrants Since 1882.* New York: Hill and Wang, 2004.

Dash, Mike. *The First Family: Terror, Extortion, Revenge, Murder and The Birth of the American Mafia.* New York: Ballantine Books, 2010.

Davenport, John I. *The Election Frauds of New York City and Their Prevention*, vol. 1: *Eleven Years of Fraud, 1860–1870.* New York: J.I. Davenport, 1881.

Davis, Sarah Lawrence. *Authentic History of the Ku Klux Klan, 1865–1877.* New York: American Library Service, 1924.

De Stefano, George. *An Offer We Can't Refuse: The Mafia in the Mind of America.* New York: Faber and Faber, 2006.

Dewees, Francis P. *The Molly Maguires: The Origin, Growth and Character of the Organization.* Philadelphia: n.p., 1877.

Dickie, John. *Blood Brotherhoods: A History of Italy's Three Mafias.* London: PublicAffairs, 2014.

Dillingham, William P. *Importing Women for Immoral Purposes.* Washington, D.C.: U.S. Government Printing Office, 1909.

Dixon, Edward H. *The Terrible Mysteries of the Ku-Klux Klan.* New York: n.p., 1868.

Domanick, Joe. *To Protect and To Serve: The LAPD's Century of War in the City of Dreams.* New York: Pocket Books, 1994.

Dorr, Goldthwaite, and Sidney Simpson. *Report on the Cost of Crime and Criminal Justice in the United States.* Washington, D.C.: U.S. Government Printing Office, 1931.

Dray, Philip. *At the Hands of Persons Unknown: The Lynching of Black America.* New York: Random House, 2002.

Dyer, David P. *Autobiography and Reminiscences.* St. Louis: William Harvey Miner and Co., 1922.

Einstein, Isidor. *Prohibition Agent No 1.* New York: Frederick A. Stokes, 1932.

Enright, Richard T. *Capone's Chicago.* Lakeville, MN: Northstar Maschek Books, 1931.

Erie, Stephen P. *Rainbow's End: Irish-Americans and the Dilemmas of Urban Machine Politics, 1840–1985.* Berkeley: University of California Press, 1988.

Ettinger, Clayton J. *The Problem of Crime.* New York: Ray Long and Richard R. Smith, Inc., 1932.

Evans, Chris, and Howard Kazanijian. *Ma Barker: America's Most Wanted Mother.* Lanham, MD: Rowman and Littlefield, 2017.

Fentress, James. *Eminent Gangsters: Immigrants and the Birth of Organized Crime in America.* Lanham, MD: University Press of America, 2010.

Fijnaut, C., and L. Paoli, eds. *Organized Crime in Europe.* New York: Springer, 2004.

Finch, Stanley. *The White Slave Traffic: Address by Stanley W. Finch, Chief of the Bureau of Investigation of the Department of Justice, before World's Purity Congress Louisville KY May 7, 1912.* Washington, D.C.: International Reform Bureau, 1912.

Finney, Guy W. *The Great Los Angeles Bubble: A Present Day Story of Colossal Financial Jugglery and the Penalties Paid.* Los Angeles: Forbes, 1929.

Flynn, William J. *The Barrel Mystery.* New York: n.p., 1919.

Folsom, Robert G. *The Money Trail: How Elmer Irey and his T-Men Brought Down America's Criminal Elite.* Washington, D.C.: Potomac Books, 2010.

Fox, Craig. *Everyday Klansfolk: White Protestant Life and the KKK in 1920s Michigan.* East Lansing: Michigan State University Press, 2011.

Fox, Stephen. *Blood and Power: Organized Crime in 20th-Century America.* New York: Penguin, 1990.

Funderburg, J. Anne. *Bootleggers and Beer Barons of the Prohibition Era.* Jefferson, NC: McFarland, 2014.

Gilfoyle, Timothy. *City of Eros: New York, Prostitution and the Commercialization of Sex 1790–1920:* New York: Norton, 1992.

_____. *A Pickpocket's Tale.* New York: W.W. Norton, 1992.

Ginger, Ray. *The Age of Excess: The United States From 1877 to 1914.* London: Macmillan, 1971.

Glenny, Misha. *McMafia: Seriously Organized Crime.* London: Anansi, 2009.

Goldman, Emma. *Anarchism and Other Essays.* New York: Mother Earth, 1911.

Golway, Terry. *Machine Made: Tammany Hall and the Creation of Modern American Politics.* New York: Liveright, 2014.

Goodwin, Doris Kearns. *The Bully Pulpit: Theodore Roosevelt, William Howard Taft and the Golden Age of Journalism.* New York: Simon & Schuster, 2013.

Gottlieb, Robert, and Irene Wolt. *Thinking Big: A History of The Los Angeles Times.* New York: Putnam's, 1977.

Guinn, Jeff. *The Last Gunfight.* New York: Simon & Schuster, 2011.

Hammack, David C. *Power and Society: Greater New York at the Turn of the Century.* New York: Russell Sage Foundation, 1982.

Hammond, Bray. *Sovereignty and an Empty Purse: Banks and Politics in the Civil War.* Princeton, NJ: Princeton University Press, 1970.

Hartmann, Rudolph H., and Robert H. Ferrell, eds. *The Kansas City Investigation: Pendergast's Downfall 1938–1939.* Columbia: University of Missouri Press, 1999.

Henderson, Thomas M. *Tammany Hall and the New Immigrants: The Progressive Years.* New York: Arno Press, 1976.

Higham, John. *Strangers in the Land: Patterns of American Nativism 1860–1925.* New Brunswick, NJ: Rutgers University Press, 1988.

Honey, Michael K. *Southern Labor and Black Civil Rights: Organizing Memphis Workers.* Urbana: University of Illinois Press, 1993.

Hoover, J. Edgar. *Persons in Hiding.* Boston: Little, Brown, 1938.

Horn, Stanley F. *The Invisible Empire: The Story of the Ku Klux Klan, 1866–1871.* Boston: Houghton Mifflin, 1939.

Hostetter, Gordon L., and Thomas Quinn Beesley. *It's a Racket!* Chicago: Les Quin Books, 1929.

Hoy, William. *The Chinese Six Companies.* San Francisco: Chinese Consolidated Benevolent Association, 1942.

Hu, T.Y. *The Liquor Tax in the United States.* New York: Columbia Business School, 1950.

Hunt, Thomas, and Martha Macheca Sheldon. *Deep Water.* New York: CreateSpace, 2007.

Hutchinson, John. *Imperfect Union: A History of Corruption in American Unions.* New York: E.P. Dutton, 1970.

Iorizzo, Luciano. *Al Capone: A Biography.* Westport, CT: Greenwood, 2003.

Jacobs, James B. *Mobsters, Unions, and Feds: The Mafia and the American Labor Movement.* New York: New York University Press, 2006.

Jeffreys-Jones, Rhodri. *The FBI: A History.* New Haven, CT: Yale University Press, 2007.

Johnson, David R. *Policing the Urban Underworld: The Impact of Crime on the Development of the American Police, 1800–1887.* Philadelphia: Temple University Press, 1979.

Kantowicz, Edward R. *Polish-American Politics in Chicago, 1880–1940.* Chicago: University of Chicago Press, 1975.

Keefe, Rose. *The Starker: Big Jack Zelig, The Becker-Rosenthal Case and the Rise of Advent of the Jewish Gangster.* Nashville, TN: Cumberland House, 2008.

Kelly, Robert J. *The Upperworld and the Underworld: Case Studies of Racketeering and Business Infiltrations in the United States.* New York: Kluwer, 1999.

Kenny, Kevin. *Making Sense of the Molly Maguires.* New York: Oxford University Press, 1998.

Kobler, John. *Capone: The Life and World of Al Capone.* Cambridge, MA: Da Capo Press, 1971.

Kyvig, David. *Repealing National Prohibition.* Chicago: University of Chicago Press, 1979.

LaGumina, Salvatore J. *Wop!: A Documentary History of Anti-Italian Discrimination.* Toronto: Guernica Editions, 1999.

Lalor, John J. *Cyclopedia of Political Science,* 3 vols., rev. ed. New York: Maynard, Merril and Co., 1899.

Langum, David J. *Crossing Over the Line: Legislating Morality and the Mann Act.* Chicago: Chicago University Press, 2006.

Leinwand, Gerald. *Mackerels in the Moonlight: Four Corrupt American Mayors.* Jefferson, NC: McFarland, 2004.

Lemman, Nicholas. *Redemption: The Last Battle of the Civil War.* New York: Farrar, Straus and Giroux, 2006.

Lens, Sidney. *Left, Right and Center: Conflicting Forces in American Labor.* Hinsdale, IL: H. Regnery, 1949.

Lester, John C., and D.L. Wilson. *Ku Klux Klan: Its Origins, Growth and Disbandment.* New York: Da Capo Press, 1905.

Lindberg, Richard C. *To Serve and Collect: Chicago Politics and Police Corruption from the Lager Beer Riot to the Summerdale Scandal 1855–1960.* New York: Praeger Press, 1991.

Lloyd, Henry Demarest. *Wealth Against Commonwealth.* Boston: Harper Brothers, 1894.

Lombardo, Robert M. *Organized Crime in Chicago: Beyond the Mafia.* Urbana: University of Illinois Press, 2013.

Lombroso, Cesare, and Guigielmo Ferrero. *Criminal Woman, The Prostitute and the Normal Woman.* Durham, NC: Duke University Press, 2004.

Long, Kim. *The Almanac of Political Corruption, Scandals and Dirty Politics.* New York: Delacorte Press, 2007.

Lowi, Theodore J. *The End of Liberalism: The Second Republic of the United States.* New York: W.W. Norton, 1979.

Luthin, Reinhard H., and Allan Nevins. *American Demagogues: Twentieth Century.* Boston: Beacon Press, 1954.

Lyle, John H. *The Dry and Lawless Years.* London: Prentice Hall, 1960.

Lytle, Hal McLeod. *Tragedies of the White Slave.* New York: Padell, 1910.

Maas, Peter. *The Valachi Papers.* New York: Putnam, 1968.

McCabe, Charles R., ed. *Damned Old Crank: A Self-Portrait of E.W. Scripps Drawn from His Unpublished Writings.* New York: Harper and Brothers, 1951.

McClellan, Robert. *The Heathen Chinese: A Study of American Attitudes Toward China, 1890–1905.* Columbus: Ohio State University Press, 1971.

McClintock, John S. *Pioneer Days in the Black Hills,* rev. ed. Norman: University of Oklahoma Press, 2000.

McIllwain, Jeffrey Scott. *Organizing Crime in Chinatown: Race and Racketeering in New York City 1890–1910.* Jefferson, NC: McFarland, 2003.

McWilliams, Carey. *Southern California: An Island on the Land.* Salt Lake City: Gibbs Smith, 1948.

Mailes, Gene, and Mike Nielsen. *Hollywood's Other Blacklist: Union Struggles in the Studio System.* London: British Film Institute, 1995.

Mason, Paul, ed. *Criminal Visions: Media Representations of Crime and Justice.* Cullompton, UK: Willan, 2003.

Masselli, Joseph, and Dominic Candeloro. *Italians in New Orleans.* Mount Pleasant, SC: Arcadia, 2004.

Melanson, Philip H. *The Secret Service: The Hidden History of an Enigmatic Agency.* New York: Basic Books, 2005.

Menard, Orville D. *Political Bossism in Mid-America: Tom Dennison's Omaha, 1900–1933.* Lanham, MD: University Press of America, 1989.

Mihn, Stephen. *A Nation of Counterfeiters: Capitalists, Con Men and the Making of the United States.* Cambridge, MA: Harvard University Press, 2007.

Millis, Harry, and Royal Montgomery. *Organized Labor.* New York: McGraw-Hill, 1945.

Mitgang, Herbert. *Once Upon a Time in New York: Jimmy Walker, Franklin Roosevelt and the Last Great Battle of the Jazz Age.* New York: Cooper Square Press, 2000.

Mittelstaedt, Walter. *Herman "Baron" Lamm: The Father of Modern Bank Robbery.* Jefferson, NC: McFarland, 2012.

*The Molly Maguires: Cut-Throats of Modern Times.* Tamaqua, PA: Eveland and Harris, 1969.

Nadeau, Remi. *Los Angeles: From Mission to Modern City.* New York: Longmans, Green, 1960.

Nelli, Humbert S. *The Business of Crime.* Chicago: University of Chicago Press, 1976.

Nevins, Allan. *Hamilton Fish: The Inner History of the Grant Administration,* 2 vols. New York: Fredrick Unger, 1936.

Okrent, Daniel. *Last Call: The Rise and Fall of Prohibition.* New York: Scribner's, 2011.

Orsi, Richard J. *Sunset Limited: The Southern Pacific Railroad and the Development of the American West, 1850–1930.* Berkeley: University of California Press, 2005.

Ostrogorski, Moisei. *Democracy and the Organization of Political Parties,* vol. 2: *The United States.* New York: Macmillan, 1902.

Paoli, Letizia. *Mafia Brotherhoods: Organized Crime, Italian Style.* New York: Oxford University Press, 2003.

Pasley, Fred D. *Al Capone: The Biography of a Self-Made Man.* New York: Washburn, 1930.

_____. *Muscling In.* New York: Chas. H. Bohn, 1931.

Pilat, Oliver. *Pegler: Angry Man of the Press.* Westport, CT: Greenwood Press, 1973.

Pinkerton, Allan. *The Mollie Maguires and the Detectives.* New York: G.W. Carleton, 1877.

Pliley, Jessica R. *Policing Sexuality: The Mann Act and the Making of the FBI.* Cambridge, MA: Harvard University Press, 2014.

Pomerantsev, Peter. *Nothing is True and Everything is Possible: Adventures in Modern Russia.* London: Faber and Faber, 2015.

Potter, Claire Bond. *War on Crime: Bandits, G-men, and the Politics of Mass Culture.* New Brunswick, NJ: Rutgers University Press, 1998.

Potts, Ralph Bushnell. *Seattle Heritage.* Seattle: Superior, 1955.

Proulx, Annie. *Accordion Crimes.* New York: Scribner, 2009.

Puzo, Mario. *The Godfather.* New York: Putnam, 1969.

Raab, Selwyn. *Five Families: The Rise, Decline, and Resurgence of America's Most Powerful Mafia Empires.* New York: Thomas Dunne Books, 2006.

Rayner, Richard. *The Associates: Four Capitalists Who Created California.* New York: W.W. Norton, 2008.

_____. *A Bright and Guilty Place: Murder, Corruption and LA's Scandalous Coming of Age.* New York: Doubleday, 2009.

Reid, Ed. *Mafia: The History of the Ruthless Gang That Rules the Nationwide Crime Syndicate.* New York: Random House, 1952.

Reppetto, Thomas. *American Mafia: A History of Its Rise to Power.* New York: Henry Holt, 2004.

Richardson, James H. *For the Life of Me: Memoirs of a City Editor.* New York: Putnam's, 1954.

Riordan, William L. *Plunkitt of Tammany Hall.* New York: McClure, Phillips, & Co., 1905.

Riviere, Mary Ann. *From Palermo to New Orleans.* Lake Charles, LA: n.p., 1991.

Roe, Clifford George. *The Great War on White Slavery, Or Fighting for the Protection of our Girls.* Philadelphia: P.W. Ziegler, 1915.

_____. *Panders and Their White Slaves.* Chicago: Fleming H. Revell, 1910.

Rosen, Ruth. *The Lost Sisterhood: Prostitution in America. 1900–1918.* Baltimore: Johns Hopkins University Press, 1982.

Ross, Edward Alsworth. *Sin and Society: An Analysis of Latter-Day Iniquity.* Boston: Houghton Mifflin, 1907.

Roth, Michael P., et al. *Historical Dictionary of Law Enforcement.* New Haven, CT: Greenwood, 2000.

Russo, Gus. *The Outfit: The Role of Chicago's Underworld in the Shaping of America.* London: Bloomsbury, 2001.

Ruth, David E. *Inventing the Public Enemy: The Gangster in American Culture, 1918–1934.* Chicago: University of Chicago, 1996.

Samito, Christian G., ed. *Changes in Law and Society during the Civil War and Reconstruction: A Legal History Documentary Reader.* Carbondale: Southern Illinois University Press, 2009.

Schalck, Adolf W., and David C. Henning. *The History of Schuylkill County, Pa.,* vol. 1. Philadelphia: n.p., 1907.

Seidman, Harold. *Labor Czars: A History of Labor Racketeering.* New York: Liveright, 1938.

Shughart, William F. *Taxing Choice: The Predatory Politics of Fiscal Discrimination.* New Brunswick, NJ: The Independent Institute, 1997.

Sifakis, Carl. *The Encyclopedia of American Crime.* New York: Facts on File, 1982.

_____. *The Mafia File: The A–Z of Organized Crime in America.* New York: Equation Books, 1988.

Sims, Edwin W. *The White Slave Trade Today.* Chicago: n.p., 1910.

Sinclair, Andrew. *Prohibition: The Era of Excess.* Boston: Little, Brown, 1962.

Smith, Dwight C. *The Mafia Mystique.* New York: Basic Books, 1974.

Soderlund, Gretchen. *Sex Trafficking, Scandal and the Transformation of Journalism 1885–1917.* Chicago: University of Chicago Press, 2013.

Starr, Kevin. *The Dream Endures: California Enters the 1940s.* New York: Oxford University Press, 1997.

Stead, William T. *If Christ Came to Chicago: A Plea for the Union of All Who Love in the Service of All Who Suffer.* London: Review of Reviews, 1894.

Steffens, Lincoln. *The Shame of the Cities.* New York: McClure, Philips and Co., 1904.

Stephens, Albert Clarke. *The Cyclopaedia of Fraternities,* rev. ed. New York: n.p., 1907.

Sterling, Bryan B., and Francis N. Sterling. *Will Rogers' World: America's Foremost Political Humorist Comments on the '20s and '30s and '80s and '90s.* New York: M. Evans & Co., 1993.

Sterling, Claire. *Octopus: The Long Reach of the International Sicilian Mafia.* New York: W.W. Norton, 1990.

Sterling, Dorothy, ed. *The Trouble They Seen: Black People Tell the Story of Reconstruction.* Garden City, NY: Doubleday, 1976.

Stolberg, Benjamin. *Tailor's Progress: The Story of a Famous Union and the Men Who Made It.* New York: Doubleday, Doran, 1944.

Stolberg, Mary M. *Fighting Organized Crime: Politics, Justice and the Legacy of Thomas E. Dewey.* Boston: Northeastern University Press, 1995.

Stout, Charles. *The Eighteenth Amendment and the Part Played by Organized Medicine.* New York: Mitchell Kennerley, 1921.

Sutherland, Edwin H., ed. *The Professional Thief.* Chicago: University of Chicago, 1937.

The Tax Foundation. *Facts and Figures on Government Finance,* vols. 17–18. Baltimore: Johns Hopkins University Press, 1973.

Ter Haar, B.J. *Ritual & Mythology of the Chinese Triads: Creating an Identity.* London: n.p., 2000.

Theodoris, Athan, ed. *The FBI: A Comprehensive Reference Guide.* Phoenix, AZ: Oryx Press, 1999.

Tooze, Adam. *The Deluge: The Great War and the Remaking of Global Order, 1916–1931.* New York: Penguin, 2014.

Trelease, Allen W. *White Terror.* Baton Rouge: Louisiana State University Press, 1995.

Turkus, Burton B., and Sid Feder. *Murder Inc: The Story of the Syndicate.* New York: Permabooks, 1951.

Turner-Zimmermann, Jean. *Chicago's Black Traffic in White Girls.* Chicago: Chicago Rescue Mission, 1912.

Tygiel, Jules. *The Great Los Angeles Swindle: Oil, Stocks and Scandal During the Roaring Twenties.* Berkeley: University of California Press, 1994.

Varese, Federico. *Mafias on the Move.* Princeton, NJ: Princeton University Press, 2011.

Wallace, Anthony F.C. *St. Clair: A Nineteenth Century Coal Town's Experience with a Disaster-Prone Industry.* Ithaca, NY: Cornell University Press, 1988.

Weinstock, Matt. *My LA.* New York: Current Books, 1947.

Wendt, Lloyd, and Herman Kogan. *Big Bill of Chicago.* Indianapolis: Bobbs-Merrill, 1953.

White, Richard. *It is Your Fault and None of My Own: A New History of the American West.* Norman: University of Oklahoma Press, 1991.

White, William Allen. *Masks in a Pageant.* New York: Macmillan, 1928.

Wiebe, Robert. *The Search for Order, 1877–1920.* New York: Hill and Wang, 1967.

Willebrandt, Mabel Walker. *The Inside of Prohibition.* Indianapolis: Bobbs-Merrill, 1929.

Willemse, Cornelius. *Behind the Green Lights.* New York: Alfred A. Knopf, 1931.

Williams, Kadapa E. *Eight Negro Biographies.* New York: n.p., 1970.

Witwer, David. *Shadow of the Racketeer: Scandal in Organized Labor.* Chicago: Illinois University Press, 2009.

Wohl, Anthony S., ed. *The Victorian Family: Structure and Stresses.* London: Croom Helm, 1978.

Woodiwiss, Michael. *Crime Crusades and Corruption: Prohibitions in the United States 1900–1987.* London: Rowman & Littlefield, 1988.

_____. *Organized Crime and American Power.* Toronto: University of Toronto Press, 2001.

Woodward, C. Vann, ed. *Mary Chesnut's Civil War.* New Haven, CT: Yale University Press, 1981.

Writers Program of the Work Projects Administration in the State of Ohio. *Cincinnati: A Guide to the Queen City and Its Neighbors.* Cincinnati: Cincinnati Historical Society, 1943.

Yeager, Matthew G. *Illegal Enterprise: The Work of Historian Mark Haller.* New York: United Press of America, 2013.

Zhao, Xiaojian, and J.W. Park, eds. *Asian Americans: An Encyclopedia of Social, Cultural, Economic and Political History.* New Haven, CT: Greenwood Press, 2013.

# Index